An Evolutionary Paradigm for International Law

Philosophy, Public Policy, and Transnational Law

Series Editor: John Martin Gillroy, Professor of International Relations and Founding Director of the Graduate Programs in Environmental Policy Design at Lehigh University, Pennsylvania.

http://ir.cas2.lehigh.edu/content/john-martin-gillroy

A Note from the Editor

This new series for Palgrave Macmillan seeks, for the first time with a major publisher, to take the philosophical and public policy foundations of legal practice seriously; that is, not in terms of bits and pieces of theory or policy used to illustrate empirical claims, but as a systematic and integral basis for the study of codified law. The series will pursue scholarship that integrates the superstructure of the positive law with its philosophical and public policy substructure, producing a more three-dimensional understanding of transnational law and its evolution, meaning, imperatives, and future.

For the purposes of this series, transnational law includes the traditional categories of comparative and international law and seeks to understand the role of not just states, but persons, international organizations, nongovernmental organizations, and governments that create or use law that transcends sovereign states. The series encourages an interdisciplinary approach to transnational law and seeks research reports, original manuscripts, or edited collections that explore the essence of legal practice in both the public policy arguments that inform legal discourse and the philosophical precepts that create the logic of concepts inherent in policy debate. The series aims to expand the types and use of philosophical and policy paradigms exploring the nature of transnational law, so that its empirical dimensions are better illuminated for practitioners and scholars alike.

An Evolutionary Paradigm for International Law

Philosophical Method, David Hume, and the Essence of Sovereignty

John Martin Gillroy

Philosophical Method, Policy Design, and the International Legal System

Volume I

palgrave
macmillan

AN EVOLUTIONARY PARADIGM FOR INTERNATIONAL LAW

First published in 2013 by
PALGRAVE MACMILLAN®
in the United States—a division of St. Martin's Press LLC,
175 Fifth Avenue, New York, NY 10010.

Where this book is distributed in the UK, Europe and the rest of the world, this is by Palgrave Macmillan, a division of Macmillan Publishers Limited, registered in England, company number 785998, of Houndmills, Basingstoke, Hampshire RG21 6XS.

Palgrave Macmillan is the global academic imprint of the above companies and has companies and representatives throughout the world.

Palgrave® and Macmillan® are registered trademarks in the United States, the United Kingdom, Europe and other countries.

ISBN: 978–1–137–37662–6

Library of Congress Cataloging-in-Publication Data

Gillroy, John Martin, 1954–
An evolutionary paradigm for international law : philosophical method, David Hume, and the essence of sovereignty / John Martin Gillroy.
pages cm
Includes bibliographical references and index.
ISBN 978–1–137–37662–6 (hardback)
1. Sovereignty. 2. International law—Philosophy. 3. Hume, David, 1711–1776.
4. Recognition (International law) I. Title.

KZ4041.G55 2013
341.26—dc23 2013024133

A catalogue record of the book is available from the British Library.

Design by Newgen Knowledge Works (P) Ltd., Chennai, India.

First edition: December 2013

10 9 8 7 6 5 4 3 2 1

For Margaret M. Murray
(Writer, Editor And Much More)

Contents

Illustrations

Figures

Matrices

Table

Preface

> *The status of sovereignty as a highly ambiguous concept is well established. Pointing out or deploring, the ambiguity of the idea has itself become a recurring motif in the literature on sovereignty. As the legal theorist and international lawyer Alf Ross put it, "there is hardly any domain in which the obscurity and confusion is as great as here."*[1] *The concept of sovereignty is often seen as a downright obstacle to fruitful conceptual analysis, carried over from its proper setting in history to "plague and befog contemporary thought."*[2]*...So contested is the concept that, rather than pursuing the contestation, many political theorists think we should give up so protean a notion. Granting that the debate on the relevance of sovereignty frustratingly oscillates between claims that it will either continue to exist or that it is about to disappear, forgetting it altogether, and thereby escaping this seemingly endless argument, can easily appear as the most urgent task for political theory.*[3]

The following argument makes a case that the "urgent task" is not the abandonment of the concept of sovereignty, but an understanding of its essential philosophical nature as an integrated and evolving expression of practical reason. Sovereignty is neither ambiguous nor obscure once its fundamental presuppositions are laid bare and its many philosophical and historical manifestations shown to be the product, in actuality, of a single, dialectally dynamic but integrated set of metaphysical elements.

This is the first of three arguments describing the evolution of international law as a manifestation of practical reason through an application of philosophical method to the *source*, *locus*, and *scope* of the concept of sovereignty. It moves from a dialectic balance favoring *utility* to a balance dominated by *legal right* to a dialectic of *duty* to humanity and nature. All three arguments are meant to be a contribution to the new field of *International Legal Philosophy* as defined by Phillip Allott.[4]

This field combines a sensitivity to legal practice with an effort to understand the underlying philosophical determinants of empirical choice and behavior. One purpose of international legal philosophy is to "remove" from the minds of those who study the law what Diderot defined as "the sophism of the ephemeral," and what Allott calls "the disempowering idea that what happens to exist now is inevitable and permanent."[5] A core imperative is to "reunderstand what it is to be a thinking being"[6] and to rediscover the dialectic between the private and the public as it determines, and is redetermined by, legal practice. This requires a "revolution in the human mind"[7] so that we may transcend the current dependence on positivist methods and empirical fact as an end-in-itself, and try to understand the underlying and more constant and essential ideas and inherent dialectics that constitute the substructure or "metaphysics" of international law. I will approach this "revolution" with the use of R. G. Collingwood's philosophical method[8] and the philosophy of David Hume, applied to international law as an expression of practical reason.

The goal of philosophical method is the construction of a comprehensive policy argument (CPA) for a public policy or legal issue. In addition to the conventional use of empirical models and their logic of investigation in the study of policy and law, CPA requires that an underlying philosophical logic of concepts be deciphered to identify the ideas within the issue, and their definition, overlap, and systematic interdependence. Philosophical method is a means with which to interpret and understand competing systematic and complete conceptual logics, existing at the core of an issue and pertinent to policy change.

Philosophical method is therefore not meant to be a replacement for the empirical investigation of a policy or legal issue, or the use of scientific method in social studies. Rather, it is a complimentary and prerequisite method that seeks to transcend the limitations of positivism and present a more complete understanding of the philosophical presuppositions of positivist ideas like power, interest, or strategic rationality. Philosophical method is meant to be used with the facts of the policy or legal issue to match an illuminating *logic of concepts* with a pertinent *logic of investigation*. Within the CPA, the use of philosophical method and the metaphysics of a policy or legal issue is assumed to be critical to the full understanding of the overlapping concepts, dialectics, and scale of forms that determine, and are determined by, the empirical context of the policy or legal topic.

Specifically, instead of utilizing bits and pieces of various theoretical arguments to address narrowly focused empirical questions, as positivism prescribes, I will address the evolution of international law as practical reason in three phases. Each will be approached through a single integrated logic of philosophical concepts from a particular philosopher (i.e., David Hume, G. W. F. Hegel, Immanuel Kant). This philosophically holistic approach to the law is based on the assumption that only through the use of a single integrated argument in legal analysis can sovereignty, or any concept, be understood as a truly systematic and logical whole. A complete philosophical paradigm has a dialectic integrity and systematic logic that can more adequately describe the evolving essence of a concept like sovereignty. This approach also has the advantage of generating a number of distinct holistic descriptions of the law through the application of different philosophical systems, one at a time, to its factual structure.[9] Positivism does not seek holism, and rejects the idea that "theory" has such a characteristic. The essential or comprehensive substructure of any idea is therefore ignored in a method that recommends the observation of empirical problems through the use of whatever hodgepodge of theoretical elements is seen fit to frame its superstructure. This failure to deal with metaphysics has retarded both an essential understanding of international law as a species of legal system, and any holistic and dialectical conceptualization of its inherent concepts, like sovereignty.

A second positivist convention expects modern theorists to create new theory rather than to refine and apply that of existing philosophy. This predisposition is driven by the positivist goal of *discovery* that ignores *refinement* as a possible purpose of philosophical analysis. Collingwood argues that philosophy must take that set of ideas already known and utilize existing systematic philosophical arguments to refine them so that they evolve closer to their essence as concepts. Considering this imperative, the idea of sovereignty can be assumed to have had valid usage for hundreds of years, over which time, the concept has evolved to mean different things, each a refinement of the definition that preceded it. Transcending positivism means that the scholar's search is not for "new" material, but to decipher the metaphysical essence of a concept as it has been made manifest over time and context. These manifestations are rooted, and refined from, the known terms of that concept's inherent idea(s).

Rather than depending exclusively on positivism and its conventions, my work utilizes, in addition to Collingwood, the intact philosophical systems of Hume, Hegel, and Kant to trace the refinement of international law as a product of human practical reason. These paradigms, or integrated systems of logical concepts, will be applied to legal practice individually, so that each CPA can be deciphered separately. This provides a set of integrated and logically intact paradigms for the evolutionary stages of practical reason in international law. Because each argument is applied systematically, a deeper understanding of the source, locus, and scope in the development of law in general, and international law in particular, is possible where it is not with the application of various disconnected components of many theories. Each CPA based on Hume, Hegel, or Kant can then be used to describe a distinct context that its logic of concepts best illuminates; specifically, the (1) genesis, (2) contemporary dilemmas, and (3) future of the international legal system. By widening the perspective of international lawyers and policymakers, they can more easily perceive the dialectic of ideas that has created, and is refined by, the legal practice in which they participate. We also move toward Allott's goal of "human self-perfecting."[10] And, in addition, by providing a more complete knowledge of the origins of legal practice and its evolution, we illuminate the practical possibilities for what we might "choose to be"[11] in the future.

To achieve this, the essential metaphysical elements of state sovereignty and its inherent evolutionary scale of forms will be deciphered and described. This will transform what appears to be a multitude of definitions and practical realizations of the concept of sovereignty into a set of interdependent manifestations of a single substructure, made of a single set of dialectic elements. The interpretation of international law through practical reason sorts and integrates a diverse and discordant literature and defines state sovereignty as a single concept evolving on a scale of forms that allows it to exhibit diverse character traits, all arising from different combinations of common and essential metaphysical elements. This approach, compared to positivist methods and legal realism, allows one to transcend current agreement that sovereignty is, at best, a narrowly focused set of empirical characteristics or, at worst, "organized hypocrisy."[12] This method also encourages the scholar and practitioner to understand the predispositions and pitfalls of the concept of sovereignty, as well as its potential future paths, more effectively.

The use of philosophical method to create policy paradigms out of preexisting philosophical systems and apply these to international law will be called *Philosophical-Policy & Legal Design.* This approach allows the use of preexisting and complete philosophical arguments that provide an adequate logic of concepts to chart the evolution of the idea of sovereignty along its scale of forms. An examination of the source of practical reason in human social convention with the employment of a philosophical-policy drawn from Hume's logic of concepts about human nature will demonstrate this new approach.

Why Hume? Because, up to now, without an adequate substructure we have arguments, like Brunneé's and Troope's,[13] that may correctly identify international law as an "interactional" system, but cannot present any argument as to why it is, where this empirical reality comes from, or what its implications are for the future.

Comparatively, Hume provides a logic of philosophical concepts that answers these concerns. First, he fulfills the requirements for a fuller understanding of the origin and evolution of law from social convention and the dependence of social convention on the human imperative for society. Second, he offers a more adequate delineation of the overlapping concepts of the law in terms of the ideas and institutions that deal with norms and justice (e.g., principle, process, practice, rule, power, interest). Third, he provides a fundamental understanding of the essential dialectics at the core of a conceptualization of the law with both unconscious and conscious human participation (i.e., passion⇆reason, process⇆principle). These differences provide for the establishment of a dialectic and evolutionary scale of forms that conceptualizes law as applied practical reason. It creates both a two-stage legal system where principle, within its dialectic with process, can redress an inherent process-bias, and a fuller and more systematic explanation of the presuppositions of the concept of sovereignty, than positivist models alone can provide.

In this book, the genesis of the modern international legal system takes shape in the process⇆principle dialectic and Hume's concept of law as social convention. For Hume, the process side of this dialectic that finds social stability, as it transforms convention into positive law, is most critical. But his paradigm is limited; it fails to consider what the rise of critical principle in the law (e.g., human rights) means for the evolution of sovereignty. Since his argument cannot deal with critical principle or its full integration into the law, a second philosophical-policy to inform the next moment of legal evolution is required.

In the second book, Hegel's philosophical-policy is pertinent to understanding the rise of critical principle in the law. Applied to contemporary dispute resolution it illuminates the struggle between a Humean or conventional definition of state sovereignty and the requirements of international human rights. Hegel's argument for "recognition" combines process and principle by engaging "abstract right" in dialectic with social "morality" to create a synthesis product of "ethical life." Hegel, defining the *locus* of sovereignty through practical reason, places it, not in the individual or the community, but in the synthesis of the two through legal right. This grants the process⇆principle dialectic a new field of application with a better balanced tension that creates and defines the responsibilities of the modern state. But beyond its manifestation in the state, Hegel cannot help us understand the process⇆principle dialectic. Since international law is a distinct mode of law that deals with more than just states we require yet a third philosophical-policy to completely understand the evolution of international law as a product of practical reason.

In the third book of the series, Kant's critical philosophy is employed to define the *scope* of sovereignty as practical reason beyond the state, allowing us to move to the final stage of transnational legal development, including an imperative for what I will call an "Ecological Contract." Kant's philosophical-policy defines the scope of sovereign protection in one's duty to the integrity of humanity and the environment as dialectic representatives of the synthesis of the realm of freedom with the realm of nature.

Overall, the three-stage dialectic that defines the evolving concept of sovereignty maps onto both Collingwood's argument that practical reason moves from *utility* (Hume), to *right* (Hegel) to *duty* (Kant) and Bartelson's[14] argument (see Prologue) that a full analysis of sovereignty requires attention to its *source* (Hume), its *locus* (Hegel), and its *scope* (Kant). The ultimate purpose of this project is to explain international legal practice as an integrated manifestation of human practical reason. The motivation for this effort is to represent the entire philosophy and history of international law through a single coherent set of dialectic precepts that provide an essential, yet evolving, metaphysics for international law from its origins, through its modern dilemmas, and into its future. Let us begin with the application of Hume's philosophical-policy as the initial manifestation of practical reason in international law.

Acknowledgments

I wish to acknowledge the places that made this work possible, including The Law Faculty, the Lauterpacht Center For Research in International Law, and the Fellows and Staff of Wolfson College, all at the University of Cambridge, The School of International Studies, Simon Fraser University, The Fellows and Staff of Exeter College, the librarians at the Codrington Library, All Souls College, and the Collingwood Archive at the Bodleian Libraries, as well as the Facilities of Law and Philosophy at the University of Oxford, and Lehigh University. People, including Philip Allott, James Crawford, Vaughn Lowe, John Harriss, Roger O'Keefe, Chester Brown, Amanda Perreau-Saussine, Susan Marks, and David Braybrooke, as well as the manuscript reviewers, inspired and improved the argument herein. I have also drawn on components of previously published articles for this effort, including "Justice-As-Sovereignty: David Hume & the Origins of International Law," *British Year Book of International Law*, 79 (2007): 429–479; "A Proposal for 'Philosophical Method' in Comparative and International Law," *Pace International Law Review* (*Pace International Law Review*, Online. 1, no. 3 (2009): 1–14; http://digitalcommons.pace.edu/pilronline/3/); and "Philosophical-Policy & International Dispute Settlement: Process⇆Principle and the Ascendance of the WTO's Concept of Justice," *Journal of International Dispute Settlement*, (2012): 59–73. I sincerely thank the editors of these journals. A special thanks also goes to Mr Brian O'Connor at Palgrave-MacMillan for his enthusiasm about this entire project, and its publication.

John Martin Gillroy
Exeter College, Oxford, June 1, 2013

Prologue: Sovereignty and Practical Reason

Sovereignty is a central concept in international law. But there is no concept that generates as much confusion among scholars and practitioners. While there is general agreement that sovereignty, as the absolute power of the state to exist without transnational restrictions, has no application within the contemporary international system, this is where the agreement stops. Social science cannot seem to provide any single conceptualization of sovereignty that can not only describe the past and understand the dilemmas of the present but also predict the trends of the future with reasonable authority.

I both agree with, and challenge, this conclusion. I agree with it because sovereignty, like all social concepts, cannot be definitively classified as a single empirical phenomenon, but evolves dialectically over time, producing a variety of manifestations with the same underlying metaphysical essence.[1] But I also challenge it by contending that an essential concept of sovereignty does exist that encompasses most of the variant definitions and claims about its past and future. This unitary metaphysical foundation contains a tension of component ideas that relate sovereignty, as a manifestation of practical reason, to various definitions of justice, which are time-sensitive synthesis-moments or "snapshots in law" of sovereignty's metaphysical character. This seeming contradiction, that sovereignty is both pluralistic and unitary, is accessible through the transcendence of scientific method by philosophical method. I propose to show that sovereignty can be considered a dialectical concept with a stable metaphysical essence that produces plural manifestations over time as its component dialectics rebalance themselves.

In a definitive study of the concept of sovereignty, Jens Bartelson[2] examines the effort to apply scientific method to the idea of sovereignty in both international and sociological theory. He concludes that, first and foremost, problems of conceptual definition arise primarily when "a scientific understanding of sovereignty is attempted…the problems confronted by conceptual analysis are intrinsic to the meta-language guiding this analysis…[a meta-language preoccupied with] what it means to be scientific."[3]

Bartelson's deconstruction establishes that questions about the *source*, *locus*, and *scope* of sovereignty[4] must shift from an emphasis on the "quest" for its empirical essence to embrace a study of the epistemological context of the word itself, or the language of sovereignty in distinct historical periods. "If we are to understand the concept of sovereignty historically, the problem is not so much a matter of what *sovereignty* is, as it is a matter of what this *is* has come to mean."[5] For him, the chronology defines the concept.

He defines two possible routes to a conceptual understanding of the idea of sovereignty: first, through a scientific search for essence or, second, through an historical search for contextual truth as historical knowledge. He chooses the latter path, because he concludes that sovereignty is not a physical thing subject to essential scientific investigation.

> sovereignty has no essence, since it is what makes differen[t] spheres of politics empirically representable and intelligible; as soon as we start to demand that the concept of sovereignty should refer to something present in the world of empirical beings, our understanding of the concept itself must presuppose the same line in the water which is drawn in and through its meaningful use in political discourse…[t]hus, if we want to make sense of sovereignty…without itself being a mysterious prior essence, we should pay attention to the internal connections between sovereignty and knowledge.[6]

Bartelson's arguments about both the limits of empiricism in matters of conceptual analysis and the positive attributes of his historical epistemology are persuasive. However, while critical of any effort to use scientific method as a way of understanding sovereignty, his work is nevertheless encased within the methodological conventions of social science. For example, he definitively sorts empirical from normative conceptual worlds as a basis for his study and identifies the former as the source of meaning.[7] He also links empiricism with the existence of an object, and then with the idea of essence, so that in order for sovereignty to have any essence it must be an empirical object, which it is not.[8]

But perhaps, in addition to the deconstruction of sovereignty as a source of knowledge, which Bartelson accomplishes, there is another way to approach the subject of its essence: a philosophical-metaphysical approach. If the concept of sovereignty can be considered a metaphysical dialectic of normative and positive, rather than an empirical ontology, then we may be able to locate a new source for its essence.

R. G. Collingwood's philosophical method offers such an alternative to the social science methodology. His philosophical method attempts to treat the unique qualities of social concepts, like sovereignty, not as objects, but as metaphysical subjects of reason. That is, subjects of reason understood from the application of a set of (i.e., absolute and relative) philosophical presuppositions that are argued to be foundational to the way humans create, and are created by, the empirical world around them.

Here, Immanuel Kant is also helpful in that he describes two forms of reason that map onto, and can represent, the distinct subject matter of scientific and philosophical reason. For him, the application of human reason in the world must be defined in two ways. Kant distinguishes between

(1) *theoretical reason* in the realm of science, objects, and their causality and (2) *practical reason* in the realm of the application of human will to ends guided by logical systems of concepts establishing rules.[9] The realm of practical reason for Kant is the realm of human affairs, society, policy, and the law, where, for example, metaphysical concepts like autonomy are realized through the ideas and institutions of various definitions of justice. Combining Kant's distinction between theoretical and practical reason and his idea that practical reason is empirically accessible through rules of justice with Collingwood's philosophical method, we have a means of recognizing practical reason in international law and understanding its metaphysical properties through their affects on the changing ideas of justice in legal practice.

The use of philosophical method generates a search for the inherent dialectic character of the ideas and institutions of justice as they move, not toward the idea of a particular physical essence, but toward a metaphysical essence on what Collingwood calls a "scale of forms." In other words, the metaphysical essence of a concept like sovereignty is to be found in tracing the makeup and interaction of its dialectical components. These, over time, will surface as various definitions of justice representing synthesized iterations of practical reason on a scale of ever-increasing conceptual sophistication.

Specifically, Collingwood identifies three stages in the scale of forms for practical reason: justice as *utility*, justice as *right*, and justice as *duty*.[10] My first concern is with the genesis of justice in international law. For this purpose, if practical reason has a source, locus, and scope in international law, as Bartelson argues, then our initial task is to decipher the core "source" of sovereignty-as-utility or a genesis definition of justice within the international system. Here the concept of sovereignty, or more specifically, Justice-As-Sovereignty becomes the focus of study. With philosophical method, we can access an argument from practical reason, and with Justice-As-Sovereignty, we have a first manifestation of reason's changing content in legal practice.

Therefore, I propose a reconsideration of sovereignty through a search for its metaphysical essence; that is, a search for the distinct conceptual logic of dialectics that first defined sovereignty, as an expression of practical reason, in the rules of international justice. This will illuminate the normative and empirical, as well as the theoretical and practical, dimensions of sovereignty simultaneously by transcending the physical essence of sovereignty. From the standpoint of philosophical method, attention to the absolute and relative presuppositions of the metaphysical elements of Justice-As-Sovereignty, in stage one, is key. The intangible sets of ideas and their dialectic relations, which are its metaphysics, are critical to an understanding of the essence of the concept of sovereignty. This is true at all three stages of relative and absolute presuppositions (the latter two stages to be treated in future arguments) that define the progression of practical reason as justice in international legal practice. Each stage will have its own concept of sovereignty. Overall, I see the metaphysical essence of sovereignty through philosophical method, an essence revealed as a persistent feature of the changing ideas of justice made manifest as the international system evolves.

Delving more deeply into the history of sovereign practice in international law will reveal the essential logic of interlocking metaphysical presuppositions that make up the stages of sovereignty's scale of forms. This will show that the many seemingly diverse conceptualizations of sovereignty have but one common metaphysical root. This common root is found by applying the precepts of philosophical method, rather than those of scientific method. Further, this will reveal that sovereignty is inherently a dialectic concept composing a narrative of shifting emphasis among its inherent components. Being dialectic, its superficial manifestation changes through the creation of various practical synthesis solutions in law that define justice in the international system for particular contexts.

A strictly positivist idea of the context of sovereignty divorces it from its dialectic and metaphysical essence and defines it as a distinct set of physical properties: observable independent of normative value. Bartelson agrees that using science to understand the essence of ideas with nonphysical applications, like sovereignty, is problematic and, further, renders insight into sovereignty impossible.[11] By contrast, philosophical method assumes that the law is a dynamic and evolving concept within a changing social context, where the philosophical complexity of the idea of sovereignty will respond and change accordingly. The balance of dialectic elements within sovereignty must correspondingly shift to integrate new elements demanded by justice. For example, currently Justice-As-Sovereignty must respond to a growing legal concern for human rights as a responsibility of state legitimacy if it is to maintain its role in terms of the effective control of territory.

Bartelson's basic questions about the *source*, *locus*, and *scope* of sovereignty are useful here when combined with Collingwood's three dialectic stages of practical reason as representing justice as *utility*, justice as *right*, and justice as *duty*. I suggest that there are three distinct but interdependent definitions of justice involved in a full understanding of the metaphysical essence of the concept of sovereignty. First, one based on *utility*, which describes the genesis or *source* of sovereignty as practical reason in international law; second, one focused on *right* and the *locus* or proper attribution of sovereignty as practical reason between individuals, states, and international society; and a third dealing with *duty* and the *scope* of sovereignty as practical reason, or what it encompasses.

The application of philosophical method should show that instead of a multiplicity of independent and conflicting conceptual definitions of sovereignty, what results is a set of interdependent synthesis snapshots of Justice-As-Sovereignty in legal practice. These mark the outline or scale of forms for its shifting essence as a metaphysical concept in positive law. These snapshots reflect a common core of inherent ideas that change over time as human practical reason is expressed in an ever more refined idea of justice. This first book of three, each representing the analysis of one of the three stages of practical reason's scale of forms, will focus on the *source* of practical reason in a concept of justice as *utility* or sovereignty.

Utility for Collingwood is the first manifestation of practical reason in human affairs and, for him, is connected to the idea of the basic order and stability of society. Within the context of international law, utility means the most basic or essential definition of order in international affairs, which suggests the concept of sovereign equality. Collingwood's definition of utility depends on the unconscious evolution of social convention and no discussion of this topic can exclude consideration of David Hume, who argues that the essence of law lies in the social conventions evolved as the basic standards of order or public utility for the common good. In our effort to understand the source of practical reason in the essence of sovereignty, social convention must be acknowledged as playing a pivotal role.

If the essence of sovereignty begins in the social conventions of the international system, then we need to acknowledge the power of these social conventions in instantiating certain definitions and components of our conceptual world with almost sacred, yet unconscious, assumptions. Social convention is not originally a conscious habit but that collective pattern of behavior which evolves out of unconscious human interactions creating stable social relations over time. This stability makes formal rules as law, or justice, possible. The conventional definition of sovereignty, like all primary legal concepts, originates in the idea of justice created by the inherent dialectics of those social conventions that are initially codified as law. This imbues the concept of sovereignty with a seemingly essential definition that is, in fact, only the first stage along its scale of forms. Combined with a positivist predisposition, which denies any dialectic possibility, social convention imbues the initial conceptual logic of sovereignty with validity that grants it definitive status. However, it is limited validity.

To understand the *source* of practical reason that exists in the *essence* of sovereignty, we must use philosophical method to decipher its dialectic character as social convention; that is, to map the concepts that overlap to form its metaphysical system of absolute and relative presuppositions at this primary stage of conceptualization. This requires that we understand how sovereignty arose as a utilitarian definition of justice from social convention, to become the core of international law, as a form of practical reason, in its initial stage of development. This, in turn, requires a systematic philosophical logic of concepts describing the generic rise of social convention, its components and inherent dialectics, and explaining how these underlie and establish the essence of the concept of sovereignty through a logic of investigation that adequately explains the modern practice of international law.[12]

A systematic theory of social convention will aid our understanding of not only the source but, eventually, the locus and scope of sovereignty as a metaphysical concept. This will, in turn, provide a more expansive and useful definition of sovereignty with both unitary and plural characteristics. Rather than create a theory of social convention from scratch, the philosophical logic of David Hume can be adapted to the purpose of understanding the rise of the concept of sovereignty in the modern international system.

Some may dismiss Hume's relevance to these issues, as he only devoted a few pages of his work to the specific subject of international law. However, his entire philosophical output on human nature is an integrated and systematic argument about the human need for society and the rise of social convention, and eventually law, to stabilize human understanding and human community. The comprehensive and systematically integrated argument his philosophical logic of concepts offers about the generic rise of social convention is therefore suitable to our need to decipher a conceptual logic for the source of sovereignty in international law.

With the addition of Hume, we have created a four-tiered hierarchy that describes the project as a whole. First, at the most general level is a Kantian intuition that law should be interpreted as an expression of practical reason. This is not possible within the confines of positivism, as it primarily addresses theoretical reason through scientific method. The next tier down offers a solution to this problem. Utilizing Collingwood's philosophical method, we are able to place the idea of practical reason within a framework of assumptions that allows for the examination of the systematic nature of the law as a field of human action. Its dialectic and metaphysical characteristics become accessible, as does its capacity to be a systematic logic of concepts. The question then becomes: what specific content will enlighten us most when understood through philosophical method? In other words, how should we define practical reason for the purposes of applying it to international law? And, in addition, how are we to understand the implications of a metaphysical argument that by definition has no empirical landmarks?

The third tier of our model answers these questions. Because Kant argues that justice in legal practice is an empirical manifestation of practical reason in the world, we need to isolate the central concept that will act as a definition of justice at the genesis of international law. International law has been created around the concept of sovereignty. Therefore, the metaphysical elements of Justice-As-Sovereignty are of interest to an understanding of international legal practice as an expression of practical reason. But we must locate a systematic philosophical argument to inform our conceptualization of justice in international law.

The most specific and final tier of the hierarchy specifies the content of our definition of practical reason. Our examination of international law begins with the assumption that law has its genesis in social convention and that, because of this, a philosophical argument based on society derived from conventional roots is a reasonable point of departure. Here David Hume's logic of concepts can be utilized. Specifically, by sorting its components through the standards of philosophical method, we can organize Hume's philosophic argument into a *philosophical-policy and legal design* paradigm ready to interpret international law and its central norm of Justice-As-Sovereignty from the standpoint of the origin and evolution of social convention.

1

Philosophical Method, Hume's Philosophical-Policy, and Legal Design

Abstract

To conceptualize international law as an expression of practical reason, I adopt a procedure that applies philosophical-policy through legal design and has six steps: (1) A policy or legal issue is chosen (international law); (2) A philosophical system is selected to illuminate the issue (Hume's, because of its focus on social convention as the source of law); (3) The philosophical system is then sorted through the categories of Collingwood's philosophical method allowing one to identify the core dialectic, a scale of forms and the essential metaphysical structure of the philosophical system; (4) The fundamental assumptions for making policy and legal choices are then segregated transforming the philosophical system into a philosophical-policy paradigm; (5) The policy paradigm is then applied to international law as legal design and tested in the light of legal practice, linking the superstructure of codified law to the substructure of philosophical precepts that created it; (6) A feedback loop allows the comprehensive policy argument (CPA) and its interpretation of international law to be evaluated in terms of its utility.

Superficially, Hume does not appear to be concerned with the philosophical concept of reason but with human passions.[1] However, upon closer examination, Hume's concept of human nature treats the persons, their understanding, character, and social context, within a comprehensive argument about the power of social convention. For Hume, convention is rooted in the practical application of human rationality, both conscious and unconscious, to action, given one's circumstances, to generate collective practice.[2] Hume's perspective attempts both to understand the employment of theoretical reasoning to one's physical surroundings and to apply "practical" reasoning to the creation, stability, and persistence of human social ideas and institutions.[3]

The dialectical essence of Hume's "practical reason" is the tension between reason and passions. Passions, because of their role in moving human action toward social interaction and stability, are the root of social convention and therefore the necessary point of focus for his argument. However, for our purposes, what is of interest is not that the passions dominate reason in Hume's consideration of the human approach to the practical world, but that both reason and passion are dialectic agents in the persistence of human nature. This renders Hume's effort one we can classify as an application of practical reason.

Hume not only identifies the origins of society in human passions, but uses them to trace the evolution of social convention, which acts as a base for progressively codified legal rules. These rules assure the stability of social order, while collective action increases in size and complexity. Overall, Hume offers a complete and systematized philosophical argument about the genesis or creation of law from the evolution of social convention. Within Hume's philosophy, international law is a logical entailment of a general evolution of law from practical reason. International law and its established definition of Justice-As-Sovereignty can thus be viewed in a systematic and developmental way.

Recognition of the application of Hume's philosophy for such practical matters as international law can be traced to Duncan Forbes. He describes the philosophy of David Hume as an applied philosophy, or a "*Philosophical-Politics*."[4] I propose to employ Hume's logic of concepts, supporting the rise and maintenance of social convention in society, as a basis for the genesis of "sovereignty" in international legal practice. My goal is to understand how the nexus of philosophy, public policy, and law, represented in Hume's argument for social convention, is useful in illuminating the origins of international law. This will provide the study of international legal practice, as a *logic of investigation*, with an underlying philosophical *logic of concepts*. In this way, we shall transcend and enhance traditional positivism and empirical or scientific method and be able to proffer a different, more complete, flexible, and comprehensive understanding of the roots of sovereignty in law.[5]

Here Collingwood's[6] philosophical method can be used to provide a foundation of standards and categories for the application of philosophy to law. This method assumes a dialectic between theory and practice where the understanding of a policy or legal issue requires that the philosophical systems that provide the logic of concepts both for the existing law, and for competitive policy arguments, be deciphered. These newly identified systems can then be used for a deeper understanding of a superficial practice that includes the underlying reasons for such a practice. The use of philosophical method, in this way, transforms the systematic and whole philosophical systems under examination into philosophical-policy paradigms, which then can be applied to legal practice. Consequently, both the substructure of the status quo legal practice, its strengths and weaknesses,

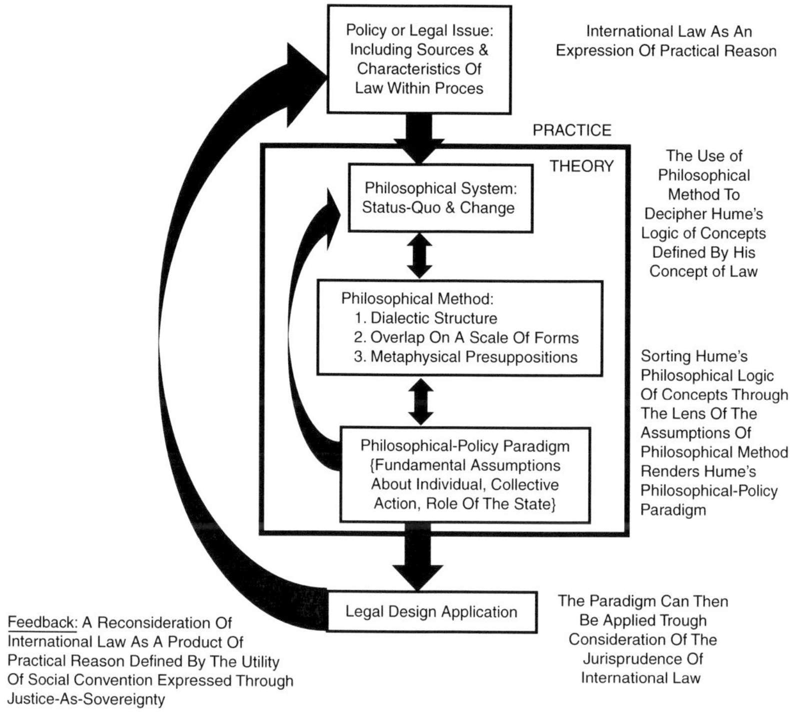

Figure 1.1 Philosophical-policy and legal design: The creation of a comprehensive policy argument (CPA).

and the dynamic parameters of change in the evolution of the concept under study are revealed.

To use philosophical methodology, (Figure 1.1) one itemizes the characteristics of the policy or law under scrutiny, then matches a preexisting philosophical system to those characteristics in order to provide a theoretical substructure for legal practice.[7] Next one takes the tenets of this philosophical system and examines them through the lens of philosophical method to decipher the core dialectic(s), the overlap of concepts defining the subject and its scale of forms. From these, the absolute and relative presuppositions of its metaphysics can be deciphered. Next, the system, understood through the philosophical lens, is turned into a philosophical-policy paradigm by segregating its fundamental assumptions, operating principle, material conditions, and shorthand decision-making procedure. Philosophical method, like its scientific counterpart, provides a set of categories and procedures, a particular point of view from within which the cross-section of social matter, viewed through any number of conceptual logics (i.e., philosophical systems) can be uniformly studied.

Hume's philosophy requires adaptation before its full application to international law can be undertaken and analyzed. To do this, I shall examine Hume's philosophical system or logic of concepts through the lens of Collingwood's philosophical method. Simultaneously, I will decipher its "philosophical-policy paradigm"[8] by defining its fundamental assumptions about the individual, collective action and the role of the state. The resulting paradigm, with its foundation of philosophical method, can then be used to describe the genesis of the international legal system, mapping theory onto practice as an expression of practical reason.

But why Hume? Hume provides a logic of philosophical concepts that fulfills the requirements for a fuller understanding of the origin and evolution of law from social convention. Specifically, he offers a more adequate delineation of the overlapping concepts of the law in terms of the ideas and institutions that deal with norms and justice (i.e., principle, process, practice, rule, power, interest). He also provides an understanding of the essential dialectics at the core of a conceptualization of the law with both unconscious and conscious human participation (i.e., passion⇆reason; process⇆principle). A Humean perspective establishes an evolutionary scale of forms based on these dialectics that conceptualizes law as applied practical reason. It creates both a two-stage legal system and a fuller and more systematic explanation of the presuppositions of the concept of sovereignty, than positivist models, alone, can provide. Most importantly, Hume's idea of science makes his argument ideally suited for examination through philosophical method, philosophical-policy, and legal design.

Hume's Idea of Science as Philosophical-Practical Reason

Although coopted by positivists[9] to support a modern social-scientific method, Hume's specific definition of philosophy-as-science was based on a more comprehensive understanding of its interdependent application to the empirical and philosophical dimensions of both nature and *human* nature. The more comprehensive character of Hume's approach to humanity, which employs what Collingwood enumerated as the characteristics of philosophical method, is a result of the definition of "science" that was prevalent in his era. The Enlightenment approach to "science" included concern for the application of reason to both humanity and nature and was founded on a recognition of the dialectic and interdependent makeup of life. For Hume and his contemporaries, approaching the world "scientifically" entailed combining philosophical and scientific method.

Many social arguments have been written since the mid-nineteenth century and, all are, in one way or another, and to a greater or lesser extent, derived from positivism with its roots in scientific method alone. Even those who criticize positivism still buy into its empirical presuppositions and produce noncomprehensive "normative" critiques of specific applications of positivist argument using components of, rather than integrated, philosophical systems. Others collapse into nihilistic "post-structural-modernism," giving up on the possibility of truth altogether. In either case, the dichotomies and assumptions of scientific method remain the foundation of contemporary research.

Nihilistic modernism demonstrates the most profound power of positivist method in forcing critics to reject the idea of "enlightenment" itself. By wrongly accepting that scientific method was the sole legacy of Enlightenment thinking, critical theory, for example, sentenced its descendants to follow the maxim that those wishing to depart from the dominance of the material, the efficient, the instrumental value, or quantitative reductionism, should reject the entire Enlightenment project. This is aptly reflected in a seminal argument for modernism made by Horkheimer and Adorno.

> For the Enlightenment, anything which cannot be resolved into numbers, and ultimately into one, is illusion; modern positivism consigns it to poetry. Utility remains the watchword from Parmenides to Russell. All gods and qualities must be destroyed.[10]

But the comprehensive idea of philosophy-as-science also arose during the Enlightenment and is a cornerstone of Hume's argument.[11] Hume's "science" of society is indeed a descriptive account of the origin of social cooperation. But it is simultaneously a prescriptive account of the normative obligations created by this human interaction that define just relations in the persistence of social organization that gain salience through levels of sanction seeking to assure certain expectations and acts. Hume was not writing in an era dominated by a dichotomizing positive methodology, but one where philosophical logics of concepts and empirical logics of investigation were assumed to be interdependent. Social presuppositions were assumed to have a dynamic context more akin to the dialectic idea of positive⇆normative.

Two strains of thought emerged from the Enlightenment. The first was the application of theoretical reason, or reason-in-nature, to classify empirical objects. Here the scientific method of Galileo and Newton was perfected in a quantitative logic and a classification system based on observation and induction that responded to a universal set of presuppositions relating to our cumulative experience, up to that time, with the world of causality. Meanwhile, a second parallel effort refined our application of practical reason to the individual as moral agent, to political organization in general, and to the universal and necessary roots of human social evolution. This effort aimed at freeing human studies from the dominance of theistic explanation, and law from determination by revelation. In response to the Reformation, a core imperative of the Enlightenment was the refinement of a universal and secular standard of practical reason as a basis for the study of society, as well as its inherent concepts and institutions.

This imperative of the Enlightenment responds to the perception that humanity and nature are related dialectically but require different sets of methodological presuppositions. Rousseau, Kant, and Hegel, among others, worked to develop this method for the application of practical reason to human affairs, but they were not as successful as the natural scientists in establishing a unified and practically-reasoned basis for their systems of thought. Perhaps this is because the superficial examination of social life suggests a pluralism of thought that defeats a common essential method of analysis. Perhaps the traditional integration of philosophy and theology was too powerful to be overcome in an age of Reformation and religious war. Or perhaps the extreme reaction to the unity and empirical prejudices of science by the Romantics, with their integration of social ideals and emotion, made the effort to base social life in a reasoned method seem less sure, less true, and therefore less possible.

The resulting asymmetry between a universal theoretical reason and the pluralism of practical reason contributed to the nineteenth century argument that one could avoid all of the presumed "theistic" and "ideological" problems of plural practical reasons by replacing them with a definitive scientific method for social study. Over the years, the philosophical method integrated by the scholastics and applied to human life during the Enlightenment atrophied from lack of use and was marginalized by social science. With the normative dichotomized from the positive, philosophy became an unreasoning ideology with all its didactic implications. Reason became associated primarily with its theoretical-scientific variant. Objects, their measurement, and a quantitative rationality of understanding, became dominant not only in the study of nature but in the study of humanity. Meanwhile, the qualities of human beings and their societies, associated with idiosyncratic values, dwindled in influence.

The dominance of empirical science representing reason in human affairs led, by the mid-nineteenth century, to theoretical reason being divorced from the practical and given status as the point of departure for "social science." With the implementation of a "social" scientific method, the analysis of human context through physical objects and the application of theoretical reason classified human life into a system of definitive or eristic bins. Consequently, the positivist ideal that one could replace revelation most effectively with theoretical reason-as-science was adapted for use on human and social phenomena and became the dominant ideal in the following centuries for advocates, critics, and opponents alike.

Hume's philosophy is not a specific theoretical effort to define "a corner" of the greater social landscape, but a comprehensive effort to argue for a specific definition of practical reason in human social life that contains both a logic of philosophical concepts and a logic of empirical investigation. Hume is not concerned with the specific struggles of any particular individual, group, or society, or any single aspect of human social cooperation (e.g., economic, political, legal) segregated from all others. While he promotes justice as a neutral process-norm, he recognizes that critical principle, based on reason, does exist and must be accounted for, if only in a secondary role within the dialectic of process⇆principle.

Hume treats both normative and empirical science comprehensively. Even though his idea of justice is descriptive in that it arises from the social interaction of persons, he also argues that, without a moral foundation, justice is impossible. A concept of sovereignty described within the framework of Hume's philosophical-policy will be a dynamic one, with its source in a set of overlapping concepts and an evolutionary scale of forms where justice is refined until codified in formal institutions. Hume's philosophical-policy offers a comprehensive philosophy-as-science, rather than compartmentalized theory, with an inherent metaphysics of absolute and relative presuppositions that, in the following chapters, will be applied to understand the metaphysical essence of the concept of sovereignty in international law.

Traditional positivist interpretations notwithstanding, Hume's philosophy is scientific in that it is a comprehensive and inherently metaphysical application of human practical reason to social life.[12] Although he seeks a description of the evolution of convention in society, and he contends that an *improper* theological metaphysics has been invoked to try and understand the social world, he neither rejects nor denies that metaphysics is necessary for the full understanding of human social evolution. As shall be seen, his metaphysical argument generates a crosscurrent of dialectics within the concept of Justice-As-Sovereignty, all containing relative presuppositions that overlap in their dynamic refinement toward the essence of social order in one absolute presupposition: the human passion for a stable international society.[13]

Hume intends to describe how human social cooperation originates and then perpetuates itself over time, context, expanding population, and social complexity. His philosophy is simultaneously normative and descriptive to this end, where these concepts overlap and are inherently interconnected within the conceptual logic of his greater philosophical system. His synthesized solution to the question of human nature and social order is based on the recognition that the moral or normative arises and changes, on a scale of forms, from the empirical interaction of human beings.

From a twenty-first century standpoint, Hume is a "scientist" of human nature and social evolution. But for reasons just explained, this categorization is a misleading one. Hume's descriptive analysis of causality in the natural world is akin to, but not the same as, his argument for ethics and society. Overall, there is no doubt that his effort is to apply science to society. But his is science as a comprehensive and universal philosophical subject, and employs a method of observation encased within a deeper metaphysics of human nature. This is science as it was for Isaac Newton, not Bertrand Russell.

Hume argues that society is not just a result of probability theory and sense impressions, but the dialectic complexity of human characteristics as they both seek society and short circuit its viability. Hume's argument reflects the inherent tensions between the human and natural world. For example, while reason and understanding are sufficient to decipher causality, human social nature requires both an acknowledgment of the interactions between understanding and impression in the mind, and ideas and actions that result from the struggle between two faculties of the mind trying to define human practical action. They represent opposites with an inherent dialectic tension and therefore equal status in the definition of one another: reason⇆passions. Although Hume's eventual synthesis argument makes reason the "slave of the passions," the latter is neither dichotomized from the former nor treated in total isolation in terms of one's control over choices and actions. The master–slave dynamic,[14] understood through the dialectic of process⇆principle, is still relational, even given the dominance of the former within Hume's logic of concepts.

David Hume is useful to us because he is neither an idealist nor a utopian with a prescription for humanity's future. The utility of Hume's philosophical-policy to international law is that he offers a systematized "philosophical" argument that tells a comprehensive "origin" or source story for the concept of sovereignty in international law. This argument includes a metaphysics of absolute and relative presuppositions that, as we shall see, maps onto our experience of international legal practice. By offering a detailed application of Hume's philosophical-policy paradigm as legal design, we can begin to see the details of how practical reason describes the origins of human social life and the evolution and refinement of social, political, and legal institutions. By using philosophical method to understand Hume's logic of concepts as a philosophical-policy paradigm, a deeper understanding of the essence of sovereignty as an expression of practical reason in international law becomes possible. To begin to see how this is possible, Collingwood's philosophical method and my use of it to create philosophical-policy and legal design paradigms needs explanation.

The Lens of Philosophical Method

Collingwood's philosophical method can be simplified into five specific characteristics that underlie the application of practical reason to human affairs. To apply philosophical method is to promote:

1. Comprehensive philosophy over compartmentalized theory;
2. Dialectic argument over eristic;
3. Refinement of ideas over the imperative of discovery;
4. Overlap of concepts rather than their definitive classification;
5. An essential metaphysics of absolute and relative presuppositions, not a primary dependence on surface validity.

First, practical reason expressed through philosophical method, requires a shift in modern thinking from a positivist focus on compartmentalized *theory* to the study of comprehensive *philosophy*. Since the positivist revolution of the mid-nineteenth century, we have been trained in our distinct disciplines to pursue theory adequate to explaining our particular corner of the sociopolitical or legal landscape. Unlike our predecessors in the seventeenth and eighteenth centuries, we no longer seek a comprehensive and essential philosophical understanding of how human practical reason applies to its social milieu, how it shapes and is shaped by the individual humans within it, and how and why it renders, in particular circumstances, particular institutional and legal structures for its persistence over time. Hume's argument, for example, begins with human psychology and understanding and ends with a general theory of social origin and persistence for human nature, while integrating the empirical and normative dimensions of the interdisciplinary subjects. Contemporary theorists are trained, first, to classify themselves as exclusively normative or empirical and then focus on a very specific application of their social or political or ethical theory that assumes only local validity for their particular subject.[15] One is no longer responsible to understand the systemic philosophical whole of human nature nor to apply universal and necessary sociolegal ideas to specific cases and controversies.[16] The immediate and practical are the only positivist objectives.

Theory is most often applied piecemeal and does not attempt to generate a comprehensive understanding of any philosopher's greater conceptual system, as we will do here. Positivists employ bits and pieces of exegesis (e.g., Hobbes' state of nature, Rousseau's general will) applied in isolation from a philosopher's greater logic of concepts, to make specific theoretical points. Positivism discounts metaphysics or integrated philosophical systems and seeks only those components of theory that aid in the specific understanding of an explicit empirical question. But concepts like sovereignty or macro-trends like globalization or climate change and how contemporary international law and policy might apply human reason to regulate them may require more than the exploration of "theoretical" corners, or isolated components of a greater philosophical space.

The second characteristic of philosophical method is the recognition of the dialectic nature of human reason. We have abandoned the ancient assumption that the core of human practical reason is *dialectic* for the modern idea that political and scholarly discourse are essentially *eristic*. The dialectic is a logical form of reasoning built on the idea that no philosophical concept exists in isolation. Dialectic concepts are assumed to be connected to webs of other concepts that influence and are influenced by them. The tension between a concept, and its opposite, or system of interacting concepts, makes up its metaphysical context and generates its conceptual essence. In dialectic, no idea can be assessed without reference to its dynamic interface with related concepts that, by affecting each other, become mutually interdependent.

The eristic approach, familiar to us through positivism, assumes that ideas should be definitively classified and isolated, for both study and practical application, like physical objects classified within closed systems. Any ensuing debate is based on creating confrontational sets of definitive and isolated precepts that will then be pitted against one another and defended without compromise to create one winner and one loser in a policy or legal debate.

While both eristic and dialectic approaches involve argument, the goals are distinct. Eristic argument creates ideological confrontation over normative matters as the rule and assumes that truth is in the integrity of an ideological position. In eristic debate, one is right or wrong before the discussion of ideas commences, while in dialectic argument all positions within the conversation are assumed to have a piece of the truth that can be synthesized into a result that allows most parties to the discussion to contribute to the "truth" of the outcome.[17]

The eristic approach to ideas fails to acknowledge that normative⇆positive or theory⇆practice are integrated dialectic pairs where one component cannot be assessed in the absence of the other. As the core of positivist political and legal scholarship, eristic studies begins with one component of a dichotomized pair (viz., empirical without normative), and requires a distinct literature for each. Eristic positivism requires that an idea be definitively classified and assessed without benefit of its inherent dialectic counterarguments. Eristic "debate" assumes that discourse and argument are a contest of established "truths," each containing an integrity of ideological position that fails if compromised by any admission that opposing arguments contain value.

A third characteristic of philosophical method is its focus on *philosophical refinement and justification* rather than scientific discovery. Philosophical method assumes that all social concepts are known to us, making the task of analysis the refinement and use of their meaning to justify a distinct range of action in changing contexts. In science, one aims to discover; in philosophy, one aims to further refine and justify new conceptions of a known idea.

The predisposition toward scientific discovery has led to a focus, within a "science of law,"[18] on the validity of static concepts, rather than the assumption of the evolution or refinement of a concept over time. Bartelson's argument about sovereignty, for example, assumes that each historic epoch studied has a separate and contextually sensitive definition of sovereignty that is valid only in those circumstances. But, because of its dialectic nature, philosophical method assumes that all the contextual manifestations of a concept, like sovereignty, are essentially interrelated. Philosophical method suggests that concepts are already known to us at some level of sophistication, and our task, through dialectic analysis, is to refine our understanding of them and their inherent complexity as applied ideas.

With a focus on refinement, philosophical method moves away from a concentration on the observable surface, to a search for the "essence" of a concept that transcends particular manifestations of its practice. This is the concept's *metaphysical* essence, indigenous to the idea itself and revealed through the progressive philosophical analysis of its transcendent ideas. A metaphysical essence is not a point of departure, but the result of the growing sophistication of a concept as its inherent dialectic ideas rebalance in more and more sophisticated combinations.

The fourth characteristic of philosophical method, *overlap* on a *scale of forms*, provides the means to access the essence of a concept. Unlike scientific concepts definitively classified by genus and species, philosophical concepts, because of their dialectic character, overlap with one another and create a scale or continuum of forms as they evolve to the increasing demands of practical reason, toward their essence.[19]

The overlap of categories into which a single philosophical idea simultaneously fits, frustrates the scientific classification of social, political, and legal ideas into one and only one observational classification. But the predisposition to define a concept by its empirical surface alone should be resisted. It is best understood in terms of both what can be observed and the underlying ideas that define and justify the concept's distinct manifestations over time. The development of a legal concept like sovereignty, along its scale of forms, toward its essence, involves all of those variables that contribute to its essential integrity,[20] defined by its dialectic and overlapping relations.

> The result of this identification [of essence] is that every form, so far as it is low in the scale, is to that extent an imperfect or inadequate specification of the generic essence, which is realized with progressive adequacy as the scale is ascended.[21]

As Bartelson contends, the essence of a concept cannot be understood in physical terms. A philosophical concept cannot be treated as a strictly positive object uniquely classified and studied in the absence of its dialectic context. In the same way, to seek the refinement and justification of the generic essence of sovereignty requires more than treating the law as a valid, isolated, and static concept, which is what positivism prescribes.

Linking distinct levels of overlapping complexity creates a philosophical "scale of forms" for a concept.

> for if the species of a philosophical genus overlap, the distinction between the known and the unknown, which in a non-philosophical subject-matter involves a difference between two mutually exclusive classes of truths, in a philosophical subject-matter implies that we may both know and not know the same thing; a paradox which disappears in the light of the notion of a scale of forms of knowledge, where coming to know means coming to know in a different and better way.[22]

With the assumption of a scale of forms as an expression of practical reason, we can use philosophical method to create ever deeper and interdependent definitions of the nature of sovereignty in international law.

Fifth, and finally, the *metaphysical*[23] nature of "essence" is more specifically defined by philosophical method in terms of a hierarchy of *relative* and *absolute* presuppositions. Here, hierarchy means that a series of dialectically interrelated relative presuppositions lead, finally, to an absolute presupposition that defines the source of the concept. The absolute presupposition is the moral primitive of the concept, its source, and the fundamental point of departure for finding its essence. The absolute presupposition is necessary to the concept's wholeness or integrity; no further presuppositions inform it. As Kaldor efficiency is to market policy methods, as autonomy is to Kant's theory of morality, and as the need for society is to Hume's argument for human nature, "[a]n absolute presupposition is one which stands, relatively to all questions to which it is related, as a presupposition, never as an answer[24] which means that 'metaphysics is the science of absolute presuppositions.'"[25]

Justification is the currency of human ideas and norms for philosophical method. The capacity of a particular set of absolute and relative presuppositions to properly inform the design of a policy argument, and the legal rules thus rendered within the context of practice, as well as its sufficiency to support its standards in practice, mark a policy idea as persuasive in legal discourse.

A well-justified and persuasive policy argument advances both the concepts involved and the degree of their success in amending the institutional structure of legal practice. Seeking ever-greater depth for legal concepts also responds to the need for a progressively more complex and sophisticated system of interlocking legal ideas and institutions that produce an ever-more sophisticated concept of justice. The refinement of rights and rules as dispositive in law is especially important given the present flux of practical reason in legal practice, which must respond to globalization and climate change as challenges to the established international rule of law.

Within positivism, a metaphysics of absolute and relative presuppositions is replaced by layers of equally relative physical presuppositions, all assumed to be true based on empirical argument and experimentation.[26] This perspective overlooks the separate roles of absolute and relative presuppositions and ignores their distinct philosophical character, metaphysical interrelations, and dynamic dialectic evolution.

When a legal argument, for example, assumes all its presuppositions to be relative, it is not assuming a dynamic dialectic connection between them, but a circular logic, as each relative presupposition is an "answer" to one level of questions, while it poses questions for the next level of similarly relative presuppositions. By assuming that all of these relative presuppositions are independently true without analysis, the purpose of any inherent metaphysical scale of forms is defeated and concepts become isolated in time and space. It becomes impossible to create a logical scale of forms for the intellectual refinement of a concept, as one has no grounds to sort and justify connections between the concept's presuppositions. Also, without a single common and fundamental foundation as a point of departure for the repeated dialectical interaction between theory⇆practice as they move toward essential refinement, the practice connected to a concept like sovereignty remains superficial. Consequently, sovereignty is less useful in understanding an ever-more complex international legal system.

From the perspective of philosophical method, fundamental presuppositions are singular and foundational within the system of metaphysics for any philosophical logic of concepts, and necessary to define a persuasive policy argument and its application to practice.

> Metaphysics is concerned with absolute presuppositions. We do not acquire absolute presuppositions by arguing; on the contrary, unless we have them

> already arguing is impossible to us. Nor can we change them by arguing; unless they remained constant all our arguments would fall to pieces. We cannot confirm ourselves in them by "proving" them; it is proof that depends on them, not they on proof....We must accept them and hold firmly to them; we must insist on presupposing them in all our thinking without asking why they should be thus accepted. But not without asking what they are.[27]

Both relative and absolute presuppositions exist in every facet of human life. But an *absolute* presupposition is one that "stands, relative to all questions to which it is related, as a presupposition, never as an answer."[28] These exist, however, only at the most primitive and essential level of conceptual understanding. They are fundamental components in a greater logical-philosophical system of relative presuppositions that are dynamic both within themselves, on the scale of forms, and with other interrelated concepts that dialectically connect theory to practice.

Absolute presuppositions are necessary in-and-of-themselves to argument, discourse, and the logical structure of the social or legal system, but can exist untested by argument only to the extent that they are nested within a system of relative presuppositions that are constantly so tested. Absolute presuppositions should also be openly acknowledged and tested by the analyst in terms of their capacity to support a logically intact, and therefore persuasive, argument.

In effect, because of a reliance on a narrow definition of empirical practice as a source of both normative and positive legal argument, we who study and use international law have accepted a definitively classified underlying set of relative presuppositions related to the observational history of practice that are treated as a set of absolute and isolated presuppositions (e.g., sovereignty, intervention, justice, norms).[29] This makes international law static and, without an absolute presupposition, logically circular. It grants us neither a scale of forms with a dynamic dialectic, nor an underlying metaphysics with an integrated system of logical concepts. Consequently, international law lacks foundation to support the source, locus, and scope of practical reason as it faces new and more demanding global challenges.

In order to accommodate the complexities involved in these challenges, and avoid a positivist bias, the whole philosophical system must be transformed into a policy paradigm fit for application to the analysis and design of international law.[30] By taking Hume's logic of concepts and applying the two-step procedure of *philosophical-policy* and *legal design* it can be demonstrated that he offers a philosophy that synthesizes the intricate social context of justice with an underlying metaphysics of sovereignty that defines the origins of international law in terms of practical reason.

Philosophical-Policy and Legal Design

A fundamental premise of philosophical method is that *dialectic* rather than eristic relations exist between policy argument, process, and the codification of law, creating and recreating justice and the rule of law as these evolve over time. Focusing on an overlapping logic of legal concepts makes legal *design*, or the understanding and refinement of the concepts of law through philosophical method and its policy paradigms, key to comprehending the core conceptual questions in international politics, policy, and law.[31] The immediate problem is operationalizing philosophical method to create an adequate metaphysical map of the dialectic constituents of the concept of sovereignty that can then be applied to practice. Here, the use of existing philosophical systems examined through the lens of philosophical method, with applicability to the concepts under scrutiny, provides the shortcut to the systematic logic of concepts necessary to investigate practice.

To provide a metaphysical map of the concept of sovereignty we need to appreciate its role as a basis for the current definition of justice-as-order in the international system. This requires that we have a philosophical argument that illuminates the origin and persistence of human social cooperation and the norms that assure its stability over time. Hume offers a philosophical argument about precisely this. His origin story of social convention generating law offers a philosophical-policy paradigm. Using legal design, this paradigm can provide an understanding of the metaphysical substructure of positive practice. By understanding the essence of Justice-As-Sovereignty as a source of practical reason, we gain a more complete picture of the origin of international law.

Philosophical-policy, or the application of philosophical method to the organization and integration of a particular system of thought, like Hume's, provides a lens that allows one to explicate the categories and ideas of a particular policy paradigm. The resulting paradigm organizes the context, metaphysical components, and history systematically, as a *logic of concepts*, prior to, and rather than relying solely on, the traditional empirical *logic of investigation* that marks standard positivist legal analysis.[32] Unlike the typical social science approach to law, the essential definition of the legal concepts involved are systematically identified and argued, rather than assumed; that is, they are studied through the tenets of Collingwood's philosophical method. A philosophical-policy paradigm is assumed to be made up of dialectically interconnected ideas that overlap within a given philosophical system, while existing on a scale of forms, self-refining toward essence over time through continued application and analysis. To the degree a philosophical system can be understood as having this structure, it has the potential to be a philosophical-policy paradigm.

To create a philosophical-policy paradigm, the details of a philosophical system are sorted into fundamental categories that, in our case, must be addressed by all philosophical arguments seeking to influence policy and law. Specifically, these fundamental categories define who the individual is, what collective action problem informs the need for policy, and the role of the state in regulating justice through the law. This method also segregates the absolute presupposition of the philosophical system built on these definitions and generates a set of systematic policy precepts (SPPs) that decode the paradigm's inherent concept of law. The resulting paradigm has a capacity to expose the essential ideas within a particular legal issue or set of issues through application as legal design. It also determines the metaphysical content of the logic of concepts involved in, and determines the process of investigation for, the legal issue under study.

Overall, systematically treating the ends and means characteristic of a philosophical-policy paradigm allows one to match an appropriate logic of concepts or set of critical presuppositions to the characteristics of a legal question. This enables us to identify the essential components in the creation of specific areas of law. For example, instead of assuming that a traditional market logic can determine policy in all cases, one has access to many systematic philosophical paradigms for the analysis of various categories of public policy.

Legal design, the second component in the application of philosophical method, is the implementation phase of philosophical-policy. Instead of creating policy with a single set of unexamined and nonsystematic superficial values, within a primarily retrospective and empirical methodology for collective decision-making, one relies on a paradigm of philosophical-policy, and its integrated logic of concepts, for both a retrospective and prospective understanding of the design of law from policy choice. In this way, an investigation of the law is backed by a full and systemized logic of philosophical concepts. This enables one to examine empirical policy and law with a variety of philosophical paradigms where each, given the existent facts or characteristics of the issue, may lead to a distinct explanation of the law.

Legal design creates codified law through a dialectical synthesis that integrates an empirical logic of problem investigation with a detailed and systematic philosophical logic of concepts. Legal design assumes that a sound legal recommendation requires accommodation of a series of dialectics that are common to all philosophical-policy paradigms, but configured or balanced in distinct ways. These dialectics include joint concern with, for example, the theory⇆practice, normative⇆positive, local⇆universal, and individual⇆collective dimensions of law, associated, in the immediate case, with the genesis of sovereignty in public international law. Legal design relies on philosophical-policy to judge the dynamic and essential relationship between ideas⇆institutions as dialectic components involved in the creation of, and solution to, any public policy or legal question.

To analyze and understand legal scholarship, or the possibilities for generating paradigms, *philosophical-policy* with *legal design* also synthesizes the several means that are currently available for one to write, think about, or discuss ethical, legal, or political thought and argument. For example, traditionally, a lawyer or policy maker might reconstruct an argument from a writer's published and unpublished work, or examine how a policy scholar's writing is understood by contemporary thinkers and deployed in their work, through modern tools like game theory. Or one might focus on the body of subsequent scholarship inspired by the writer's work but which may not necessarily conform to the logic of the original exegesis of that work.

Philosophical-policy and legal design integrates these distinct approaches to legal scholarship into a single method, employing a two-stage process of study and dialectic synthesis.

In stage one, the philosophical-policy paradigm, drawn from a greater philosophical system derived from a body of scholarship, is considered as a whole, prior to and independent of any application to practice. One begins, not with selected bits and pieces of a philosopher's writing, but with his or her ideas considered as a dialectically interconnected and synthesized whole logic of concepts. This allows one to approach that philosophy with more integrity than if one extricates selected components of the philosopher's thought to justify an isolated idea within the context of an otherwise non-philosophical argument. The emphasis in stage one is in applying the logic of philosophical method; that is, deciphering any existing *dialectic* relations and understanding the system's *metaphysics*. The philosopher's work is considered independently, and as a comprehensive system, before applying it, through an investigatory logic, to a specific legal or policy context.

In stage two, legal design applies the resulting philosophical-policy paradigm to a context-driven empirical logic of investigation in order to understand it more fully and, if necessary, to create an argument for change. While one requires philosophical-policy to set the standards of evaluation for analysis from the integrated philosophical argument alone, this second stage can employ modern analytic tools, such as game theory or statistical methods, to investigate the internal logic and implications of the philosophical system under study without compromising its conceptual logic. These modern tools, as well as the context of application, are interpreted *ex post* through the logical and structural requirements of the philosophical-policy paradigm itself, and not the other way round. These tools can only be legitimately used if they fit into the categories and context of the preexisting philosophical logic of concepts, and illuminate the inherent conceptual scheme of the philosopher's systematic exegesis, rather than prejudice or corrupt it. The combined use of philosophical-policy with legal design generates insights that are consistent with both the spirit and the letter of the philosopher's original system of ideas, as well as the facts-on-the-ground.

Intended to be inclusive, the two-stage method of philosophical-policy and legal design can describe the integrated application of any philosophical paradigm or system to the context of politics, public policy, or the law, with the objective of transcending its prevailing intellectual environment so as to identify its source, locus, and scope anew. Philosophical-policy and legal design embody an application of philosophical method that provides both a deconstruction and synthetic reconstruction of practical reason in the law. Unlike positivism it acknowledges that no concept exists in isolation and considers the source of practical reason in international law in terms of the dialectic makeup of the concept of sovereignty. This provides a more comprehensive understanding of both the many faces of sovereignty in legal practice and the common metaphysical foundation from which they all spring.

Philosophical-policy is more than the study of a philosophical system for its own sake, or the use of selected philosophical concepts in a practice- or context-driven analysis. It is an application of philosophical arguments to collective experience in order to synthetically integrate questions of what *ought* to be with questions of what *is*. Applying Hume's philosophical-policy, through legal design, determines "practice" from within the logic of his "theory," without compromising the parameters of his philosophical argument by prior concerns for context, practice, or the tools of empirical analysis.

Hume's Philosophical-Policy Paradigm and Legal Design

To convert Hume's philosophical system to a philosophical-policy paradigm, and apply it to international law, the terms of philosophical method must be mapped onto the categories of fundamental assumptions (i.e., about the individual, the collective action problem, and the role of the state) as defined within the conceptual logic of Hume's system.

The First Fundamental Assumption: The Individual—Hume's Dialectic of Human Nature and the Circumstances of Justice

The core of David Hume's philosophical system, and the first component of his philosophical-policy, concerns the roots of human nature, or the psychological fundamentals of how an individual's practical reason influences interaction with other human beings, rendering social organization. For Hume, human nature is not atomistic but universal; it is not static but evolutionary. Not dominated by a single predisposition or set of unbending principles that require eristic argument, human nature forms, and is formed, through the dialectic interaction of inherent characteristics as these adapt to context.

Hume's individual is a creature of circumstance, immersed in a multifaceted world that does not succumb to any static classification or dichotomies. Hume's definition of justice and the core component of his approach to human nature pits practical rationality against the barriers to cooperative interaction where the level of sanctions necessary to maintain collective action are continually adjusted.

According to Thomas Hobbes, nothing exists before the social contract or "covenant," but war and disorder. Our natural right to self-preservation[33] and natural law that dictates that reason should seek peace[34] determines the shape of the covenant where law at the collective level defines and determines values at an individual level. Charles Beitz, as well as most other scholars of the international system, have used this Hobbesian description of anarchy, the stark self-interest of states, and the international "state of nature," to describe the assumed background conditions in which international law arose.[35]

By contrast, Hume's state of nature is not a war "of all against all," but an inconvenient social condition of significant instability where individual agents seek community in order to find a process of interaction that yields stable social order and coordination. Hume claims this is our essential human predisposition, what we might call the source, or *absolute presupposition*, for a metaphysics of social convention.

> In all creatures,...there appears a remarkable desire of company, which associates them together...This is still more conspicuous in man, as being the creature of the universe, who has the most ardent desire of society, and is fitted for it by the most advantages. We can form no wish, which has not a reference to society. A perfect solitude is, perhaps, the greatest punishment we can suffer.[36]

The need for fellowship comes directly from the psychological makeup of all persons whose "passions" move them to act on "sensations" that invoke "sympathy,"[37] which synthesized with a natural self-interest produces a limited "generosity"[38] toward others. Unlike Hobbes, Hume's society is not a desperate solution to chaos, but a natural extension of one's propensity for community to ever-greater levels of sociopolitical complexity.

Hume contends that there is a natural tendency[39] for the individual to extend his "strongest attention" to his own welfare, while nevertheless giving some attention to the welfare of his immediate relations, and even some to the welfare of strangers.[40] Herein lies the genesis point for the power of limited generosity, and his dialectic rejection of egoism, as self-interest is balanced along broader sympathetic lines. Hume's recognition of this inherent opposition and its synthesis product [self-interest⇆sympathy = limited generosity] defines the individual within his philosophical system.

> So far from thinking that men have no affection for any thing beyond themselves, I am of opinion, that tho' it be rare to meet with one, who loves any single person better than himself; yet 'tis as rare to meet with one, in whom all the kind affections, taken together do not over-balance all the selfish.[41]

In seeking ever more complex sociopolitical relations, however, agents confront the reality of the empirical world and find that while society becomes increasingly important to them, it also makes their lives less secure.

Hume argues that there are three "different species of goods, which we are possess'd of; the internal satisfaction of our mind, the external advantages of our body, and the enjoyment of...possessions."[42] He acknowledges that the first two species are secure because they are internal and safe from the designs of others. However, the third species of goods, our possessions, are not protected from others and are therefore inherently unstable. The scarcity of possessions and their easy transfer between individuals, combined with humanity's tendency to want more than the limited nature of unclaimed property will allow, causes a competition for possessions that works against the social fabric so inherently important to each and all.[43] In addition, humans are relatively equal in their capacity to secure additional property or interfere with its acquisition on the part of others, both as individuals and in concert with one another. This rough equality further adds to the instability of social relations.

Equality and *scarcity*, as social realities, in combination with the *limited generosity* that is a dialectical product of self-interest and sympathy, combine to establish what Hume calls the "*circumstances of justice*."[44] Since the juxtaposition of all three circumstances works against the coordination necessary to maintain fundamental social stability, justice is necessary to secure more stable coordination than the state of natural equality allows.

The threat posed by property instability requires that humanity evolve social "convention" to set expectations, generate rules, and insure coordination of behavior, using justice to counter empirical circumstances. Since individual tendencies can conflict with the collective interest, Hume contends that we must create artificial virtue to circumvent our human nature and secure our collective ends. In this way "convention" is created, over time, from unconscious overlapping ideas and actions, to stabilize property and to correct for the facts of equality, scarcity, and limited generosity, within the process of human interaction.

> 'Tis certain, that no affection of the human mind has both a sufficient force, and a proper direction to counter-balance the love of gain, and render men fit members of society, by making them abstain from the possessions of others.[45]
>
> From all this it follows, that we have naturally no real motive for observing the laws of equity, but the very equity and merit of that observance; and as no action can be equitable or meritorious, where it cannot arise from some separate motive...we must allow, that the sense of justice and injustice is not deriv'd from nature but arises artificially, tho necessarily from education, and human convention.[46]

Applying Hume's philosophical-policy to the history of international law, we would expect that the *inter-national* instability of possession and scarcity, for example, during the Reformation and the wars that followed, caused humanity, first by instinct and then upon reflection, to reorganize their patterns of interaction through the development of alternative sets of conventions, with new positive law to support them. In a world where social conventions are the primary human means to social security, the failure of pre-Reformation international practices required the search for better ways of coordinating national and regional behavior to protect property and establish reciprocity at a more universal level of social organization.

The solution to the pressure of increasing complexity within the international system is to coordinate on a specific social convention that offers a norm fit to safeguard the persistence of the process of coordination itself. This *process-norm*, required to maintain the utility of social order, is represented, for the international system, in the concept of sovereignty. The process-norm of sovereignty defines *justice* for, in this case, the society of states, and more narrowly delimits the collective sense of morality. What evolves is a more formal and fundamental coordination convention to protect the process of ongoing social cooperation. Order, as that most essential and utilitarian definition of the concept of justice, provides this norm, given the circumstances of its creation. In this way, Hume opts not for a narrow theory of human psychology or sociology of mass behavior, but for a comprehensive conceptual philosophy of human nature and its consequent effect on the passions of the persons, their dynamic social interaction with others, and the policy, politics, and law that define and administer justice among them.

> 'tis impossible for men to consult their interests in so effectual a manner, as by an universal and inflexible observance of the rules of justice, by which alone they can preserve society, and keep themselves from falling into that wretched and savage condition, which is commonly represented as the *state of nature*.[47]

The contextual circumstances, which evolve with the complexity of human society, continually interact dialectically[48] and produce variable levels of risk to society that require human social interaction to fabricate distinct types and levels of sanctions in response. For Hume, the survival of the passion for society, caught in a dynamic and philosophical maze of metaphysical and empirical crosscurrents, requires the creation of artificial virtue and artificial institutions to circumvent antisocial pressures on our human nature and secure a consistently stable means to the contextual end of social order. Thus, justice evolves through the trial and error of human interaction to "conventionally" provide the requisite stabilization of property and correct for the circumstances of justice. Humanity, therefore, collectively evolves a definition of justice as a further means by which to coordinate society and respond to the passion of human nature for social organization.

For Hume, humanity would approach international cooperation as it approached intra-national cooperation: through the evolution of social convention. From a Humean perspective, international society is the product of the circumstances of international justice and the evolution of convention. This is true both in the choice of states as convenient institutional structures, and in the coordination of these states toward more *global* stability of property. Thus international rules of behavior (i.e., law) originate in scarcity, the rough equality of states, and a diplomacy of limited generosity. All of these factors are reactions to intersocietal instability, triggering the imperative to seek social convention as the basis of that artificial virtue necessary for the reestablishment of order, and the coordination of action in international relations.

The circumstances of justice prevail in terms of the limited generosity of the agents (i.e., states) who seek order and stability for their territory and internal possessions in the face of scarcity, and the roughly equal capacity and ability of others to threaten these possessions by themselves or through the formation of alliances and the disruption of international commerce. To counter these threats, the prime directive becomes the coordination of one's collective choices with the collective choices of others, so that, in the long run, one's social need finds strength in unity with others, cooperating in the stability, ownership, and transfer of possessions between sovereign states.

This is the genesis of social convention in international law. In a Hobbesian world the origins of *jus gentium* are traced to war and chaos. But for Hume, the origins of pre-legal relations lie in the natural propensity of human beings to seek more and higher levels of social order and coordination, thereby creating law to counter the circumstances of justice on an ever-larger scale of complexity. Law originates in habit and practice between states and creates a set of choices, behaviors, and expectations that establish the limited generosity of "diplomatic" conventions; that is, the set of initially informal rules and norms by which nations coordinate themselves.[49] At first, the "dignity"[50] of each agent and the "approbation"[51] of other such roughly equal "civilized" agents are the only tools of enforcement.[52] But these minimal sanctions soon need to be supplemented, as human propensities for ever more complex social organization place increasing stress on convention as it tries to coordinate larger and more heterogeneous groups of actors.

The Second Fundamental Assumption: Collective Action—Justice-As-Sovereignty and the Overlapping Evolution of Convention and Social Justice

In deciphering the second fundamental assumption of Hume's philosophical-policy, he argues that the status of the individual is both the motivation for, and the logical result of, the requirements of collective action. Through the maintenance of the proper synthesis product of limited generosity, humanity creates the empirical reality of its society. The structure of collective action sets the parameters in which human practical reason finds synthesis and persistence, while both dialectically overlap in the quest for the continued coordination of social order as the absolute presupposition of Hume's philosophical-policy.

Hume's system allows for a complexity of overlapping dialectics where the essence of the concepts involved have utility to the degree their interaction produces and protects the social stability of property. From within the context of Hume's argument, it is impossible to definitively classify or segregate any of these concepts for separate study, or to assume that one can analyze the importance of any one in the absence of the others. A social scale of forms cannot be understood as a set of isolated empirical or normative processes nor depend on a simple causal or linear progression, but must integrate the interactions and complex context of dialectically overlapping ideas to judge the socio-ecological[53] dynamic involved and adjust to it.

Interpreting Hume's argument through philosophical method highlights the central dialectic in the complexity of overlapping concepts that determine both the manifestation of practical reason in society and the condition of individual and collective, or public utility within his philosophical-policy:

the tension between *process⇆principle*. Hume does not separate the empirical from the normative, but describes these as interrelated concepts, so that justice is simultaneously both an empirical condition of stable coordination and a normative imperative to maintain that equilibrium. In the same way that passion determines reason, his argument for justice creates a dialectic where process, or the absolute need to stabilize property as a means to cooperation, outweighs any substantive definition of justice in terms of specific principles or ends independent or critical of social convention. But just as he promotes the passions over reason without eliminating the latter as a part of human social life, he promotes process over substantive principle without denying the existence of substantive principle in shaping the process-norm of justice. For Hume, the use of reason to inform principle is left to the idiosyncrasies of each society, as long as these principles do not disrupt the stability of the process of collective action, which is the paramount requirement of the fundamental human passion for society. To the degree that the introduction of a substantive principle critical of this process would be disruptive to its stability, it is discounted and discouraged within the logic of concepts that generate social convention. In this way, Hume's definition of justice is necessarily process-based.

Explaining the genesis and evolution of moral obligation from empirical behavior Hume demonstrates that social convention comes about through human interactions, creating allegiance to those normative standards that work to facilitate collective action over a long term. In effect, practical passions are applied in the world through an evolving practice that allows stable human coordination to progress up a scale of forms from the genesis of small-scale family relations to state and then interstate levels of social organization. Sovereignty offers a definition of justice fit to regulate and maintain this process. As humans proceed up this ladder of complexity, overlapping legal, political, and moral concepts are refined and redesigned so that the dialectical dynamics of ideas produce synthesis solutions for changing coordination dilemmas.

Game theory has been used by scholars to understand the strategic interactions that turn individual choice into collective outcomes.[54] However, disagreement exists about the precise nature of Hume's strategic context. In a nutshell,[55] the controversy is whether Hume is describing the rise of convention as a prisoner's dilemma or as a coordination game.[56] Only by approaching the strategic context dialectically, through Hume's philosophical-policy, can both of these positions be understood to exist simultaneously.

Initially he seems to be describing the standard game for the creation and distribution of public or collective goods: the prisoner's dilemma. Because the outcome that is best for each individual player is nonoptimal for society within a prisoner's dilemma, the participants, playing out their self-interest, and facing the possibility both of exploiting the cooperation of others and being exploited in the act of unilateral cooperation, prefer to be last into a cooperative equilibrium and first out of it.

This is unlike the standard evolution of a social convention, which is assumed to result from a coordination game, where multiple equilibria are possible and where individual behavior and unconscious choice find and maintain coordination that is optimal for both the individual and the society, simultaneously. Language conventions are a common example of this. Therefore, if Hume is truly talking about social convention then he should be describing a coordination game. But he seems to be describing a prisoner's dilemma in the stabilization of property; so the claim is that his normative standards are either not from social convention or do not describe cooperative behavior toward collective goods. The usual solution to this supposed paradox is to argue that since there is no doubt Hume is using convention, then the prisoner's dilemma must be capable of producing conventions.[57] But this solution still replaces the coordination game and its strategic context with the noncooperative environment of the prisoner's dilemma, which creates a distinct type of convention raised on conflictual foundations, requiring a different set of assumptions and expectations.

Those involved in this debate assume the validity of positivist assumptions. They do not consider dialectic, overlap, and the refinement of concepts on a scale of forms. Nor have they examined the particular complexity of the international level of organization as a dialectic, but distinct, strategic reality, separate from the context of municipal law that characterizes its component states. In fact, as defined by dialectical argument, both sides of this debate are simultaneously correct at different levels of systemic organization. What Hume is describing is a global coordination game creating standard international social convention built on hundreds of solved municipal prisoner's dilemmas. Before we explain this complexity, we need to understand the context of the coordination game itself.

Lewis' coordination game describes a cooperative strategic interaction where two self-interested players (Row and Column) prefer joint decision-making to the independent variety. The motivation of the players is to conform to the predominant pattern of behavior, which can arise without conscious choice. Here, knowledge that all other players will choose a specific strategy to cooperate is enough incentive for any other player to choose an identical strategy: all a new player needs to know is which equilibria—what latent norm—defines the cooperative solution.

Both players do best if they each choose the same solution by choosing the same strategy. In Matrix 1.1, the points of equilibria are (R1, C1) and (R2, C2). A point of equilibrium is defined as that combination of payoffs where no one agent could have produced more utility for himself by acting differently. It is to the advantage of both Row and Column to cooperate on either of the two points of equilibria. With these strategy pairs, each player gains a payoff of 1. There is no incentive for either to fail to coordinate, for this would result in a payoff of 0. Consequently, the actors seek to coordinate themselves on one of the two (1,1) solutions.

Matrix 1.1 Coordination game.

	C1	C2
R1	(1, 1) [Equilibrium]	(0, 0)
R2	(0, 0)	(1, 1) [Equilibrium]

These two *coordination equilibria* are said to be indifferent to the players and represent stronger-than-normal points of equilibrium.[58] When one player has chosen a strategy, neither player's situation can be improved by making any other choice or by defecting from cooperation with the other player.[59] In order for a game to be a Lewis coordination game, it must have at least two equal points of equilibrium between which the players are, at least initially, indifferent. These multiple indifferent equilibria dictate that the game has no dominant strategy for either player.[60] There is no clear choice between R1 and R2 for Row or C1 and C2 for Column, no matter what the other player chooses. Each player's strategy is dependent on the choice of the other player in order for a preferred outcome to be achieved. The players' choices are therefore interdependent.

The logic of the coordination game is based on the expectations of the players, from which the solution also emerges. The pure coordination game is best described as a game of iteration, or dialectical evolution, where players gradually build expectations of each other's choices based on the repeated trial and error of synthesis solutions. Each player is eventually better able to anticipate the other and achieve coordination, which is, for Hume, the absolute presupposition of social order. The establishment of a coordination equilibrium defines a manifestation of social sympathy and self-interest (i.e., limited generosity) that integrates the utility of the individual with that of the collective.

Lewis relates his pure coordination game to the evolution of social convention. He defines a convention in the following way:[61]

> A regularity R in the behavior of members of a population P when they are agents in a recurrent situation S is a convention if and only if it is true that, and it is common knowledge in P that, in almost any instance of S among members of P,
>
> 1. Almost everyone conforms to R;
> 2. Almost everyone expects almost everyone else to conform to R;
> 3. Almost everyone has approximately the same preferences regarding all combinations of actions;
> 4. Almost everyone prefers that one more conform to R, on condition that almost everyone conform to R;
> 5. Almost everyone would prefer that any one more conform to R' on the condition that almost everyone conform to R'.

Social convention is, therefore, a solution to an iterated pure coordination game where a system of concordant mutual or social expectations are established over time. This solution is inherently self-enforcing.

> Once the process gets started, we have a measurable self-perpetuating system of preferences, expectations, and actions capable of persisting indefinitely. As long as uniform conformity is a coordination equilibrium, so that each wants to conform conditionally upon conformity by the others, conforming action produces expectations of conforming action and expectations of conforming action produces conforming action.[62]

Lewis maintains that Hume's concept of convention fits within his model[63] and I agree. However, dialectically, the international level of organization produces social convention through the coordination game, while the municipal level stabilizes property within a prisoner's dilemma. A critical distinction is that, at the municipal level, the player's motivation to cooperate is different. The tendency of each player is to take advantage of the conventions of property and to free-ride on the cooperation of others in order to protect himself or improve his own lot. Here, it takes more than the knowledge that everyone else is cooperating for any particular actor to look past his limited generosity, and cooperate in collective goods provision without legal background institutions as a security net. In order for Hume's individual to cooperate and maintain society, additional incentives, in the form of coercive institutions, must be evolved.[64]

But in a pure coordination convention, such as driving on a specific side of the road, it is not in one's interest unilaterally to ignore the convention and drive against traffic. One need only know which side of the road is used, or to which set of process-based property rules the convention pertains. It is in one's interest to coordinate one's behavior with the other players; that is, to adopt the established way of doing things. Lewis' coordination game does not require a strong central government, as all any individual needs to know in order to coordinate himself is where the coordination point, the equilibrium, lies.

However, a type of free-riding is possible within Hume's coordination game that is not about cooperation itself, but about the perceived indifference between the solutions. Once coordination is established, it is possible for an individual player to discount both the utility of their cooperation and the comparative justice of any specific equilibrium. By the definition of justice as an artificial virtue, any equilibrium can, in any specific instance, be unjust to a particular state and not be in its interest. For example, the equilibrium supporting European colonialism may not have been as advantageous to the colonies as to the parent states.[65] To maintain long-term coordination, Hume argues that even though any single act of justice may or may not be advantageous to an individual player, each needs to focus on the overall interplay of all acts of justice, which are cumulatively of public utility and to everyone's advantage.

> A single act of justice is frequently contrary to public interest; and were it to stand alone, without being follow'd by other acts, may, in itself, be very prejudicial to society. When a man of merit, of a beneficent disposition, restores a great fortune to a miser, or a seditious bigot, he has acted justly and laudably, but the public is a real sufferer. Nor is every single act of justice, consider'd apart, more conducive to private interest, than to public.... But however single acts of justice may be contrary, either to public or private interest, 'tis certain, that the whole plan or scheme is highly conducive, or indeed absolutely requisite, both to the support of society, and the well-being of every individual.... Property must be stable, and must be fix'd by general rules. Tho' in one instance the public be a sufferer, this momentary ill is amply compensated by the steady prosecution of the rule, and by the peace and order, which it establishes in society. And every individual person must find himself a gainer, on balancing the account; since, without justice, society must immediately dissolve.[66]

Discounting and seeking other, seemingly more advantageous, points of coordination or alternative equilibria, which are accessible within a coordination game, must be discouraged. A conventional concept of justice may need to be supported, not only by the disapprobation of one's peers, but by the further sanctions of some form of decentralized governance. This would guarantee the origin or persistence of international social order once a particular equilibrium has been conventionally established.[67]

One of the most important differences between the rise of convention on an intra-state level, and its evolution between actors internationally, is that the international strategic situation is built on multiple, solved, prisoner's dilemmas at the municipal level. This makes the rise of social convention through coordination at the international level more stable and more authentically conventional. Simultaneously, the strategic reality now prescribes that, when no established legal systems preexist, the evolution or first stabilization of property would be more akin to a noncooperative prisoner's dilemma, solved by a stronger and more sanction-oriented type of social contract-by-convention.

The coordination game that originates the conventions of international justice and generates international law is built on the stability of many established constituent legal systems, each with its own operational and codified conventions. This provides a more secure atmosphere in which the states can seek an international point of coordination among the multiple equilibria present. This represents justice, or the process-norm that insures the persistence of a common point of social equilibrium. This one point of coordination is a socially and philosophically refined convention that builds on the past success of its constituent actors in protecting the process that has created and maintained international social order.

The coordination game stands as a reasonable model for the strategic reality in which the European-based international system was formed and stabilized. Individual states preexisted, having solved their municipal prisoner's dilemmas in the wake of the Thirty Years War. The treaties of Westphalia created a point of normative focus, or moral equilibrium, for the further development and spread of international social conventions supporting states and their interrelationship as means to the ends of social order and coordination of international behavior. This was done by creating rules of membership in the society of states and by forming a definition of the state, its power, and defining the control each had in domestic and international affairs. In other words, a formal operationalization of preexisting social convention in the process-norm of *Justice-As-Sovereignty*.[68]

Once the *Westphalian Equilibrium* was established as the solution to the coordination game, it represented a set of shared procedural values that then came to dominate a refined definition of joint decision-making made necessary by growing systemic interdependence and the need to stabilize property at the international level. Characteristic of a coordination game rather than a prisoner's dilemma, the motivation to conform to the requirements of this equilibrium spread beyond the original membership and universal standards came to support and spread the predominant conventional pattern. It was not that the Westphalian Equilibrium was particularly valued (viz., there were other alternatives—for example, empire), but it represented the original and predominant point of coordination, which made it valuable and eventually obligatory for all new states.

Solving a coordination problem requires a synthesis process-norm, that defines the equilibrium to which the actors coordinate to form a consensus. As a solution begets order and stabilizes property, this gives it a sense of permanence, and a prerogative over other competing points of equilibrium as it soon becomes obvious that any national society wishing to participate in international affairs has to accept, for example, the Westphalian Equilibrium, to gain a place in the "*club*" as a *sovereign* state. Like driving on the left- or the right-hand side of the road, once the pattern is established, no single actor, or group for that matter, has a strong incentive to fight the predominant pattern of convention and drive against traffic. There is no divergence of individual and social interests, as exists in a prisoner's dilemma, nor the requirement of a strict structure of enforcement. To get anywhere, you join the established conventional consensus, as no individual agent has any incentive to work against that consensus.

The positivist definition of prudence as "self-help"[69] is replaced with an imperative to protect the means and end of mutual coordination, acknowledging the interdependence of one's sense of order and purpose with others in developing an international system of utility to all. As Justice-As-Sovereignty informs international law, the concentration shifts to *mutual-aid* and *expanding reciprocity*. Any one state succeeds only by recognizing that it can achieve more for itself by cooperating with the established social conventions that stabilize international property. To fight the pattern or try to invent a new consensus on an alternative equilibrium is impossible without a significant erosion in the power of preexisting social convention.

Once the coordination convention is established, an international system is created. Then, Lewis' requirements for a definition of international social convention can be restated in the following way:

> A regularity (R = Westphalian Equilibrium) in the behavior of states in international relations (P) when they are agents in a recurrent situation S is a convention if and only if it is true that, and it is common knowledge in P that, in almost any instance of S among members of P,
>
> 1. Almost every state conforms to the Westphalian Equilibrium;
> 2. Almost every state expects almost every other state to conform to the Westphalian Equilibrium;
> 3. Almost every state has approximately the same preferences regarding all combinations of actions that allow the Westphalian Equilibrium to persist;
> 4. Almost every state prefers that one more state conform to the Westphalian Equilibrium, on condition that almost every state conforms to the Westphalian Equilibrium;
> 5. Almost every state would prefer that any one more state conform to an alternative to the Westphalian Equilibrium on the condition that almost every state conforms to the same alternative to the Westphalian Equilibrium.

In addition to the strategic setting, the international collective action problem cannot solve itself in a long-term and stable coordination convention unless it is tied to a specific concept of justice that is of public utility to the society of states. This requires that a consensus form over a process-norm that has the coordination of the whole, and its utility, as its sole concern.

Hume's concept of natural law helps us understand this *sense* of justice. His philosophical-policy does not define "natural law" in the traditional terms of a priori or independent principles of justice. Justice is the virtue of respecting other's property;[70] it is the result of a social *process* through which humans unconsciously coordinate themselves, and set mutual expectations, creating the stability they seek in the society they crave. For Hume, justice begins with the "appetite betwixt the sexes."[71] The resulting family is a natural field for the transposition of individual habits into patterned social behavior. Education in the family, the original conveyer of social convention or pre-legal norms, provides children with expectations for social life as learned from the experience of adults. In humanity's innate passion for social stability, Hume defines the absolute presupposition of his metaphysics and the source of his argument for sovereignty in the international system. This also provides the point of origin for a unique concept of *natural law*, one based on the socialization of individuals and the natural evolution of patterns of behavior and expectation that create social convention.

> In a little time, custom and habit operating on the tender minds of children, makes them sensible of the advantages which they may reap from society, as well as fashions them by degrees for it, rubbing off those rough corners and untoward affections, which prevent their coalition.[72]

To extend humanity's natural but limited generosity to include an ever larger group of agents on a global scale requires the establishment of a more formal sense of justice focused on a specific social convention able to regulate collective action to the advantage of global society. Our dialectical refinement of the concept of convention is not a departure from the agent's limited generosity but, rather, a reflection of its long-term security within a greater social order with growing complexity.

> Instead of departing from our own interests, or from that of our nearest friends, by abstaining from the possessions of others, we cannot better consult both these interests than by such a convention; because it is by that means we maintain society, which is so necessary to their well-being and subsistence, as well as to our own.[73]

Social convention is at first derived from unconscious action that creates mutual expectations, and then from habitual acts that produce more fixed and conscious expectations that become enforceable through rules as sanctioned, and therefore, *proper* and *expected* behavior. The social conventions of diplomatic behavior predated diplomatic law. The practice of states did not originate in explicit contracts or covenants, as Hobbes argued, but rather lay in tacit agreements that were voluntary and enforced through a system of mutual restraint and approbation.[74] The rules of the international system, as confirmed by Hume's philosophical-policy, have their beginnings in the social context, or trial and error, of interaction between states as social constructions. These created expectations and then patterns of acceptable behavior that were anointed as the procedures of those "civilized nations" that established a consensus at the Westphalian Equilibrium.[75] This conventional standard then sets the expectations upon which treaties, and other, more conscious, international legal acts became possible.

These natural or unconscious patterns of behavior and reciprocity eventually created a recognizable system of practice on the level of international society. At this point, a core social process norm arose to protect social convention: Justice As Sovereignty. Justice arose in response to its success in correcting for the rough equality, limited generosity, and scarcity of property that Hume argues creates the need for justice in the first place. Justice-as-convention regulates customary behavior at a point of coordination that corrects for these "circumstances of justice." The "artificial virtue" of justice as a manifestation of the coordination equilibrium, and a shorthand for it, represents legal practice for a specific representation of the international social order, allowing it to persist, and granting its process-norm moral weight. The essence of justice lies in the natural and unconscious dialectic of human passions.

> There is no passion, therefore, capable of controlling the interested affections but the very affection itself, by an alteration of its direction.[76]

Globally, sovereignty is a *conventional process-norm*, a normative standard, evolved from the dialectic between action and expectation. From this, agents can create and maintain coordination for their mutual benefit; that is, for the stability of the property of each and all and to execute collective action free of disruption.

> This convention is not of the nature of a promise: For even promises themselves,...arise from human convention. It is only a general sense of common interest; which sense all the members of the society express to one another and which induces them to regulate their conduct by certain rules. I observe, that it will be for my interest to leave another in possession of his goods, provided he will act in the same manner with regard to me. He is sensible of a like interest in the regulation of his conduct. When this common sense of interest is mutually express'd, and is known to both, it produces a suitable resolution and behavior. And this may properly enough be call'd a convention or agreement betwixt us tho' without the interposition of a promise...Two men who pull the oars of a boat, do it by an agreement or convention, tho' they have never given promises to each other. Nor is the rule concerning the stability of possession the less deriv'd from human convention, that it arises gradually, and acquires force by slow progression, and by our repeated experience of the inconveniences of transgressing it. On the contrary, this experience assures us still more, that the sense of interest has become common to all our fellows and gives us confidence of the future regularity of their confidence.[77]

With the establishment of the process-norm of Justice-As-Sovereignty, international society evolves a regulatory precept for the refinement of obligation, promise, treaty, and transference by consent. In addition, the process-norm is the standard by which distinctions are made between, for example, a law of peace and a law of war.[78] It is important to note that Hume, when he describes the evolution of social convention as the stabilization of property, is not concerned with how, or how many, particular objects are assigned to specific people or social groups.[79] Justice, for him, is simultaneously about allocation and distribution, but only in terms of the process or procedures by which these acts are carried out, so that they result in a stable system in support of social convention. Hume's logic is both actual and metaphysical but has no required or substantive outcome in terms of critical principles of justice.

Given the context of our international legal system, Justice-As-Sovereignty protects the Westphalian Equilibrium and anchors custom and experience, initially in practice, and then in law. The norm of sovereignty is a process-norm because it holds no substantive definition of the right or the good, but evolved in order to maintain the public utility of coordination, which is the end-in-itself. Sovereignty supports that definition of convention that best compensates for the international circumstances of justice. It solves and secures the collective action problem.

Justice-As-Sovereignty is the process-based and context-driven foundational or "Grundnorm" of our international system. Offering a fundamental definition of justice, it simplifies the terms of coordination by segregating the essential utilitarian element of cooperation and inserts itself as the imperative within the system for the later conscious codification of social convention in law. For international society, Justice-As-Sovereignty becomes the basis for stability, coordination, and coexistence through reciprocity.[80] Representing the Westphalian Equilibrium, Justice-As-Sovereignty reinforces approbation of diplomacy and adds a layer of sanction redirecting those who might free-ride on the cooperation of others and disrupt this particular conventional solution or coordination equilibrium.[81]

But why is sovereignty the source of practical reason in international law? Because the imperative of a Humean convention is to find consensus in the stabilization of property, which, in the international context, means giving each actor in the international system control of its own affairs. A nation's resources, whatever they wish to do with them, can best be stabilized through Justice-As-Sovereignty. Social convention on a national level solidifies the interdependence of persons within social community through rules relating to property that separate each person's possessions and make each the master of that which belongs to him as long as he restrains from interfering with the possessions of others.[82] Justice-As-Sovereignty, within the international system, creates the same order on a global level. It does this by separating the effective control of possessions for each nation and granting each dominion over its own territory and wealth, as long as it restrains from interference in the domestic affairs[83] of other "civilized" nations.[84] Civilization is here defined as sharing the international circumstances of justice and acknowledging an obligation to Justice-As-Sovereignty and the Westphalian Equilibrium as the consensus solution to the global coordination game.

The artificial virtue of Justice-As-Sovereignty, however, does not exist in a static environment. States are presented with continuing challenges when applying justice within a dynamic, open,[85] and ever-changing international system. As we have already acknowledged, the nature of justice as an artificial virtue is such that, while the *sovereign* coordination equilibrium is generally in every nation's interest, it may act against a single actor's interest in any specific instance.[86]

In the operationalization of Justice-As-Sovereignty, those whose self-interest is infringed in specific cases will be motivated to discount the status quo convention of justice and, subsequently, work against the particular coordination equilibrium that disadvantages them, striving for an alternative. The problem of discontent is increased with the growing complexity of global society as more and more nations evolve into states with aspirations to be granted Justice-As-Sovereignty and become part of the established international system.

With many heterogeneous potential cooperators, the individual nation also strategically loses touch with the direct effect of its behavior on collective action. In a larger and more complex international society, it is not as evident that individual actions against sovereignty undermine global society, or coordination as a whole, even if such agency has a higher probability of disrupting coordination at the Westphalian Equilibrium.[87] Hume's contention that international society can and does establish itself without government is based on the premise that a society of nations remains small, homogeneous, and the purview of but a few "civilized" nations with shared values and circumstances. This critical mass of cooperators have common expectations realized in Justice-As-Sovereignty and controlled by their own mutual sense of moral approbation and justice.

Although "free-ride," in this context, does not mean that coordination itself is threatened by these complexities, a specific Lewis equilibrium and its particular definition of convention may be threatened by alternative equilibria that arise and are argued to be more efficient or effective in maintaining international coordination as circumstances change.[88] As global society grows in complexity, the moral approbation or disapprobation of civilized nations may no longer be enough to maintain a particular coordination equilibrium. At this point, the acknowledgment and further legal codification of social convention becomes necessary to defend Justice-As-Sovereignty against emergent norms.

Consequently, the Westphalian Equilibrium, and the emergent process-norm of Justice-As-Sovereignty, need to be institutionalized in a governance structure that further protects them against the growing complexity that empowers the disruptive quality of the circumstances of justice. To secure the normative prerogative of the status quo convention, defining as it does the point of coordination for the international system, conscious rule-generation though policy argument and legal design, toward a stable international society under law, becomes necessary.

The overlapping dynamics of social evolution, to compensate for the circumstances of justice and the dialectic complexity of human social interaction, has settled upon a process-norm; that is, a norm that is neutral between specific manifestations or principles of property, but created by a process of consensus that stabilizes collective action. For Hume's philosophical-policy, justice is order, or the stable coordination of human interaction where one's sympathy with fundamental social interests requires an additional level of sanction to persist. Justice is also that pattern of allocation and distribution that works for a stable social order. In effect, as the dialectic between sympathy⇆self-interest evolves and overlaps with the dynamics of the empirical world, justice is a means for incorporating new social facts while protecting the essential coordination of society.

> But tho' it be possible for men to maintain a small uncultivated society without government, 'tis impossible they shou'd maintain a society of any kind without justice and the observance [of the]...fundamental laws concerning the stability of possessions....These are, therefore, antecedent to government, and are...to impose an obligation before the duty to civil magistrates has once been thought of...Government upon its first establishment,...derive(s) its obligation from those laws of nature.[89]

Viewing the international system as a coordination game, more than one equilibrium always exists. An alternative that commands no consensus may nevertheless act in competition with the status quo and its conventional stabilization of property without threatening coordination itself. Against the challenge from alternative norms, like "efficient global trade" or "the responsibility to protect," Justice-As-Sovereignty and the Westphalian Equilibrium must be empowered to remain effective. Moral, legal, and political rules must be more tightly ascribed to the support of *sovereign* states.

Blackletter international law is not discovered but refined from social convention as protected by Justice-As-Sovereignty. Hume contends that we have a natural obligation to observe this conventional standard, and he notes its power to coordinate behavior and set expectations even before the advent of codified rules, law, or government. This natural obligation to social convention, Hume's sense of *natural law*, provides international society, through the circumstances of justice and the limited generosity of states, with a moral obligation to joint decision-making and to the preexisting coordination equilibrium based on sympathy, which contributes to the increased security and longevity of the public interest in collective social action.

> Thus self-interest is the original motive to the establishment of justice: but a sympathy with public interest is the source of the moral approbation which attends that virtue.[90]

When both approbation and the conventions of justice are insufficient to correct the tendency of human nature to work against settled social patterns of behavior, Hume supports a further refinement of the idea of convention expressing a stronger force for the redefinition of human nature: governance institutions and positive law.

The Third Fundamental Assumption: The Role of the State—Contract-By-Convention Refining Justice

Applying philosophical method to the third fundamental assumption of Hume's philosophical-policy, human social life is defined, not in terms of the discovery of peace and order but, in the dialectical refinement of social convention in response to the changing circumstances of justice. The continued application of layers of sanction ends, for Hume, with a role for the state in the persistence of the absolute presupposition of his philosophical-policy: the stability of society.

Government is the final stage of sanctions. Refinement of the justice-norm creates, an empirical institutional structure and codified law that is more inherently adaptable, in compensating for evolutionary change, than the norm of justice alone. Understanding Hume's argument as a philosophical-policy paradigm points out that the same overlapping ideas and processes that create social convention are expected to evolve through different stages of refinement along what Collingwood calls a "scale of forms": both internally, from approbation to justice to government, and externally, from local to global social organization.

Contract for Hume, is not based on independent critical principle that would give imperative force to the achievement of an end that can be either materially produced (e.g., a treaty) or is a nonproducible end-in-itself (e.g., an autonomous moral agent).[91] Justice-As-Sovereignty is a process-norm where the means of collective action are the end-in-itself. This contrasts with Hobbes' concept of social covenant, which is a one-shot agreement based upon *critical* principles drawn from *prior* laws of nature, common to humanity as a whole and based on conscious reason.[92]

Since Hume's social contract is logically based on preexisting social convention,[93] it is therefore a *contract-by-convention*, internal to a sociological process based on an established idea of Justice-As-Sovereignty that makes convention manifest and persistent in social relations. Here, positive law is an extension of Justice-As-Sovereignty, which adds another layer of sanctions to those conventions already established to maintain stability within the international system.

The institutionalization of Justice-As-Sovereignty encourages the creation of sovereign states. The dialectic between ideas⇆institutions requires convention, which then demands a unit of organization that can operationalize sovereign dominion over territory, and stabilize possessions globally. The social construction of the sovereign state is the effective vehicle for Justice-As-Sovereignty and allows for all to share equally in the advantages of reciprocal stability. But Hume's sovereignty is not Hobbes'. In *Leviathan*, sovereignty is the conscious product of a two-stage contract[94] that renders the origin of society, justice, and law at the same time. Hume describes each as a separate developmental stage in the philosophical refinement of social convention on a scale of evolving forms. Within Hume's logic of concepts, Justice-As-Sovereignty is antecedent to institutional law and politics, but has evolved from the moral approbation and norms of social convention.

Through political negotiation and legal contract, based on social convention, voluntary and codified law is created, enshrining the preexisting practices, expectations, and traditions of the conventionally-based international system within a positive law created around the process-norm of Justice-As-Sovereignty. The concept of sovereignty thus routinizes conventional sources for positive rules and becomes institutionalized. This codified law provides assurance that the rules of ethical life will be honored as the complexity of global society grows in the continued persistence of the process equilibria by which social convention was created and continues to be maintained.

Through this codification process, policy establishes procedural rules of recognition, adjudication, and change that *validate* or *legitimize* the rule of law.[95] At this stage of social evolution, the creation of a valid legal system refines one's moral obligation beyond a concern for one's private honor (i.e., approbation) or public dishonor (i.e., informal norms of justice) and into policy institutions that codify positive law derived from the process-norm (i.e., Justice-As-Order or Sovereignty). This ensures continuous supervision of the dynamic effects of the circumstances of justice and the protection of the universal passion for society. Contract-by-convention moves practical reason into conscious policymaking and the codification of positive law.

Before international law and institutions are established, a combination of enlightened self-interest (limited generosity), moral approbation, and social utility foster social convention and define Justice-As-Sovereignty. But just as nested municipal systems give added incentive to the creation and solution of the international coordination game, Hume's philosophical-policy also supports the argument that the municipal experience in solving the prisoner's dilemma tends to give states a more urgent municipal obligation and a less pressing allegiance to the international coordination equilibrium. Specifically, Hume claims that "tho' the morality of princes has the same extent, yet it has not the same force as that of private persons, and may lawfully be transgress'd from a more trivial motive."[96]

As humanity's social framework becomes more complex, the human tendency to discount the long-term public interest and prefer the immediate satisfaction of desires, which works against established social convention, gains power and requires more conscious institutional regulation for the equilibrium to persist. Especially on an interstate level of organization, "the natural obligation to justice, among different states, is not so strong as among individuals, the moral obligation, which arises from it, must partake of its weakness."[97] Considering the less secure status of international moral obligation, the evolution or refinement of sanctions that protect the Westphalian Equilibrium must keep pace with the growing size and heterogeneity of international society. This makes *discounting* Justice-As-Sovereignty more probable without tighter global institutionalization and codification.

> Now as every thing, that is contiguous to us, either in space or time, strikes upon us with such an idea, it has a proportional effect on the will and passions, and commonly operates with more force than any object, that lies in a more distant and obscure light...This is the reason why men so often act in contradiction to their known interests; and in particular why they prefer the trivial advantage, that is, present, to the maintenance of order in society, which so much depends on the observance of justice.[98]

Unlike the realists,[99] Hume describes selfishness and self-interest as dialectically dysfunctional tendencies that overtake our wider and more foundational sympathy and work against social stability. Contract-by-convention is necessary because Justice-As-Sovereignty is limited by the extent to which it can compensate for this "limited generosity" on the part of individual agents. Humanity needs society at multiple levels of organization and society requires the provision of collective goods for its persistence. The origin of international legal institutions, through contract-by-convention, builds on approbation and the process-norm of Justice-As-Sovereignty to maintain stability over time, space, and the increasing complexity of social organization.

> Two neighbors may agree to drain a meadow, which they possess in common; because 'tis easy for them to know each others mind; and each must perceive, that the immediate consequences of his failing in his part, is the abandoning the whole project. But 'tis very difficult, and indeed impossible, that a thousand persons sho'd agree in any such action; it being difficult for them to concert so complicated a design, and still more difficult for them to execute it; while each seeks a pretext to free himself of the trouble and expense, and wou'd lay the whole burden on others. Political society easily remedies both these inconveniences.[100]

For the global "meadow," coordinating a diversity of nations toward a recognition of, and adherence to, the global public interest becomes more difficult as the expansion of the legal design space encourages any one state to abdicate its global social responsibility and "free-ride" on the participation of others. But this is not a positivist's definition of defection, where size and heterogeneity encourage independent "self-help" actors to abandon the socially-optimal equilibrium in order to indulge their national self-interest and exploit others. Hume's international system is not a prisoner's dilemma but a coordination game, where a system of international cooperation and a specific, Westphalian, equilibrium is conceded to be in the interest of all, but where change or evolution between indifferent equilibria may occur without destroying fundamental coordination itself.

Within Hume's philosophical-policy, defection from cooperation in the context of a coordination game, unlike the prisoner's dilemma, is not for mere exploitation, but is evidence of disgruntlement with the prevailing definition of public utility. It is an effort to seek a new, more socially-optimal, coordination equilibrium that is indifferent to the players in terms of payoffs (i.e., stability and order), but which might achieve a *more just* and preferred definition of utility with a redefined process-norm. Defection is an act of state intended to substitute a norm that is expected to be more beneficial to the community, given the flux of evolving international social history and its dynamic scale of forms.[101]

In a society of two, the fact that limited generosity may be influenced more by self-interest than by sympathy for others, does not detract from the general understanding of the coordination equilibria that represents the common interest and what is needed to secure it. The limited population and common values make general cooperation both expected and sanctioned. In a grand alliance, for example, a small set of like-minded states protecting the sovereignty of all would not defect casually from the "common good" that brought them together.[102]

However, in a more populous or complex context, the natural tendency to limit one's field of concern and neglect international obligations is intensified by the fact that global-social ends become more removed from the perception of the individual nation-state and further discounted. For a disadvantaged agent, the immediate gain from satisfying desire in a new equilibrium is all the more tempting when the current equilibrium seems less exclusively necessary to a stable international social order.

In addition, discounting coordination is exacerbated by the intuition that unanimous participation in any one coordination equilibrium is no longer necessary to produce global collective goods. With so many sovereign states and only a subset of them necessary to produce the collective good, a state may decide that they need not continue to contribute to a particular definition of justice, when an alternative may create more order at less cost for them. With a population of two, each state must contribute to the alliance or no good will be provided; but for 200 states, free-riding on the participation of others is possible, and not directly detrimental to any specific global good.[103] Each state will have a stronger inclination to consider that a transgression on its part will entail no immediate collective repercussions. Under these conditions, global society, the Westphalian Equilibrium, and the established norm of Justice-As-Sovereignty are in danger of erosion and replacement by another process-norm, point of equilibrium, and definition of justice. That is, unless the established equilibrium is reinforced.

Considering that social stability is still of paramount importance to humanity, and that the conventional equilibrium has proven effective in maintaining it, a further adjustment or philosophical refinement of the status quo idea of social convention must be made in order to reinforce Justice-As-Sovereignty and the integrity of global collective action. The conscious creation of political-legal rules from the process-norm of Justice-As-Sovereignty, as well as the creation of the international governance institutions to operationalize and enforce them, reaffirm international utility in the collective interest of this particular solution to the global coordination game.

> It is evident that, if government were totally useless, it never could have place, and that the sole foundation of the duty of allegiance is the advantage which it produces to society by preserving peace and order among mankind.[104]
>
> When men have once perceiv'd the necessity of government to maintain peace, and execute justice, they wou'd naturally assemble together, wou'd chuse magistrates, determine their power, and promise them obedience.[105]

As justice empowers limited generosity to compensate for the tendencies of self-interest that undermine society, legal institutions and actors add needed sanctions and organization to the established social convention of Justice-As-Sovereignty. With the application of Hume's philosophical-policy, collective action, which previously had only the process-norm of Justice-As-Sovereignty backed by approbation to insure performance, now has definitive legal sanction (i.e., rules and rights) to back it up. This makes the growth and progressive codification of international law a necessary component of the evolving metaphysical complexity of the international legal system. It is possible, through "[p]olitical society,"[106] for ever-greater and more diverse international societies to coordinate themselves using Justice-As-Sovereignty to create an ever-wider "civilized" world.

> Tho' there was no such thing as a promise in the world, government wou'd still be necessary in all large and civiliz'd societies; and if promises had only their own proper obligation, without the separate sanction of government, they wou'd have but little efficacy in such societies.[107]

Originally, a social convention dealing with Justice-As-Sovereignty commands a moral obligation from the enlightened limited generosity of states. However, the pre-institutional obligation to fulfill diplomatic expectations is predominantly dependent on the value that each state places on its reputation (i.e., moral character) as a state upholding Justice-As-Sovereignty.

> There is nothing, which touches us more nearly than our reputation, and nothing on which our reputation more depends than our conduct, with relation to the property of others.[108]

However, reputation alone will not ensure that every nation develops a proper *sense of justice*,[109] especially if the community of nations becomes more heterogeneously cultural. Hume's introduction of the "Knave" at the end of the second *Enquiry* acknowledges these limitations.

Hume describes "a sensible knave [who] in particular incidents, may think that an act of iniquity or infidelity will make a considerable addition to his fortune, without causing any considerable breach in the social union" (viz., any considerable disruption of the overall stability of the coordination equilibrium). This defection from a particular definition of social cooperation is condemned by moral sensibilities, convention, and justice, showing that such actors "themselves are, in the end, the greatest dupes, and have sacrificed the invaluable enjoyment of a character, with themselves at least, for the acquisition of worthless toys and gewgaws."[110] International actors commonly known as "rogue states" that "free-ride" on established coordination conventions may be described by Hume's philosophical-policy as having "lost a considerable motive to virtue"[111] that leaves their sovereignty beyond social, or because of the broader context, international protection.

In order to ensure that global society survives despite member states who continue to discount the collective interest or search for alternative process-norms, Hume adds the "artifice of politicians" to justice and the desire for reputation as an ultimate layer of sanctions in support of coordination conventions.[112] Specifically, global politics and international legal rules and institutions employ people whose limited generosity is said to be informed by the global public interest rather than their own narrower interests, thus reinforcing the public utility of Justice-As-Sovereignty. These individuals are charged with imposing sanctions on Knave-like antisocial behavior, publicly rewarding participation in and punishing defection from the conventional coordination equilibria. Transforming Hume's philosophical-policy into a legal design argument for the international system, lawyers and policymakers can be said to have a vested interest in the utility of global society and are better able to recognize, define, and keep tabs on the health of nations.[113]

> Education, and the artifice of politicians, concur in bestowing a farther morality on loyalty, and branding all rebellion with a greater degree of guilt and infamy. Nor is it a wonder, that politicians shou'd be very industrious in inculcating such notions, where their interest is so particularly concern'd.[114]

With lawyers and policymakers leading supranational governance institutions, built from contract-by-convention and the process-norm of Justice-As-Sovereignty, the cumulative effect of social convention on the cooperation of individual nations is more fully institutionalized and, therefore, at its most powerful. One builds on the other, with more complex sanctions to regulate more complex social relations. The social stability of the global society remains both the fundamental presupposition and the moral imperative for the process-norm of Justice-As-Sovereignty.[115]

With an understanding of the fundamental assumptions about the individual, the collective action problem and the role of the state, Hume's logic of concepts renders a Philosophical-Policy Paradigm (Figure 1.2) that

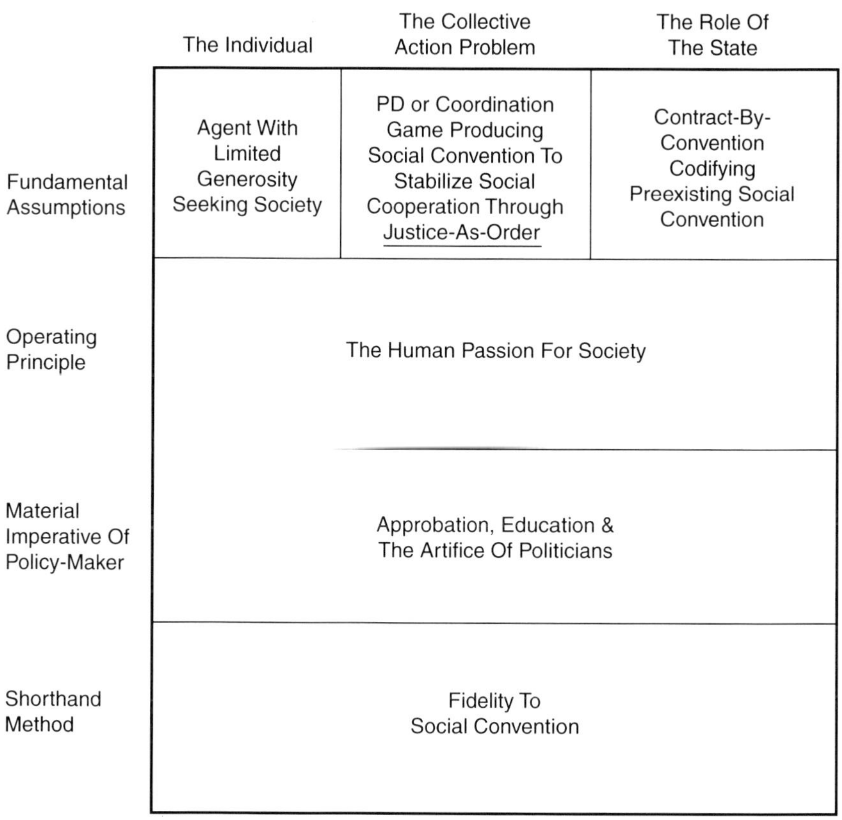

Figure 1.2 Hume's philosophical-policy paradigm.

generates an *operating principle* for policy in the absolute presupposition of the human need for stable society. This in turn logically defines the *material conditions* of law and policy; that is, what the lawyer or policymaker allocates in order to operationalize the core principle in terms of approbation, education, and the artifice of politicians. The policy paradigm also defines fidelity to social convention as the *primary method* by which policy and law are assured social persistence over time.

The "Essence" of Sovereignty in International Law

From the perspective of Hume's philosophical-policy, the law of nations arises as legal design from the absolute presupposition that humanity seeks society and social order on all levels of organization. Hume creates a dialectic metaphysics of presuppositions where convention arises from custom with levels of sanctions that protect the human need for society as the absolute presupposition of local, municipal, and international cooperation. In the concept of limited generosity, sympathy and self-interest synthesize to generate an imperative to discover a coordination equilibrium that can take humanity from an inefficient state of nature to a more collectively optimal international system. Social convention, represented by the process-norm of Justice-As-Sovereignty, stabilizes territory and creates, in the fullness of time, that system of international law and those governance institutions that are needed to progressively adapt human coordination to a dynamic, open, and ever-more complex world system.

Justice-As-Sovereignty offers a refined philosophical solution to the international need to express practical reason as justice-in-utility. It is created out of the imperative for cooperative social behavior as a collective good. It synthesizes the greater dialectic between normative and positive law by creating a definition of natural law that regards moral obligation[116] as evolved from the experience of finding and stabilizing a coordination equilibrium. This equilibrium is the result of the positive actions, expectations, and interactions of humans in the natural course of their agency.

However, we know from the precepts of philosophical method that the essence of a concept is not its starting point but the culmination of its series of "moments"[117] along a scale of forms. The full and proper consideration of sovereignty as international legal practice will come with an understanding of its essential nature, which is illuminated by Hume's integrated philosophical system of metaphysical presuppositions. In order to appreciate the evolution of sovereignty and the dialectic between process⇆principle, the chapters that follow will identify four specific Humean philosophical insights that more fully define Justice-As-Sovereignty. These insights, along with their policy ramifications and evidence in law, will detail the metaphysical geography of sovereignty as a source-definition of practical reason in international law and demonstrate its utility in application to legal practice.

Each subsequent chapter will be composed of three parts. In the first section, a *philosophical insight into sovereignty* will be identified and a specific

SPP deciphered. In the second section, the SPP will be used to extrapolate those *legal design* tools that create a logic of investigation derived from Hume's logic of philosophical concepts. This application of practice to theory is accomplished by employing the catalogue of contemporary methodological tools (e.g., game theory) or theoretical models (e.g., Hart's concept of law) that are available to illuminate Hume's arguments in more contemporary terms. In the third and last section of each chapter, Hume's insight will be tested against existing legal practice. Are the specific insight, and the policy design tools rendered by it, reflected in the evidence of international legal practice? Here, practice will be defined by the terms of international dispute resolution and its jurisprudence.[118] This case analysis tests whether or not the comprehensive policy argument or *concept of law* created by Hume's philosophical-policy can illuminate international dispute settlement.

* * *

Before we move on, however, the SPP and its role in this argument must be more completely defined. Metaphysically, the SPP is a relative presupposition arising from an absolute presupposition (e.g., passion for society) and represents a dialectic component of the core process norm (e.g., Justice-As-Sovereignty). The imperative of the SPPs are to provide procedural rules for the operationalization and persistence of the process-norm. Hart has already argued that those rules meant to sort the procedural priorities of a legal system can be defined in terms of either *adjudication*, *change*, or *recognition*. SPPs fulfill these functions.

Each SPP is *systematic* because it is created from a philosophical-policy paradigm as a direct logical entailment of the insight under consideration. It concerns *public policy* as each SPP is identified, not to justify and direct individual moral or ethical choices,[119] but to solve sociopolitical collective action problems and facilitate legal design. Lastly, each SPP is a *precept* because it provides, as a relative presupposition in a dialectic argument on a scale of forms, a metaphysical guidepost for the empirical evaluation and logical delineation of the positive law.

The purpose of philosophical-policy and legal design is to illuminate the underlying metaphysics in legal institutions and codified law, enhancing a positive logic of policy investigation with a philosophical substructure that specifics the ideas from which that reality arises.[120] In order to accomplish this, the presuppositions of a philosophical system must be translated into procedural "rules of thumb" or precepts of policy and legal design. The SPPs are these "reasonable" rules of thumb for political judgment that, although components of the metaphysical geography of the concept of sovereignty, also practically actualize it within the tangible framework of a comprehensive policy argument for international law.

Being a direct product of exegesis, each SPP results in an identifiable, logical, and epistemological connection between a specific philosophical insight and a practical rule of thumb that can then be used as a standard for the application of theory to practice. These *precepts*, or presuppositions, empirically represent the metaphysical content and logic of their corresponding philosophical insights for legal design. They interact with the law to set expectations and influence the collective action that subsequently determines the synthesis product of ideas⇆institutions that is the positive law. Collectively, the SPPs act as procedural rules or standards for the law. They first create and then guide the configuration of collective political action, as it integrates the "is" of the empirical world with persuasive arguments for how it "ought" to be. The SPP prescribes change consistent with moral standards provided by the inherent metaphysics of the philosophical-policy paradigm. The aim of locating the SPPs is to identify the constituents of the core process norm in its first moment of essence, or conceptualization, as the genesis, or source, point of practical reason in international law.

2

"Effectiveness": A "Local" Rule of Recognition and the Foundation for Justice-As-Sovereignty

Abstract

Based on the core dialectic of process⇆principle and the effectiveness of social convention as a foundational means to the stability of human social life, Hume's argument for natural law defines both the municipal and international level of social organization. Hume's comprehensive policy argument is extrapolated by the elaboration of his concept of law. Accentuating the procedural rules of recognition, adjudication, and change as prerequisites to substantive rules reverses the positivist priority between the two as asserted by H. L. A. Hart. Hume's concept of law promotes policy design backed by a process-norm of Justice-As-Sovereignty interpreted through the systematic policy precept (SPP) of effectiveness as a "local" rule of recognition. Lastly, jurisprudence provides evidence for the salience of Hume's philosophical-policy.

I. Hume's Logic of Concepts: A Natural Law of Process⇆Principle

Francisco Vitoria confronted a basic philosophical problem in the application of practical reason to positive law: finding a new metaphysics for the positive law, when the previous definition of natural law fails.[1] The infancy of modern international law coincided with an age of exploration that would bring Europeans into contact with aboriginal peoples around the world. Meanwhile, the definition of natural law, that since Aquinas[2] had been based on an idea of human reason directly inferred from divine and eternal law as interpreted by the Catholic Church, no longer held universal acceptance. The Reformation had made God's revelation a local and diversified cultural phenomenon, inadequate to provide a common definition of natural law for European nations, let alone native populations of "foreign" lands. Vitoria, being concerned with using natural law as a basis for *jus gentium*, but having to abandon Papal revelation, required a "new" natural law, a secular natural law based on reason, which could justify the practice adopted by post-Reformation Europeans in both their interstate relations, and in their contact with aboriginal populations in the new world.[3]

Here, Vitoria's effort to separate practical reason from revelation and make it the common denominator[4] of jus gentium for all men, including, aboriginal people,[5] becomes an exercise in circular logic. Vitoria's new metaphysics for the decatholicized definition of reason, deals primarily with matters of faith (e.g., barbarian baptism and conversion), based on a substantively Christian, if not Catholic, interpretation of revelation. By replacing the Pope with temporal rulers and by making "human" reason ostensibly Christian, Vitoria arrives where he started with a substantive basis for natural law that is still locally circumscribed and significantly less than universal.[6]

From the standpoint of Hume's philosophical-policy, Vitoria's dilemma was that he conceptualized natural law in terms of *substantive* rather than *procedural* moral and legal rules and he therefore had to rely on a universal set of critical religious principles when these were becoming increasingly localized. His substantive natural law, whether from revelation or reason, was built upon divine law and was becoming localized both in terms of the circumscription of Christian ethics and the replacement of the Pope with local rulers. So Vitoria was faced with either having to accept Reformation pluralism and settle for local or regional critical principles as the basis for his idea of practical reason, or deny Reformation breakdown altogether, an ahistorical alternative. Vitoria, rightly, separated human reason from religious principles, but failed to see that natural law could be a function of either substantive or procedural principle. Substantive universal principles had been destroyed in the Reformation, but he required them, so he fell back on "Christian" revelation although it was inadequate to the task. Whatever its attributes, his circular logic is, at best, a weak substitute for the ideal of a natural law from a secular practical reason that represented all humans.

However, using the logic of philosophical method, Vitoria's dilemma can be addressed through the fundamental Humean dialectic between *process⇆principle*. Examining Vitoria's dilemma from the standpoint of Hume's philosophical-policy, one can identify an argument for a universal set of *procedural* rules and obligations that better supports a universal metaphysical basis for practical reason, and therefore, a distinct definition of natural law that respects the facts of the post-Reformation world.

Social conventions, like Justice-As-Sovereignty, are not universally valued in terms of ex-ante or a priori aetiological-norms[7] or critical/reasoned principles, but in terms of their capacity to maintain coordination of the international *process* itself. Hume makes a distinction between the practice of social convention focused on procedural rules and the derivative duty-producing rules of substantive law that come after contract-by-convention. For Hume, justice in natural law is a synthesis of process⇆principle, where the former holds the initial highground.

Applying this dialectic to Vitoria's dilemma allows international law to be universally procedural and securely based upon *process-norms* like Justice-As-Sovereignty, while acknowledging pluralist or local substantive law, based upon contextual critical principle. In effect, Hume's philosophical-policy allows for two definitions of practical reason, or natural law, to exist simultaneously for a single and stable international system: one *local* and *substantive*; the other *global* and *procedural*.

In this way, Hume's philosophical-policy provides a universal definition of "natural law," not beholding to the inherent dictates of critical principle or ideal-regarding, aetiological-norms. For this reason, it avoids the pitfall of substantive definitions of natural law, like Vitoria's. Rather, Hume describes the origin of social cohesion and long-term social stability in a natural law based on universal passions as the human motivation to action. Although initially unconscious of the passions at issue, humans seek social interaction and coordinate themselves so as to obtain it. Hume's argument concentrates on the "process" of locating and maintaining a cooperative equilibrium as the end-in-itself for any social system. In this way, stability is built from procedural practice and a universal common law, based on the process-norm of Justice-As-Sovereignty, without denying the substantive pluralistic ends of any particular sovereign state.

Hume's philosophical-policy would explain the Reformation,[8] and the conflict that follows, in terms of substantive ends being forced on unreceptive audiences with resulting social instability.[9] Social convention, on the other hand, focuses on the creation of obligation from a set of universal but neutral and procedural common laws that provide a process-base for a minimal jus gentium. Justice-As-Sovereignty, as a procedural norm, simultaneously coordinates a single universal international community through process, while allowing substantive principle to find legal voice on the municipal or local level.

Hume's argument for natural law is distinctively procedural. It is based in social convention rather than critical principle, it provides the point of departure and the central presupposition for the application of all of his philosophical insights into international law. It also provides a foundation for an argument that avoids Vitoria's dilemma. Hume's unique theory of natural law is the first, and central, philosophical insight created by the application of Hume's philosophical-policy to the genesis of legal design in international law. It results from Hume's dedication to the integration of philosophical method with empirical or scientific observation. As I have argued, Hume is more than a "British empiricist."[10] His writing treats the normative and empirical as interactive dynamic components engaged in what philosophical method defines as dialectic relationships along a complex scale of forms.[11]

But why call this a concept of "natural" law? Because Hume's philosophical-policy allows for development of a process that generates morality, justice, and politics from the natural social behavior of human beings.[12] In Hume's philosophical-policy, our behavior is rooted in a set of normative presuppositions, where the human need for society or stable social interaction is absolute. Hume's "science" is a "moral-science of collective action." He defines the "natural" in terms of what the individual applies his or her unconscious passions to, as well as how other humans respond to these choices. The resulting interactions then set up social conventions and resultant expectations that are the foundry for ethical, political, and legal rules in moral support of the absolute presupposition of social order.

For Hume's philosophical-policy, "natural law evolves and is learned by experience"[13] as individuals interact and create process-norms in order to coordinate their behavior and find the stable society they seek. Social convention, based on the social sympathy and the human need for society, is the core of this solution and creates a normative character from the morality of natural human interactions.

> Conventions of property, coordination and reciprocity are natural laws as they are not conscious but evolve spontaneously out of repeated interactions and diverse interests.[14]

Obligation to social convention also arises naturally from the setting of human expectations and the need for enforcement of these conventions by approbation (the first stage of social sanction). As the international coordination game indicates, it is in our individual interests to follow a convention once it is established, and to establish it in our collective interest in order to coordinate ourselves toward political or legal stabilization. The laws of nature, as they render social convention, create expectations of "ought" in our and others' behavior from their inherent evolution and existence.

> Around these conventions a system of morality grows up; we come to recognize a moral obligation to play our part in cooperative arrangements and learn to condemn those who try to take free rides on other people's efforts.[15]

Hume integrates a "sense of justice" as an evolving universal morality into his natural law. However, it is assessed methodologically by the empirical logic of process rather than any independent moral principle. It is moral because "we believe that we ought to keep the Laws of Nature";[16] it is empirical because it is not *prior* principle that provides the imperative to moral choice but process-norms and their "[c]onventions [that] ought to be kept."[17]

This natural order springs from Hume's passion-based idea of practical reason. Beginning as social convention represented by Justice-As-Sovereignty, reason seeks a higher and higher level of moral complexity, in an evolutionary scale of forms or progressive codification process, that spreads order across successive levels of social organization.

> And indeed, when we consider how aptly *natural* and *moral* evidence link together, and form only one chain of argument, we shall make no scruple to allow that they are the same nature, and derived from the same principles.[18]

At the foundation of his metaphysics, Hume's argument for natural law is rooted in sentiment. Collingwood argues that human history "is a history of thought."[19] Hume's philosophical-policy adopts a Newtonian approach to the origin of collective action with his dependence on the observation of "real" human behavior as the core of justice and its inherent moral obligation. In both his effort to analyze human understanding and decipher social justice, Hume seeks to "cultivate" a "true metaphysics"[20] of presuppositions dealing with passions, sentiments, impressions, experience, custom, or what he calls the "internal fabric, the operation of the understanding, the working of the passions."[21] The normative dimension of this metaphysics emphasizes the obligation one feels to the project of social cooperation itself as a unique base for natural law. Hume "aims to ground moral obligations firmly in the soil of human nature itself, in the natural workings of the human mind, and thereby fulfill the bold ambitions of the theory of natural law."[22]

At the foundation of this effort lies an absolute metaphysical presupposition; namely, that all human beings naturally seek, and are incomplete without, a stable social order. Hume acknowledges that obtaining a metaphysical understanding of how ideas generate observable action is not as easy as accepting the outward signs of experience at face value. But, unlike a modern positivist,[23] Hume, tackling a philosophical rather than a technical subject, recognizes the importance of the metaphysical dimensions of action and choice.

> How painful soever this inward search or enquiry may appear, it becomes, in some measure, requisite to those, who would escribe with success the obvious and outward appearance of life and manners.[24]

Within Hume's philosophical-policy, human thought, as ideas, are products or "copies" of "impressions."[25] Motivated primarily by one's passions, the person deciphers the facts of the material world through his capacity to translate habitual interpersonal experience into a causal inference by the employment of what Hume calls "customary transition."[26] The integration of human character with one's experience of the world through social convention is the core of both his argument for justice, and the prior notion of human understanding. It also provides the "true"[27] metaphysical core for his greater philosophical-policy.

From these presuppositions, Hume's philosophical-policy also provides a definition of "natural" as *fundamental* law. This is an important distinction. For Hume, justice and convention are not *natural* in the sense of being an a priori component of human nature, but are, instead, *artificial*, and fundamental or first manifestations of human social interaction. Human nature is made manifest in the natural passions and their outward expression, which are the content of his natural law. This fundamental natural behavior is then expressed and protected by artificial social and legal constructs, like justice.

When Hume speaks of "natural law," he is therefore describing a fundamental law or system of just rules that is an artificial creation of the dialectic between reason⇆passions and that pre-dates social order as critical to it. Being fundamental, natural law is a direct outgrowth of unconscious human interaction. The natural passion for society needs protection as it evolves, and this security is provided by *artificial* constructions like family, tribe, or nation. Being artificial, Hume argues that the conventions of justice (e.g., Justice-As-Sovereignty as an international process-norm) and their moral obligations may act to serve the public interest even when they do not serve any particular individual's wants.[28] This phenomenon makes justice "artificial," but at the same time dialectically *natural*, in terms of one's moral obligation to that evolution of convention called for by the social needs and requirements of one's natural sentiment for public order.

Only an inherent understanding of the dialectic tension between natural⇆artificial could render the argument Hume makes for a natural law that is simultaneously both. The synthesis of artificial justice in natural law with a natural morality in artificial rules of behavior is beyond positivist dichotomy or scientific classification. The artificial roots of justice as law are not in the tradition of divine command,[29] nor are they the universal a priori principles of human nature determining the will of the individual.[30] Hume's philosophical-policy is unique because it focuses on human action, or more definitively, interaction. Specifically, it considers how human encounters naturally produce expectations built on a metaphysics of humanity's inherent need for society and one's use of artificial social convention to translate such sentiments into both an understanding and a transformation of the practical world.

At the same time, Hume's conceptualization is compatible with the tradition of natural law theory. This is because his greater philosophical system depends upon a metaphysical structure of absolute and relative presuppositions within a scale of forms that provides a point of departure for the extrapolation of both an a priori theory of human understanding and an a posteriori theory of justice. That Hume favors the passions in his account of human understanding reflects his effort to replace "superstition" with science and an "abstruse" with a more "easy and obvious" philosophical system based on human agency.[31] Hume considers his methodology more practical and, therefore, of more utility to the understanding and improvement of human behavior as well as to our success in creating the ordered social cooperation we, as humans, require.

> It [the easy philosophy] enters more into common life; moulds the heart and affections; and, by touching those principles which actuate men, reforms

> their conduct, and brings them nearer to that model of perfection which it describes.[32]

The dialectic between the artificial⇆natural that marks Hume's "Newtonian" approach to society and its origins is measured in the sentiments, passions, and actions of individuals. In this way, Hume's philosophical-policy explains how human collective action (subnational, national, or international) is initiated and what characteristics of the person motivate or inhibit the effort to find order in coordination.

This approach to natural law is also dynamic as it indicates that a scale of forms exists, first, in terms of the evolution of different levels of sanctions (i.e., from approbation to justice to political society). In addition, the imperative of growing social complexity causes the expansion of society from small group life in the family, to tribal community, to the state, and then to the interstate relations of a global social order.

> But suppose the conjunction of the sexes to be established in nature, a family immediately arises; and particular rules being found requisite for its subsistence, these are immediately embraced; though without comprehending the rest of mankind within their prescriptions. Suppose that several families unite together into one society, which is totally disjoined from all others, the rules, which preserve peace and order, enlarge themselves to the utmost extent of that society; but becoming then entirely useless, lose their force when carried one step further. But again suppose, that several distinct societies maintain a kind of intercourse for mutual convenience and advantage, the boundaries of justice still grow larger, in proportion to the largeness of men's views, and the force of their mutual connexions. History, experience, reason sufficiently instruct us in this natural progress of human sentiments, and in the gradual enlargement of our regards to justice, in proportion as we become acquainted with the extensive utility of that virtue.[33]

Within this interacting scale of forms, Hume's natural law creates an imperative for progressive expansion of social complexity, while it maintains the advantage of being truly secular and expressed through a universal and practical reason, in both unconscious behavior and conscious choice. Hume's focus is on the "process" by which human interaction leads to repetition, custom, and then, social convention as secular, yet ultimately moral, phenomena. This approach does not depend on any particular a priori precept or independent principle as a basis for cooperation, and therefore allows a value pluralism to exist within systems of evolving social convention, depending on the context and circumstances of each human society.

Human consciousness is not necessary to this evolving natural process, at least not at its genesis. Although human enlightenment grows as levels of sanctions move from unconscious convention to very conscious contract-by-convention in political society, Hume's argument assumes that individuals seek society and apply their passions to the material world based on universal social predispositions, regardless of the degree to which they are conscious of them. Unlike a scholastic definition of natural law[34] that assumes knowledge of a specific set of divine revelations, or a Hobbesian idea of the laws of nature that requires conscious and reasoned contractual choice based on one's will, Hume reveals a natural law that begins with human passion and the unconscious desire for society. This natural law allows for the evolution of legal order as society geographically expands and social sanctions, consequently, become more complex in response.

Lastly, for our purposes, Hume's practical metaphysics of natural law has the capacity to decipher varying problems of interplay between sentiment and action that are common to ever-greater levels of evolving social stratification. Specifically, he describes international political society as an evolutionary step in providing "peace and order among mankind."[35]

> When a number of political societies are erected, and maintain a great intercourse together, a new set of rules are immediately discovered to be *useful* in that particular situation; and accordingly take place under the title of Law of Nations.[36]

However, as we shall see in chapter 5, Hume also notes that each distinct level of organization has specific dilemmas in terms of both the origin and maintenance of collective action. These specific problems are characteristic of the power of the absolute presupposition of social order. In the same way that strategic rationality, driven by different degrees of passion, creates the environment of a prisoner's dilemma on the municipal level and the conditions for a coordination game internationally, Hume's process-based sense of natural law allows room for distinct definitions of order and different understandings of public utility, as well as the moral obligation that is generated by it, for each level of society.

> Human nature cannot by any means subsist, without the association of individuals; and that association never could have place, were no regard paid to the laws of equity and justice. Disorder, confusion, the war of all against all, are the necessary consequences of such a licentious conduct. But nations can subsist without intercourse. They may even subsist, in some degree, under a general war. The observance of justice, though useful among them, is not guarded by so strong a necessity as among individuals; and the *moral obligation* holds proportion with the *usefulness*. All politicians will allow, and most philosophers, that reasons of state may, in particular emergencies, dispense with the rules of justice, and invalidate any treaty or alliance, where the strict observance of it would be prejudicial, in a considerable degree, to either of the contracting parties. But nothing less than the most extreme necessity, it is confessed, can justify individuals in a breech of promise, or an invasion of the property of others.[37]

This approach to natural law creates a flexible basis for an understanding of the origins of human cooperation on each level of social organization.

Hume's attention to the "inner fabric" of a primarily "social" humanity and his effort to place justice, defined as that process-norm bringing order to society as "absolutely requisite to the well-being of mankind and [the] existence of society,"[38] supports a universal theory of natural (or fundamental) law. This "fabric" can be recognized as a central character in the application of his systemic philosophy to the origin and persistence of international law as well as municipal law.

Therefore, in addition to the universal metaphysical dimension of Hume's theory of natural law, a local component is also provided for. Hume stresses context, circumstance, and the actions of persons. These are the critical dimensions of Hume's philosophical-policy that accommodate the "facts on the ground" that coalesced to create the practice of international law as we know it. If Hume is correct about the determinative nature of circumstance on the advent of justice and its particular form and content, it becomes crucial to determine if his philosophical-policy is reflected in the social history that provided for the genesis of contemporary international law in the Westphalian Equilibrium.

> Thus, the rules of equity or justice depend entirely on the particular state and condition in which men are placed, and owe their origin and existence to that utility, which results to the public from their strict and regular observance.[39]

If our history was launched from a natural law that creates a dialectic scale of forms integrating stronger sanctions with larger social orders, as Hume's philosophical-policy prescribes, then its application to the contextual prehistory of modern international law ought to provide evidence for this narrative. This task requires that we first examine the dialectic between local⇆universal and its effects on uncertainty as these create a generic justification for law.

The Context of Modern International Law

Hume's philosophical-policy, with its idea of natural law, is built upon the generic role of *universality* and *certainty* as factors that create a human need for law. These two ideas are critical in turning a human craving for society, Hume's absolute presupposition, into the legal regulation of social order. Both ideas operate within the local⇆universal dialectic. Specifically, *universality* is the tendency to find communion and commonality in rules producing the largest scope for fairness and equality that is possible. *Certainty* deals with the affects of fear and uncertainty that require rules that introduce some level—local or more universal—of security through law.

Social history is, for Hume, a philosophical subject. Collingwood argues that, where an historian might seek the particular, the philosopher seeks the universal.[40] Hume's philosophical-policy confirms metaphysics through observation. The resulting argument is that the *universal* experience of humanity is in seeking and keeping social order and cooperation through law as a necessary component of humanity's long-term stability.[41] The dialectic relations between the certain, which has a tendency to the immediate and local, and the universal, which is inherently connected to distance and uncertainty, lie in the tension between one's simultaneous need for personal security and social stability.

In a world of random chance, human beings seek certainty in their expectations of social interaction, while in a condition of biological isolation or uniqueness, they seek the universality of society and its fellowship. This is why most people fear alienation, seek community, value loyalty, and protect allegiances. It explains why our institutions resist change to situations that maintain established patterns of social relations, why empire and unification in politics compel us, why family as security and immortality engages us as a common imperative, and why centralization of power invokes both irrational fear and zealous devotion. From the standpoint of Hume's natural law, this system of dialectic tension is why humanity requires *law*.

For Hume, the experience of insecurity creates morality within one's obligation to the rules of law as a means of creating certainty in human life.[42] In this way, habit, and the expectations connected to it, can be regularized and granted universal validity in a world of seeming randomness. But this "normative certainty" is only effective to the degree that it is based on generally-held human traits and relevant to all, equally, within some definition of social or universal community.

If morality had no common roots or applications, it would not constitute a public obligation, but a very personal and atomistic or existential ethics, applied in a world of random behavior without common sanction or legitimate authority. Like a saint in a concentration camp, law would be strictly a personal and theoretical subject requiring supererogatory acts, while the practice of moral behavior, assuming it is mediated by collective action problems, might add to the chaos instead of lessening it.

Philosophical method, or any intellectual method for that matter, seeks commonality of trait and generalization to facilitate theoretical understanding and its extrapolation. Even with philosophical method, where overlap of concepts causes definitive classification to be impossible, the search for universal traits or predispositions attributable to humanity as fundamental assumptions persists. Regardless of one's condition or circumstance universalization is the primary means for the generalization and logical extrapolation necessary to establishing an integrated system of thought that has general and practical application. Especially with the subject of law, the *universality* of one's presuppositions is a key to fostering the practical *certainty* humanity seeks in an ordered society.

Hume's natural law supports social organization and the creation of order out of chaos by focusing on neutral process rather than critical principle, and empirical action rather than intrinsic states of mind. Hume is a philosopher before he is a scientist. His attention to the metaphysical undergirding of social convention, with its inherent universal passion for society, provides the key to the practical certainty rendered by his argument for law, justice, and social order, both municipally and internationally.

The search for a universal basis to establish certainty in human life is the point of origin for most theories of both natural and positive law. The primary, that is universal, predispositions attributed to humanity are not just a factor in our unconscious actions but form the framework for argument within which the reasonableness of public policy, law, and social institutions are ultimately debated.

The dialectic interplay between ideas and the legal institutions they create, and which support or are critical of them, is central to any application of Hume's philosophical-policy and its definition of sovereignty. To understand the historical and metaphysical context of international law as global social order, we should consider the idea of a fundamental law of basic process-rendering rules, like sovereignty. With its universality and certainty, Justice-As-Sovereignty creates an international context of order in tribute to the absolute presupposition of humanity's need for sociopolitical stability.

All legal philosophy can be said to originate in either the moral universality and certainty of natural legal theory, or its rejection in lieu of the universality and certainty of local or common positive practice. The cleavages within legal thought and the terms of scholarly debate in which we now operate have an evolutionary history that begins with the idea of natural law as the foundational definition of practical reason and, therefore, the fundamental presupposition of legal theory and practice. Hume's philosophical-policy is part of this tradition but also an innovative reaction to it, based on his interpretation of human and intellectual history.[43] Specifically, for Hume, law is the result of the metaphysical need for society creating the universality and certainty of an ordered social existence through the process of evolving social convention and an artificial norm of justice. But is this scientific-metaphysics reflected in history?

Hume's Natural Law: Evidence in History

Natural law, like modern politics, is primarily a creature of European origin.[44] Arguments have been made that the physical geography of the West facilitated the progress of technology and the advance of liberal values.[45] A concurrent argument for the contextual origins of law cites the dialectic between particular ideas/values, like *individualism* and the *primacy of reason*, which grew out of the European circumstance fostering Christianity.[46] The original idea of natural law finds voice in a Western concern for reason, individualism, and right. This is the ascendance of a priori critical principle, and the innate character of human reason as a product of divine instigation where revelation serves as the only legitimate basis for human critical will and the thought, choice, decision, and action it creates.[47]

To apply Hume's philosophical-policy to the rise of a positive law derived from a process-based natural law, we begin where humanity first found certainty and order in a social manifestation of universal law: the Papal international system. The ambition of Pope Gregory VII in *Dictatus Papae* fueled his effort to use the "role of law as a source of authority and a means of control"[48] to make all, then developing, systems of municipal or royal law subservient to the Papacy, which would become the primary agent in the international system of late eleventh-century Europe.

> During the last decades of the eleventh century, the papal party began to search the written record of church history for legal authority to support papal supremacy over the entire clergy as well as clerical independence of, and possible supremacy over, the entire secular branch of society. The papal party encouraged scholars to develop a science of law which would provide a working basis for carrying out these major policies. At the same time, the imperial party also began to search for ancient texts that would support its cause against papal usurpation. There was, however, no legal forum to which either the papacy or the imperial authority could take its case—except to the pope or the emperor himself.[49]

This choice, from our metaphysical point of view, was not a choice at all. For both the royal and the ecclesiastical structures of law, created simultaneously, obtained their universality and certainty from a common base within the revelations of Christ as interpreted by the Catholic Church. This *revelation-based* universality and *revealed* certainty gave Pope Gregory's ambition a political advantage in the creation of social convention and then codified law, as he could offer a more certain social order under universal Canon Law than under any secular alternative.

> Both canon law and royal law were grounded in the authority of external sources of law, to which they looked for objectivity and generality. Both found such sources in divine law and in natural law...the secular order was, by definition, more chaotic, more disorganized, more aimless than the spiritual order. The secular order was more in need of reform and redemption....was subject to reason...intended to be scientific...but it was closer to custom than Canon law, and therefore closer to disorder...it was more difficult to systematize.[50]

As reflected in Hume's logic, the moral certainty and theological universality of the Christian Church in the Middle Ages provided the institutionalized and stable social order sought by human passion to stabilize collective action. Within this context, both universality and certainty are created by a coordination equilibrium focused on the dominance of the "one, holy, catholic, and apostolic Church," where secular or civil law is considered subservient to, and a creature of, the primary development of Canon Law. Here, natural law is not external to, but an integral component of, the evolution of positive law itself.[51]

In the competition between less stable secular legal systems and the transnational certainty of Christian revelation in law, the system of Papal government and Canon Law actually created the dialectic synthesis for social order. This was necessary to the growth and persistence of its many nested secular legal systems, which gained strength within the greater or universal certainty provided by the Church.

> The Canon law as a system was more than rules; it was a process, a dialectical process of adapting rules to new situations. This was inevitable if only because of the limits imposed upon its jurisdiction, and the consequent competition which it faced from the secular legal systems that coexisted with it.[52]

From within Hume's philosophical-policy, the success and stability of this "Papal Revolution" can be described within the context of the institutionalization of the Christian principles of individuality, reason, and progress for humanity.[53] Informed by a Humean narrative, we might anticipate that the integration of these principles as representative of Christian social convention, within the Papal legal system, set the tone for the future evolution of institutional forms through contract-by-convention anticipating the modern "Western" state as well as the idea of the "rule of law" at all levels of social organization. History confirms this pattern.

> The Papal Revolution,...made Christianity into a political and legal program. The church became a state. Canon law became a specific means, first, of holding the church-state together, and second, of reforming the world. The other emerging law systems also sought to reform custom in accordance with reason and conscience. Yet this was not meant to destroy the old communities; on the contrary, it was intended to strengthen them. To apply reason to custom, that is, to weed out the mass of unreasonable customs and to cultivate the reasonable ones into a system of law was a bold program...a new dialectical method...taught the West to synthesize cases into rules, rules into principles, principles into a system.[54]
>
> In the case of the Papal Revolution, two of its major goals, rule *by* law and rule *of* law—that rulers must seek to effectuate their policies systematically through legal institutions and that they are themselves to be bound by the legal institutions through which they govern—were quite new to Western society.[55]

Unlike other "universal" religions,[56] Christianity, and the Papal State it generated, formed a conventional legal context punctuated by the dialectic between the conventions of the universal Christian Church and the scriptural certainty its principles provided. By basing this first international system of law on the universality and necessity of common theistic revelation, the international "Christian" society also built itself upon the potentially nontheistic pillar of individuality. In this way, they created a set of "modern" aetiological-norms and a critical metaphysics that would eventually transcend its Catholic religious-institutional structure, generate the Reformation, and eventually lead to our complex but coordinated secular interstate system.

However, over time, the institutional structure that contained these theistic principles was separated from them through critical argument. The Papacy no longer held the monopoly on what became the aetiological-norms of individual freedom and progress, which transcended the Church's context as reasoned critical principles and sparked the Reformation. When the cooperative equilibrium created by the international Papal system began to crumble through defection, the Church tried to save itself through a tighter conventional grip on its subjects. Here, the conventional status of Church institutional rules were promoted over what had been its inherent principles, which had been usurped by Protestants. Dogmatic loyalty to the Church as an administrative institution became the sole test of universality and certainty.

In effect, the Papacy's international law had been based upon a coordination equilibrium of revealed principle, that then evolved beyond the institutional structure that had been created to maintain it, becoming universal-critical principles. With the loss of its principles to the forces of the Reformation, the Papacy desperately sought to preserve its administrative and legal façade of rules. The resulting ideological zeal made the rules and institutions more brittle; theistic principle split into non-Catholic critical principle and static Papal dogma. Consequently, eristic ideologies replaced dialectic engagement producing hard, fast, and mutually exclusive definitions of truth that eventually led to war. This caused the universal failure of the Papal legal system that had heretofore provided stability for the essential dialectic between process⇆principle. This failure portended the need for a new international coordination equilibrium.

The ultimate clash of this essential dialectic came in the post-Catholic fruition of the principle of individual freedom during the Protestant Reformation. In its critical form, it not only conflicted with Catholic dogma but its resulting synthesis splintered the universal church into many sects and the certainty of revelation into the vast confusion of each person's individuated relationship to God. This particular manifestation of process⇆principle provided the background conditions for the spread of intellectual expression and the steady progress of study in both science and philosophy, while it also destroyed the universality and certainty of the established "Papal" international system and its Canon Law.

When the Catholic Church was secure in its domination of both the religious and secular world,[57] its processes were able to provide the stability necessary for the advancement of freedom and individuality in terms of science as well as the exploration of the philosophical and social conditions of humanity through divine revelation. The conditions of certainty and universality provided by the Church fostered the creation of a critical and non-conventional scientific method that encouraged the application of reason to both the empirical and the metaphysical world.[58] For a time, the substance of the inter-European social system was manifest in a synthesis of process and principle. It gave both theory⇆practice a common home in the *eternal law* as revealed in the *divine law*, shown to humanity in *natural law*, which then became the point of origin for *positive* law or practice.[59]

Divine revelation, in the first European international system, provided universal certainty, or justice-as-social-order, that supported what Hume might invoke as the "passion" for a stable society of science, politics, and law. In addition, revelation mapped universal substantive principles, and their concurrent obligations, from the common religion onto legal institutional processes. This era of theological-monism provided both the material and spiritual world an integrated legal certainty and truth that all humans seek in both their private and public lives. Divine and eternal law inform natural law, which creates a single set of rules for human behavior within the security of a Christian world system.

Hume's philosophical-policy provides an explanation for the rise of what we might call "justice-as-revelation," in its establishment of the fundamental dialectic between process⇆principle and the consequent rise of the latter to challenge the former in law. It also can be used to predict the failure of this conventional point of equilibrium within the international coordination game. The synthesis policy solution transcends the status quo as the substantive layer of common critical principle evolves past the institutional structure of the Church and fractures into many ideas of revelation with the onset of the Reformation. In consequence, the universal certainty of both layers of process and principle became unstable. In order to reclaim certainty or universality, a movement toward an alternative point of coordinated equilibrium became imperative. In effect, the principles of Catholic revelation transcended the conventional institutions and became the basis for many local applications of principle to process. Now, transcendent, independent, reflexive, and critical principle as aetiological-norm (e.g., freedom, individuality, progress) shifted the human search for certainty to the local level of social organization where context, although narrow, was more certain.

Using the argument for natural law derived from Hume's philosophical-policy, we can both anticipate and predict a compensatory move in finding a new coordination equilibrium. Specifically, as long as the Papal System was stable on that equilibrium created by the general social conventions of the Catholic Church, the process was reinforced by whatever contextual principles were contained within the idea of Christianity. However, when these contextual principles moved to a new level of complexity, and a new idea of independent substantive principle emerged—one that transcended the processes of any single set of institutions and became critical of that stable process equilibrium—there was conflict. The Church's reaction was to emphasize their sociotheistic institutional conventions as dogma; rules now independent of justification but nonetheless obligatory.

With the advent of dogmatism in the Church, the resulting entrenchment put the Papacy in the position of persecuting the logical entailments of those critical principles of freedom and individuality upon which it gained its original status. Consequently, widespread social instability ensued. What was needed was a new sense of universalism and certainty beyond the substantive dogma of the Church. One system of natural law as critical principle was broken by the Reformation. However, another, reemphasizing the cooperative *process* through new conventions that avoided a dependence on revelation and a priori principle, was about to evolve and take its place.

As the Catholic definition of social stability was disturbed by the transcendence of critical principle, so society searched for another set of process conventions that could settle the inherent transnational tensions created by the, now eristic, conflict of Catholic–Protestant principle. Hume's conceptual logic would suggest that, with principle so dysfunctional, what was needed was a different foundation for natural law, focused on process rather than principle. The imperative for collective action did become a search for neutral social "means" that could accommodate a host of substantive or principled ends, all finding some measure of local–contextual expression within the framework of more universal social conventions.

As the flaw in "justice-as-revelation" became increasingly obvious because of its dependence on a law of dogmatically-revealed principle, which had been localized by the Protestant cooption of former Catholic principles, a change of both equilibria in the coordination game and metaphysics became necessary. This exemplifies Hume's argument for a "true" metaphysics. Specifically, a new understanding of natural law as process-based would now undergird the establishment of an alternative coordination equilibrium for international social order.

Since the not-so-universal Church and its Canon Law had lost control of critical principle, which had, through its Protestant use, become disruptive of intersocietal coordination, the "universal" salience of Papal metaphysics and its definition of natural law was at stake.

> The analytical integration of Canon law, that is, its explicit logical systemization, proceeded from a belief that underlying the multiplicity of legal rules and procedures was a set of basic legal principles, and that it was the task of jurists to identify those principles and to help shape the law so that it would conform to them. The jurists thought in principles.... It was believed, further, that the underlying legal principles had not only a logical aspect, being subject to reason, but also a moral aspect, being subject to conscience. Therefore, not only an analytical or logical systemization was required, which would strive for consistency in the law, but also a moral systemization, which would strive for equity. In addition, the principles underlying the law were believed to have what today would be called a political aspect: they were, on the one hand, the principles already implicit in the law, but they were also on the other hand, a program, a standard by which to judge and correct and, if necessary, to eliminate particular existing laws. They were supposed to be realized in practice.... a political element of reformation, or development, or growth.... The logical, moral, and political aspects of basic legal principles were summarized in the concept of natural law.[60]

With a loss of the prevailing definition of natural law, the metaphysical foundation of Papal rule no longer provided a point of international coordination. As Vitoria argued, to reestablish universality, a new set of presuppositions, divorced from revelation, were needed. What he did not consider was a shift in the dialectic from principle to process, and a consequent redefinition of natural law. Hume's philosophical-policy would recommend an international system independent of God, a "secular" international law that, through a focus on a natural law of process, simultaneously supported majority and minority faiths.[61]

The application of the metaphysics of an international system as suggested by the Humean dialectic between process⇆principle, supports a narrative by which the clash of critical principle in the Reformation causes humanity to seek a process-based, trans-societal coordination equilibrium in order to reestablish intersocietal stability. If we examine the origins of international law from a positivist's perspective, ignoring the fact that positive law has a philosophical or metaphysical dimension, then we have but a binary choice: maintain a dogmatic natural law with no basis in shared principle or reject natural law completely for the consent of states in practice.[62] Hume's philosophical-policy suggests a third alternative.

Hume's True Metaphysics and the Genesis of the International Legal System.

Hume argues for a "true" metaphysics, one rooted in humanity's unconscious need for society and social order. He employs a natural law of social convention, evolving from the behavior instigated by the philosophical presupposition to elevate political *means* over moral *ends* and social *convention* over aetiological-norms and *critical* principles. This innovation of placing the evolution of social relations as the ultimate foundation for the universality and certainty sought in law, allows his argument for justice to attain more flexibility, stability, and utility within the "Post-Reformation" context of value pluralism.

Simultaneously, Hume's philosophical-policy retains a more dynamic metaphysical substructure that allows international law after Westphalia to establish itself as more than a mere set of positive rules. It also becomes a durable system of legal metaphysics where authority and legitimacy are the flexible product of dialectics between philosophy⇆science, normative⇆empirical, and theory⇆practice. In this way, Hume's natural law anticipates not only the historic transition of international law from the Papal Equilibrium to Westphalia, but the dynamic evolution of the international system afterward.

This more dynamic natural law begins as the world shifted toward the value pluralism of the Reformation and the revealed substance of foundational Canon Law was stripped of its certainty. Canon Law and its scholastic underpinnings are no longer a valid basis for international legal order nor for municipal law.[63] In the resulting vacuum, the Protestant cooption of critical principle, outside the established institutional rule structure of a preexisting Catholic order, resulted in a breakdown of the universality and certainty that maintained the existing coordination equilibrium, resulting in the Thirty Years War.

When the established international equilibrium lost its metaphysical imperative, and the human need for society outgrew one set of circumstances and moved toward another, the local and secular municipal subsystems, which had evolved their own social conventions, became more prominent in terms of the search for certainty and stability in human society. During the time of the Papal Equilibrium, these local legal systems benefited from stability created by the universal protection of justice-as-revelation. Consequently, they were the natural alternative when the Papal system collapsed. However, these legal systems were not well developed and also lacked adequate rule universality and certainty.

Municipal and Royal systems were still too few and too weak to establish order at more than a local level; no one or no group was sufficient to create a stable system of intersocietal law that could absorb the "fact" of value/religious pluralism. Because all were operating in a world of ideas where critical principle was elevated over process, and therefore was disruptive of it, people lacked a sense of neutral conventional process as a proper and more universal metaphysics for "natural" law. In the Reformation, moral pluralism was accompanied by metaphysical uncertainty and social disintegration. There was a war of critical principle against itself. In these new circumstances, Royal Law[64] was the only fit substitute for Papal Law.

> When the attack on the Canon law of the church came in the sixteenth century, it was the law of kings and princes that played a leading role against it; manorial law had disappeared almost entirely, feudal law survived chiefly as a residue of the past, and urban and mercantile law had become increasingly subordinate to royal law.[65]

Specifically, the erosion of "justice-as-revelation" had both an external and an internal source. Externally, it was Reformation and war. Internally, the growing human insecurity from the breakdown of the dialectic of Church ideas⇆institutions no longer controlled the conceptualization of those imperatives of reason and individuality with which Catholic social conventions first institutionalized. Hume's philosophical-policy, based on his "true" metaphysics, provides an explanation for the two-tiered international system that arose from the failure of "justice-as-revelation."

Protestantism caused the most serious shift in equilibrium by its attack on the universality and certainty of conventional Papal metaphysics and the particular definition of certainty that it was based upon. In its place, an alternative "positive" law had to be invented that was independent of, and applicable to, the myriad of "divine," "natural," and "human" laws bred by the new era of religious freedom. For the first time, universal Canon Law lost primacy. A new sense of local "civil law" was empowered and legal positivism was born.

> The Lutheran Reformation, and the revolution of the German principalities which embodied it, broke the Roman Catholic dualism of ecclesiastical and secular law by delegalizing the church. Where Lutheranism succeeded, the church came to be conceived as invisible, apolitical, alegal; and the only sovereignty, the only law (in the political sense), was that of the secular kingdom or principality. The Lutheran reformers...were skeptical of man's power to create a human law which would reflect eternal law, and they explicitly denied

> that it was the task of the church to develop human law. This…made possible the emergence of a theory of law—legal positivism…a means and not an end, a device for manifesting the policy of the sovereign and for securing obedience to it.…by freeing law from theological doctrine…the Reformation enabled…a brilliant development…the power of the individual…to create new social relations through the exercise of his will.[66]

With the disappearance of natural law's universal a priori metaphysics, a separation of law and morals was instituted. Critical principle had demonstrated its capacity to disrupt coordination and, because the Church was now removed from politics, the practice or "process" of the positive law became the focus of jurisprudence and legal analysis. When the Church could no longer provide stable cooperation, the agreed point of coordination and its definition of justice was abandoned as it no longer had the allegiance of its constituents, or utility for the persistence of international society. Certainty and social order disappeared with the Protestant Reformation. A vacuum was created into which the local mix of pre-state principalities were drawn.

Universality as a basis for law was the first casualty of these transcendent ideas. Instead of a single source of divine revelation at the core of natural and human law, a new sense of individuality and the uniqueness of each person's relationship to God took on salience. The ability to render one's own interpretation of scripture through the use of one's own "reason," causes the certainty of a universal "justice-as-revelation" to fracture into many voices, institutions, and distinct arguments about the will of God. This chaos created a dependence on one's *local* positive law to provide a more restricted universalism and certainty, marked by the walls of one's principality. Because universality and certainty were no longer supported at the international level by "justice-as-revelation," the idea of the state was born as a result of the fact that local-municipal governance had more experience with both positivism and secular governance.

Through the lens of Hume's definition of natural law, local principalities promoting the *process* of cooperation rather than critical principle, as the end-in-itself, would give their social conventions a flexibility and a value pluralism that provides a backstop of stability when critical principle breaks the system apart. The particular facts of any legal context, in terms of its local ability to produce convention, and therefore order, become the "proper" locus of moral value and the obligation generated by any legal system, not its substantive or principled ends. The promotion of process over principle in the evolution and establishment of any future international system proffers a solution. This consequently requires a new metaphysics of process to provide a more stable foundation for positive practice; this is Hume's "true" metaphysics operationalized in his formulation of natural law.

In addition to the rise of local governance, the positivist imperative can also be understood in a more flexible way from within Hume's philosophical-policy. The loss of international equilibrium found in "justice-as-revelation" engendered a search for certainty and universality in a separation of religion from truth. As we see in Vitoria's work, an effort was underway, in both the sciences and philosophy, to base certainty and universality in practical reason. While the scholastics who employed "analysis…synthesis…and dialectic,"[67] first developed to create Canon Law,[68] could have offered a philosophical method for the analysis and synthesis of secular law, this is not what happened. As Vitoria found, without the uniform revelation that once provided its metaphysics, Scholasticism's definition of natural legal method was either discarded with "justice-as-revelation" or useless without it.

Instead, politics, and law, sought new metaphysical foundations to reestablish some form of universality and certainty and turn a principle-driven Thirty Years War into what would become a process-based Westphalian legal peace. That is, the dysfunctional and violent clash of uncompromising Catholic and Protestant *principle* required that law be shifted to the other pole of its essential dialectic in search of a neutral *process* that could end the violence and maintain a lasting peace. With one universal God and church, theological-monism was obvious. With the replacement of one church with many, this monism was inadequate. However, when philosophy and religion are so historically intertwined, and when philosophy no longer had a solid universal foundation in any single end, philosophy was replaced by a focus on the empirical "science" of positive law and practice that ushered in the era of a positivist dualism or dichotomy for law and morality. Dialectic monism was replaced by the seeds of eristic positivism in the separation of practice from morality, science from metaphysics, law from morals, and philosophy from politics, each as a separate classification of subject matter, or "species" to be studied individually.

This focus on positive practice as the only secure route past a failed system built on justice-as-revelation becomes obvious with the application of Hume's philosophical-policy, which provides an explanation of the origins of contemporary international law. In this context, the Treaties of Westphalia eventually ended the chaos of the Thirty Years War by separating principle from process and accentuating the latter in a focus on the universal sovereignty of states and local religious rights of practice. Each of these ideas supports the other and the latter is guaranteed by the former.[69] With this change of venue, from principle to process, a new international law begins its evolution in the creation and recognition of what comes to be a sovereign system of "civilized" states.[70]

In the same way that the Reformation created a scientific method that claimed "truth" because it was independent of revelation, the original definition of natural law, dependent on religious principle, made the separation of reason and revelation in law and morals, a foregone conclusion afterwards. Scholastic methods notwithstanding, the rise of Protestantism began the process that created our contemporary intellectual world, where science and the humanities take increasingly separate, nondialectic, and nonparallel tracks.

Because "justice-as-revelation" failed, a new definition of practical reason and universality was sought, not in alternative aetiological-norms or nonreligious critical principle, but in the safer and less vulnerable process-based character of a conventional definition of justice. Here, Justice-As-Sovereignty was removed from the disputation of a priori principles and found a secular definition of reason in positive method (e.g., practical observation, experimentation, and induction of established practice from sense experience) resulting in a focus on the effective control of territory. In scientific analysis, the separation of the positive and normative enabled a secular definition of reason as methodical procedure. These circumstances granted it, as an intellectual pursuit, a new and conventionally-based certainty, replacing dependence on disputed substantive principle or "moral laws of nature" with a search for the more tangible "physical laws of nature"[71] as these related to the sociopolitical processes necessary for the existence and behavior of states.

With the demarcation of the physical from the metaphysical, a new foundation also had to be sought for the philosophical component of human thought. But here, the damage caused by the fracturing of theology and the tight historical bonds between the theological, the spiritual, and the philosophical, caused problems that could not be addressed by scientific method alone. As Collingwood argues, philosophical matters are by nature categorical and systematic.[72] Further, within a world of secular positive–normative dualism, there is no longer a categorical set of principles, or a systematic argument, that can be claimed or sought as universal, certain, and true. Without a single source of revelation, and its resultant values, argument becomes opinion, pluralism breeds uncertainty, and truth is reduced to the prejudice and relativity of competing ideologies. Truth and certainty become confined by empirical context and social convention, while substantive moral *principle* becomes subordinate to secular and scientific *process*.[73]

This state of intellectual confusion created an Enlightenment *asymmetry* that Hume's concern for the relationship of science and philosophy transcends. The historical context in which Hume created his philosophical system resulted in a philosophy having explanatory power beyond the ascendancy of any one set of substantive critical principles. With the association of the scientific with the positive and secular, and with a lingering doubt that principle, especially religious principle, could create a stable social order, scholars failed to overcome the asymmetry between the success of scientific method and the separation and seeming stagnation of philosophical method in human studies.

Hume embraces the dialectic of both scientific and philosophical method, making the process of conventional evolution the substance of natural law. With a continued concern for dialectic process and philosophical method, he supplemented the idea of science with a "true" metaphysics that integrates moral and social theory into the context of an already proven descriptive methodology. Hume argued that a philosophy based on a definition of reason backed by revealed principle is too "abstract" and is to be censured for not just being "painful and fatiguing, but as the inevitable source of uncertainty and error," which make it of little use. The problem is that a "considerable part of their metaphysics…[is]…not properly a science."[74]

> but arise either from the fruitless efforts of human vanity, which would penetrate into subjects utterly inaccessible to the understanding, or from the craft of popular superstitions, which, being unable to defend themselves on fair ground, raise these intangling brambles to cover and protect their weakness.[75]

The idea of a principle-based natural law had too many connections to the "vanity" and "superstitions" of a pre-reformation Catholic Church. Hume appears to be concerned that this disreputable metaphysics, although no longer in vogue, was being used by some Enlightenment scholars to kindle an approach to the dialectic reintegration of science and revelation-based (Roman Catholic) metaphysics, which he argues is retrogressive.[76]

Although separated from the demise of "justice-as-revelation" by hundreds of years, Hume worried that "Papist" metaphysics was waiting for a new opportunity to defeat a more practical and secular philosophy, like his, with its focus on deciphering practice and the passions behind human action.[77] "Chaced from the open country, these robbers fly into the forest, and lie in wait to break in upon every unguarded avenue of the mind, and overwhelm it with religious fears and prejudices."[78] The specter of this "enemy" to rational thought, agued Hume, must be replaced with a "true metaphysics."[79] His definition of natural law provides this metaphysics.

Specifically, Hume argued for a new definition of practical reason, an "enlightened-monism," where reason becomes the "slave of the passions."[80] Reason is not eliminated or dichotomized from passion, but, while recognized as a component of human thought, his focus on human passions demotes it to a secondary status in this dialectic: as a slave or dependent of human sympathies and the social conventions that evolve from these passions. Meanwhile, passions, especially those directed to the origin and persistence of human society, create a "natural" foundation for a definition of fundamental law, based on the "fact" of a need for social cooperation, which is also its artificial result.

The advent of human artifice, in turn, creates an overlapping scale of forms that begins with social convention and finds fruition in justice and contract-by-convention. In this way, Hume dialectically reconciles process⇆principle and makes the science of human nature more dynamic and complex. The categorical substance or *principled* end of social cooperation becomes the *process* or means of cooperation. Hume also acknowledges reason and the aetiological-norms behind it, but only as a secondary source of the normative, dependent on social convention. Critical principles are tamed by context; *universality* can be found in local sociability; and *certainty* located in the universal reciprocity and social convention in which that sociability is nested.

The attempt to unite science and metaphysics makes Hume's philosophical-policy unique and its application to, in this case, international law, revealing. Hume refuses, first, to depend on a conscious list of aetiological-norms or critical principles, built on reason, as the absolute presuppositions of his natural law. Second, he refuses to give up the idea that a universal theory of morality cannot be rendered by an empirical or scientific approach to social order. These characteristics make his work exceptional and inherently more complex than modern positivism.

Hume is successful in establishing a dialectic relationship between the components of reformation-dualism. By tying together "scientific *reason*," defined as observation, induction, and experiment (i.e., the process of scientific method), and the *passions* as normative motivation, sentiment, and practice based upon specific metaphysical presuppositions (i.e., the process of philosophical method), one can decipher a moral foundation for social order, at all levels of organization.[81] This moral foundation provides the universality and certainty necessary to law without a dependence upon a priori or critical principles that have proven disruptive to international social order.

Hume frees the "philosophical" from the "theological," while scientifically reintegrating human reason and the passions as integral components in a reconstituted dialectic of social convention.[82] The theoretical and the practical are now components of a single definition of science through a Humean Enlightenment monism that restores the symmetry between practical reason, science, and philosophy. Rather than these dimensions of human social life being dichotomous independent variables, they are interrelated components of a greater social reality.

Hume was not to know that the components of enlightenment-monism have since developed unevenly, and that his work would be used to permanently separate scientific method from any normative or philosophical concerns for humanity, which would be treated dichotomously outside of any dialectic method. An isolated "social science" has since become more readily associated with truth, certainty, and universality, while the scholars of the moral world continue to argue over the relationship between the theological, spiritual, and sociopolitical dimensions of human agency and collective action.

This failure is built on the Enlightenment asymmetry and produces a permanent chasm between the "objectivity" of scientific method, and the corresponding "subjectivity" of philosophical pursuits. A secular priority has been granted to "experience" as a much more reasonable foundation for social as well as scientific analysis. Meanwhile, the moral or philosophical dimensions of social life continue to be segregated and associated with either fragmented theology, fuzzy thinking, subjective preference, or unreflective ideology.

Hume's philosophical-policy takes advantage of the Enlightenment asymmetry and can be said, in retrospect, to alleviate it. Rejecting neither philosophical or scientific method but recognizing that they are not distinct but, rather, interrelated means for providing universality and certainty, Hume attempts a dialectical synthesis with the idea that "[c]ustom, then, is the great guide of human life."[83] Hume's definition of natural law is, therefore, an inimitable response to the theoretical and practical problems he faced within the historical context in which he wrote. Both in his life and in his study of history, he experienced major disruptions to the coordinated social order of humanity and he strove to create a philosophy that more nearly describes how human passions actually achieve cooperative social outcomes.

The SPP of Effectiveness

From this foundation of natural law, our examination of the metaphysical constitution of Justice-As-Sovereignty suggests that its first presupposition is the Systematic Policy Precept of *effectiveness* as a *local rule of recognition*. This SPP arises from the dominance of process, the focus on social convention and its process-norms, and the central role played by the *effectiveness* of such process-norms as they define public utility. Effectiveness also provides the standard of procedural validity for a process-norm, like Justice-As-Sovereignty, which, by its stability, provides for the universality and certainty necessary to Hume's concept of law.

As a *local* rule of recognition this SPP of effectiveness represents the local dimension of Justice-As-Sovereignty and the vital role the stability of local governance plays in the persistence of the greater international system. This dimension of Justice-As-Sovereignty runs parallel to what Krasner calls "domestic sovereignty" or "the formal organization of political authority within the state and the ability of public authorities to exercise effective control within the borders of their own polity."[84]

This conventional, and therefore process-based, idea of law creates an inferior place for critical principle, discouraging it as disruptive to coordination and therefore demoting it to a "secondary" source of moral authority for international law. Hume's unique insight is a multifaceted and interactively engaged definition of natural law in a dialectic between process⇆principle. This approach provides a solution to Vitoria's dilemma. Hume's natural law locates the certainty and universality of law in the effective coordination of the international system itself, rather than in any transcendent principles.

Meanwhile, to argue from the standpoint of a procedural common law of international affairs, effectiveness as coordination depends on the process-norm of Justice-As-Sovereignty to empower the creation of law as those rules of utility in providing for global stability. The consequences that distinguish and demote substantive critical principle elevate that which effectively expresses the human passion for social order. They also make effectiveness the first metaphysical component of Justice-As-Sovereignty and a standard upon which the Humean legal design process will judge good from bad public decision-making and valid from invalid international law. Effectiveness, like all SPPs, is rendered from the process⇆principle dialectic as a relative presupposition of the metaphysics of sovereignty. Its role in defining the source of practical reason in justice-as-utility finds expression in establishing and maintaining coordination at the Westphalian Equilibrium. This, in turn, defines the requirements of certainty and universality for the Westphalian international legal system.

Dialectically, Hume's system is both validated and made obligatory by the ability of process-norms to stabilize social life and give it order, certainty, and universality through the production of social convention and cooperative equilibrium. Hume's definition of natural law creates a new definition of the *concept of law* itself. To this, we now turn.

II. Legal Design Implications for Policy Investigation: Transcending Hart's Concept of Law

Once philosophical method has been utilized to understand a philosophical logic of concepts as a philosophical-policy paradigm, the next step is to apply this paradigm to a legal context, as a logic of policy investigation, in order to see how those particular circumstances turn theory into practice. This transmutation of philosophical paradigms into applied policy and law through the pairing of a logic of concepts with a logic of investigation for legal design results in a comprehensive policy argument about Hume's concept of law.

By deciphering Hume's *concept of law*, a transitional model can be created that will allow us to faithfully render the entailments of Hume's philosophical insights into legal design. As we seek to decipher the metaphysical elements of Justice-As-Sovereignty, our point of departure will be the greater concept of law itself, in which passions, social conventions, and process-norms like sovereignty all operate. By mapping the systematic policy precepts or SPPs, that support the process-norm of Justice-As-Sovereignty for the international legal system, into Hume's more general concept of law, we will place the particular context of international law into a more generic model of law and legal evolution as drawn from Hume's philosophical-policy.

Hume's concept of law is founded on the SPP of *effectiveness*. Metaphysically, effectiveness is a relative presupposition, providing a standard of utility and validity for local universality and certainty. Hume's philosophical-policy creates a connotation of law as valid practice contained within the evolution from coordination, to convention, to justice, and only then to codified rules of law. This makes the origins of the concept of law unique in that its inherent logic places *practice* as a prerequisite to the existence of either informal, or formal, legal *rules*. Practice becomes the most critical component in the Humean description of a generic legal system; it is the basis for the study of legal genesis based on his philosophical paradigm and its concept of law.

David Hume's Concept of Law

The distinctions of Hume's concept of law can be best revealed by comparing and contrasting it with the authoritative concept of law within legal positivism, as conceptualized by H. L. A. Hart.[85] Specifically, the increased complexity and norm-sensitivity of Hume's philosophical-policy must be noted and, then, the greater philosophical space for the practice of international law created by Hume's logic of concepts described.

The essential foundation for Hume's concept of law lies in the evolution of social convention. The formal rules of law do not preexist for Hume, nor are they primarily creatures of critical reason and idea generation. Formal legal rules are rendered by social conventions that have previously evolved through human interaction within society, in reaction to that society's particular circumstances of justice. The strategically neutral process by which alternative coordination equilibria are made attractive, routinized, and turned from unconscious, informal, collective action solutions into conscious rules or laws for human behavior, is anchored by the idea of a social convention and the subsequent practice it produces. This is a prime example of Hume's philosophical-policy reversing the positivist priority between practice and rules.

> Hume denies that a general rule or principle could be established out of nowhere, prior to all practice. Rather, each individual recognizes that it will be beneficial to refrain from taking another's possessions only if others reciprocate this behaviour; given that we all have roughly the same psychology, significant numbers of persons will come to this conclusion separately, and be fairly assured that they are not alone in their understanding; they will begin to make tentative first moves, always checking for reciprocity; the longer this goes on, the more the practice gets established. While this is happening, their conscious awareness of the rule-qua-rule, or convention-qua-convention, becomes stronger. This developing form of life, this practice, has made them capable of explicitly formulating the idea of a convention. The convention emerges out of the practice, and only then can take on a life of its own...actions are only explicitly *guided by a rule* once practice is well established.[86]

Within this process of social evolution, in which a codified legal system is one result, Hume's philosophical-policy and legal design suggests that the formal rules of law that make up a legal system originate in a social setting where individuals attempt to coordinate their behavior and their choices so that order may arise and society persist. As may be recalled from the previous chapter, this unconscious coordination leads to informal rules and sanctions. We see them first in terms of approbation and then in terms of the identification of a process-norm that integrates the idea of justice as an outgrowth of practice and the effort to secure or stabilize that social practice. Only at this point can one proceed from convention to contract-by-convention and the codification of informal rules into formal and dispositive law through governance institutions.

Unlike Hart's concept of law Hume's set of formal legal rules begins with unconscious human interaction that creates the foundation for the eventual formalization or codification of legal practice. Social convention shapes a system of accepted practice through the association of certain choices with the imperative to coordinate in society. It also connects social convention with the idea of a norm of justice, like sovereignty, that forms the central standard of a concept of law, from which the positive law is thereafter created and evaluated.

With a substantial social history of sanctions evolved before the advent of formal legal rules, the concept of valid lawful practice takes on a very important role for Legal Design within Hume's philosophical-policy. Indeed practice, and its progressive sanctions of approbation and justice, stabilizes preceding stages of social order and, in this way, clears the way for law by establishing a template for both the procedure and contextual substance of its codification process.

The idea of governance, let alone government, is not a precondition for the creation of a legal system of rules, as Hobbes argued.[87] For Hume, governance is merely another transitionary stage in the scale of forms that institutionalizes conventional behavior for the continued persistence of society as its complexity grows. The promotion of conventional *practice* over *rules* makes Hume's argument both distinct from and more normatively complex than Hart's argument, which originates with legal rules.

Hume's philosophical-policy transcends Hart's dependence on a non-dialectical system of primarily substantive law based on primitive custom. Hume also adds complexity by acknowledging the connection between morality and law, as well as obligation and validity. Additionally, Hume creates a pre-law "sense of justice"[88] that acts to give his argument more persistent and universal application.

Building formal law on a foundation of social convention, Hume accounts for the inherently dialectic character of law and integrates the empirical with the normative, justice with order, and moral obligation with the primacy of procedural over substantive law. This gives Hume's concept of law a unique character reflected in experience and an inherent normativity from within the validity of the coordination process. Here, also, Hume has something in common with Hart, but with a twist.

A Humean definition of justice focuses on the process-law that Hart denotes as secondary rules of *recognition*, *adjudication*, and *change*. Hume discounts the primacy and particulars of specific commands or principles and fealty to them, which Hart defines as chronologically prior and "primary" in his concept of law. The twist is that Hart's "secondary" rules are Hume's primary, while Hart's "primary" rules are Hume's secondary in the creation and refinement of a concept of law. This is not the only difference.

Hart's argument in the *Concept of Law* begins with the distinction between habit or custom, and law. Specifically, his approach to the evolution of law is that "convergent habitual behaviour"[89] is only the first step in a process that eventually arrives at a system of rules that are, in contrast to habit or custom alone, "effective, normative, and create a sense of justice among a population."[90] Hart, like Hume, acknowledges that the first regulation of human interaction is through the process by which habits are formed and then expanded to a social level of operation. However, Hart, unlike Hume, does not see this stage of evolution as a legal one. Hart argues that there is no "internal"[91] aspect to this behavior, an attribute which is necessary from within Hart's logic for anything to have the character of law.

> the *internal aspects* of rules....When a habit is general in a social group, this generality is merely a fact about the observable behaviour of most of the group. In order that there should be such a habit no members of the group need in any way think of the general behaviour, or even know that the behaviour in question is general; still less need they strive to teach or intend to maintain it. It is enough that each for his part behaves in the way that others also in fact do. By contrast, if a social rule is to exist some at least must look upon the behaviour in question as a general standard to be followed by the group as a whole. A social rule has an "internal" aspect, in addition to the external aspect which it shares with a social habit and which consists in the regular uniform behaviour which an observer could record.[92]

Hart argues that custom, unlike the law it is built upon, does not impose duty, nor is it necessarily effective in any way for the social cohesion or progress of the society. Custom is merely convenient and the manner in which people work out their collective action problems. These informal customary guidelines are therefore nonnormative.

Hart's informal patterns of behavior are capable of producing law, but only of a type that utilizes command to invoke obedience or impose duty. A customary system of rules breeds what Hart calls substantive or "primary rules."[93] Habits turn into orders to maintain established patterns of behavior and these, in turn, invoke obedience through command. Hart sorts international law into this preprocedural state of affairs.

> though it is consistent with the usage of the last 150 years to use the expression "law" here, the absence of an international legislature, courts with compulsory jurisdiction, and centrally organized sanctions have inspired misgivings,...The absence of these institutions means that the rules for states resemble that simple form of social structure, consisting only of primary rules of obligation, which, when we find it among societies of individuals, we are accustomed to contrast with a developed legal system.[94]

His classification of international law as a "simple form of social structure" is the basis on which Hart then proceeds to create a full model of what he considers a "developed legal system."

The key to a fully developed concept of law, for Hart, is the presence of *rules* rather than mere *practice*. Hart's logic makes practice a nonlegal arena where the system of primary rules alone is incapable of adequately defining "the *content* of laws...their *mode of origin*...or their *range of application*,"[95] all of which are necessary for a fully developed legal system to emerge. Hart argues that with a base in custom (as he defines it), substantive or primary rules evolve to create the appearance of a legal system, but, since there are no specific legal rules that establish the general validity of these practices, this breeds uncertainty.[96] Customary practice also offers no way to overcome what Hart calls the "static quality"[97] of primary rules of command and obedience. Lastly, he argues that a system of customary primary rules is inefficient[98] for the settlement of conflict and the dissolution of disputes.

To solve these shortcomings, Hart suggests that uncertainty requires a "rule of recognition,"[99] that the static quality of primary rules needs a "rule of change,"[100] and that the inefficiency of an undeveloped legal system is reversed by a "rule of adjudication."[101] All three of these rules are contained within a single class of what Hart calls "secondary rules."

> Under rules of one type, which may well be considered the basic or primary type, human beings are required to do or abstain from certain actions, whether they wish to or not. Rules of the other type are in a sense parasitic upon or secondary to the first; for they provide that human beings may by doing or saying certain things introduce new rules of the primary type, extinguish or modify old ones, or in various ways determine their incidence or control their operation. Rules of the first type impose duties; rules of the second type confer powers, public or private. Rules of the first type concern actions involving physical movement or changes; rules of the second type provide for operations which lead not merely to physical movement or change, but to the creation or variation of duties or obligations.[102]

Paraphrasing Austin,[103] Hart claims that "in the combination of these two types of rules there lies...'the key to the science of jurisprudence.'"[104] Only with the addition of these secondary rules, according to Hart, will international law take that "step from the pre-legal into the legal world."[105]

> It is indeed arguable, as we shall show, that international law not only lacks the secondary rules of change and adjudication...but also a unifying rule of recognition specifying "sources" of law and providing general criteria for the identification of its rules.[106]

From the standpoint of Hart's concept of law, international law is an undeveloped system of customary behavior and primary rules that has evolved from habit without a connection to that sense of obligation necessary to all legal systems.

> The most prominent feature of law at all times and places is that its existence means that certain kinds of human conduct are no longer optional, but in *some* sense obligatory.[107]

Hart's concept of law finds its distinction in the introduction of secondary rules. Law does not originate in custom because of the lack of a normative or "internal" character in the latter, its failure to invoke obligation, or create universality and certainty. However, with the creation of a class of procedural rules that speak to the validity and legitimacy of those rules, law is born. Hart's logic distinguishes law and morals so that the judgment of a valid law is distinct from an evaluation of its normative weight or status. He also separates law and justice so that "[j]ustice constitutes one segment of morality primarily concerned not with individual conduct but with the ways in which *classes* of individuals are treated."[108] Overall, while the "internal" aspects of the rules of law are important, and obligation to the law is one of its "prominent" features, the division in application of the concept of law between primary and secondary rules allows Hart to promote the latter over the former and value law primarily in terms of its positive validity.

The conclusion of his argument is that the internal, moral aspect of legal rules becomes an external, critical point of reference that allows valid law to exist independently of any normative entanglements. Hart describes this as an advantageous situation.

> What surely is most needed in order to make men clear sighted in confronting the official abuse of power, is that they should preserve the sense that the certification of something as legally valid is not conclusive of the question of obedience, and that, however great the aura of majesty or authority which the official system may have, its demands must in the end be submitted to a moral scrutiny. This sense, that there is something outside the official system, by reference to which in the last resort the individual must solve his problems of obedience, is surely more likely to be kept alive among those who are accustomed to think that rules of law may be iniquitous, than among those who think that nothing iniquitous can anywhere have the status of law.[109]

Overall, Hart separates law and morals, diminishes international law as a legal system, oversimplifies an understanding of custom, and promotes rules over practice. The reason for these failures is that Hart's concept of law is created within a positivist ethos and suffers from a lack of dialectic, a failure to understand scale of form, and an idea of custom that lacks the complexity of Hume's definition of social convention.

Hart's definition of custom depends on establishing a dichotomy between practice and rule where the former has no necessary legal or moral effectiveness in terms of human society, while the latter requires it. His definition of "primary rules" also depends on a dichotomy between the external observation of behavior and its "internal aspect" that grants rules legal status. Here, a primary rule is only possible when the internal or normative aspect of the "law" is added to an observed pattern of practice. However, the normative and observationally positive aspects of an act are not inherently related by Hart. Finally, Hart's definition of a secondary rule depends on a dichotomy between positive validity and normative obligation. Here, the morally neutral rules of recognition, adjudication, and change make practice *legal* through the valid acceptance of the secondary rules involved. This validity is then, and only then, as law, ready to be tested against the moral and obligatory requirements of primary rules with their post-customary "internal aspect." For all secondary rules, the separate aspect of moral obedience remains external and distinct form the rule's validity. Legal status is bestowed by the rule's distinctive but nonnormative validity.

Overall, the difficulties of Hart's argument can be traced to his promotion of *rule* over *practice* and his focus on the attribute of validity for his specific types of rules, rather than on the pattern of practice that predates them. Hart devalues the role and normative complexity of prelegal custom and, most important for our purposes, he presents a philosophical logic that prevents international law from being more than a "primitive" concept of law.

In contrast, Hume's philosophical-policy, avoids these difficulties and allows international legal practice full status as law. For Hume, formal law is a product of informal legal-conventional development where both are stages in a scale of forms for his concept of law. This makes a place for international law within the multiple levels of evolving human organization on the scale of forms that is social convention. Here, Hume's philosophical-policy suggests a more complex international legal system that heeds the requirements of its particular circumstances, on a distinct yet dialectically connected tier of social organization, and with a sense of governance distinct from most municipal systems of law.

First and foremost, Hume's philosophical-policy promotes *practice* over *rule* in his description of a concept of law. Within Hume's logic, practice not only predates the existence of rules, but creates the legal content of rules through the evolution and codification of *social convention*. Within Hume's philosophical-policy and legal design, social convention is a more complex idea than custom because it replaces the series of dichotomies relied upon by Hart with dialectics that engage the normative and positive, the external and internal aspects of practice, and the interaction of practice and rules to provide a more persuasive argument for the generic evolution of the international rule of law. The evolution is determined by the metaphysical balance of dialectics within Justice-As-Sovereignty.

Specifically, social convention has three critical distinctions from the standard positivist assumptions about custom adopted by Hart. First, Humean social convention, unlike Hart's definition of custom, is built on an innate dialectic between practice and the generation of rules that makes social convention inherently *efficacious* in that it exists specifically to solve a collective action problem and is motivated by the passion for society and social order, upon which its public utility depends.

By engaging the tension between practice, and the need for certainty and universality in expectations that are provided by law, and by promoting practice over the rules of law, Hume transcends the mere social habits of individuals by infusing human interaction with an *internal* foundation in our passion and sympathy for the creation and persistence of society.

This passion is the root motivation of the search for stability[110] and creates the need for legal rules of behavior as well as the normative obligation to heed these rules that regulate and counteract the existing circumstances of justice.

Hume's philosophical-policy elevates mere habit to a prelegal practice rendered from one's natural propensity to create artificial rules reflective of specific focused motivation, even in terms of the unconscious choices and actions of persons. Within Hume's logic of concepts, the evolution of social convention is the creation of *effective* conventional practice regulated, internationally, by Justice-As-Sovereignty. This rise of convention may originally be unconscious, but is never mindless; nor is it ever without legal purpose. The human passions generally, and the passion for society in particular, create practice that is a synthesis between habitual behavior and those informal rules necessary for social cohesion and order. This makes convention, as social practice, of inherent utility to human society, both immediately in an informal sense, and eventually, in a formal sense as codified rules are created from preexisting practice with the advent of political society.

Second, conventional practice, within Hume's philosophical-policy, endows all informal and formal legal rules with a dialectic between external patterns of human behavior and the "internal" moral aspects of those rules. These external and internal aspects of Hume's concept of law, form a dialectic that acknowledges the integration of the normative character of a convention with specific empirical behavior generating, first, rules of procedural validity (what Hart called secondary rules) and, second, rules of substantive obligation (what Hart called primary rules).

Since social convention is the result of human interaction, normative obligation to it is produced by those effective actions that create and protect society and, therefore, the absolute presupposition of social stability. Transcending the positivist dichotomy between normative and positive, Hume's inherent dialectic is simultaneously *normative* because it is connected to a specific definition of *justice*, and both the result of, and motivation for, specifically sanctioned *empirical* behavior. The *observable* and the *motivational*, or the external and the internal aspects of social convention, and the resulting legal rules, are simultaneously present in this dialectic. Their synthesis is made evident, for international law, in the metaphysical components and evolution of the process-norm of Justice-As-Sovereignty.

Unlike Hart's concept of law, which assumes custom has no inherent sense of justice or morality, Hume argues that social convention, even in its prelegal stage, evolves the sanctions of justice before the advent of political society or codified law. The process-norm of sovereignty has status because of its public utility to a stable international society, and because, as Hume states, justice is "impossible without antecedent morality" that provides the content of Justice-As-Sovereignty.[111] This makes utility and justice dialectic prerequisites, and integral components, of both substantive and procedural rules of law.

A third difference between Hart and Hume is that Hume's philosophical-policy identifies a core dialectic of process⇆principle that is generic to the concept of law and foundational to all rules generated by practice. By synthesizing the validity of the law and its moral authority from a dialectic between, respectively, procedural and substantive rules, Hume's philosophical-policy avoids the problematic dichotomy between valid law and moral law, as law is simultaneously both (at least in terms of providing for social coordination). In effect, the relationship between Hart's primary and secondary rules is a creature of Hume's essential dialectic between process⇆principle; rule validity is inherently part of this moral geography.

Within this essential dialectic, each rule has a role in deciphering a system of conventional practice that contains both passion and reason, process and principle, but in synthesis snapshots that grant the dominant role to the former of both pairs. This results in a concept of law where the dominance of process is fundamental and a system of procedural/process rules are primary. What Hart calls rules of recognition are, for Hume, the first and primary product of prelegal practice and social convention. Hume's concept of law then makes substantive rules secondary, both in chronology and importance.

Hume's philosophical-policy grants validity an inherent normative character connected to the stability of social convention, as his argument maintains that the procedural rules of social convention create the proper definition of natural law, or those inherent and *universal* assumptions about humanity and its social conditions that make the law necessary. Meanwhile, the rules that create substantive moral duty are *local* and address the particular circumstances of justice faced by each evolving legal system. These substantive rules yield to process-based convention and the specific normative sense of justice that is made manifest in the particular process-norm that stabilizes property. This also defines Hume's idea of justice, which in turn is the basis for governance institutions.

Hume's philosophical-policy seeks universality in procedural *process*-norms, like sovereignty or rules of validity, that invoke obligation to the coordination equilibrium that it protects. Rather than a dependence on substantively moral or principled duties, that are the primary source of morality for Hart, Hume's philosophical-policy makes such substantive ends secondary and dependent on the prior evolution of a procedural, legal system.[112] Process-norms create cooperation and maintain it over time as society becomes more complex, without the involvement of any specific universal substantive normative end, except that of validity itself.[113]

Hume's moral dialectic is not about substantive duty, but the duty or obligation one has to the maintenance of the cooperative system of norms and rules. The normative point of departure for Hume's philosophical logic are the procedural rules that make convention valid by stabilizing the allocation of property, and therefore, society, which is its absolute presupposition. By facilitating the persistence of society and the passions behind it, the dialectic of procedural⇆substantive rules makes the former universal, while it bends the substance of the law to the local requirements and specific contexts of the circumstances of justice.

From the standpoint of Hume's philosophical-policy, Hart's model does not adequately emphasize the interactive and dynamic role of norms as the progenitors of legal rules. For Hume, two sources of normative value overlap two layers of evolving law. First, he identifies social convention as related to universally valid process. Second, principle is related to local substantive rules of behavior. Both have a normative character with different content and level of application, where the latter is "slave" to the former.

Hume's philosophical-policy defines the international legal system as a fundamentally justice-based system with a process-norm of sovereignty making Hart's "primary" rules "secondary," in that they lack core status within the Humean model. In this way, Hume's concept of law creates a richer, multitiered philosophical space with evolving institutional governance structures at both local and universal levels that can apply sanctions through contract-by-convention to integrate policy argument and legal design as these effectively support the end of the cooperative process itself.

Hume's comprehensive policy argument, or his concept of law, directs us to focus on the process-rules of recognition, adjudication, and change (that are here defined as SPPs), as the metaphysical underpinning for the source of Justice-As-Sovereignty in practical reason.

Two Definitions of Principle

Within Hume's concept of law, the process-rules or SPPs denote what Hart called a secondary system of rules, but how about Hart's primary or substantive rules? How does Hume's concept of law handle them?

Before the advent of contract-by-convention and the political society it ushers in, the evolution of social convention illustrates an effort to produce that pattern of practice based upon Justice-As-Sovereignty that assures social coordination and the persistence of society. In Hume's concept of law substantive rules and their deontic ends are not the focus of the social system. What is paramount are those procedural practices that establish and maintain cooperation through convention and assign valid roles to those who decide the ends of the society and the application of social convention to public affairs. Within the logic of Hume's philosophical-policy and legal design, process precedes substantive rules within all evolving legal systems, as substantive duty-imposing rules are created for their support of procedural social convention.

For example, applying Hume's philosophical-policy, one would expect that before identifying a specific or codified definition of murder and generating universal rules about this "crime," a society must establish processes that validate practice as law, and procedurally determine who is allowed to decide life or death issues, how, and under what circumstances they can act. This is Hume's primary rule. It is not substantive like Hart's, but a procedural practice speaking to the circumstances in which recognition, adjudication, and change determine the validity of a society's expectations and behavior.

Historically, one can see that process is a prerequisite to substantive law. If one becomes King under established procedural conventions (e.g., divine right, family, strength, trial by combat), one can kill a subject within valid practice. Meanwhile, for a peasant to do the same thing, even to one of his own class, is procedurally invalid and brings punishment.

The Humean argument posits that process and rules of normative validity are the first, conventional elements bestowing certainty and universality on any informal substantive rules of behavior. The King has the a priori benefit of expectations, based on practices of recognition, adjudication, and change. These validate substantive contextual principles of behavior before any specific legal rules of criminality emerge, that, for example, might define murder independent of context.

The conventional pattern of practice, which is first sanctioned by approbation and justice and then by the advent of political society and contract-by-convention, establishes a pattern of effective behavior coalescing on a point of equilibrium necessary for the stability of the society. These existing prelegal practices are therefore the prime candidates for codification as legal rules with the advent of design institutions and the creation of positive law. With the establishment of governance institutions within Hume's logic of concepts, the primary focus is on the elevation of procedural rules from practice to codified law.

> When men have once perceiv'd the necessity of government to maintain peace, and execute justice, they wou'd naturally assemble together, wou'd chuse magistrates, determine their power, and promise them obedience.[114]

In his methodical separation of law and morals, Hart fails to integrate this dynamic tension between practice⇆rules. He also fails to recognize the simultaneous presence, in the generation of the latter from the former, of the dialectics of both the normative⇆positive and external⇆internal aspects that Hume's concept of law proffers. Hart, unlike Hume, does not distinguish the prerequisite dialectic between *process-norms* that create "secondary" rules of recognition, adjudication, and change, and *aetiological-norms* that are the source of the reasons and prior ends that inform the commands of "primary" duty-imposing rules.

This discrepancy makes another more evident. Hart assumes only one type of primary or substantive rules within a legal system. But Hume's approach to the concept of law demonstrates that this is a more complex question than Hart allows. With two normative routes to the law, one through process and the other through critical principle, and with the former initially dominating the latter but then allowing for a richer sense of critical substance with the advent of contract-by-convention, Hume's philosophical-policy exposes the need for two distinct definitions of a substantive rule for international law.

The inherent complexity of Hume's concept of law offers a more expansive normative foundation for policy argument and international legal design. Within Hume's philosophical-policy, the priority of social convention and its process-norm of Justice-As-Sovereignty create the background conditions necessary to the effective stability and order of international society. Only through contract-by-convention and its process-based normative foundation does the possibility of law become real. The universality and certainty provided by social convention then allow for the full inclusion of critical, substantive, and procedural norms and rules in policy and legal design.

For Hume's idea of legal design, the evolution of law is initially a conventional process that creates governance structures through contract-by-convention. With the advent of contract-by-convention, policy argument has a full set of political-legal institutions. The fundamental dialectic of the law, that between process⇆principle, is thus enabled to fully engage its components as the institutions of the political society that come from social convention have the capacity to process both procedural and substantive norms⇆rules for law-in-society. The core dialectic can now be more completely utilized by legal design, with both passion and reason fully interacting with one another as a basis for argument and institutional codification. Passion-based *process* and reason-based *critical principle* can now both seek validity or codification as dispositive law.

However, before the advent of contract-by-convention, there is still a need for informal prelegal rules on substantive issues. Under these conditions, the substantive as well as the procedural rules are determined by the context of social convention; that is, by the process-norm of Justice-As-Sovereignty as the groundwork of the international legal system. While this is to be expected for procedural rules, as they are inherently means-based like social convention itself, it is unusual for substantive rules, given the basic understanding of the idea of principle as critical of convention and related to *ends* not *means*. Here, the word "principle" must be bifurcated by policy argument into the two functional definitions required by Hume's concept of law: *contextual* and *critical*.

Normally, we think of a "principle" as a precept focused on a substantive end rather than any particular means, and as having a critical or a priori source that is inherent within the principle itself and backed by human practical reason.[115] Given this definition of principle, Hume contrasts reason and the passions, and his philosophical-policy renders the distinction between *process-norms* and *aetiological-norms*, the latter containing a self-referential core with an inherent "reason" or "cause." This definition of critical principle, as a slave of passion and process, has no significant status before the advent of contract-by-convention, because there has been no opportunity for critical principle to formally influence social convention on equal terms in the codification of legal rules. However, any system of social convention has "principles," which are necessary to what Hart calls "primary" rules.

Before critical principle arose from *aetiological-norms*, the principles that existed within Hume's concept of law were established standards without independent content. They were determined by the requirements of Justice-As-Sovereignty and exist to maintain the cooperative process that social convention supports. Substantive rules at this stage of evolution find their meaning in the specific moral duties necessary to the persistence of social convention. Therefore, the functional definition of "principle" is not critical but *contextual*; that is, not focused on an independent substantive end but, dependent on a circumstantial end necessary to the persistence of social convention and the cooperative process established by Justice-As-Sovereignty.

Consequently, for international law, both procedural and substantive rules are initially derived from Justice-As-Sovereignty. For example, when self-defense is interpreted by the United Nations (UN) as a valid reaction only for states, it is contextual to the "principle" of Justice-As-Sovereignty. If self-defense were considered a critical principle it would make it dependent on a foundation in human reason, and the rights of the individual to defend themselves. Only with the rise of critical principle, enabled by institutionalization under contract-by-convention, do aetiological-norms and their rules take on an internal *cause* and become independent of the conventional system of process and obligation that has been created solely to protect stable coordination.

With government, substantive ends can have a critical or independent status within institutions that they do not have in a society dominated by social convention. But when substantive ends are no longer exclusively based on the context of social convention or the process of cooperation as an end-in-itself, their aetiological manifestations, and the rules they prescribe, can act as critical standards on which to judge the legal status of the preexisting conventional norms and rules (both procedural and substantive). For example, were the substantial ends of international jurisdiction no longer predominantly contained within the context of state sovereignty, the fuller operationalization of universal jurisdiction, as the aetiological manifestation of the universal responsibility to enforce international law, could act as the critical standard for the judgment of jurisdictional claims.

This creates a more balanced dialectic between substantive and procedural rules where their dialectic is more complete and fully engaged. With aetiological or critical rules generating legal obligation, the scale of forms for the process⇆principle dialectic becomes much more complex and more fully operationalized. It is now possible to critically judge those conventions that truly support the substantive, principled ends of social or individual value, as opposed to those that do not. With critical principle as a full participant in the application of practical reason, a legal system produces rules (both procedural and substantive) that both reinforce and challenge social convention. Legal practice can now accommodate both the process rules of recognition, adjudication, and change, as well as preexisting contextual principles. Critical principle can then assess both as to their proper role in the positive law.

Within Hume's model of the concept of law, international legal practice is not, as Hart argues, a system of primary rules without secondary rules, but a system of stable procedural or secondary rules, like Justice-As-Sovereignty, that produces contextual principles to stabilize the international system. All rules arise from social convention, which also determines that set of contextual substantive principles necessary to the persistence of international society, even before the full interaction of process⇆principle creates a completely fleshed-out international legal system.

This important switch in pride-of-place, making procedural rules from social convention "primary," changes our conception of international law to include multiple paths of dispute resolution and complex governance structures. Its institutions and sources of law may be distinct from those usually seen in municipal systems, but they contain both procedural rules and substantive/contextual principles that make international law a legal system in its own right. Treating international law as a system of social convention that is formalized into codified law takes note of both the foundations of law in sovereignty and the Westphalian Equilibrium. In addition the relevance of critical human rights and environmental principles will become more prominent as the scale of forms that defines the international concept of law evolves.

International law is, therefore, not simply a moral system, but a fully intact and evolving legal system just at the point where contract-by-convention, and its resultant governance structures, are becoming stronger and more three-dimensional. International law is a system of conventional procedural rules (e.g., *in dubio mitius*) and contextual substantive rules (e.g., *pacta sunt servanda*), recently faced with challenges from critical aetiological-norms (e.g., *jus cogens* principles and *erga omnes* obligations). The use of Hume's philosophical-policy in legal design offers the potential for a new perspective on sovereignty in international law that has profound implications for how we understand the global evolution of practice and the rule of law given the future path of its inherent dialectics.

For example, Hume's approach allows us to explain the legal status of "general principles of law recognized by civilized nations" as a source of international law.[116] These principles are not a priori critical principles based on practical reason, like human dignity or environmental integrity, but have their foundation in the informal evolution of social convention, and are contextual to "civilized" social rules supporting the process-norm of Justice-As-Sovereignty and the international society so rendered. The human need for these principles to substantively support the procedural rules of the status quo in the form of Justice-As-Sovereignty gives these contextual principles their utility and their status as a definition of justice and a source of law.

As contract-by-convention on the international level provides increasingly complex governance (i.e., sanctioning) structures, through which a more balanced idea of practical reason can find expression in the legal design process, concern for universal human rights or universal jurisdiction as critical substantive ends should play a larger role in the international rule of law. Current dilemmas, such as the full legalization of universal jurisdiction or finding legal justification for humanitarian intervention, may demonstrate that this administrative or political institutionalization is underway. Within Hume's concept of law, these dilemmas are created by the rise of critical, aetiological, or universal principle, escalating the dialectic between process⇆principle and challenging the dominant status of conventional practice and Justice-As-Sovereignty.

In a fuller engagement of process⇆principle, critical principles should be expected to remain secondary to passion-induced process-norms because a considerable amount of time and persuasive argument will be necessary to erode the power of established social conventions and their contextual principles. This is because, within Hume's philosophical-policy, critical principles based on inherent ends are independent of process, so their ends are assumed to challenge the status of the core process-norm of Justice-As-Sovereignty. As a result, critical principles will be unconsciously assumed to be disruptive to the established coordination equilibrium. Thus they are devalued within the international governance system to the advantage of conventional process-norms like Justice-As-Sovereignty.[117]

Explicitly, Hume's natural law of "process" combines the normative with the empirical as two ever-present halves of the same social reality. Even though Hume's synthesis solutions ultimately may fall on the empirical side of the current (and artificial) divide between positive and normative, his philosophy is a combination of the two. Applying Humean philosophical-policy suggests how the current study of the international system might be normatively reconsidered and redefined within his legal design process.

One result of applying Hume's logic of concepts to the normative geography of international legal design is that we can make distinctions, not fully articulated within contemporary international law, between three types of "norms," all of which are present in the international legal system. It is possible to distinguish a reasoned principle (*a priori end*) from a passion-based process-norm (*justice*) or a legally-valid rule (*positive law*). Each appears as a distinct component of the Humean concept of law. Each type of norm plays a distinct role as international society becomes more complex and convention becomes more ingrained in the legal system, first by approbation, then by justice, and finally by governance institutions under contract-by-convention. In making these normative distinctions, however, Hume's philosophical-policy also creates a hierarchy or scale of forms through which law is codified.

The importance of an a priori principle, which is the traditional starting point of a natural law argument, is made posterior and secondary to the prior evolution of convention from human social interaction. Passion is deemed more fundamental than reason and is much more critical to establishing a stable society. Our "passion" for society is the "natural" driving force for the metaphysics of Hume's philosophical-policy; the rendering of Justice-As-Sovereignty as a manifestation of the passion for society is the basis for contract-by-convention, governance institutions, legal design, and the codified rules of the international positive law.

Anticipating Kelsen[118] and Hart, Hume makes his concept of law simultaneously empirical, sociological, and constructivist in nature. But unlike either Kelsen or Hart, Hume's philosophical-policy maintains the interdependence of normative and positive as dialectic elements of the evolution of law. Hume's definition of justice is a perfect fit for Collingwood's first moment in the scale of forms for practical reason: utility. Hume's concept of justice is based on social convention created to give order and stability to society to provide for the public utility.

Hume's philosophical-policy defines justice as order. Sovereignty insures a stable synthesis equilibrium for the international coordination game. As humans seek order at the international level, Justice-As-Sovereignty is adopted as the core standard or process-norm to gauge the utility of positive rules as they support or disrupt collective action within the developing legal system. Hume's conceptual logic creates a more universal level of social order in which the normative metaphysics of Justice-As-Sovereignty is *integrated* into positive practice creating stability for international property. Order becomes the natural means of justice—a means that is at the same time an inherent end-in-itself for Hume's concept of law. Henry Sidgwick described Hume's definition of justice in this way.

> What Hume (e.g.) means by Justice is rather what I should call Order, understood in its widest sense: the observance of the actual system of rules, whether strictly legal or customary, which bind together the different members of any society into an organic whole, checking malevolent or otherwise injurious impulses, distributing the different objects of men's clashing desires, and exacting such positive services, customary or contractual, as are commonly recognized as matters of debt.[119]

For this reason, Hume's idea of "sovereignty" does not have the status of a reasoned a priori principle. Rather it is a process-norm that protects social cooperation. If legal sovereignty is but the product of a process that creates social convention, then it has no a priori or necessary moral status within international law as a critical or contextual principle focused on a specific end (producible or nonproducible).

Rather, the SPP of *effectiveness* is a rule of recognition by which sovereignty is created and through which its validity persists. Being an effective process-norm grants sovereignty its status as a core element in the recognition of statehood. Recognition carries both an empirical and normative status within Hume's philosophical-policy. The process-norm is not a critical principle with an essential end without which its character as a normative precept fails. The moral value or validity of a process-norm is in its capacity to maintain the cooperative process. And while it arises before government and contract-by-convention exists, a process-norm eventually, with the size and complexity of the society it orders, faces more complex challenges and responds to them through law.

For example, Justice-As-Sovereignty is necessary to international social convention, at least at its origin, but can be overtaken if and when it no longer is *effective* in maintaining coordination. Especially after the advent of contract-by-convention, other process-norms may contest its status, as can a priori regulative or critical principles that originate within legal and policy design institutions. Both of these possibilities challenge the order and stability of the Westphalian Equilibrium, but to different degrees.

In the same way that the dialectic between justice⇆utility synthesizes into a definition of justice as sovereign order, Hume's sense of natural law integrates the idea of core moral precepts and their universal application with the idea of positive convention, observable behavior, and the coordination of elective agency. Although Hume's natural law describes the primacy of the passions, application of his natural law establishes the process-norm of Justice-As-Sovereignty as both the "is" and "ought" of social coordination and international law. Overall, Hume's philosophical-policy acknowledges both normative argument and positive methodology. Applying Hume's philosophical-policy to legal design, his concept of law has four basic characteristics:

1. The human need for society is the absolute metaphysical presupposition of the argument for sovereignty;
2. process-norms are made distinct from critical principle and have validity in terms of their effectiveness and utility;
3. process as social convention is made distinct and a prerequisite to contract in policy and law; and
4. convention and its contextual principles form the primary moral foundation for universality and certainty within Hume's concept of law while critical principle is reduced to secondary moral status in creating codified law.

This produces a process-model of Hume's concept of law (see Figure 2.1) that has two sources supporting the synthesis of social convention, contextual, and critical principles, as these express practical reason in international law.

The focus of legal discourse for Hume's philosophical-policy is not the particular rule or set of rules, nor the legal principle from which they may have arisen, but, rather, the system of practice in which property stabilization through coordination is embedded. The effectiveness with which the process-norm of Justice-As-Sovereignty provides for this universality, certainty, and consequent stability of international society grants it validity within the system. The process-norm must provide that stability which is necessary to the persistence of an ordered international system at equilibrium. This role also grants Justice-As-Sovereignty its moral authority. The SPP of *effectiveness* becomes a relative presupposition in the metaphysical structure of sovereignty within Hume's concept of law. It also plays the role of a local rule of recognition for the transformation of philosophy into municipal public policy and then into international law through design.[120]

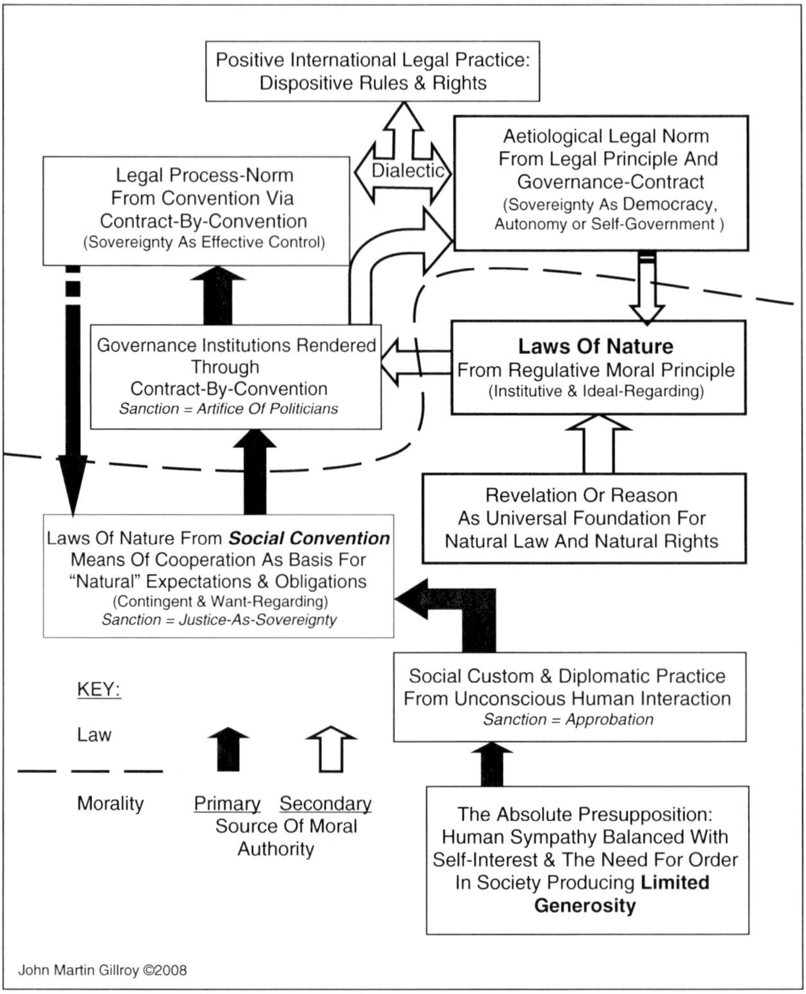

Figure 2.1 Hume's concept of law.

Overall, Hume's philosophical-policy inhibits any source of international law within the legal design process to the degree that it does not effectively represent the system's coordination conventions and their persistence. Critical principle is inherently disruptive to process and so we might expect that principle, as a recognized source of international positive law and practice, is primarily *contextual* rather than *critical*. Any presence of critical principle in contemporary international law will likely be considered inherently destabilizing and a threat to order that should be distrusted and "[c]hased from the open country" by social convention and its local rule of recognition, the SPP of effectiveness. Here, reason and its critical products remain the "slave of the passions."

III. Evidence in Legal Practice

Within a Humean logic of concepts, the genesis of sovereignty as an expression of legal practice lies in its metaphysics as social convention. In the following chapters that flesh out sovereignty as a metaphysical concept, evidence for the philosophical insight examined will be sought within the jurisprudence of international dispute settlement. Using Hume's philosophical-policy and legal design, international case law can be read as a chain of decisions based on a common view of the world created by the evolution of social convention, its process-norm of sovereignty, and its inherent dialectic of process⇆principle. Legal practice should reasonably map onto Hume's concept of law with its focus on Justice-As-Sovereignty.

Hume's worldview assumes that social conventions first create and then stabilize the sovereign state as an institutional manifestation of municipal-level society. Justice-As-Sovereignty, in its role as a process-norm, then simultaneously assures international stability and local validity as it protects and empowers each nation in its relationships with other sovereign states. Overall, Justice-As-Sovereignty creates a stable international society through its facilitation of the Westphalian Equilibrium.

As social convention, rather than mere custom, Justice-As-Sovereignty is endowed with two specific characteristics. First, social convention implies "effectiveness." To evolve over its scale of forms, the process-norm for a system of social convention must be an effective means to achieve stable social coordination. Second, sovereignty as social convention focuses, primarily, on procedural means to establish an effective point of coordination or equilibrium. Although social convention may require certain substantive rules to provide for the ends of coordination, these instrumental principles will never be independent moral standards but context-driven principles, dependent upon the procedural nature of convention for their character. The SPP of *effectiveness* is, metaphysically, both the standard of validity and the source of moral obligation for Justice-As-Sovereignty.

Therefore, a full metaphysical understanding of Justice-As-Sovereignty requires the identification of two interrelated levels of *rules of recognition*: one *local* and dealing with the "effectiveness" of the sovereign state from its internal social perspective; and the other *universal*, and dealing with the external affects of sovereignty in the establishment of legitimate reciprocal cooperation and the security of international society. This additional "universal" rule of recognition will produce a separate SPP as a dialectic partner for effectiveness to recognize the validity of international law in terms of interstate obligation within an international society. It will be the subject of chapter 4.

At this point in our analysis, Hume's logic of concepts must first focus on effectiveness as a local rule of recognition and the conventionally dominant component of those dialectics that create Justice-As-Sovereignty as an expression of practical reason. Hume's philosophical-policy builds the idea of rules of recognition on the foundation of local social convention and its scale of forms, and more particularly, the dialectic between local⇆universal as this impels the law forward. Therefore, society, within the social construction of the state, requires a local rule of recognition that validates international law as those rules that honor Justice-As-Sovereignty in terms of the stability of that municipal system.

Local recognition will, at least initially, have priority in the synthesis that is the practice of Justice-As-Sovereignty. It arose with the Westphalian Equilibrium when peace at the international level allowed for sets of municipal social conventions to take hold as the foundation for an interstate structure. However, as the local becomes more stable, and states more numerous, the international system of social convention may change to adapt through a dialectic balance weighted toward the priority of the universal rule of recognition.

If the metaphysics of sovereignty gives synthetic priority to the municipal stabilization of property, then this will affect where the burden of proof is placed by international legal practice. Specifically, the burden should be placed, not on the local level of recognition to demonstrate that international law permits a particular act, but on the universal level to demonstrate that it prohibits a particular act so as to maintain the stability of the Westphalian Equilibrium. This dialectic balance toward the priority of local effectiveness supports an international law created as a system of specific prohibitions. This is where the examination of international case law begins.

This particular definition of the burden of proof is precisely the position established in 1927 by the Permanent Court of International Justice in the *Lotus* case.[121] Within this case, substantially about criminal jurisdiction on the high seas, the court recognized the minimum parameters of international legal practice as if they were an evolving set of social conventions existing to protect the local stability of municipal systems cooperating at the Westphalian Equilibrium.

> all that can be required of a State is that it should not overstep the limits which international law places upon its jurisdiction; within these limits, its title to exercise jurisdiction rests in its sovereignty.[122]

If international law is evolving so that sovereign municipal conventions can maintain effectiveness, stabilized and protected from international disturbances, then it makes sense to have a rule of recognition based on a system of prohibitions, so that municipal societies are only regulated (recognizing valid international law) when their actions threaten the fundamental stability of the international level of social organization. Otherwise, a level of international legal restraint endangering Justice-As-Sovereignty could result. Intrusive international regulation would threaten the effectiveness of the Westphalian Equilibrium by its inhibition of municipal social convention, which has already demonstrated its effectiveness in maintaining order within a state-based governance structure and therefore has attained pride of place in legal practice.[123]

> international law governs relations between independent States. The rules of law binding upon States therefore emanate from their own free will as expressed in conventions or by usages generally accepted as expressing principles of law and established in order to regulate the relations between these co-existing independent communities or with a view to the achievement of common aims. Restrictions upon the independence of States cannot therefore be presumed.[124]

From the vantage point of Hume's concept of law, the equilibrium of coordination is such that only a prohibition-based system of international law is reasonable. Law at the international level is required only to prohibit such state action as threatens Justice-As-Sovereignty. Consequently, *Lotus*, as a point of departure, gives priority to local-state rule of recognition and creates a system of international law on the back of established municipal social conventions. *Lotus* grants primary legal status to municipal government, and its contract-by-convention, that has stabilized each of the states to make up the international order. This also creates a narrow field for universal recognition of an international jurisprudence, which has the burden of proof to find a specific prohibition to extend transnational jurisdiction.

> The Court therefore must, in any event, ascertain whether or not there exists a rule of international law limiting the freedom of States to extend the criminal jurisdiction of their courts to a situation uniting the circumstances of the present case.[125]

But setting this burden of proof is only the first step in the legal scale of forms as defined by the rules of recognition within Hume's philosophical-policy. Once social convention establishes the contextual liberty of each state in the law, it then needs further refinement of the process-norm of Justice-As-Sovereignty, so that the SPP of effectiveness gains further definition in legal practice.

The next step in the conceptual refinement of Justice-As-Sovereignty on a Humean scale of forms can be found in the *Isle of Palmas* arbitration. Here, the burden of proof for local recognition was further defined by the idea of the *effective control* of territory. The first task of Justice-As-Sovereignty is to make sure that local effectiveness is protected in the most basic legal terms. Hume defines justice as the stabilization of property, so a rule of recognition based upon social convention would first seek a material definition of the state by focusing on the empirical "effectiveness" of its local social conventions in the stability of its territory.

> Sovereignty in the relation between States signifies independence. Independence in regard to a portion of the globe is the right to exercise therein, to the exclusion of any other State, the functions of a State. The development of the national organization of States during the last few centuries and, as a corollary, the development of international law, have established this principle of the exclusive competence of the State in regard to its own territory in such a

> way as to make it the point of departure in settling most questions that concern international relations.[126]

For social convention, practice is much more important than rules; in fact, the evolution of practice creates the basis for codified rules within Hume's concept of law. Consequently, it is not surprising that an international legal practice arising from social convention uses the material conditions of "effective control" to judge the legal status of territory.

In the *Isle of Palmas* arbitration, existing treaties granting control of the territory in question could have been decisive. These treaties and their historical power, as well as their codified status within the realm of universal recognition, formed a dialectic with the material evidence of effective control. Yet the treaties were not dispositive. Why not? Perhaps because the ends of social convention in terms of stability of property are unconsciously understood to be the essential test for the persistence of the system of law created by social convention and its process-norm of Justice-As-Sovereignty.

The *Isle of Palmas* case is about legitimate governance as defined by international social convention. Convention creates effective stability as a local rule of recognition for the future of social order, and therefore, from a Humean point of view, it is the instrumental end of a stable property scheme that ought to decide the validity of sovereign legitimacy. Adjudication should be expected to seek evidence of social stability as valid material verification of proper ownership. Max Huber, the arbitrator in the *Isle of Palmas* case,[127] does just this.

> discovery alone, without any subsequent act, cannot at the present time suffice to prove sovereignty over the Island of Palmas.[128]

> The Netherlands title of sovereignty, acquired by continuous and peaceful displays of state authority during a long period of time going probably back beyond the year 1700, therefore holds good.[129]

Making the argument that ownership of the islands is rooted in the social conventions evolved through the circumstances of Justice-As-Sovereignty, he granted legitimate governance on the basis of "effective control" of the territory. This decision is a natural extension of *Lotus* where social convention is both refined and substantiated as the foundation of international rules of recognition. The history of effectiveness with which a territory is administered, or the local stability of property within the norm of Justice-As-Sovereignty, is of paramount importance for valid title; not the legal contracts, treaties, or titles that had been won or lost by the other states involved in the dispute.

> The principle that continuous and peaceful display of the functions of state within a given region [a]s a constituent element of territorial sovereignty is not only based on the formation of independent states and their boundaries...as well as on an international jurisprudence and doctrine widely accepted; this

> principle has further been recognized in more than one federal state, where jurisdiction is established in order to apply, as need arises, rules of international law to the interstate relations of the states members.[130]

If effective control is a fit definition of state sovereignty and defines its legitimacy to participate in a prohibition-based international law of coordination, then does this not grant substantive status to the idea of the sovereign state? It does not. The core focus of social convention is the stability and persistence of society, not its institutional structure, which has only instrumental value. Current legal practice is built on a system of states. But, within Hume's logic of concepts, the state as an institutional representation of the society is only of utility to the extent that it successfully allows the persistence of both municipal and international social order. Rather, the degree of social cohesion and the ongoing utility of the process-norm of Justice-As-Sovereignty determines the status of the state structure in international law.

So the state is not an end-in-itself; nor is sovereignty a substantive critical principle that might trump the fundamental process that established order at the Westphalian Equilibrium. Justice-As-Sovereignty is only a process-norm generated to ensure that the law respects the core status of social convention within the international legal system.

The instrumental status of the state as a creature of Justice-As-Sovereignty, with its measure of effective control, can be further demonstrated by examining the arbitration decisions over the status of Yugoslavia. The Badinter Commission,[131] set up to determine the status of the former Yugoslavia, placed the burden of proof on those who would maintain the state's existence rather than on those who would proclaim its demise. This shifted the decision criteria to concern for the stability of the social system rather than the institutional presumption of statehood. If the state was a moral or legal end-in-itself, it would have privileged status in the adjudication, as a necessary element to the persistence of international law.

However, the decisions are worded as if no such essential element existed. Rather than adopt the fundamental assumption that a quality or characteristic of a state is substantive and necessary in some critical way, the opinion assumes that the status of the state is dependent on the effectiveness of the local rule of recognition, the viability of effective control, and the continuing utility of the process-norm of Justice-As-Sovereignty. The Badinter Commission made its recommendations as if social convention and the SPP of effectiveness were the ultimate arbiter of which state survives and which disappears.

In its report, the Commission appears to recognize that the legitimacy of Yugoslavia was directly tied to the local rule of recognition: effective control. Yugoslavia was judged in terms of how its state governance system guarded the stability of its society(ies). Since the state is a social construction built on the utility of social stability and recognized through its effective local control, the societies involved, and their persistence within any state structure, determined the range and character of that state's validity. The federal system is of less importance than the degree to which it fostered social convention and the maintenance of the international cooperative equilibrium.

> In a federal State, the existence of the State implied that the federal organs represented the components of the federation and wielded effective power. In the case of the SFRY, the essential federal organs no longer met the criteria of participation and representativeness inherent in a federal state.[132]

Within this system of Humean standards, with the state's existence subject to a process-norm of Justice-As-Sovereignty, it is logical to withdraw recognition of statehood when it is judged that any particular institutional structure is unable to provide for the stability of its territory and the persistence of its society. Such is the conclusion reached by the Commission; that is, Yugoslavia was no longer in effective control, its institutions were "in the process of dissolution," and it had lost its legitimacy.[133]

This judgment is made on the basis of established practice. The Commission is both sanctioned by, and finds its mandate in, international law.

> The Commission's answer to the question put had to be based upon the principles of public international law which defined the conditions on which an entity constituted a State.[134]

Consequently, state sovereignty was judged by established legal practice as if it were based on Hume's definition of social convention. The judgment implies that the process-norm of Justice-As-Sovereignty was determinative of a state's status within the international community. Here the institutional structure of the state is being treated as if its value were merely instrumental to social stability; as if cessation of a state's ability to provide the essential "effective control" over its people and territory is the measure of its validity.

The willingness of the Commission to abandon Yugoslavia can be criticized as a failure to understand the character of federal structure. But it may have more to do with the Commission's unconscious fealty to international social convention and its local rule of recognition. It acted as if international law was a system of social convention where it is not the state as an entity in itself that is critical to the international rule of law, but rather, the stability of property and the persistence of its constituent societies, judged by the state's effective control.

Under this logic of concepts, the state of Yugoslavia had no further utility and should be replaced by smaller units supportive of the needs of the stability of the distinct societies involved. The decision may be described as a logical outgrowth of an understanding of the dispositive rule of recognition, arising from the evolution of the international rule of law as a system of social convention, building on *Lotus* and *Isle of Palmas*.

In this sequence of cases, a loss of effective control meant a loss of legal existence for the state structure. But what about a state that is successfully providing stability for its society but has other objections to its legitimacy. To what extent should the viable "effective control" of a state be respected by a *Lotus*-based system of international legal practice? Examining the *South West Africa* case and the advisory opinion of the International Court of Justice on the *Legality of Nuclear Weapons*, using the metaphysical structure of Hume's philosophical-policy, will begin to address this question.

In the *South West Africa* case,[135] the Court was faced with the territorial administration of Namibia under the legally-appointed responsibility of the state of South Africa. The League mandate, an established process-friendly manifestation of Justice-As-Sovereignty, was considered by the Court as dispositive in and of itself. For Hume, social convention is simultaneously empirical and normative. So if the mandate is backed by convention, it provides a moral imperative. With the dialectic between process⇆principle engaged, the Court's majority focuses on the determination of "moral well-being." Is it substantially a creature of process or principle?

> Article 2 of the Mandate...require[s] the mandatory to "promote to the utmost the material and moral well-being and the social progress of the inhabitants of the territory."[136]

This case was precipitated by South Africa's attempt to expand its domestic policy of apartheid into Namibia. Two other African states, as members of the then extinct League of Nations, challenged the legality of this decision within the League mandate that granted South Africa the territorial administration. The question then became whether the moral objections of Ethiopia and Liberia created a separate right, based on critical principle, to reinterpret the particulars of the mandate in light of the morality of its "sacred trust." The Court argued it did not.

> even as members of the League...the Applicants did not, in their individual capacity as States, possess any separate self-contained right which they could assert, independently of, or additionally to, the right of the League, in the pursuit of its collective, institutional activity, to require the due performance of the Mandate in discharge of the "sacred trust"...to set themselves up as separate custodians of the various mandates. This was the role of the League.[137]

The Court ruled for South Africa and dismissed the complaint. A minority of the Court argued for a definition of "sacred trust" enhanced by a more universal idea of "civil rights," external to South African sovereignty. This dissent is one from the standpoint of critical/substantive moral principle. According to the dissenting voices, because apartheid was morally wrong, international law should allow intervention to prevent apartheid from being transplanted to Namibia.

> if the Court had considered the question of the existence of an international standard or criterion as an aid to interpretation of the Mandate it would have

> been pursuing a course to which no objection could be raised. In my opinion, such a standard exists and could have been and should have been utilized by the Court in performing what would then be seen as the purely judicial function of measuring by an objective standard whether the practice of apartheid in the mandated territory of South West Africa was a violation of the Mandatory's obligation to "promote to the utmost the material and moral well-being and the social progress of the inhabitants of the territory."[138]

This decision was controversial,[139] and the Court did not recover its moral authority until the *Barcelona Traction* case of 1970, where they recognized erga omnes obligations. But in recognizing that the decision in this case was driven by the power of social convention, the logic of the majority's decision is more understandable.

Logically, the sovereign state exists, not as a principled end-in-itself, but as an institutional manifestation of the process-norm of Justice-As-Sovereignty. It was initially created by social convention for the effective maintenance of the municipal society that requires a coordinated international system for its persistence. Convention is about process and property stabilization, which defines Justice-As-Sovereignty. Consequently, the point of the law in relation to a sovereign state is to sanction effective control of all mandated territory. Protecting the mandate as effective control is, simultaneously, normative, because social convention finds its morality in the maintenance of cooperative equilibrium and Justice-As-Sovereignty, which would be disrupted by the use of critical principle (e.g., a rights-based definition of "sacred trust"). If these points are understood as the key to the continued stabilization of international property and persistence of the Westphalian Equilibrium, then the majority position in *South West Africa* has an inherent logic that is empirically and normatively justifiable.

Specifically, within Hume's concept of law, the core value of social stability to coordinate behavior and expectations around an international equilibrium corrects for the natural instability of property and provides for the legal and moral persistence of social order. The human predisposition to find points of coordination, like the Westphalian Equilibrium, creates both municipal and international social conventions protected by a process-norm of sovereignty that assures the maintenance of the conditions of cooperation over time.

Social conventions, that promote process over principle, are challenged or disrupted by the introduction of policy or legal design arguments based upon critical principle or aetiological-norms (e.g., human/civil rights). Therefore, institutions created by social convention have a distinct bias against allowing such principled arguments to be legitimized in law. If Hume's concept of law accurately reflects the evolution of international legal practice, then the *South West Africa* case established that process held the balance of power within the dialectic of process⇆principle for the Court. The decision can be read as in support of sovereignty's local rule of recognition (i.e., effectiveness) carrying a legal and moral status higher than, and resistant to, critical principle.

Within the process⇆principle dialectic, one can expect the bulwark of process-law built upon social convention to provide the foundation for judicial thinking and decision-making. From this perspective, one can assume that legal arguments based on values other than international social coordination have a high potential to undermine established social stability and violate the local rule of recognition, making process less effective and therefore risking social cohesion. The Humean predisposition suggests that arguments built on critical principle are disruptive to an established and proven status quo equilibrium. The combination of these assumptions and predispositions creates a very heavy burden of proof for critical principle to overcome social convention and determine the synthesis solution in law from this dialectic confrontation. Even if critical principles, like those connected to civil rights, gain status in general discourse and other political institutions, the judiciary, the ultimate protectors of the law, will continue to treat social convention as the "common sense" or predominant legal "form" and critical principles as mere "interests."

> Humanitarian considerations may constitute the inspirational basis for rules of law, . . . Such considerations do not, however, in themselves amount to rules of law. All States are interested—have an interest—in such matters. But the existence of an "interest" does not of itself entail that this interest is specifically juridical in character.[140]

In the United States, the power of the bulwark of social convention, as it confronted a dialectic with substantive moral/legal principle in civil rights, can be illustrated by the 1896 decision of the Supreme Court to support segregation in the south. In *Plessy v. Ferguson*,[141] the Court rejected arguments based on the substantive aetiological-norms of freedom and equality and upheld the contextual or conventional process-norm of "separate but equal" that had secured a long-established social order. In a case very similar in argument to *South West Africa*, the highest Court in the United States was faced with a dialectic between process⇆principle. Presented with a choice between one line of argument based on long-established law evolved from preexisting social convention, or an alternative argument from substantive and critical concepts of equal civil rights, they found for the security and stability of the former.

In *South West Africa*, the argument was over the character of the mandate held by South Africa and whether the transplantation of apartheid was within the legal parameters of said mandate. As in *Plessy*, the dialectic was between an argument about the procedural sanctity of social convention versus the substantive requirements of critical moral/legal principle. In identical fashion, the Court in *South West Africa* opted to protect law based on social convention against the possible destabilization of equilibrium by a substantive civil rights argument based on critical principle. Below the surface of their technical argument about Article 22, the majority was, in fact, simply reaffirming Justice-As-Sovereignty as a moral and legal baseline.

> In the present case, the principle of the sacred trust has as its sole juridical expression the mandate system. As such, it constitutes a moral ideal given form as a juridical regime in the shape of that system. But it is necessary not to confuse the moral ideal with the legal rules intended to give it effect. For the purposes of realizing the aims of the trust in the particular form of any given mandate, its legal rights and obligations were those, and those alone, which resulted from the relevant instruments creating the system, and the mandate itself, within the framework of the League of Nations.[142]

Although discounting human rights appears surprising from a twenty-first century viewpoint, if considered from within the framework of Hume's philosophical-policy and its scale of forms, they are logical entailments of a deep, and perhaps unconscious, trust in established social convention. Social convention and its process-norm have what Thomas Franck calls a "compliance pull."[143] Justice-As-Sovereignty is what Jackson calls "a concept fundamental to the logical foundations of traditional international law."[144] Its requirements have an inherent rationality when viewed from within Hume's concept of law, that can only be overcome gradually.

In the 1960s, when the *South West Africa* case was decided, the world of international human rights was in the same dialectic context for process⇆principle that American civil rights law was at the turn of the twentieth century, when *Plessy* was decided. Specifically, both contexts were situations where critical or substantive principle, dealing with racial discrimination, had only been in full dialectic with law from social convention for a decade or two. The bulwark of social convention was strong and the codification of critical principle into the rule of law was a relatively new phenomenon that was still, unsurprisingly, assumed to be very disruptive of a well-established global social order.

The social conventions that establish the foundation for codified law have a distinct power to limit the effect of principled arguments when they are finally introduced into the dialectic process of institutional governance after contract-by-convention. The introduction of aetiological-norms into the law inherently requires that process sometimes be overridden by critical principle. This means that the institutional structures created by the process-norms of social convention will also create a language and a set of social predispositions that define legal validity and governance legitimacy within a pragmatic logic that promotes *effective* process in the face of *disruptive* principle. Consequently, to those trained within the context of these conventions, legal rules created in support of social convention are perceived to be more reasonable; that is, valid and legitimate "form" within established legal practice.

When an established practice is first challenged by substantive principle, these critical arguments are no competition for the requirements of rules based on Justice-As-Sovereignty as valid law from social convention. In the *South West Africa* case, the majority ostensibly interpreted the "sacred trust" connected to the Mandate as not amenable to arguments from critical principle that were not already validated by effective control and its normative weight as the local rule of recognition. As they argued, "[r]ights cannot be presumed to exist merely because it might seem desirable that they should."[145]

That the dialectic between process⇆principle is a matter of the evolution or progressive codification of substantive principle within a legal system initially dominated by social convention is a reality all but acknowledged, in dissent, by Judge Tanaka. He shows an understanding of an emerging role for human rights, and argues that the evolution of critical principle has progressed further than the majority of the Court allows.

> Without doubt, under the present circumstances, the international protection of human rights and fundamental freedoms is very imperfect.... But there is little doubt of the existence of human rights and freedoms;... the existence of such rights and freedoms is unthinkable without corresponding obligations of persons concerned and a legal norm underlying them. Furthermore, there is no doubt that these obligations are not moral ones, and that they also have a legal character by the very nature of the subject-matter. Therefore, the legislative imperfections in the definition of human rights and freedoms and the lack of mechanism for implementation, do not constitute a reason for denying their existence and the need for their legal protection.... Accordingly, the dispute concerning the legality of apartheid comes within the field of the interpretation and application of the provision of the Mandate situated in Article 7, paragraph 2, of the Mandate.[146]

Although both the *Plessy* and *South West Africa* decisions have since been ostensibly overturned by law that reflects the minority human rights arguments therein presented, this transcendence of process by principle required persistent critical argument over many years. Rights, being disruptive of process, must wear-away the trust of social convention to find a place in the synthesis of dispositive legal solutions.[147] The result of this evolution in international law is a growing effort to amend Justice-As-Sovereignty in terms of the inclusion of basic rights as a measure of a state's legitimacy. This position, however, has not fully replaced the local rule of recognition and effective control. Hume's philosophical-policy establishes the prior status of social convention in the human unconsciousness and therefore should lead us to expect that any erosion of the idea of Justice-As-Sovereignty on its scale of forms will be slow and require repeated efforts.

In *South West Africa*, effective control is the guiding SPP for the majority. The protection of the proven process norm of state sovereignty and the state's ability to establish and maintain stability set the burden of proof for the case. Two assumptions appear to dominate the decision: first, ceteris paribus, a state should be allowed to make its own internal decisions, second, any definition of "sacred trust" that transcended the process-based mandate was not a legal but a political matter and not the valid purview of the courts. The Court acted as if this matter should be decided within the greater context of Justice-As-Sovereignty that, in this case, required that a good deal of weight, even in the face of questions of human rights, should to be given to effective control. Is this case unique, or can its essential point be confirmed and perhaps even further refined on a scale of forms by adding to our case chain?

Consider the advisory opinion of the International Court of Justice on the *Use of Nuclear Weapons*,[148] which both confirms and refines the finding of the Court in *South West Africa*. It demonstrates the full power of the social conventions connected to "effective control" because the state, in its contextual right to preserve its basic stability, makes Justice-As-Sovereignty the trump card of international legal practice regarding nuclear weapons.

The complicated decision of the majority in *Nuclear Weapons* is the next link in the chain of our argument about the dominance of process over principle. By relying on social convention, contextual process-norms, and legal custom, *Nuclear Weapons* verifies and further defines a process-centered international law based on Justice-As-Sovereignty. By allowing the use of nuclear weapons it clearly discounts the critical principles within international humanitarian and environmental law.

In the first procedural decision of the Court, the judges decided to switch the question from whether international law existed that would permit the use of nuclear weapons to a search for a specific "prohibition" against the use of such weapons. This reconceptualization of the argument, built on *Lotus* and *Palmas*, recognizes that sovereignty is a process-norm, while it relies on the underlying assumption that the burden of proof lies with those who would prohibit a state's actions.

> The use of the word "permitted" in the question put by the General Assembly was criticized before the Court by certain States on the ground that this implied that the threat or use of nuclear weapons would only be permissible if authorization could be found in a treaty provision or in customary international law. Such a starting point, those States submitted, was incompatible with the very basis of international law, which rests upon the principles of sovereignty and consent; accordingly, and contrary to what was implied by use of the word "permitted," States are free to threaten or use nuclear weapons unless it can be shown that they are bound not to do so by reference to a prohibition in either treaty law or customary international law. Support for this contention was found in dicta of the Permanent Court of International Justice in the "Lotus" case…[quoting ICJ Reports 1986 p.135 ¶269-Nic] "in international law there are no rules, other than such rules as may be accepted by the States concerned, by treaty or otherwise, whereby the level of armaments of a sovereign State can be limited."[149]

With the establishment of *Lotus* as the point of departure for the examination of the question, the Court is faced, like its counterpart in *South West Africa*, with sorting out the dialectic between process⇆principle, given the established status of social convention and Justice-As-Sovereignty. The difference in this case was that, in the years between the two cases, the status of critical principle in legal argument had advanced. In addition to the progress of human rights law that had been established by both treaty and the

UN Charter, humanitarian law had progressed in its influence both within the context of war and peace. International environmental law, seeking to protect the integrity of nature in the face of human perturbations, had also been incorporated in treaty, principle, and custom. Most critically, the ideas of erga omnes obligations, containing the seeds of universal jurisdiction, and jus cogens critical principles, as the most important class of aetiological-norms or substantive moral principles of law, were both codified, the former in case law and the latter in treaty.[150]

Consequently, the Court was not able to dismiss the principled argument of all of these areas of law offhand and was forced to consider each in the search for its prohibition of the use of nuclear weapons. Within each of these searches, the issue area under consideration produced aetiological or substantive arguments about the destructive power of nuclear weapons, the resultant violations of international environmental, humanitarian, or human-rights law, and the consequent responsibility of states. None of this analysis produced a specific prohibition against states using nuclear weapons. The most that can be said is that it illuminated a more fully engaged dialectic between process⇆principle thereby creating a situation where the sovereign actions of states, at least at the margins, were more encumbered. For example, consider the limiting effect of a "respect" for the environment on the use of nuclear weapons.

> The existence of general obligation of States to ensure that activities within their jurisdiction and control respect the environment of other States or areas beyond national control is now part of the corpus of international law relating to the environment.[151]
>
> The Court thus finds that while the existing international law relating to the protection and safeguarding of the environment does not specifically prohibit the use of nuclear weapons, it indicates important environmental factors that are properly to be taken into account.[152]

The Court seemed to acknowledge that, while not yet dispositive, the "principle" side of the dialectic had redefined the range and affect of the process-norm of Justice-As-Sovereignty. Instead of easily dismissing the entire question of prohibiting the use of nuclear weapons, as their counterpart completely dismissed the idea of an enhanced "sacred trust" for South West Africa, the Court found that even without an outright ban, humanitarian, environmental, and human-rights law required a more subtle and more well-reasoned argument that conditioned the circumstances in which nuclear weapons could legally be used.

Instead of confirming a simple and absolute idea of Justice-As-Sovereignty, the Court needed to refine its protection of this process-norm by bringing a contextual principle of self-defense into their opinion. The majority settled on a narrowed idea of sovereign self-defense, where the "effective" rule of recognition was further refined by the dual conditioning norms of *proportionality* and *necessity*.[153] This demonstrated that while Justice-As-

Sovereignty retained its character as a core norm protecting process, "effective control" was conditioned by necessity and proportionality. In this way the Court admitted to the growing power of critical principle within the primary dialectic of international law.

At the beginning of this case chain, the process-norm was measured only in terms of the material conditions of effective control of territory; that is, by a state's ability to stabilize property for the persistence of international social order. At that juncture in the creation of an international legal system, the synthesis of legal practice created by the dialectic between process⇆principle was weighted substantially toward the bulwark of social convention that supported process. However, with the advent of contract-by-convention and international governance structures, aetiological-norms or substantive critical principles found voice in the evolving international legal system and began to gain codification in the sources of international law (i.e., principle, custom, and treaty). This new presence for critical principle was acknowledged by the Court in *Nuclear Weapons* in the tortured logic of the complicated argument for the conditions under which use of these weapons might be justified.[154]

Meanwhile, this additional argument for necessity and proportionality in the use of nuclear weapons is also further evidence that the idea of Justice-As-Sovereignty is indeed a process-norm evolving on a scale of forms, and not a critical principle or end-in-itself. A critical principle, which is always argued in relation to an end-in-itself, is, by definition, a matter of inherent necessity. An aetiological-norm contains its own moral causality and is never measured continuously but discreetly; it either exists (e.g., within the law, or within morality) or it does not. For example, a right against being tortured does not bend to necessity or the proportionality of circumstance, but, once acknowledged, continues to exist regardless of degree. This is why a state's argument that exigent circumstances make torture legal does not change the international law on the subject, nor the state's responsibility.

Proportionality is also not a test of aetiological-norms. One cannot be proportionately tortured, nor is the torture of one states' citizens a fit legal basis for the proportional torture of another's nationals. If self-defense was a critical principle in the mind of the Court, then the tests of necessity and proportionality would not be necessary. The fact that they do apply these conditioning norms is evidence that they understand self-defense in terms of what Hume's concept of law defines as a contextual principle. Here, self-defense as a contextual principle, evolved from, and for the purpose of the persistence of, social convention, protects only the state, which would not be the case were it a critical, or jus cogens, principle.

This decision can be described as an effort on the part of the majority to further define the requirements of Justice-As-Sovereignty, thereby refining the essence of social convention up its scale of forms without fundamentally removing it as the dominant imperative for the process⇆principle dialectic. This action provides additional support for the contention that the Court's frame of reference is compatible with Hume's philosophical-policy and its concept of law.

The Court concludes that there is no direct prohibition on the use of nuclear weapons. This is only because the Court cannot rule out the circumstances in which necessity and proportionality may require one state to use these weapons in self-defense to prevent its total annihilation.[155] One explanation for what is commonly considered a complex argument is that the Court was desperately trying to avoid a *non liquet*.[156] While this may be the case, the critical dimension of the majority decision, from the standpoint of Hume's philosophical-policy and legal design, is in an acknowledgment by the Court, on the one hand, that critical principles were involved, and, on the other, that it is important to provide for those extreme circumstances where the existence of a sovereign state's effective control is at dire risk.

The Court's opinion can be interpreted, first, as recognizing the conventional roots of the contextual principle of self-defense as a creature of Justice-As-Sovereignty. Second, in the same way that this definition of international legal practice was critical in the reorientation of the case toward "prohibition," it also provided the conventional basis for the dialectic between process (self-defense measured by necessity and proportionality) and principle (jus cogens) that characterizes the central arguments about nuclear weapons and the laws of force, humanitarian law, and environmental protection that make up the opinion.

Further evidence for the Court's unconscious recognition of the evolving dialectic between process⇆principle can be found in the core argument of Judge Weeramantry's dissent. He acknowledges the predominance of social convention from *Lotus* with the contention, like that argued by Tanaka in *South West Africa*, that the progress of principle over process had already pushed international law, and consequently, the metaphysics of sovereignty, to the point where critical principle was determining sovereign legitimacy.

> In the half century that has elapsed since the "Lotus" case, it is quite evident that international law—and the law relating to humanitarian conduct in war—have developed considerably, imposing additional restrictions on state sovereignty over and above those that existed at the time of the "Lotus" case....This Court cannot in 1996 construe "Lotus" so narrowly as to take the law backward in time.[157]

Nevertheless, the majority decision in this case is a continued, although considerably strained, defense of the established and conventional international system. It acknowledges the absolutely fundamental role of Justice-As-Sovereignty within the international legal system and the continued dominance of the local rule of recognition (i.e., effective control) as traced from *Lotus*.

The chain of cases considered demonstrates how the structure of the state finds protection in a local rule of recognition (i.e., effectiveness) that acknowledges legitimate international law where it is compatible with foundational social convention. These cases also demonstrate the dominant default position of social convention in determining how the dialectic between process⇆principle translates into dispositive international legal practice. Lastly, it illustrates that, as part of the refinement of process in the face of evolving critical principle, there has been an erosion of the power of the dominance of social convention. As the status of legal arguments from aetiological-norms becomes more determinative, the essence of sovereignty as the source-point for practical reason in international law proceeds on its scale of forms to encompass a new sense of its own legitimacy; one that includes critical principle. But this has not yet been fully institutionalized. Process still controls the core dialectic.

Overall, the Court can still not allow the essential nucleus of Justice-As-Sovereignty and its SPP of effectiveness as a local rule of recognition to yield to even the most critical jus cogens principle. To do this would place the Westphalian Equilibrium, and the stability of its society, at risk. But, as we will see in the next chapter, Hume's concept of law, its institutional governance structure, and the SPP of progressive codification will continue to more fully engage the process⇆principle dialectic, applying continued pressure to Justice-As-Sovereignty.

3

"Progressive Codification": A Rule of Adjudication and the Evolution of Justice-As-Sovereignty

Abstract

Hume's philosophical-policy provides a dynamic definition of governance drawn from social convention that is neither as static nor as demanding in terms of enforcement as is normally assumed within a positivist conceptualization of a legal system. Instead, governance through process-norms allows many different levels and complexities of sanctions to be judged equally as international law, with the sole criterion that they ensure the process of cooperation. For Hume, international governance is an evolving set of prelegal and legal sanctions measured by the amount of institutional practice needed for the persistence of convention in the face of growing social complexity. This makes sovereignty a creature of the systematic policy precept of progressive codification as the rule of adjudication within Hume's concept of law. Next, the legal design extrapolation describes international law in terms of a multistage model for the balancing and rebalancing of process⇆principle. Lastly, case analysis provides evidence that Hume's philosophy-policy illuminates legal practice to a degree positivism cannot.

I. Hume's Logic of Concepts: Governance on a Scale of Forms

Superficially, there is a theoretical disagreement between *Emer de Vattel*, who suggests that basing international law in human choice and the consent of states precludes the existence of a substantive theory of natural law, and *Hugo Grotius*, who relies on a fundamental theory of natural law to frame his argument about *jus gentium*. But, on a deeper level, both attempt to transcend Vitoria's dilemma by suggesting that, for a secular version of international legal governance to bring universality and certainty, it must be based upon the consent of states. Vattel designates his argument as a "voluntary and positive"[1] argument for international law, where the only perfect right is sovereignty, a perfect right being defined as that on behalf of which, all nations agree to act. Grotius builds his argument for universality in the common practices of states on the contention that international legal practice reflects something "necessary and natural"[2] in human reason.

Vattel and Grotius fundamentally agree. Both prescribe a positive theory of state consent as the foundation of law or governance in the international system. Both argue that international law is based on a essential norm of sovereignty that limits the law to that to which states consent. They may disagree as to the degree to which consent has a metaphysical foundation, but they agree that the positive law of states is derived from an assumption of sovereignty defined, not in social stability, but in the *presumptive*, *express*, or *tacit* agreement of states as moral persons in interstate relations. By promoting a theory of positive consent as the core of international law, both discount the importance of metaphysics or natural law. Vattel, writing after Grotius, was able to drop his predecessor's theory of natural law altogether, without greatly affecting the basic argument for a jus gentium regulated by justice-as-consent.

But building governance institutions on an international law of consent, is problematic. In addition to the many issues inherent in the ideas of tacit and presumptive consent,[3] a focus on law by consent erases the normative supports and the metaphysical context of international law. It eliminates the standards necessary to analyze why a state or states may, or should, consent to one governance arrangement rather than another. It also loses any normative justification for sovereignty as that norm that maintains international cooperation. If consent is the measure of the law, then sovereignty can be compromised in the name of choice. Grotius' effort to reinforce consent with natural law is an effort to create a remedy for this problem. But his effort collapses into consent as a positive act, significantly unsupported by any other normative motivation or systematic justification.[4]

Hume's philosophical-policy and legal design, with its unique perspective on sovereignty, avoids a dependence on consent as a basis for governance. Hume's idea of natural law uses social convention as a positive manifestation of humanity's normative passion for society. His definition of natural law integrates local empirical practice with a universal metaphysics of process, creating a prerequisite for the validity of any act of consent in Justice-As-Sovereignty. Consequently, Hume's idea of governance is not defined by what states will consent to, but by what promotes the persistence of social convention and the social order it creates through Justice-As-Sovereignty at the Westphalian Equilibrium.

Justice-As-Sovereignty is a direct outgrowth of Hume's metaphysics for property. Social convention, unlike mere custom, exists to stabilize property. However, the measure of stability is not conscious preference or consent. Hume's normative standard is the utility of that allocation to the persistence of social convention as a manifestation of the absolute presupposition of the human passion for society. This is the metaphysical imperative behind property law that grants one legal scheme more "moral" and "legal" value than another. Here, Hume differs from Grotius, whose theory of property relies on positive consent supported by a concept of natural law that contains no inherent or necessary metaphysical standards. Like his idea of international practice, Grotius' theory of property provides little in addition to an empirical idea of consent as the measure of the law.[5]

> For the very nature of man, which even if we had no lack of anything would lead us into the mutual relations of society, is the mother of the law of nature. But the mother of the municipal is that obligation which arises from mutual consent; and since this obligation derives its force from the law of nature, nature may be consulted, so to say, the great-grand-mother of municipal law. The law of nature nevertheless has the reinforcement of expediency.[6]

Hume's philosophical-policy and legal design describes governance as the institutional phase of a process of evolving levels of sanction. This scale of forms suggests a more complex understanding of international law as a progressive effort to continually create the global governance structures necessary to a changing sense of international Justice-As-Sovereignty. Within the conceptual logic of Hume's philosophical-policy, the pillars of international law are contained by, and channeled toward, the progressive support of social convention as it continually seeks social stability.

Within a Humean framework, an expression of consent is secondary and not strictly positive. Like all the terms of law, it is considered a product of the process⇆principle dialectic. Consent then becomes a dynamic concept built on a metaphysical framework created to support a continued refinement of conventional international relations under Justice-As-Sovereignty. This includes, for example, concepts of promise and promise-keeping that are the moral foundations of the international law of treaty.

With a normative focus on the dialectic between process⇆principle, Hume offers a dynamic and normative foundation for law and its governance structures that can adapt institutional forms depending on changes in requirements for international social cooperation. Hume argues that social convention is normative practice backed by a definition of justice, which not only can exist without consent, but must be a prerequisite to any form of promise or expectation of performance in positive law.[7]

Consequently, Hume's philosophical-policy creates a stable and fully realized prelaw environment where approbation and justice exist before consent, the institutionalization of policy norms, or their codification as rules of law. If there is a preexisting stability of norms and an established coordination equilibrium before the advent of positive law (i.e., legal consent), then the concrete transition process is already metaphysically configured, as its "rules" of behavior have been tested and maintained as social conventions.

Hume's concept of law assumes that the institutionalization of governance, after contract-by-convention, establishes a formal legal system based on the conventional root of the passion for society and its process-norm of sovereignty. However, institutions also support the rise of critical principle and its contribution to a full-blown process⇆principle dialectic. This makes Hume's concept of law dynamic because it changes and evolves in order to adapt governance and Justice-As-Sovereignty given balance within the core dialectic. In effect, the process model of Hume's concept of law, identified in chapter 2 has at least two stages or configurations given the initial dominance of process followed by the growing influence of critical principle in making public choices. If the international legal system is to be acknowledged in its full metaphysical and practical complexity, we need, not just a rule of recognition as we saw in the last chapter, but a *rule of adjudication* that sets process standards for decision-making that validate preexisting social convention through Justice-As-Sovereignty. This is achieved by the systematic policy percept (SPP) of *progressive codification.*

As the scope and complexity of society increases and municipal systems become stable and attempt to order international affairs, international society evolves sanctions of approbation, justice, and, finally, "political society."[8] On the municipal level, these sanctions provide a solution to the prisoner's dilemma (PD) that supports collective action within the state. These sanctions are consequently created in the form of a centralized enforcement mechanism to solve the PD, gain "effective control" of territory, and establish peace and order.

On the international level, within the context of a coordination game, the strategic demands are different and require other governance arrangements in support of Justice-As-Sovereignty. Specifically, if the PD was the strategic reality of both municipal and international law, as it is assumed to be within the Hobbesian model, the transnational state of nature would still exist and preclude the centralization and enforcement institutions necessary for the existence of international law. When an international system has an anarchic environment and a global PD to solve, the only governance that can be considered legal is governance derived from an integrated and centralized sovereignty. This forms Hobbes argument that government is what "holds men in awe"[9] and creates a single, central, top-down governance structure. Without this idea of law as command from central government, governance does not exist in terms of collective action that can overcome a PD. This makes what we now call international law suspect in terms of its status as law, if not its necessity.[10]

Hume's philosophical-policy does not require one specific and hierarchical governance solution to find international property stabilization equilibria within a coordination game. Rather, Hume's concept of law rests on constantly refining governance solutions with varying degrees of sanctions. Because of the background conditions of Lewis' coordination games, we do not require a centralized enforcement regime to establish initial coordination of international society; nor, indeed, to have a well-developed sense of international justice. Even before the full institutionalization of an international "political society," approbation and Justice-As-Sovereignty create a dispute settlement compliance regime that is a decentralized means to find and secure an international coordination equilibrium based on social convention. In effect, Hume's legal design endows the international strategic situation with much more metaphysical complexity than either Grotius or Vattel do and more institutional flexibility than Hobbes grants.

The Westphalian Equilibrium was founded on the support of a dynamic set of constituent municipal governments that solved their collective action problems, and whose requisite stability supplied enough "awe" so that international governance could be less centralized and still persist. Unlike a noncooperative PD, the act of seeking a coordination convention or equilibria is consciously in the interests of all. So when a new state is granted sovereignty through legal recognition by the international community, it has already agreed to Justice-As-Sovereignty and the conventions of the Westphalian Equilibrium as the "prominent solution" to global social stability. A new state has no rational interest in alienation from this conventional equilibrium but will work within it, even when it proves burdensome.[11]

Overall, the idea of governance provided by Hume's logic of concepts has a number of philosophical connotations and levels of possible complexity, depending on which of the multi-equilibria of evolving convention is chosen to represent justice-as-order for the international system. For Hume's philosophical-policy, international law is not created to contain or express state power, but to stabilize property on a global level, ensuring interstate coordination and the international social order sought by human passion. Maintaining the Westphalian Equilibrium through Justice-As-Sovereignty means coordinating the many municipal governments with transnational legal rules and institutions, and producing a dynamic international society that changes with its context to continually encourage peaceful social, commercial, and political interaction while honoring the sovereign equality of each and every participant.

As rules of recognition abate uncertainty, a rule of adjudication abates inefficiency in the legal system by "empowering individuals to make authoritative determinations of the question whether, on a particular occasion, a [substantive] rule has been broken."[12] Within the context of Hume's concept of law, this means granting the authority to judge the pace and application of substantive rules as the balance shifts between process⇆principle in the course of the progressive codification of international law.

With the creation of dispositive law from social convention, which happens with the advent of transnational political society and contract-by-convention, Justice-As-Sovereignty is progressively codified in reaction to the growing validity of critical principle in the law. Using the policy and legal processes of emerging governance institutions, social convention grants power to adjudicate in order to maintain its status within the system. This establishes the capacity of international society to make justice, as a process-norm, more than just something people ought to obey, or do obey out of the pattern of their unconscious expectations and actions. Progressive codification, as a rule of adjudication, gives Justice-As-Sovereignty conscious legal validity in the normative utility of its persistent rendering of peace, order, and good governance for international society.

The municipal level of social organization focuses on the integration of social convention by a coercive enforcement system that requires compliance. But within an international governance system, this is not necessary. With distinct institutions and a tangible and organized policy process to progressively codify the law, the transnational level of social organization, in its own way, addresses the requirements of the passion for society. It also, addresses the ongoing dialectic between process⇆principle through the persistence of Justice-As-Sovereignty, as the core process-norm of Hume's concept of international law.

Building on the imperative for effective sovereignty as the key to the local rule of recognition, a more complex legal system requires a more complex metaphysics. Procedural rules also must deal with the disposition of property over which no one has effective control. This, in turn, implies a need for the process-norm of Justice-As-Sovereignty to be further refined by a system of adjudication for international law. This system must efficiently design, set, and encourage compliance with basic rules for the "occupation, prescription, accession, and succession" of property between states, and for the "promise-keeping" that makes transfer by consent work and, simultaneously, implies a moral, if not legal, obligation.[13]

Initially, in a decentralized legal system, this adjudication process will rely on ideas such as good faith, transfer by consent, and promise-keeping as core precepts.[14] Adjudication procedures, in this way, build on "effective control" of territory by encouraging any and all interstate contract that increases a state's obligation to reciprocal behavior, concurrently preserving the Westphalian Equilibrium and the state's sovereign space while adapting to the shifting mix of process⇆principle created by governance institutions.

The procedural rules of adjudication, built on informal social convention, will create international social conventions of a diplomatic type. A Humean diplomat expects that the circumstances of justice will define the law. As those circumstances change he will work to integrate the changing forms of substantive and procedural law into an ever-more refined and distinct international rule of law. A Humean diplomat would be ever-mindful that justice is utility, defined in this case by the process-norm of sovereignty, and would recognize that space between international actors is critical to the maintenance of coordination at the established equilibrium. The *process* of coordination is a normative end-in-itself, and therefore the system of adjudication created to represent this dynamic process must empower it as it evolves levels of sanctions to match the requirements of international social complexity.

Within this dynamic, Justice-As-Sovereignty establishes formal international law from informal social convention in order to create synthesis snapshots, for the confluence of dialectics represented by the SPPs, that create a legal design reinforcing that social convention. Moral compliance as a product of social convention is not, as in a noncooperative context, a matter just of coercion, but is created by the common sense imperative to coordinate oneself on the established equilibrium. As long as the coordination equilibrium remains intact, the concept of Justice-As-Sovereignty represents both a state's internal and external affairs in a dynamic synthesis of law.

Hume's philosophical-policy creates an argument for governance where some degree of sanction is *necessary* to the end of the cooperative practice that insures international society. But it allows for degrees of sanctions and a more decentralized compliance process that can rely, in response to growing complexity, on moral approbation, Justice-As-Sovereignty, or the institutions of government with the "artifice" of bureaucrats and judges.

A critical element of this environment is the continually evolving nature of the law and the prerequisite imperative for social convention to adapt to the dynamic complexities of international social life. Because of this, the SPP for sovereignty as governance, is located in the tendency of the international concept of law to generate a *rule of adjudication* defined by *progressive codification*. Governance structures translate social conventions and their process-norms, as well as both contextual and critical principles, into black-letter law, operationalizing philosophical norms by legal practice. This is achieved through the evolution of what Hart calls "rules-of-adjudication,"[15] or procedural rules recognized by society as the legitimate process by which disputes about ideas are eventually settled in valid law. The objective at each level of social complexity is for sanctions to preserve social convention by creating coordination, then justice, and then institutional governance. This ensures that both the municipal and international tiers of social organization have a stable pattern of metaphysical refinement given the dialectic of process⇆principle.

From a Humean point of view, the stability of social convention on the municipal level, through the sanctions of municipal government, allows the initiation of coordination at the international level of organization. Once begun, the evolution of global governance at the international level reinforces both its own social convention and that of its municipal counterpart. This creates a stable two-tiered system allowing for progressively more complex global governance institutions.

Overall, the process of governance is one of finding a synthesis between a state's sense of its domestic and foreign sovereignty. The process requires setting rules of international adjudication that support international social convention without interfering with municipal stability and social order. However, with the advent of Hume's international "political society" and contract-by-convention, the potential for a full engagement of the dialectic between process⇆principle exists. Because social convention finds critical principle disruptive, it not only fails to support it, but discourages it, slowing progressive codification.

But with the creation of legal institutions that can process critical principle as well as social convention into law, the possibility of a legal design synthesis snapshot containing both *process-* and *aetiological*-norms exists. As the process-based core of sovereignty evolves, it establishes a progressive governance teleology.[16] It originates in the unconscious creation of social convention, moves to a focus on a cooperative process-norm of justice, and finally creates a transnational policy framework within contract-by-convention that supports a continuing dialectic, between process⇆principle, through public policy argument and legal design.

This teleology produces a progressive scale of forms within international law moving from contextual "civilized" *principle* to *customary* law to *treaty*. Each of these sources of law employs moral precepts as, first, legal principles, then legal norms, and then dispositive rules in law. This multilevel refinement process is part and parcel of the metaphysical scale of forms, that is, international law expressed as practical reason. The SPP of progressive codification makes international governance a continuing means to the end of social order.

The role of the law as ultimate stabilizer for each level of social organization makes it imperative that the law actualize, through rules of adjudication, its capacity to create order through valid action, rendered and applied universally in order to establish certainty of expectations. The *trust* engendered by the progressive codification of law and the growing complexity of governance institutions allows the metaphysics of social order within Hume's philosophical-policy to encompass an ever more complex concept of sovereignty.

Trust in a rule of adjudication allows a governance structure to legitimately and continually define the law. Within international law, this means elevating principle as a source of law, to a custom, and customary law to a treaty, through a recognized legal process that gives the progressive codification of the sources of international law legitimacy in the eyes of international society. As the adjudication process is forming in response to the interaction of social convention and the complexity of the material world, the system is best characterized, not as a Hobbesian world of power and self-interest, but as a Humean world, focused on the growth and persistence of international society, the stabilization of property, and the idea of progressive codification under the process-norm of Justice-As-Sovereignty.

Unlike power, which is a zero-sum good where one person's gain is another's loss, property stabilization as a synthesis solution is in everyone's interest. Whatever one possesses by habit, then convention, then by codified law is more secure than relying on another's preferences with resulting vulnerability. Humean governance focuses on the universal human passion for society, the limited generosity of international agents, and the stabilizing influence of political society, given its circumstances of justice.

Within Hume's philosophical-policy, the state is not an end-in-itself, but an instrumental means for stability and a receptacle for the complex metaphysics of sovereignty on both the municipal and international level of the global legal system. As a social construction, the state seeks coordination to stabilize territory and possessions given the circumstances of justice as the point of departure for the progressive evolution of the international legal system. Hume's concept of law does not describe self-interested states seeking power, trying to replace an anarchic state of nature with a centralized civil state in one, risky, all-or-nothing act. Rather, governance is realized, over time, on a scale of forms, through the dialectic of process⇆principle that is operationalized in varying levels of municipal and international adjudication.

Because of the imperative of progressive codification as a rule of adjudication, Hume's philosophical-policy and legal design is helpful in understanding the process-norm of sovereignty as "*first possession*" of territory necessary to the initial *stabilization* of international society. Governance also has utility for the continued persistence of Justice-As-Sovereignty through legal support for *transfer by consent* and *promise-keeping*, which, combined with initial *stabilization*, is defined by Hume as the "*three laws of convention*."[17] The creation of public policy and legal design arguments through contract-by-convention thereby allows the concept of sovereignty to be philosophically and practically refined given the complexity of international society. In this progressive codification, promise-keeping, and the laws of private and social contract on which it is based, humanity is further conditioned for coexistence where transference by consent and stability of property have already been established.

> The invention of the law of nature, concerning the *stability* of possession, has already render'd men tolerable to each other; that of the *transference* of property and possession by consent has begun to render them mutually advantageous: But still these laws, however strictly observ'd, are not sufficient to render them so serviceable to each other, as by nature they are fitted to become.[18]

Each level of governance is created in response to the progressive evolution of the moral/legal motive for society that, as the absolute presupposition of Hume's argument, must adapt on a scale of forms to changing social circumstance in order to persist. The motive of social order, in this way, responds to social complexity through the adaptation of governance institutions. Change is based on human experience and the repetition of a signaling system that is first sanctified by moral approbation, then justice, and is codified by promise and the law of contract through contract-by-convention.

> They are the conventions of men, which create a new motive, when experience has taught us, that human affairs wou'd be conducted much more for mutual advantage, were there certain *symbols* or *signs* instituted, by which we might give each other security of our conduct in any particular incident. After these

> signs are instituted, whoever uses them is immediately bound by his interest to execute his engagements, and must never expect to be trusted any more, if he refuse to perform what he promis'd.[19]

> When each individual perceives the same sense of interest in all his fellows, he immediately performs his part of any contract, as being assur'd, that they will not be wanting in theirs...Afterward a sentiment of morals concurs with interest and becomes a new obligation upon mankind. This sentiment of morality, in the performance of promises, arises from the same principles as that in the abstinence from the property of others. *Public interest, education,* and *the artifices of politicians,* have the same effect in both cases.[20]

Hume argues that a duty "supposes an antecedent obligation."[21] The reciprocal nature of the duty⇆obligation dialectic creates both an obligation in promising and the subsequent trust in one's duty to keep the promise. "Now 'tis evident we have no motive leading us to the performance of promises, distinct from a sense of duty."[22] The moral quality of action, and not centralized enforcement mechanisms, ensures its persistence, especially during transitional periods when the integrity of coordination is most threatened and choice more uncertain.

For Hume, promise-keeping is, first and foremost, a social convention, one that would be neither intelligible nor invoke an obligation without its metaphysical foundation in sentiment, human action, and the moral obligations so generated.[23] The background of social convention and the process-norm of Justice-As-Sovereignty grants international promising its validity and its value as a representation of the public interest or utility. Social convention further depends on sovereignty's inherent signaling system, which sanctions a "proper" point of coordination while it creates a moral obligation through the act of making a promise and engendering the trust that those promises will be kept. A role for promises and trust is a necessary component for any rule of adjudication and for any set of governance conventions aspiring to set the terms of an international coordination equilibrium, whether status quo or to create change.

Whenever "a sentiment of morals concurs with interest, and becomes a new obligation upon mankind,"[24] stability is increased and the risk of changing equilibria is lessened. "A promise creates a new obligation,"[25] argues Hume, and this supposes that "a new sentiment" has arisen and been codified in that promise.[26] Passion, as a basis for the stability of social convention, can be traced up the scale of forms in terms of layers of governance sanctions and becomes a component of the effort, not only to stabilize the status quo, but to create and confirm alternatives to it. The rule of adjudication is critical in this process as it segregates the valid and relevant law that supports Justice-As-Sovereignty. It also establishes the collective action policy necessary to maintain what Krasner calls "interdependence sovereignty," or "the ability of public authorities to regulate the flow of information, ideas, goods, people, pollutants, or capital across the borders of their state."[27] The obligations and duties created by international governance, given its rule of adjudication, support the persistence of social convention in the public interest by setting expectations of trust that buttress social stability at both municipal and international tiers of organization, while they provide the essence of legal certainty and universality.[28] This certainty in application of the local rule of recognition also requires that trust not only exist internally to the state, but externally in its relationship with other states, especially in the form of the negotiation and agreement to treaty as a source of international law.

The laws of social convention are, in this way, realized by the reinforcement of both morality and law as these evolve more and more effective sanctions for treaty compliance. The evolution of the law from social convention carries with it the idea that law and policy are both processes that find their purpose in the persistence of society itself (i.e., those conventions that empower the human need for community). Political society, government, or less coercive governance structures allow for the creation of law not just in a positive sense, from practice, but, in a moral-metaphysical sense, from the imperatives of sentiment and the obligation of making and keeping promises.

Since the persistence of social convention in law requires both promise and trust, no player wishes to be in a position where they "must never expect to be trusted any more."[29] This type of alienation, especially when backed by the sanctions of justice and legal governance, is a sad fate for any agent assumed to be primarily social. In fact, the full progressive codification of the new law of international contract, which is an expression not only of contract in a private sense but of social contract and the public law necessary to regulate it, is not only the culmination of one sense of social convention, but the point of origin for a much more complex policy space than positivism allows.

The basis for this complexity, given the SPP of progressive codification, is the dynamic balance between process⇆principle that requires sanctions and rules for the persistence of Justice-As-Sovereignty. As social convention is refined on a philosophical scale of forms, it battles the inherent instability of the shifting balance of process⇆principle as society grows in size and complexity. But Hume's philosophical-policy and legal design assumes that the correlative evolution of levels of sanctions and layers of convention can address this conflict through reliance on the progressive codification of Justice-As-Sovereignty.

As we know, Hume's argument for natural law assumes a dialectic between process and principle that gives the former priority as the primary means for the creation of moral, legal, and political imperatives within the international system. Critical principle, unlike contextual principle, has value independent of social convention. Demoted to secondary status within Hume's concept of law, it is only accessible within the system after the creation of governance institutions that can process them. Progressive codification, through formal legal institutions, allows for procedures that grant critical principle the possibility of legitimacy through the policy and legal design process.

The evolution of convention and its process-norms are the initial and the primary means for the evolution of both procedural and substantial rules in society. Initially, convention as the evolution of order from habit and custom was the sole means for the creation of society at the international level, up to the point where governance institutions and an international policy space become possible. With legitimate institutions and laws based on prior social convention, the possibility of a substantive ethics with a reflective or critical law, emerges in full dialectic with the procedural ethics and law of the process-norm of Justice-As-Sovereignty. The role of the rule of adjudication is to assign procedures, through progressive codification, by which substantive rules are created. Within Hume's argument, the status of principles as the substantive ends for the policy and legal process is downplayed, because of their proven propensity to disrupt the social order. Nonetheless, Hume provides for a dynamic system based on a natural law that anticipates the slow synthesis of contextual and critical principle with preexisting process.

Social convention has the capacity to absorb a plurality of values, cultures, and religions by focusing on the process of coordinating society and giving it order rather than any particular substantive or principled end. In this way, social convention trumps critical principle as a source of morality and as a foundation for the evolution of Hume's international legal system. The focus on positive practice and its concern for effective cooperation creates a metaphysics where the procedural means becomes the preferred route for the evolution of moral and legal rules and the legal systems' "end-in-itself."

However, with the creation of governance institutions in international political society, the previous inhibited status of critical principle finds a new policy channel for expression. In international forums of political debate, the jurisprudence of tribunals creates policy and legal rules that include distinct substantive-critical principles. Aetiological-norms or critical principles, unlike contextual principles, arise from reason rather than the passions, and support the transcendence of context and circumstances in the name of a priori ends. These invigorate discourse as alternative, nonconventional points of coordination or new equilibria for international coordination (e.g., *jus cogens* principles).

Justice-As-Sovereignty must adjust and, through its SPPs, synthesize the full potential of both process and principle inherent in the core dialectic. This is accomplished through a reordering of its synthesis priorities, so that justice gains complexity with a growing and more codified legal system. But the process also demonstrates the disruptive quality of critical principle because its substantive ends can only be sustained if decision-makers are willing to transgress process in order to uphold them. Critical principle is focused only on its substantive end, necessary to the character of the principle, as opposed to the validity or stability of the coordination process or its equilibrium. As Hume's logic of concepts suggests, the risk of disturbance to social convention is greatly increased with the introduction of critical principle into the policy space.

As de facto possession becomes de jure through the application of the laws gleaned from social convention and their progressive codification, the rise of critical principle becomes the most considerable legal design threat to the peace and order of society provided by social convention. Justice-As-Sovereignty, although able to counteract the size and complexity problems inherent in the evolution of social convention, achieved dominance because critical principle was inhibited by the power of social convention to create order and stabilize society.

Because critical principle has been demoted to a secondary source of norms, at least until governance through political society or contract-by-convention arises, social convention has flourished with a relatively simpler idea of sovereignty. Critical principle is an external threat because, unlike size and complexity inherent to the passion for society protected by Justice-As-Sovereignty, critical principle requires rebalancing the reason⇆passions dialectic in favor of the former, which erodes the absolute presupposition of Hume's concept of law. Critical principle exists to measure social convention and change it. It provides a distinct and dialectic source of moral approbation, justice, and law that can both transcend and judge process, but also has the imperative to do so.

The evolution of a rule of adjudication based upon the SPP of progressive codification creates governance institutions from an initial, established point of coordination chosen from a number of possibilities, such as the selection and maintenance of the Papal System as an international coordination equilibrium. The stability of this definition of international society is maintained first within the social convention of Justice-As-Sovereignty, and, second, by dispositive law with the advent of formal governance institutions. At some point, however, a status quo equilibrium may no longer command the allegiance necessary for its persistence. Then local interaction on another alternative coordination equilibrium may begin to gain force. Through signaling and other interaction dynamics, an alternative point of coordination may gain the sanction of approbation as an alternative definition of justice.

The alternative may be another process-norm that has been acknowledged as more effective at maintaining stability in international society. If so, then the gradual defection from the status quo norm and movement to the alternative will be disruptive but less violent and therefore less troublesome. But the alternative might also be based on an aetiological-norm or critical principle, for example, when equality called for desegregation of the United States in the 1960s. Internationally, disruption would follow the full elevation of universal jurisdiction as an *erga omnes* obligation or the classification of the precautionary principle as jus cogens. In these cases, the transcendence of the established process by critical principle rather than a process-norm is more disruptive to the status quo. In what could be a revolutionary scenario, the environment of trust and promise-keeping created by conventional process may not be enough to halt the serious interruption of social cohesion.

In either case, but especially with the evolutionary replacement of one process-norm with another, the same conventions of promise-keeping and trust will be used to lessen the risk of defection from one equilibrium and allegiance to another. In effect, Justice-As-Sovereignty can be rebalanced to adjust through the reorientation of its metaphysics; its SPPs. The task of the governance system is to maintain the persistence of Justice-As-Sovereignty, making changes with as little disruption to the social order of the society as possible.

It may not be possible to manage these critical principles so that they cause minimal disruption, but a convention-based international system will try nonetheless. The imperative of a process-based system of convention is to make any transition to an alternative equilibrium as stable as possible. This is of less concern when one process-norm is replacing another as a theory of justice for the coordination of social order. All process-norms are based on procedural rules of reciprocity and support the background conditions of social convention, as this is beneficial to both the status quo and alternative equilibria. The intransigence of social convention is in the human predisposition to think that there is no aetiological imperative to replace a process-norm and no reason to override a stable systemic process that is generally necessary to social persistence.

Critical principle, on the other hand, has its aetiological character in either want- or ideal-regarding ends that do not necessarily benefit from the existing system of coordination protected by social convention. The imperative of a critical principle is to realize its end, and this may very well require the disintegration of the status quo process. For example, the Protestant Reformation required the dissolution of much of the property and moral priority of the International Papal System for the realization of its ends.

In the case of the critical principles driving the Reformation, this revolutionary shift was too fast for the Papal equilibrium to protect itself and it was not until the end of the Thirty Years War that the circumstances of the peace created an alternative possibility for the rise of process to replace critical principle as the core of the Westphalian Equilibrium. This new point of coordination for the international system, because it indicated the replacement of critical religious principle with neutral process, evolved over many decades, struggling with and adjusting to uncertainty and a lack of universality. In the end, a new point of departure for international governance was created. A new coordination convention, Justice-As-Sovereignty, came to be valued both physically, by creating stability and order out of war, and metaphysically, by focusing on the normative priority of process that could accommodate a pluralism of critical ends at a local level.

Whatever level of centralization or complexity the international governance structure may now have, Hume's philosophical-policy draws a firm line for the law's point of origin. Specifically, within Hume's philosophical framework, codified law originates with contract-by-convention (i.e., governance institutions). Although legal norms may have roots in social convention or critical moral principle, it is through the advent of contract-by-convention and a formal rule of adjudication as progressive codification that the power of the dialectic between process⇆principle is engaged. Only at this point in the evolution of sanctions are rules and rights institutionally codified by the governance structures set up to operationalize them.

Since Hume's natural law is a process-based conception where aetiological principles are the slaves of the passions, in order for critical principle to compete it needs a government and a legal design space. Practically, this requires the evolution of social convention to stabilize the fundamental social predisposition of humanity. With approbation, justice, and the artifice of politicians established, natural law as regulative moral principle can then move from the status of personal moral principle to collective legal principle, then legal norm, and then legal right or rule dispositive in specific cases.[30]

Hume's concept of law establishes social convention as the foundation for both municipal and international legal constructions and the core unit of all progressive codification on all levels of social organization. Therefore, social convention and the legal process-norm it renders have a distinct moral weight and persuasive advantage in legal and political argument. They reflect the point of departure for social evolution itself and set the expectations of individuals and collective entities for the evolution of the system, even before the advent of conscious governance.

With the advent of legal governance as the ultimate layer of sanction for the stability of the international system, the focus of governance institutions becomes the SPP of progressive codification and the creation of a system of adjudication that can regulate the synthesis of process⇆principle so that Justice-As-Sovereignty can persist. This synthesis will have conscious contract in policy choice as an additional tool for the progressive codification of international law. The codification of contract as promise in treaty law can further stabilize the obligations and duties connected to the establishment of trust within a social milieu protecting the coordination equilibrium while seeking the essence of Justice-As-Sovereignty on its scale of forms.

From this exposition of the progressive codification of social convention in governance, Hume's legal design leads us to expect that the origins of treaty law lie in decentralized moral obligation, public duty, and a definition of promising that sets expectations and establishes trust. The metaphysical elements of *real consent* or the importance of the social conventions of promising in the decision of a state to negotiate toward the establishment of better relations are emphasized by his logic of concepts. The first manifestation may be through informal, then diplomatic contact, then by negotiations moving toward a set of arbitration conventions.[31] Eventually, more formal legal agreements on specific topics, suggested by the need to stabilize social convention, will gain consent, and obligations to these promises will accrue set expectations about what a state's legal interests are and how its sovereignty is defined.

The voluntary actions of states, in the approbation stage of social convention, is policed in a trial and error method as part of the "civilized" or diplomatic behavior of states. Focusing on the particular process-norm of Justice-As-Sovereignty, more formal, private promise-keeping becomes available as a tool of legal design. With contract-by-convention, full codification of promise in public contract eventually produces a contract regime for the creation and persistence of "legitimate" treaties.[32] Progressive codification as a rule of adjudication, not only charts the evolution of treaty from custom and custom from principle but also explains why large and complex multilateral treaties only become possible when built on a substructure of more private (i.e., state-to-state) promising and the trust that evolves, conventionally, from this experience with smaller and less complex bilateral relations.

> Many conventions that cover substantial groups or populations are built up out of dyadic or very small number interactions....Most of the conventions Hume and Lewis discuss...are built out of dyadic and small-number interactions.[33]

Procedural rules of recognition and adjudication evolve within a state and secure municipal society by progressively compensating for growing size and complexity. The evolution of such procedural rules for the international system will ultimately depend on the corresponding response of its governance systems to progressively more complex roles for law in the stabilization of international society. With contract-by-convention, the institutions of governance and the parameters for negotiation become possible. At this point, treaty is added to principle and custom, as sources of legal rules codifying social convention. Simultaneously, the process-norm of Justice-As-Sovereignty grants legitimacy to the consent of a state, its obligation to promises, and its duty to keep those promises within codified bilateral and multilateral treaties.

During this evolution, the practice of states as supported by Justice-As-Sovereignty will focus on consent as a manifestation of promise and an expression of the process-norm of justice. The principle of consent in support of convention, however, should not be mistaken for a critical principle. Although many international scholars characterize the pertinent governance principle as consent defining justice,[34] Hume's philosophical-policy defines justice in terms of social convention, where the instrumental value of consent as a contextual principle is reduced to that required by said social conventions for their persistence. Justice-As-Sovereignty is not dependent on consent, but vice versa.

This is confirmed in the creation of an international strategic environment where the physical payoffs of choice are undergirded by a metaphysical system of obligations, duty, and trust, created by the imperative for social stability to support Justice-As-Sovereignty and its underlying conventional process. Real consent and the duty to perform promises has long been a core concept in international law. *Pacta sunt servanda*[35] is also a core element of Hume's philosophy.[36] This contextual principle of treaty law has meaning only to the extent that it is built on the preexistence of social convention;

it also contains a moral obligation because it empowers the passion for stability in the persistence of Justice-As-Sovereignty as it faces an ever-more complex and evolving international society.[37]

Within Hume's concept of law, treaties, as creatures of social convention, should be judged by the process-norm of Justice-As-Sovereignty, which will initially emphasize *in dubio mitius* or that interpretation of the treaty most favorable to the stability of the Westphalian Equilibrium.[38] An international system of Humean convention should also be anticipated to protect Justice-As-Sovereignty and its coordination equilibrium in terms of a liberal system of treaty reservations. Assuming that most reservations are about critical principle, a liberal system of reservations is recommended[39] because the priority for Justice-As-Sovereignty is wide subscription to a treaty, or its point of equilibrium, not the vindication of particular substantive ends. With a metaphysical focus on the stability of international society, a more open system of reservations encourages participation and submission to the rules and expectations of the international system. Here the substantive quality of that cooperation is of less importance to the maintenance of coordination and can await more mature governance institutions.

Overall, the governance process, within Hume's philosophical-policy and legal design, has an adjudication rule of progressive codification that characterizes international law as a more dynamic system of governance possibilities than positivism allows. Hume's paradigm also grounds a state's consent in metaphysical standards supplied through the SPPs of Justice-As-Sovereignty, and motivated by the absolute presupposition of humanity's passion for society.

International society must persist and progress along the scale of forms toward its essence. Hume's idea of natural law invokes a local rule of recognition defined by the SPP of effectiveness in the establishment of certainty and the inhibition of critical principle. Applying Hume to the rise of international governance institutions suggests the need for a rule of adjudication framed by the SPP of progressive codification to meet and integrate, to the extent possible, the rise of critical principle in legal design. This procedural law creates a dynamic system of governance alternatives and culminates in contract-by-convention, treaty law, and the persistence of social convention in the legitimate settlement of disputes within Hume's international "political society."

II. Legal Design Implications for Policy Investigation: The Delineation of Procedural and Critical Legal Systems

When the institutions of governance and the procedural rule of adjudication are established, the discourse of politics expands to include not only social convention and its process-norm of Justice-As-Sovereignty but critical principle in Hume's secondary path to the law (see Figure 2.1). By the introduction of critical principle to the preexisting process-norm created by social convention, a new, more intricate, design space is created. At this point the metaphysics of Justice-As-Sovereignty has the potential for a second prominent stage of complexity (what G. W. F. Hegel called "moments") on its scale of forms. The logic of policy investigation, that is, the legal design space, must now adapt given the possibility of this new "moment."

The first moment occurs when sovereignty as social convention moves from informal practice to formal law as the dominant representative of the process⇆principle dialectic. The second moment occurs when critical principles seek a rebalance of this asymmetry and Justice-As-Sovereignty responds to maintain its status within the cooperative process. These distinct levels of complexity are caused by the dynamic or dialectic nature of Hume's concept of sovereignty as social convention. A more detailed analysis of these two moments is necessary if progressive codification is to be a meaningful contributor to the metaphysical complexity of Justice-As-Sovereignty.

With the progressive development of social convention and the resulting dynamic of justice, rules are focused on the persistence of the process of cooperation and are therefore generative of procedural rules of recognition, adjudication, and change. But, recalling Hart's assertion that the transition to a legal system requires both procedural and substantive rules, an initial basis for those substantive rules is required that is not based on critical principle, because these standards must await the advent of contract-by-convention to become part of the governance structure.

As we discovered while solving Vitoria's dilemma in the previous chapter, by making the universal dimension of international law process-based, and therefore creating stability with procedural rules, the Humean concept of law allows substantive norms to find meaning within the context of local or contextual convention. Because the international legal system at this first moment of complexity originates in a procedural common law, the need for substantive norms and rules by progressive codification must also be contextual.

Hume's natural law does not have to provide universal substantive norms. This is an advantage. Rather, substantive norms and rules from within Hume's logic of concepts are left to regional or more local contexts and draw duty from religion, tradition, culture, or other normative components of one's circumstances of justice. The only requirement of Hume's argument is that these conventionally-based substantive rules do not interfere with the overall process of social cooperation, which is assured by their remaining primarily cultural or contextual. In this way, the progressive codification of international law remains primarily procedural where any substantive rules are also contextual to social convention within a universal sense of obligation to the process of joint coordination. These contextual "primary rules"[40] only play a minor role in a universal "overlapping consensus"[41] of generally cooperative values.

On the other hand, with the establishment of policymaking through contract-by-convention and the imperative for progressive codification, the ability to consciously design law through political means becomes possible. In addition to the unconscious creation and behavioral reaffirmation of social convention through the process-norm of Justice-As-Sovereignty, practical reason can also be defined in terms of independently justifiable aetiological-norms in legal design discourse. In a fuller realization of Hume's dialectic between passion and reason, *prior* ends (e.g., equality, freedom) deciphered by the latter can now be used to argue for critical principle in legal design through a dialectic or critical analysis of existing social convention. This eventuality is not fully recognized within Hume's philosophical-policy, but its contingencies are clear. If the passions are to continue to enslave reason, Justice-As-Sovereignty, or the process-norm protecting the social equilibrium, must become progressively more complex to inhibit critical principle or absorb it. Within the legal design system, sovereignty must not only blunt the increasing role of critical principle in assessing and even replacing social convention as an imperative of international law but also adapt to it.

Because of the evolutionary-progressive characteristic of the rule of adjudication, Hume's concept of law requires a more sophisticated, or second, level of complexity in its scale of forms. After all, the law must now evolve from a model that contains no critically-reasoned principles to one that does: from a one-path model of Hume's concept of law focused on convention, to the full two-path model that includes critical principle as a second foundation for law (Figure 2.1). This requires the description of a two-stage model of the legal system that can accommodate the evolving dialectic balance between process⇆principle.

Initially, the process⇆principle dialectic is drastically asymmetrical: reason is the slave of the passions. Social convention determines not only the parameters of process but the contextual product of substantive principle; both are determined by their relationship to Justice-As-Sovereignty. For example, currently the substantive principle of self-determination is defined contextually by Justice-As-Sovereignty through the "safeguard clause" to mean only the self-determination of "peoples" not significantly discriminated against by their sovereign state.[42] If self-determination were based on critical principle, self-determination would be connected to humanity in both its individual and social manifestations, independent of Justice-As-Sovereignty.

As order is established and certainty reinstituted, political society creates procedural channels for policy discourse and legal design. Critical principle is made prominent by the fact that human focus can shift to specific universal ends that are aetiological, containing inherent moral causality (e.g., freedom, equality, human rights). Through progressive codification, critical principle gains distinction and sufficient force to challenge social convention and balance the preexisting dialectic asymmetry. In the evolution of law as social convention, even with the advent of contract-by-convention, the law remains primarily about the synthesis of governance structures, based on the ability of social convention to be primary and prior to critical principle.

Social convention creates the procedural common law that allows for the formalization or codification of the law; the foundation of social convention has pride of place in policy argument and legal design, even with the challenge of critical principle.

What changes in the two-stage Humean concept of law is the dynamic quality of the dialectic and its synthesis product. Legal governance, dependent on the advent of contract-by-convention, creates the opportunity for both moral pathways to the law to have identity and provide access to power through the legal design process (Figure 2.1). With this phase of progressive codification, a definition of practical reason formerly dominated by the passions can now free reason from its "slave" status. Through the creation of critical norms and substantive rules for obligation, critical principle will provide further complexity to the metaphysical sophistication of the process-norm of Justice-As-Sovereignty. This proffers another level of legal complexity suggested by Hume's philosophical-policy: an evolutionary intricacy that implies a concept of law larger and more dynamic than Hart's positivist vision.

The legal geography of Hume's argument for Justice-As-Sovereignty, therefore, has levels of convention for both municipal and international systems with interdependent stages of sanctions and different descriptions of the strategic situations at both municipal and international levels of social organization. This evolutionary, dialectic scale of forms makes Hume's integrated system compatible with a complex and multifaceted legal design space. Explicitly, from the perspective of Hume's philosophical-policy, the institutional governance structure and its adjudication norms are responsible for the support and persistence of an ever more dynamic conventional process, as well as for the stability of an evolving and increasingly complex social order. Under these circumstances, Hume's "artifice of politicians" would not be limited to a system of decentralized or minimal sanctions but, with a more truly engaged dialectic between process⇆principle, policy and legal design is given the potential to create a more centralized polity, adequate to the new complexity of the international social order.

Through Hume's concept of law, a policy space contains basic political institutions that take an initial *idea* and the *characteristics of a public issue*, and process them, as policy argument, though a series of steps that include *political choice* by a set of legitimate rules of recognition, bureaucratic *production* of primary rules and regulations, and *final government action* with its resultant *real world outcomes*, all contained within a recognized system of legitimate adjudication.[43] In addition, the complexity of Hume's evolving scale of forms offers a more complex, inherent, moral content that is a combination of the process-norm of sovereignty, contextual principle, and aetiological-norms or critical principles. All are necessary to understanding how the passions continue to create and reinforce social convention and the sanctions to insure them in the face of independent-critical principle.

This set of contingencies requires a more complex definition of the legal design space than is normal from within positivist legal theory or established policy science. Traditionally, it is argued that, within the policy space, the political creation of law is a second-best alternative.[44] A core precept of policy science is that the decision-making necessary to collective choice is best done under one of two precedents. The preferred alternative is to leave the public choice to the private sector, in a market for goods, services, or risks that require only minimal, background legal institutions and can exist with minimal social conventions, even in a prelaw state-of-affairs. The second-best alternative is to allow the "artifice of politicians" to address public choice, but only to the extent that the governance infrastructure is used to mimic what the market would do if it could make the decision.[45] The first option suggests the privatization of public goods and collective action functions. The second offers the methodology of Kaldor efficiency and cost-benefit analysis to empower market choice and create market outcomes through public governance decision-making.[46]

Traditional policy analysis, like legal positivism, assumes a unitary decision-maker and is most comfortable with the retrospective examination of choice. Using technical assumptions, "value-free" science, and mathematics, benefit-cost methods assess policy choice where markets are the preferred allocation mechanism.[47] This school of thought rejects philosophical method and, instead, uses observation, strict classification of concepts, induction, and eristic, rather than dialectic, argument.[48]

However, when viewed comparatively with Hume's philosophical-policy, traditional market positivism provides an impoverished picture of the legal design space. First, Hume emphasizes the public nature of his definitions of interest, utility, and social convention.[49] Although social convention is created by repeated private interactions, this is merely a starting place for Hume's argument; it has no inherent prerogative, either moral or legal. The private need for the public security of society is the absolute presupposition of Hume's argument. This precludes anything but a temporary concern for private market allocation or distribution.

The stabilization of property, for example, is required, not because of a priority for private wealth generation, or to increase any one person's benefits over costs, but for the order, security, and stability of the social or public space. Critical to Hume's argument is that the process-norm of justice is a creature of public utility, as its artificial status requires it to be.[50] Justice is enacted in the public interest of a stable social order. The "social" character of convention distinguishes it and makes both informal rules and codified law susceptible to moral obligation.

Next, Hume's progressive codification of the law, over levels of sanctions, finds ultimate form, not in economic markets, but in government.[51] Commerce will arise before government, as the existence of justice, its conventions, and a stable society set the background for the rise of markets.[52] But markets cannot protect social convention as society expands and becomes more complex. For Hume, only the public institutions of "political society" are capable, over the long term, of empowering public utility drawn from the passion for society and social order.

Hume also depends on dialectic argument as the vehicle for his concept of law and its progressive codification. As I have established, he argues for a *moral-legal-science* of man. The decision-maker is required to account for the overlap of concepts, the presuppositions of philosophical method, the categorical nature of the concepts, and the synthesis of a total system derived from dialectically related components.[53]

The philosophical method used to decipher Hume's philosophical-policy employs legal design, not only for retrospective analysis, but for the prospective formulation of public policies that support social convention and its collective utility in a dynamic and multistage legal system. This adds an *ex ante* argument to an *ex post* analysis as the responsibility of officials and suggests that changing manifestations of the circumstances of justice require distinct actions and reactions on their part, all relative to the universal standard of Justice-As-Sovereignty. To represent the public interest requires that markets be understood and considered as an option for legal design, but only to the degree that markets can empower the passion for society by supporting Justice-As-Sovereignty.[54] In assessing a potential policy argument, economic, scientific, and technical data are evidence for the analysis and formulation of legal design alternatives; they are not the core, nor the priority, of the argument itself.

Given the logic of Hume's philosophical-policy, the passions create sentiments and these spark human agency. This is the core of the legal design process, both unofficially, in terms of the evolution of habit into custom into social convention into Justice-As-Sovereignty, and officially, with the advent of a formal governance system to sanction the persistence of established order, with codified law. Overall, Hume's argument exhibits an essential distrust of private choice and self-interest. Only their mutation, through dialectic synthesis, makes them suitable for the public purposes served by the rise and persistence of social convention.[55]

Legal design requires an awareness of the metaphysical context as well as the empirical circumstances of any policy issue, how it relates to human passions, and how it can advance, and be advanced by, Justice-As-Sovereignty. The evolution of social convention, and its escalating sanctions, are in dialectical relation to these circumstance; the law is rendered as a means to justice, requiring that policy analysis and legal design be flexible. The focus on process and against principle also requires that any "one-size-fits-all" methodology, like benefit-cost, be rejected.

Legal design also requires that philosophical argument take precedence over quantitative analysis and that persuasion becomes the ultimate test of a legal choice, rather than its cost-benefit ratio. In creating a synthesis solution for the dialectic between ideas, the legal designer fulfills his public responsibility through an awareness of the proper metaphysics of an issue in addition to its economic parameters. One focuses not just on what "is" but what "ought" to be.

Legal design is concerned with both the ends of a policy and the various means that can be employed to reach those ends. Adaptable to the creation of law from both process and principle (i.e., both contextual and critical), legal design is charged with the dialectic integration of both intrinsic and instrumental values. Using scientific, economic, and sociopolitical facts legal design produces a persuasive policy argument that presents reasonable choices to the public.[56] By transcending retrospective market analysis, legal design provides greater capacity to account for the complexity and uncertainty inherent in a dynamic and progressively evolving design space. In so doing, the legitimate adjudication process is better able to protect law as social convention from a variety of threats.

The evolutionary scale of forms for Justice-As-Sovereignty requires a design process that accommodates change within a fluid metaphysical environment. No assumptions give priority to any particular static context or principle. This allows for the use of philosophical method to create a seamless argument, both in terms of the dialectic between process⇆principle and the transition between local, national, and international governance.

Legal design requires that one consider multiple allocation and distribution systems. Here, government can sort issues into their best institutional setting determining the proper allocation mechanism to support progressive, that is, adaptable, synthesis solutions to the process⇆principle dialectic. Philosophical-policy and legal design recognizes that collective action and the decisions that empower it are not an exact, or even experimental, science, but philosophical subject-matter dependent on the employment of metaphysical paradigms. These paradigms add to and enrich concepts of value, expand choice beyond strictly private markets, and recognize multiple institutional contexts as legitimate avenues for the creation and implementation of the law. They do so by promoting multiple political avenues for allocation rather than maintaining a total reliance and deference to market models, means, and ends.

While the initial legal status of social convention on the international level may be contained within a decentralized and voluntary system of compliance backed by moral obligations, this minimal institutional configuration only scratches the surface of the design space. The definition of a "reasonable" legal structure for the interpretation of a strategic situation, its inherent values, and the needs of society within these will change with the imperative of progressive codification.

Explicitly, Hume focuses not on custom as a prelegal stage of social order, but on social *convention*, with its specific requirements and ramifications. Before the advent of contract-by-convention, social convention establishes a coordinated social order based on approbation and Justice-As-Sovereignty as prelegal governance sanctions. With contract-by-convention, the creation of a more complex legal design space becomes possible and codified law can be added to preexisting practice. General or customary international law, in fact, offers a reservoir of practice for this purpose.

International customary law, as a legal design component derived from Hume's philosophical-policy, can be conceptualized as a transitional legal source for principle (both contextual and critical) seeking codification as treaty law. Customary international law is a gatekeeper for a multistage international legal system that must be capable of adjudicating in a progressively more complex environment. Even though the initial development of international governance is through informal rules and practice determined by the passion for society and its social conventions, this pool of customary international law soon becomes the basis for those values to be recognized in other sources of law. This is the point of departure for Hume's two-stage concept of law.

With the distinct rules generated when law is first established, Chthonic prelegal systems evolve into convention-based legal systems where process-norms determine both procedural and substantive (i.e., contextual) rules. I will designate this first level or moment of complexity for progressive codification as a *Functional Stage-I Procedural Legal System*.

Justice-As-Sovereignty focuses primarily on the creation of procedural rules of recognition, adjudication, and change, and those contextual principles that support the preestablished conventional processes that have, heretofore, stabilized international society. By entering the legal design space, social convention is codified through contract-by-convention in a legal environment where the sole universal consideration is the achievement of a cooperative process as an end in itself.

At this stage, progressive codification initiates a dialectic that integrates process and contextual principle for the objective of empowering social convention through the transition from moral to legal obligation. Law as contract-by-convention is preoccupied with the "process" of the process⇆principle dialectic. The principles that exist as law are not critical principles that threaten process, but contextual principles that are a "slave" to the requirements of Justice-As-Sovereignty and the rules of procedure derived from codified social convention. At the international level, these contextual principles would be those that primarily exist in order to create an overlapping consensus of local values (e.g., nonintervention, good faith, self-defense).[57] Traditionally, these support the effective control of territory, the progressive codification of social convention, and the peaceful coexistence of states, allowing only changes that reinforce the established "sovereign" definition of justice-as-order.

However, this is insufficient in terms of the continued evolution of Hume's concept of law. With the introduction of governance institutions by contract-by-convention, Hume's philosophical-policy creates a dynamic and evolutionary idea of law on a scale of forms. The design of international law empowers the secondary normative path for the formulation of law: critical principle. Although the subjugation of principle to process is the point of departure for the Humean legal system, the layers of sanctions created in support of social convention are also the means for critical principle to begin its own evolution to equal status within the process⇆principle dialectic.

A second level of metaphysical complexity enhanced by aetiological-norms, and their substantive-critical rules, is now a possibility within the legal design space. With a more fully engaged process⇆principle dialectic, reason and the passions must find a new synthesis, through a rebalancing of the SPPs, in order to maintain international social order. With critical-substantive principle to challenge contextual-substantive principle, we have the full manifestation of the dialectic of progressive codification. The rule of adjudication attempts to maintain order while satisfying both the needs of established social convention and the aspirations of critical arguments for rights and rules based on aetiological-norms.

This more complex set of dialectic interactions creates additional stress on legal adjudication norms and transforms a Stage-I Procedural Legal System into a *Stage-II Critical Legal System.* At Stage-II, progressive codification addresses dialectics between the prior conventional or contextual creation of substantive rules and new substantive rules from critical principle. This adds a new complication to both the internal and external definitions of the SPP. Adjudication procedures strive to maintain the stability of international society for the *internal* codification of moral principles to legal principles, legal norms, and then to dispositive rights and rules. Adjudication also stabilizes the *external* progression from principle to custom to treaty, as critical principle challenges the hegemony of the established coordination equilibrium.

Explicitly, external progression is initially rendered by Hume's theory of natural law within a context of a predominantly procedural common law. Social convention as the foundation of natural law is vital in its use as a moral justification for a progressively more refined and legally multifaceted move from Stage-I to Stage-II. Social convention also plays a role in the evolution of compensating levels of governance as layers of sanctions are created through contract-by-convention to stabilize an increasingly more complex social context. The existence of an institutional legal design space, initiated by the advent of contract-by-convention, began with an idea of a legal system where *aetiological-norms*, and the *critical principles* deduced from them, were a secondary normative foundation for international law. In Stage-II, the secondary path to law seeks equal primary status as a component of persuasive policy argument.

With contract-by-convention and more complex forms of governance, *ends* for cooperation, in addition to the *means* of cooperation, become critical components of legal design. Rendering substantive norms from critical reason, in addition to procedural and substantive contextual norms from the passions, requires that the legal design process work with an increasingly complex conceptualization of both internal and external progressive codification. As an empirical system of law fully adapts to the process⇆principle dialectic, its adjudication rules and governance structures, created to mediate the continued role of Justice-As-Sovereignty, are more absolutely tested.

Progressive codification occurs both externally (i.e., principle to custom to treaty), and internally (i.e., practical reason as passion to practical reason as critical principle). Meanwhile, as Hume's concept of law assumes, international society is growing in size and complexity. Overall, this is a much more dynamic idea of law than the positivist conceptualization. Instead of a simple theory of interstate consent, we have a dialectic and more complex normative base for the law growing from, and created to protect, the existence of international society through a complex metaphysical concept of Justice-As-Sovereignty.

The concept of law deciphered from Hume's philosophical-policy builds on the logic of his theory of natural law, but also extends this theory to incorporate *prior* principle as a lesser component of the conventional foundations of law. Throughout his writings, Hume concentrates on the conventional roots of law and policy. He considers the existence of human coordination to protect societal cohesion to be so important that he all but ignores the role of critical principle. However, he does acknowledge its existence in relation to the passions, and within his dialectic of practical reason. This gives his concept of law a more complete natural law foundation than either positivism, which rejects natural law totally, or traditional laws of nature that are based on revelation or less-than-universal critical principles. Hume's philosophical-policy allows a more complete picture of the international legal system both at its origins, where social convention is dominant, and into contemporary times, where critical principle, focused on ends rather than means, is a major component of our empirical landscape. A concept of law that cannot synthesize social convention with human rights, erga omnes obligations, and jus cogens principles, is of less utility to the practice of contemporary international dispute settlement.

That Hume downplayed the role of critical principle is understandable. As we have seen in the last chapter, Hume created his philosophical system at a time when *prior* principle, based on Catholic revelation, had caused much social disintegration and conflict. In contrast, Hume described an evolution of law that focused on the human need for society and the social conventions created by the process of interaction and cooperation. This means, or process-oriented, approach to creating a society with justice and legal governance adequately provided the "true" metaphysics for Hume's origin story of the nature of human social life. His logic deciphers the genesis of law in human nature. This requires the argument to focus on the creation and empowerment of social convention as it allows for long-term social stability and certainty for humanity.

Hume's philosophical-policy is not ideal but empirical, not prescriptive but descriptive. The role of ideal-regarding principle is initially eclipsed by process and social convention; this is what Hume considers historical. But reason still exists as a dialectic component of the process⇆principle interaction. Hume's description of the advent of contract-by-convention and the creation of political society offers a legal design space in which critical principle eventually can play a larger role. This topology may not be fully mapped by Hume, but the key exists in the core dialectic of his legal process.

Hume's philosophical-policy begins with the premise that a system of social practice evolving from unconscious behavior to social convention to a process-norm of justice, and then to governance with contract-by-convention, is the primary model of the legal system. This legal system can exist and persist without much input from critical principle. Hume's core argument about the law is that a convention-based system is both necessary and sufficient for the genesis of the rule of law.

The Stage-I level of complexity is *functional* because it provides the means to the stabilization of humanity's need for society while it disdains critical ends or principle as disruptive to social cohesion. It is *procedural* because means are promoted over ends and ends are made conditional on the persistence of the means of coordination. This primary legal system contains the first moment on the scale of forms for the metaphysical essence of sovereignty where its SPPs define the dominance of process over principle within the law.

Effectiveness is the foundation of this model in terms of the efficacy of the idea of social convention, which, as we have argued, differentiates it from custom. Social convention and the process-norm of Justice-As-Sovereignty, forms the core of Hume's argument because of its effectiveness. The establishment of coordination and its stability at equilibrium allows Justice-As-Sovereignty to reach a standard of effectiveness necessary for its regulation of international law. Social convention is effective because it provides primary legal systems that ensure a stable social life.

With the advent of government, or international governance and the full engagement of the process⇆principle dialectic, legal design provides a more complex normative framework for the SPP of progressive codification as the rule of adjudication for the evolving international legal system. As previously described, progressive codification, has both an *external* and an *internal* definition within Hume's philosophical-policy. In its Stage-I manifestation, the legal system stresses the internal progression of the law.

First, a nonlegal or informal precept or standard of human behavior finds its origin in a *moral principle* or *social convention*. These precepts exist outside the field of international legal practice but within the field of philosophical discourse where idea-generation and argument, as well as legal design, determine those precepts that move into the legal structure and those that do not.

At this point, the social convention is a moral precept not yet included in binding or nonbinding international law, but which does appear in preparatory material (*travaux préparatoires*) for international conferences, meetings, proceedings, or in international policy debate about rights, rules, and proper adjudication. Moral principles figure in the formation of legal argument as the resulting debate sorts out more persuasive precepts for eventual establishment in law.

Next, the nonlegal precept enters the field of legal practice by its adoption as a *legal principle* that can be defined as a normative precept. Legal principles appear in domestic and international binding and nonbinding agreements as well as international treaties and institutional mandates. A legal principle can be critical or contextual and used to create or coordinate an organizational/institutional framework through the generation of structures including commissions, conferences of the parties, and treaty-based secretariats.

Hume's philosophical-policy requires contextual principles before critical ones. Contextual legal principles are a type of moral principle that take their content from the conventions that create them. While they are substantive (focused on ends) rather than procedural (focused on means), they are also characterized by their local and conventional content, which comes from context, or the common values that support the persistence of social convention, Justice-As-Sovereignty, and its Westphalian Equilibrium. For example, the international principle of "domestic jurisdiction" as described in the United Nations Charter[58] speaks to both a general contextual principle that supports Justice-As-Sovereignty and the protection of local values by the social conventions of the international system.

When a precept exists as a legal principle within the field of legal practice, it can then become a *legal norm*, in the way that international social convention created the norm of Justice-As-Sovereignty. An informal coordination principle outside the field of legal practice evolves into a legal norm accepted into general practice inside that field. Within this basic model of the legal system, a process-norm is a concept that not only appears as a contextual principle in legal discourse and institutions, but has also been consciously accepted by a sizable number of states and international agents as creating a binding legal obligation either through treaty or customary law. Here, the procedural social convention has already informed substantive contextual principle in order to acquire sufficient backing to spread its influence more widely. The acknowledgment of states that a particular principle is both a part of legal discourse and also an accepted part of the general practice of states, and perhaps even customary international law, grants a "principle" the status of a "norm."[59]

With contract-by-convention creating the means for the transition between informal social convention and formal legal practice, progressive codification can complete its transformation and a norm can become a *dispositive legal right or rule* within the field of legal practice. In the same way that codified treaty can be declaratory of custom, legal norms can generate positive law with responsibilities and obligations that are dispositive in specific facts situations. This positive law of rules and rights requires effective core institutions for implementation, enforcement, and dispute settlement that transform a moral precept into a legal norm that codifies informal rules of recognition and adjudication. This allows for the stabilization of larger and more complex societies while reflecting the moral standards of social convention in the positive law. The general, acknowledged acceptance of a legal norm grants stability and weight to rules generated in a Stage-I international legal system.

With the existence of rules from norms based on legal principles derived from social convention, the metaphysical or *internal* definition of progressive codification, within Hume's legal system, is established. In terms of the *external* or positive definition of progressive codification, legal practice and the governance of contract-by-convention provide a practical arena for the expression of the process-norm of Justice-As-Sovereignty by the transformation of international legal principle into customary law and then treaty. This codification ladder sanctifies any idea that responds to the standard of Justice-As-Sovereignty as it regulates the influence of dispositive rules and rights based upon the stability requirements of international society.

In Stage-II, the external dimension of progressive codification complicates the international rule of law. In the interaction of principle, custom, and treaty it allows governance institutions to promote substantive, inherent, and universal ends deciphered by the application of practical reason as critical principle (e.g., human rights, environmental integrity). In this way, for the first time, principle in law is not only contextual but critical and capable, through progressive codification, of trumping process in the synthesis of the legal design dialectic. Critical moral principle has its source in either revelation or reason; both become active in relation to the preexistence of social convention and its procedural and contextually-substantive rules. Critical "moral" principle is generated by the existence of *prior* conventional legal practice, but enters the field of formal law by becoming a component of the legal design process that challenges rather than supports those social conventions. Critical principle has the potential to become, like social convention before it, legal principle, then a legal aetiological-norm and then dispositive rights and rules in international law, all through the adjudication process created by progressive codification.

The Stage-II system occurs at a moment of progressive codification where social convention and its roots in the passion for society are tested by critical principle derived from the universal ends of moral agency.[60] For example, a moral concern for human dignity such as a duty to stop genocide may be suggested within the international legal design process as a critical consideration vis-à-vis a conventional concern for the *Lotus* sovereignty of a state. In a Stage-II legal system, agents must process the critical rights claim by re-sorting the dialectics inherent in the concept of sovereignty, without losing the primary concern for the persistence of collective action and Justice-As-Sovereignty. Because of the complex dialectical nature of sovereignty, the predisposition toward a conventional synthesis solution may retard critical principle, but cannot remove it from constant and persistent claims on the progressive codification process. Critical principles, as in the *Plessey* and *South West Africa* cases, take time to infiltrate the metaphysics of a dominant process-norm, effecting a new balance of dialectics and creating a new synthesis for legal design.

However, in Stage-II, the status of the international community's duty to human dignity as a moral concern may utilize the external hierarchy for progressive codification and blossom into a critical legal principle that has the potential to be more generally accepted and obligatory as a norm of customary international law or the subject of a treaty. With the establishment of critical principle in international law, the ongoing dialectic between process⇆principle creates a new moment for sovereignty on its scale of forms. This allows decision-makers to use the adjudication process, not only to continue the protection of the Westphalian Equilibrium, but increasingly to encourage the inclusion of critical principle as a refining agent in the metaphysical dynamics of Justice-As-Sovereignty.

Evidence for the evolutionary transformation from convention to the dialectic between process and critical principle can be found in the comparative analysis of contemporary systems of municipal law. For example, Patrick H. Glenn in his book *Legal Traditions Of The World* argues that while all systems of law began with informal sets of Chthonic rules built upon custom, some of them have evolved to a status that Hume's concept of law would identify as a dialectic and secular Stage-II system. Meanwhile, others have not yet fully achieved this level of complexity, and retain their Chthonic roots in a revelation-based legal system determined by eristic argument and dogmatic substantive standards.

Glenn's taxonomy of formal legal systems can be illuminated and set into comparative context with the use of Hume's two stage concept of law. Specifically, what if we consider Chthonic prelegal systems as based, not on custom, but on Humean social convention with its roots in morality and its focus on effectiveness and justice-as-utility? This primarily procedural or "tribal" law can be traced to a set of coordination decisions that were chosen, at first unconsciously and then for their specific effect, and which insured the persistence of the "tribal" context as the society grew in size and complexity and confronted other Chthonic systems.

These Chthonic systems of informal rules make a status transition to a Stage-I formal legal system. The first laws evolved are procedural rules of recognition, adjudication, and change, represented within a process-norm that stabilizes and formally creates governance structures that maintain social interaction and cohesion based upon the established collective action equilibrium (see Figure 3.1). Each has a specific process-norm that defines justice for that context of cooperation.

One would expect the first set of substantive formal rules to be contextual, drawn from the same conventional framework that created the procedural substructure of the new system of governance. These contextual-substantive rules find their original source in revelation or religious precepts, based on dogma and eristic interaction; they created "local" or cultural conventions that determined group membership and the terms of cooperation from a particular "religious" foundation.

The continuing dependence on Chthonic law, even as the functional prerequisites of a Stage-I system are being acquired, explains the existence of Glenn's systems of Hindu, Islamic, and Talmudic law. These can be described as eristic Stage-I systems of formal rules. Here, the substantive law is contextual and based upon a specific set of conventionally-based practices that define, in these cases, a specific religious tradition. Roman Law can also be classified as a conventional Stage-I system as it is a direct outgrowth of social convention and practice in Hume's definition of these concepts. However, one difference in Roman Law is its focus on process to the exclusion of any

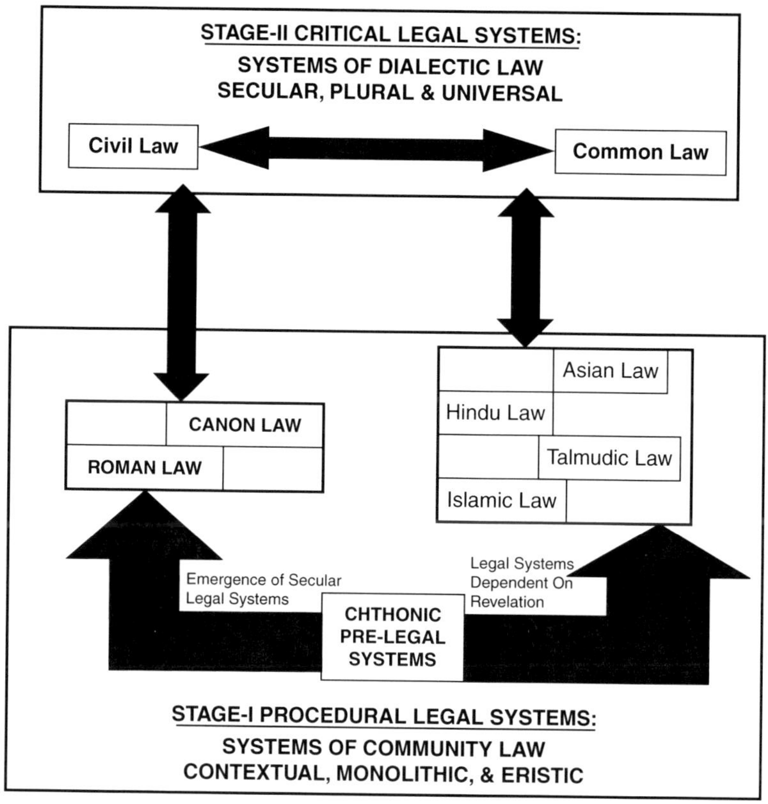

Figure 3.1 The evolution of the rule of law.

particular set of substantive principles. This allows it to continue to evolve out of its Chthonic roots, while other conventional systems maintain this status. This also gives it a capacity to integrate new ideas and concepts not directly connected to Roman culture. Thus, Roman Law transcended local or contextual substantive rules and became the foundation for a variety of secular, critical, and dialectic legal systems.

International law also shares this focus on process. The basis of modern international law is not revelation, nor reason, but secular social convention and the process-norm of Justice-As-Sovereignty. Its Stage-I system is open to the influence of noncontextual ideas; this is both its greatest strength and a serious weakness. International law, with a foundation in social convention, allows for a plurality of normative values at the municipal level, while its universality is focused on coordination and the sovereignty of states. Such openness also allows contract-by-convention to foster a more complex legal system where the process conventions come under the scrutiny of critical principle. This creates the potential for significant change in the metaphysical balance of Justice-As-Sovereignty and the viability of the Westphalian Equilibrium. A foundation in social convention as process does not carry the eristic characteristics of revelation-based Stage-I systems, but points out the pitfalls of dependence on substantive and exclusionary religious principle in a revelation-based idea of justice. Just as the Papal system was not able to maintain the status of its cooperative equilibrium when confronted with law based upon secular social convention, revelation-based Stage-I municipal systems may have to sacrifice their religious law in favor of the international and secular civil law that established the Westphalian Equilibrium.

Within the European context, secular Civil Law (*jus communes*) has evolved from the twelfth-century synthesis of Roman and Canon Law,[61] and represents most of the world's Stage-II legal systems. Secular Common Law, also with a Roman foundation,[62] took root in Britain and its Colonies. A Stage-II system, by definition, has evolved beyond reliance on substantive rules based in social convention, to incorporate a system of substantive and procedural rules, created by a dialectic between social convention and critical principle expressing secular practical reason. These systems have transcended exclusive religious values for pluralistic and secular universal dialectics. They require law to be inclusive, protecting human integrity within an open debate that considers humanity⇆utility⇆justice to be the core of law. Most importantly, through the application of conventional and critical components of the dialectic, Stage-II systems represent the effort to refine the norm of Justice-As-Sovereignty at its second moment of metaphysical complexity where process⇆principle are more fully engaged.

From the standpoint of Hume's philosophical-policy and its concept of law, all legal systems start as Stage-I Procedural Legal Systems. However, with the advent of contract-by-convention, which is a prerequisite of a Stage-I system, or any system of formal law, the possibility of critical legal principle is added to the design space and the further refinement of the concept of law becomes a possibility. With the transition to a Stage-II legal system, a greater challenge to progressive codification is created where the metaphysical anatomy of the dominant process-norm confronts the necessity to integrate conscious procedural and substantive law that is a product of critical principle. In effect, the transition between Stage-I and Stage-II is a transition from the *RULE OF SOCIAL CONVENTION* to the *RULE OF LAW*, where the latter becomes more than just a positive set of rules stemming from unconscious practice.

III. Evidence in Legal Practice

Hume's philosophical-policy and legal design requires that we understand a two-stage concept of the legal system. The primary stage is a procedural legal system where the bulwark of social convention holds sway in the metaphysics of Justice-As-Sovereignty and the rules of law are regulated by the need to maintain the Westphalian Equilibrium. In the more complex Stage-II model, critical principle emerges in the legal process. Stage-II offers a more fully engaged dialectic. Here, the process-norm can not only be challenged by critical principle, but principle, as a secondary foundation for change within Hume's concept of law, can determine positive law and influence the metaphysical balance of Justice-As-Sovereignty.

The adjudication process is that institutional framework in which the settlement of disputes creates the synthesis solution to the process⇆principle dialectic for any issue at any particular time. It represents the point where the essence of Justice-As-Sovereignty is challenged by the new complexities of a Stage-I system in transition. The chain of cases we are about to examine demonstrates how Hume's philosophical-policy and legal design maps onto a legal jurisprudence forced to accommodate increasing challenges to the conventional, process-based definition of Justice-As-Sovereignty.

In the *North Sea Continental Shelf* cases of 1969[63], the opinion of the International Court of Justice attempted to establish an "equitable" system of delimitation for a group of states where idiosyncrasies of geography made drawing boundaries difficult. The core of the decision revolves around whether or not the "equidistance principle," a component of the 1958 *Geneva Convention For the Law of the Sea*, could also be considered customary international law. Since a number of the parties to this case were not signatories to the treaty, the validity of the principle as custom, and therefore universal international law, was a prerequisite for mandating its general use in this situation.

The Court decided that the equidistance principle was not customary law. But the important dimensions of this case, from a Humean perspective, lie in an argument built on two lines of disputation. First, consider how the judges maintained the delineation between a principle codified in treaty that is not declaratory of custom and another codified from customary law. Second, consider the two distinct definitions of "principle" employed by the majority and the dissent.

In terms of the separation of treaty from customary law, the minority saw the existence of the 1958 treaty as a fact supporting the recognition of the equidistance principle in customary law. The argument of the dissenters proceeded as if the "progressive codification" of international law would have been advanced even if the 1958 treaty and its principle had not been considered declaratory of custom.

> The adoption of the Geneva Convention on the Continental Shelf was a very significant element in the process of creating new rules of international law in a field which urgently required legal regulation.[64]
>
> ...the Court by according the equidistance principle the status of a world law would make a contribution to the progressive development of international law.[65]
>
> The possibility has thus been reserved of recognizing the rapid emergence of a new rule of customary law based on the recent practice of States. This is particularly important in view of the extremely dynamic process of evolution in which the international community is engaged at the present stage of history....In situations of this nature, a convention adopted as part of the combined process of codification and progressive development of international

> law may well constitute, or come to constitute the decisive evidence of generally accepted new rules of international law. The fact that it does not purport simply to be declaratory of existing customary law is immaterial in this context. The convention may serve as an authoritative guide for the practice of States faced with relevant new legal problems, and its provisions thus become the nucleus around which a new set of generally recognized legal rules may crystallize.[66]

Meanwhile the majority, years before the *Nicaragua* opinion would make the sources of law independently valid, argued that, since the 1958 Geneva Convention was not specifically declaratory of custom, the sovereign rights of those states not party to it would be violated if it was assumed to be universally valid in customary international law.

> The Court accordingly concludes that if the Geneva Convention was not in its origins of inception declaratory of a mandatory rule of customary international law enjoining the use of the equidistance principle for the delimitation of continental shelf areas between adjacent States, neither has its subsequent effect been constitutive of such a rule; and that State practice up-to-date has equally been insufficient for the purpose.[67]

However, an examination of the majority opinion and dissents, from the perspective of Hume's legal design, illuminates more interesting reasons for the disagreement about the relationship between treaty and custom.

From the standpoint of Hume's philosophical-policy, the *North Sea Continental Shelf* cases are fundamentally a debate about the definition of the word "principle" within the metaphysics of the concept of Justice-As-Sovereignty. The majority approaches "equidistance" as if it were what we categorize as "critical principle," seeking validation as part of a shift to a Stage-II Critical Legal System. They write of principle as if it is a challenge to the recognized process-norm of Justice-As-Sovereignty and its Westphalian Equilibrium. Meanwhile, the minority tries to make the case that "equidistance" is nothing more than a contextual principle within a Stage-I Procedural Legal System that is representative of, and therefore of no threat to, Justice-As-Sovereignty.

In the language of Hume's logic of concepts, the majority assumes that the contextual rights of states must not be violated by critical principle. The contextual rights of states are based on the social conventions of effective property stabilization and Justice-As-Sovereignty whereas critical principle is always assumed to be disruptive of social stability.

> More important is the fact that the doctrine of the just and equitable share appears to be wholly at variance with what the Court entertains no doubt is the most fundamental of all the rules of law relating to the continental shelf...namely that the rights of the coastal State in respect to the area of the continental shelf that constitutes a natural prolongation of its land territory into and under the sea exists *ipso facto* and *ab initio*, by virtue of its

> sovereignty over the land...there is an inherent right. In order to exercise it, no special legal process has to be gone through, nor have any special legal acts to be performed. Its existence can be declared...but does not need to be constituted....the right does not depend on being exercised.[68]

This focus on sovereignty is complemented by the majority's description of equidistance in terms of characteristics that we now associate not with contextual, but with critical principle. They describe their search of international practice for evidence of the principle's status as custom as one for a "mandatory rule" that is "a priori" and contains "inherent necessity." This is the description of an aetiological-norm, a critical principle with an essential or necessary end, not a contextual principle built on and subservient to the social convention of Justice-As-Sovereignty that represents it.

> The conclusion drawn by the Court from the foregoing analysis is that the notion of equidistance as being logically necessary, in the sense of being inescapable *a priori* accompaniment of basic continental shelf doctrine, is incorrect.[69]
>
> ...it is clear that at no time was the notion of equidistance as an inherent necessity of continental shelf doctrine entertained.[70]

Examining equidistance as a critical principle assumes it to be inherently disruptive of an established Stage-I International Procedural Legal System. To give it legal status as custom would therefore require the Court to rebalance the metaphysics of Justice-As-Sovereignty in order to elevate critical principle over the effective control of territory. State sovereignty, as a representation of the bulwark of social convention, is at stake for the majority. They are not willing to allow critical principle, which they would not yet expect to be demonstrated in custom, to become a full part of general international law with universal authority. In effect, they are reluctant to allow equidistance to prematurely move up the hierarchy of external progressive codification.

> It emerges that from the history of the development of the legal regime of the continental shelf,...that the essential reason why the equidistance method is not to be regarded as a rule of law is that, if it were to be compulsorily applied in all situations, this would not be consonant with the certain basic legal notions which,...have from the beginning reflected the *opinio juris* in the matter of delimitation; those principles being that delimitation must be the object of agreement between the States concerned,...the continental shelf of any State must be the natural prolongation of its land territory and must not encroach upon what is the natural prolongation of the territory of another State.[71]
>
> ...the equidistance principle could not be regarded as being a rule of law on any *a priori* basis of logical necessity deriving from the fundamental theory of the continental shelf, [which] leads to the final conclusion...that the use of the equidistance method is not obligatory.[72]

At the same time, the dissenting voices in the Court, in effect, made the case that the equidistance principle, is not critical principle but contextual, and not any threat to either the conventional legal system nor Justice-As-Sovereignty. The wording of these dissents avoids the majority's use of language like "necessity," "mandatory," and "a priori," focusing instead on the functional qualities of the principle within the established context of state sovereignty and the Westphalian Equilibrium.

> if the law of the continental shelf were devoid of the provision concerning delimitation by means of the equidistance principle, satisfactory functioning of the institution of the continental shelf could not be expected.[73]
>
> ...the rule with regard to delimitation by means of the equidistance principle constitutes an integral part of the continental shelf as a legal institution of teleological construction....The delimitation itself is a logical consequence of the concept of the continental shelf that coastal States exercise sovereign rights over their own continental shelves....Delimitation itself and delimitation by the equidistance principle serve to realize the aims and purposes of the continental shelf as a legal institution....without this provision (equidistance) the institution (shelf) as a whole cannot attain its own end.[74]

This case can best be described as a debate over the power of adjudication to make progressive codification real in terms of advancing the international legal system toward a more fully engaged dialectic between process⇆principle. The process of dispute settlement is utilized to decide the legitimacy of "principle" in the evolution of international legal practice. But instead of the majority and dissent having a common definition of principle, they inherently disagree on whether equidistance is a natural outgrowth of social convention and the process-norm of Justice-As-Sovereignty, or an independent critical principle and an inherent risk to conventional rules of justice.

Essentially, this is less a debate about customary international law than an argument over the definition of principle within an evolving international legal system. Underneath the adjudication process, progressive codification is the real subject of the case. Justice-As-Sovereignty's rule of adjudication is engaged in a dispute about the character of principle and its resultant threat to established patterns of conventional practice.

In this contest, which Hume's philosophical-policy tells us to expect in the transition between a Stage-I and Stage-II legal system, the Court is adjudicating change as if it were setting the pace of the transition by dictating the definition and role of principles of law within the process⇆principle dialectic. The purpose of a rule of adjudication is for the Courts to set the parameters of their decision process and define the terms of the legal design discourse. Within the Humean model, this entails various synthesis solutions between process⇆principle with the assumption that, as a legal system achieves a Stage-II status, principle has the potential to move beyond merely being contextual and supportive of social convention to become critical of those conventions.

From the standpoint of Hume's concept of law, the majority can not envision that the equidistance principle may be compatible with social convention. Satisfied with the status quo, they are unwilling to advance the equidistance principle to customary international law. Hume's philosophical-policy informs us that this is because such a promotion would require a rebalancing of the SPP of effectiveness and the SPP of progressive codification, disturbing the metaphysics of Justice-As-Sovereignty. Such reluctance portends what Hume's logic predicts: a very slow adaptation of process to the demands of principle in transition to a Stage-II legal system. Thus, it should be no surprise that judges err on the side of established social convention.

The next case proffers a bellwether demonstration of a Court beginning to expand its adjudication rule to include principle, while still protecting essential conventional process. In the 1997 *Gabcikovo-Nagymaros* case,[75] the International Court of Justice was faced with a breach of a bilateral treaty between Hungary and Slovakia in which each party had agreed to build a complementary dam project on the Danube river. Hungary, accused of abandoning the project, approached the Court on the basis of what it called "ecological necessity," which it argued was a fit reason for termination of the treaty.

> Throughout the proceedings, Hungary contended that, although it did suspend or abandon certain works, on the contrary, it never suspended the application of the 1977 Treaty itself. To justify its conduct, it relied essentially on a "state of ecological necessity."[76]

In its opinion, the majority recognized that international legal practice had advanced to the degree that "necessity" was an established legal principle, illustrating that it had advanced on the internal hierarchy of progressive codification. This principle had achieved such status by being both an accepted piece of customary international law, through the International Law Commission's *Law Of State Responsibility*, and treaty law, through the 1969 *Vienna Convention On The Law Of Treaties*.[77] The acknowledgment of "newly developed norms"[78] can be more definitively understood if the rise of these norms is viewed as a result of the intercession of a rule of adjudication. Progressive codification is such that aetiological-norms were beginning to obtain a foothold in what was incrementally becoming a more fully actualized Stage-II international legal system.

More specifically, through progressive codification, substantive principles like those connected to "necessity," "impossibility of performance," and "sustainable development" had become legitimate considerations of adjudication for the Court. The Stage-II dialectic in this case is more fully engaged than it was for the *Continental Shelf* Court, and, in this case about infrastructure, conventional definitions had been accepted by all the Judges. However, it is also evident that the move toward a Stage-II dialectic is not complete. The very specific definitions of "necessity" and "impossibility," as well as the continued definition of the prime process-norm of Justice-As-Sovereignty in terms of "mutual consent,"[79] still conditioned the Court's consideration of the facts.

> The Court concludes...that...the perils invoked by Hungary, without prejudicing their possible gravity, were not sufficiently established in 1989, nor were they "imminent," and that Hungary had available to it at that time means of responding to these perceived perils other than the suspension and abandonment of works with which it had been entrusted....Hungary was, then, presumably aware of the situation as then known, when it assumed its obligations under the Treaty.[80]

Although the consideration of evolving norms is subsumed in their attention to treaty law and the serious matter of *pacta sunt servanda*, this Court went further than its predecessors in recognizing that the normative dimension of adjudication is a dynamic and dialectic exercise. The Court stopped short of considering whether any of the principles in the case were jus cogens or peremptory norms of international law, which would be able to trump social convention.

> Neither of the parties contended that new peremptory norms of environmental law had emerged since the conclusion of the 1977 Treaty, and the Court will consequently not be required to examine the scope of Article 64 of the Vienna Convention on the Law of Treaties....On the other hand, the Court wishes to point out that newly developed norms of environmental law are relevant for the implementation of the Treaty and that the parties could, by agreement, incorporate them...Consequently, the Treaty is not static, and is open to adapt to emerging norms of international law....The responsibility to do this was a joint responsibility.[81]

The Court did not accept Hungary's argument about "ecological necessity" and maintained both the integrity of the treaty and the responsibility of the state of Hungary. But it also placed one of the potentially critical principles considered in the case at the heart of its finding by ordering that the states renegotiate the treaty with the "concept" of sustainable development as their standard of reference.

> It is clear that the Project's impact upon, and implications for, the environment are of necessity a key issue....The Court is mindful that, in the field of environmental protection, vigilance and prevention are required on account of the often irreversible character of damage to the environment and of the limitations inherent in the very mechanism of reparation of this type of damage. Throughout the ages, mankind has, for economic and other reasons, constantly interfered with nature. In the past, this was often done without consideration of the effects upon the environment. Owing to new scientific insights and to a growing awareness of the risks for mankind—for present and future generations—of the pursuit of such interventions at an unconsidered and unabated pace, new norms and standards have been developed, set

> forth in a great number of instruments during the last two decades. Such new norms have to be taken into consideration, and such new standards given a proper weight, not only when States contemplate new activities but also when continuing with activities begun in the past. This need to reconcile economic development with protection of the environment is aptly expressed in the concept of sustainable development.[82]

The dissent of Judge Weeramantry is also telling. He contended that the majority, in admitting aetiological-norms into their adjudication, failed to go far enough. From the standpoint of Hume's philosophical-policy, he is anticipating a transition to a Stage-II Critical International Legal System. He goes further than the majority to state that "the principle of sustainable development...is an integral part of modern international law."[83] He then contends that "[e]nvironmental rights are human rights"[84] and makes reference to Judge Tanaka's dissent in the *South West Africa* case to argue that, "[t]he ethical and human rights related aspects of environmental law bring it within the category of law so essential to human welfare that we cannot apply to today's problems in this field the standards of yesterday."[85]

Invoking a full evolution to a Stage-II Critical Legal System, and a much wider range of concerns for the adjudication of international law, Weeramantry makes a case that the proper rule of adjudication should allow for a stage of progressive codification where critical principle and erga omnes obligations are dominant within the process⇆principle dialectic.

> We have entered an era of international law in which international law subserves not only the interests of individual States, but looks beyond them and their parochial concerns to the greater interests of humanity and planetary welfare. In addressing such problems, which transcend the individual rights and obligations of the litigating States, international law will need to look beyond procedural rules fashioned for purely *inter partes* litigation....When we enter the arena of obligations which operate *erga omnes* rather than *inter partes*, rules based on individual fairness and procedural compliance may be inadequate. The great ecological questions now surfacing will call for thought upon the matter. International environmental law will need to proceed beyond weighing the rights and obligations of parties within a closed compartment of individual State self-interest, unrelated to the global concerns of humanity as a whole. The present case offers an opportunity for such reflection....crossing cultural and disciplinary boundaries which have traditionally hemmed in the discipline of international law.[86]

Weeramantry's call to refine the process-norm of Justice-As-Sovereignty, through the full synthesis of process⇆principle in issues related to humanity and planetary "interests," comes with an argument for what we now understand to be a reorientation of the dialectics inherent to sovereignty. This is a perfect manifestation of what one might expect within a Stage-II system of adjudication. It occurs at a point in progressive codification where law now represents critical as well as contextual principle in full dialectic engagement. If the role of dissent in legal cases is to accelerate legal practice to achieve a more robust definition of progressive codification as a rule of adjudication, then we can have no better example than this.

The last case considers comparative law between the state of Canada and the international legal system. In the *Continental Shelf* case, we observed adjudication standards as if set in a Stage-I or very early Stage-II legal system, where protecting the conventional international system from the disruption of critical principle was the highest priority. The *Gabcikovo-Nagymaros* case, some thirty years later, demonstrated that the transition toward a more fully actualized Stage-II legal system for international law was closer to fruition. But the 1998 Canadian Supreme Court case *Reference re Secession of Quebec*[87] sets the standard for synthesizing process⇆principle in the requirement of a Constitutional framework to fully adjudicate the dialectic. This is a framework common at the municipal level, but nonexistent at the international level of social organization.

Quebec is an advisory opinion of the Canadian Supreme Court on one of the most pressing questions of Canadian and International law; namely, the meaning of self-determination for "peoples" already contained within a recognized sovereign state. The Court tackled its task in two stages: first, examining whether Canadian law exists that would sanction the unilateral secession of Quebec from Canada. Finding that no such domestic law existed, it then applied the same question of a right to unilateral secession to international law and found that no such law existed at this tier either.

Although this elegant opinion is both an historical and legal exercise, it also has a philosophical argument that is of great interest from a Humean point of view. Specifically, it demonstrates the ultimate role of Constitutionalism, in the modern democratic context, as the final arbiter of progressive codification, or the dialectic of process⇆principle within a Stage-II legal system. The argument illustrates a dependence on municipal Constitutionalism in its contention that there is no unilateral legal route to self-determination. It also highlights the dependence of international legal practice on municipal Constitutionalism to decide on the ultimate validity of self-determination claims within dispute settlement and the resulting synthesis of process⇆principle.

> Constitutional government is necessarily predicated on the idea that the political representatives of the people...have the capacity and the power to commit [them] to be bound into the future by the constitutional rules being adopted. These rules are "binding"...as defining the majority which must be consulted in order to alter the fundamental balances of political power (including the spheres of autonomy guaranteed by the principle of federalism), individual rights, and minority rights in our society.[88]
>
> In this way, our belief in democracy may be harmonized with our belief in constitutionalism.[89]

This "orderly framework" is the point of departure for the Court's philosophical argument about Constitutionalism; the Justices' perspective illustrates that a Constitution is the ultimate objective of progressive codification as a rule of adjudication.

Specifically, the case reflects a seeming recognition that, in the transition to a Stage-II Critical Legal System, adjudication norms must accommodate a much more complex social reality. No longer does the prelaw bulwark of social convention hold the moral and legal highground in the form of the simple legal process-norm of Justice-As-Sovereignty. With the advent of contract-by-convention, the concern for essential or necessary ends and their self-defining aetiological-norms becomes a much more substantial player in the core dialectic between process⇆principle.

Consequently, adjudication must fully integrate critical principle into the synthesis legal solutions of the dialectic, to the point where principle may determine the parameters of process. In the previous cases, the transition was a slow and incremental progression. However, as demonstrated in the last case, critical principle (i.e., sustainable development) does eventually appear in majority opinions as *rationes decidendi*. But in gaining ground on process, critical principle also acts as a disruptive force and can disable some of the core ideas within the conventional system of sovereign adjudication rules. So how is it that a legal system achieves progressive codification through expanding rules of adjudication without chaos breaking down the order, or fundamental stability, of a society?

The Canadian Supreme Court's answer is that Constitutional law creates the appropriate synthesis mechanism, representing both the interests of critical principle and a stable society. In effect, constitutional law segregates the essential rights or entitlements of all citizens and places them, as core critical principles, beyond the reach of majority rule. In this way, the need for what is "necessary" is judicially protected in the ongoing ebb and flow of executive and legislative decision-making that maintains justice-as-order and protects social convention. Thus, a constitution provides a set of rules for an overarching "orderly framework" that protects a baseline synthesis of both sides of the process⇆principle dialectic. Under these conditions, a society is able to simultaneously protect social convention, progressive codification, and the essential norms of critical principle.

In its argument about the lack of Canadian law to support the unilateral secession of Quebec, the Court made it clear that, while Quebec does have a separate and unique "people," the first requirement of self determination, the rights of this minority have been fully supported by the Canadian Constitutional System.

> The Quebec people is manifestly not,...an oppressed people. For close to 40 of the last 50 years, the Prime Minister of Canada has been a Quebecer. During this period, Quebecers have held...all the most important positions in the federal Cabinet.[90]

Fundamentally, the "fact" of the Canadian Constitution and its Charter of Rights and Freedoms is the decisive factor in the argument that since the "people" of Quebec have their full human rights within Canada, they have no legal reason for unilateral action. Under these conditions, the Constitutional process is the only way for secession to be legal. It is the Constitutional responsibility of Quebec, to go though a lengthy negotiation process with its people, the people of the rest of Canada, and with the federal Government in order to affect a legally-sanctioned independence from Canada.

The interesting twist in this argument comes when the Court assesses the question of unilateral secession within the practice of international law. In their analysis, the Court seems to argue consciously that self-determination as a critical principle must always be weighed against the prime concern for stable coordination of the international system and its process-norm of Justice-As-Sovereignty.

> The international law principle of self-determination has evolved within a framework of respect for the territorial integrity of existing states. The various international documents that support the existence of a people's right to self-determination also contain parallel statements supportive of the conclusion that the exercise of such a right must be sufficiently limited to prevent threats to an existing state's territorial integrity or the stability of relations between sovereign states.[91]

Within international law, as a potential Stage-II system, the prerequisite of Justice-As-Sovereignty, and the possible vulnerability of the Westphalian Equilibrium, are an ever-present component of the adjudication process. To make a case for secession, or the self-determination of a "people," even if they are not given their full rights within the "parent" state, is a matter of critical principle disturbing established international law from social convention. For the Court, intervention into the sovereign matters of a recognized state is still fundamentally a matter of finding a *Lotus* prohibition.

> It is clear that international law does not specifically grant component parts of sovereign states the legal right to secede unilaterally from their "parent" state....proponents of the existence of such a right at international law are therefore left to attempt to found their argument...on the proposition that unilateral secession is not specifically prohibited and that what is not specifically prohibited is inferentially permitted.[92]

Within this narrow legal framework, and lacking Constitutional Governance on the international tier to properly regulate the synthesis of process⇆principle, the Court in this case reverts to municipal constitutional law. Their use of "internal self-determination" sets the adjudication standard for both levels of the international system.

> The recognized sources of international law establish that the right to self-determination of a people is normally fulfilled through internal self-determination—a people's pursuit of its political, economic, social and cultural development within the framework of an existing state. A right to external

> self-determination (which in this case potentially takes the form of the assertion of a right to unilateral secession) arises in only the most extreme of cases and, even then, under carefully defined circumstances.[93]

> A state whose government represents the whole of the people or peoples resident within its territory, on the basis of equality and without discrimination, and respects the principles of self-determination in its own internal arrangements, is entitled to the protection under international law of its territorial integrity.[94]

The delineation between internal and external self-determination can be argued to be a direct outgrowth of the bulwark of social convention and the continued influence of the Stage-I level of complexity and its conceptualization of Justice-As-Sovereignty. The international legal system has no adequate process to render synthesis solutions to disputes between process and principle and, therefore, cannot accomplish a full transition to Stage-II. This logic entails that, in order for international adjudication to properly incorporate process⇆principle, a Constitutional Framework is a necessary eventuality. Only constitutional law can properly act to enshrine essential aetiological-norms without excessive disruption of established convention or procedural rules of property stabilization.

Within international legal practice, the "internal" concept of self-determination is known as the "safeguard clause"; it is customary law further codified within the 1970 *Declaration on Principles of International Law Concerning Friendly Relations and Cooperation Among States*. But this particular clause is more an international codification of municipal Constitutionalism than an independent piece of international legal practice.

Within the transition to a Stage-II Critical Legal System, it is imperative to set process⇆principle into balance by established and fundamental process. As the Canadian Supreme Court recognizes, this requires a Constitutional Governance Structure. Without one, international rules of adjudication have no ultimate normative process standards with which to establish consistent measures of the correct dialectic synthesis between well-established sovereign process and evolving critical principle. Under these conditions, without Constitutional guidelines to integrate critical principle, they are potentially a more ominous disruption to the stability of international social convention.

Consequently, progressive codification, as a rule of adjudication within the international legal system, first establishes itself as a complete and stable Stage-I Procedural Legal System, including custom, contextual principles, and the consent of states in treaty law. Next, legal adjudication must recognize the transition to a Stage-II Critical Legal System and take steps to classify the most essential critical principles jus cogens and the most necessary obligations erga omnes, so they can eventually be integrated into judicial deliberations.

However, the *Quebec* case illustrates that a fully engaged dialectic within a fully institutionalized Stage-II Critical Legal System will require a Constitutional adjudication standard. This framework of constitutional law does not yet exist at the global level. And if the implications of Hume's philosophical-policy and legal design are correct, one should expect that without Constitutional Governance to create stable adjudication rules of synthesis, the Stage-II transition will never be fully completed. International law will continue to rely on the constitutional standards of municipal systems for its gauge of the proper role for critical principle in a process-dominated core dialectic of the international rule of law.

Together, these cases illustrate what both the internal and external definitions of progressive codification will have to address in the future. The international system is currently a Stage-I system where the first consideration of critical principle is gradually being integrated into international law; first in dissent, then in *obiter dicta*, and only then in *rationes decidendi*. The cases also highlight the importance of constitutionalism as the ultimate arbiter of the process⇆principle dialectic and indicate that it is a prerequisite for a stable Stage-II legal system.

Combining the local rule of recognition, that is, the SPP of effectiveness, with the rule of adjudication in terms of the SPP of progressive codification, provides a view of international legal practice that highlights a more complex metaphysics for Justice-As-Sovereignty, anticipating the growth of critical principle in international adjudication. A reluctance to fully incorporate critical principle is not a moral rejection of the quality of those rights, but a predisposition to reaffirm the fundamental status of social convention at the heart of the international legal system.

In chapter 4, we will examine a second type of recognition rule. The universal rule of recognition is a counterweight to its local variety, defining Justice-As-Sovereignty, not in terms of domestic security, but in terms of international responsibility. This will further enhance the metaphysical essence of Justice-As-Sovereignty.

4

"Peaceful Cooperation": A Universal Rule of Recognition and the Strategic Context of Justice-As-Sovereignty

Abstract

Hume's philosophical-policy suggests a definition of the international system diametrically opposed to the common positivist assumption of a violent and chaotic Hobbesian state of nature. Justice-As-Sovereignty maintains coordination through the systematic policy precept of reciprocal cooperation which acts as a "universal" rule of recognition and offers the possibility of an international law that is much more than merely the establishment and protection of the state. Next, game theory extrapolates the legal design elements of Hume's concept of law, defining the international system as an unstable, but not anarchic, coordination game, built on a stratified foundation of solved municipal prisoner's dilemmas. Lastly, the evolution of this strategic context is verified through international case law.

I. Hume's Logic of Concepts: Customary Law From a Distinct "State of Nature"

In chapter 2, a local rule of recognition from the SPP of effectiveness was identified. But in this case, Hume's philosophical insight demonstrates that the metaphysics of Justice-As-Sovereignty is actually a multi-tier collective action problem where the additional SPP of *peaceful or reciprocal cooperation* creates a *universal rule of recognition* specifically supporting Justice-

As-Sovereignty. The process-norm is defined, dialectically, both from the municipal level up, and from the collective level down. Reciprocal cooperation is in dialectic with its local counterpart of effectiveness. It also acts in concert with the rule of adjudication toward the evolution of a definition of effectiveness that focuses more on the international than the national conceptualization of Justice-As-Sovereignty. Although there are wider implications for this systematic policy percept (SPP), as understood within Hume's philosophical-policy, it is akin to Krasner's definition of "international legal sovereignty" which "refers to the practices associated with mutual recognition, usually between territorial entities that have formal juridical independence."[1]

Hume's logic of concepts provides a foundation to make a case for a definition of *jus gentium* that, while it may have risen from the mere coordination of states, is a nonderivative, stable legal system with the capacity to transcend a simple definition of sovereignty and support the complex idea of an international rule of law for transnational or universal society. This is not a new notion.

During the Reformation, Suarez argued for "peace in a universal law of nations."[2] In support of this end, he tried to find a bulwark against the disintegration of the Catholic world system in a new global conceptualization of jus gentium. The search for norms to stabilize the international system as a single, integrated, and separate rule of law[3] was uniformly assumed to require the presupposition that both natural law and international law were, as Vitoria had argued, based on the same foundation: revealed human reason. This was the only way to give both a necessary metaphysical base and a common core imperative to the jus gentium. But, for Suarez, revealed reason was no longer universal and, therefore, of marginal utility.

Nevertheless, Suarez expanded Aquinas' distinction between the "natural" and the "civil" law. Because of the obvious lack of universalism in the Reformation's idea of revelation, which then informed natural law, and his need to make international law a distinct legal system, Suarez detached the jus gentium from natural law and made it predominantly a global variant of the civil law. While he contended that the jus gentium "derives its force from natural law,"[4] he argued that it is not "contained within the bounds of natural law,"[5] and was not a "necessary law" based on reason, but less "immutable" than the natural law.[6] This jus gentium is a "law of will,"[7] rendered from "habit,"[8] and guaranteed by "actual usage,"[9] foretelling Hume's philosophical-policy. Suarez defines the law as in "an absolute sense human and positive,"[10] and created to ensure that the international system of states is "properly ordered."[11]

Being a sound Scholastic and dialectician, Suarez posed counterarguments that he then addressed. The most telling of these is when he posits that "it seems impossible that the *jus gentium* should be common to all peoples and should nevertheless have its origins in human will and opinion."[12] Although Suarez satisfies himself that this counterargument is answered by the capacity of natural law to inform "the customs of all nations,"[13] and in this way create a universal law out of integrated customary practice, he continues to maintain that its character as civil law means that it has "no altogether intrinsic and natural necessity."[14] In effect, Suarez assumes that, with reason and revelation made moot as possible "natural" foundations for the international legal system, jus gentium, as a variant of civil law, must depend on local practice universalized through the experience and consequent expectations of interstate relations.

For Suarez, jus gentium acknowledges that custom is primarily measured in terms of the civil or positive law as a manifestation of the will of states. This "will" is, by his argument, without any "necessary" metaphysical foundation, nor a collective imperative that might make it truly "common to all mankind."[15] The goal of peace through universal law is therefore dependent upon an acknowledgment on the part of each state that they are a "member of a universal society."[16] However, Suarez expects this stable universality to be a serendipitous product of the "habitual conduct of nations," without a necessary standard to judge good from bad law. His hope seems to be that a common predisposition in all states will lead to sound and humanitarian results. But what is the basis of this predisposition, if it has no common point of origin, justification, nor imperative to action?

The problem in Suarez's argument is a misunderstanding of the international system as a single global collective action problem made up of individual state agents who are dealing with two expressions of the same civil law, one domestic and one foreign. For Suarez, the jus gentium is an "intermediate"[17] step between universal natural law and domestic civil law. But he makes it an extension of the latter without the stability of the former.

Viewed through Hume's philosophical-policy, Suarez fails to understand two crucial points. First, international law is not just an extension of civil law, but a specific strategic reality with a distinctly defined society to protect. Second, there is an additional foundation for practical reason that can provide a "necessary" basis for justice: social convention. Specifically, Hume's philosophical-policy treats international law as a separate systemic tier of law with its own strategic rationality, distinct from the municipal tier, while dialectically connected to it. In addition, Hume's conceptual logic rests all law, both in terms of municipal civil law and jus gentium, on his argument for a natural law of social convention built on the human passion for society.

Two levels of stable social interactions play out in the international legal system. They share a common base in a natural law of human passion. But they have different circumstantial expressions of law given the distinct demands on the agents involved and the conventional solutions produced by each for their unique collective action problems. The local rule of recognition, expressed in terms of the SPP of effectiveness, creates a conceptualization of Justice-As-Sovereignty incomplete without its dialectic connection to the universal rule of recognition defined through the SPP of peaceful or reciprocal cooperation. Reciprocity-As-Effectiveness, in this context, grants each tier of the international system its own dialectic role in creating the law. Each has a role in synthesizing law, contributing its particular breed of social convention to the overall process of social order. In other words, the jus gentium is a simultaneous product of Justice-As-Sovereignty defined as both domestic social stability and an evolving sense of a global or "universal society."[18]

Because the municipal collective action problem is akin to a Prisoner's Dilemma (PD), while international collective action is a Lewis Coordination Game, the distinct strategic contexts allow Hume's concept of law to stabilize the international system without the same degree of law enforcement required by coercive municipal governance structures. Given the two distinct sets of background conditions and dialectic collective action problems to consider, one can argue for different configurations of law to create distinct definitions of governance for municipal⇆international systems. This delineation acknowledges separate but interdependent circumstances of justice that require good international law to balance effective control with the state's reciprocal responsibilities to a transnational sense of law and society.

Overall, because Hume's approach elevates *process* over *principle* and focuses on procedure in his concept of law and its evolving legal system, the complexity of the strategic situation allows for distinct combinations of procedural and substantive rules to govern on municipal, as opposed to international, levels of organization. These varieties, however, are not antagonistic to mutual order but dialectically necessary to it. Engaged with one another, they produce a synthesis product that assures not only distinctly governed municipal systems built on their unique circumstances of justice, but, simultaneously, a universal set of circumstances and social conventions that also rely on Justice-As-Sovereignty to support international social equilibrium.

Under these interdependent circumstances, justice creates a dynamic jus gentium capable of evolution, coordination, and the genesis of multiple governance systems with a responsibility to enhance and promote progressive codification of international law. Justice-As-Sovereignty supports a dialectic between the collective (i.e., international) and individual (i.e., state) levels of strategic interaction. This dialectic causes legal stratification between municipal and international legal systems, while it sets the process standards for state legitimacy in terms of responsibility to contribute to the persistence of peace in a universal law of nations.

Acknowledging both the strategic reality of states and the distinct requirements of their international relations, Hume's legal design imperatives recognize that jus gentium has its own collective action problem to solve and its own requirements for cooperation and social order that allow it to evolve and persist. This begins with less centralized and coercive governance structures. A design argument drawn from Hume's philosophical-policy would focus on the process of cooperation between tiers of social organization as the critical dialectic variable. Because this interaction coordinates both *sovereignty as effective control* and *sovereignty as peaceful or reciprocal cooperation*, it creates a complex combination of recognition and adjudication standards that must be integrated to provide peace and justice on both levels of society at the same time.

In this way, Hume's concept of law creates a definition of customary international law that equals more than the aggregate will of states. International custom is inherently rooted in the passion for society at the international level of organization and grows from a natural law of social convention. Jus gentium represents the interaction of municipal and international social conventions in a search for a synthesis international system of law that allows for the coexistence of domestic and global society. In addition, the legal recognition of states, both from the local level as sovereign entities and from the universal level as responsible cooperators in a dynamic coordination equilibrium, demands a new definition of municipal/international legal stratification. In such a design, municipal systems integrate international law into the domestic context, while the international system taps municipal law as a source of innovation and change.

Hume's definition of natural law proffers a more complex and representative model of the international system and its strategic complexity with rules of recognition for *local effectiveness* and *universal reciprocal cooperation*. The two-tiered system as a dynamic whole provides the dialectic background conditions for the evolution of sovereignty in legal practice.

The two levels of recognition rules required by this strategic complexity have further effect on the "circumstances of justice" for international practice. Specifically, it is no longer reasonable to assume, as contemporary international theory does, that states are individuals while the international system is an anarchic state of nature. Instead, Hume's philosophical-policy suggests that states are social constructions representing stable societies at both the municipal and international level of organization, while law is a creature, not of rules, but of practice in a "state of nature" that is nonoptimal, yet hardly Hobbesian.

Given the historical background of modern international law, a stable social order at the Westphalian Equilibrium is the legal objective. With the disintegration of the Papal international system, and its "revealed" sense of natural law and transnational social conventions, universality was sacrificed for local stability in a series of "royal" legal systems. These evolved into modern states. To transcend the limited certainty and order experienced at the local level, an international process-norm was required to reestablish transnational cooperation and social convention so that both local and international law could develop dialectically. Justice-As-Sovereignty allows for universality and certainty in both the coordination of international law at the Westphalian Equilibrium, and the rise of the municipal state, as each principality solved its PD.

Although city-states and regional royal principalities existed before the Thirty Years War, the violent disruption of the Reformation came before their full development.[19] Local and regional governance was not sufficiently developed to substitute for the demise of the Papal System, or forestall the resulting disorder and war. So the secular royal subsystems began a process of progressive codification through both local and international social convention. This first stabilized the royal systems and then lead to an inter-national point of coordination that made a system of "states" and their reciprocal duties-in-law the preferred model for a stable global social order.

For Hume, natural law, regulated by humanity's passion for society, informs Justice-As-Sovereignty, which seeks law for the purposes of finding a stable cooperative equilibrium to provide certainty and universality for an increasingly complex international social order. The law is, in this way, primarily a transsocial or inter-national phenomenon that fosters the creation of a system of states in order to stabilize both municipal and international society.

Built on the natural law of evolving social convention that creates a customary law of practice as a prerequisite to any legal rules, Justice-As-Sovereignty supports both national and transnational social orders in moving up their scales of forms. It does so by undergirding both with a metaphysical framework that synthesizes reason⇆passion and the society's self- and social-interest in a legal design based on the dynamic balance of process⇆principle.

These dynamics began in a situation where the fracture of revelation into many streams of ideological thought assured that no universal system would replace the Church. Consequently, local secular law was called on to develop and fill the gap so society at its most basic level could find some level of certainty. This allowed cities, manors, cultures, royal houses, and religious sects to create a more localized stability as the core building blocks of international society's metaphysical scale of forms. All of these legal entities were responding to the absolute presupposition of one's need for society and social order as these arose out of the "state of nature" that was the Thirty Years War.[20]

This necessitated that a jus gentium, in terms of Justice-As-Sovereignty, be built on the basis of the dialectics of a local rule of recognition, in support of effective control within the state, and a universal rule of recognition in terms of the state's reciprocal duties to transnational stability. The resulting Westphalian Equilibrium was, therefore, a synthesis of both universal and local procedural recognition but was also the creation of a new set of international social conventions (i.e., sovereignty and minority rights) that would eventually replace the Papal system with a secular international law.

Law is the conventional means of providing order, certainty, and predictability for social life. But only two legal systems, Urban and Royal, survived the violence and stress of the Thirty Years War.[21] The conventional need to stabilize society for its own persistence caused municipal systems to seek a means to their independent circumstances of justice. However, simultaneously, this effort also provided for the joint circumstances embracing their common religious divisions, through a peace settlement that recognized the dialectic circumstances with solutions to both local security and universal coordination.[22] Within the Treaties of Westphalia were the seeds of a two-tiered metaphysical scale of forms that provided for both sovereignty⇆minority rights.[23] At this point Justice-As-Sovereignty supported the rise of customary law at the international level, while setting parameters for the recognition of states, the reciprocity of contextual rights, and the stratification of municipal and international law.

The process-norm of Justice-As-Sovereignty stabilized the Westphalian Equilibrium. Consequently, a set of practices and contractual rules from these practices set in motion what has since come to be known as customary or general international law. These are legal rules from practice, which itself has come from international social conventions that define the legitimate responsibilities of reciprocal coordination for any state seeking the protection of the system of sovereign states.

In the international dialectic, rules of local and universal recognition provide a balance between effective control and reciprocal responsibility that surfaces as synthesis legal design rules. Customary international law as transnational social convention then arose as a primary source of law for the two-tiered system. Specifically, the stratification of the law, (i.e., how and what international laws apply municipally), is a customary rule-synthesis of the dialectic balance of social conventions in the form of SPPs that provide a metaphysics for Justice-As-Sovereignty.

After the Reformation, a new scale of forms was needed to synthesize social convention in a move toward a reorganized international system based on secular values and focused on neutral process rather than divisive critical principle. Justice-As-Sovereignty provided the answer. Society finds an imperative in the generic essence of "universal" social convention and the order and certainty it provides for a pattern of collective action on the local tier. The dialectic of local and universal recognition within Justice-As-Sovereignty sustains the process of seeking the universal by creating a municipal foundation for dialectical method that eventually recreates order in the universality of a newly secular and process-based interstate system.

For Hume's philosophical-policy and legal design, Westphalia is not just a treaty solution to a long war, but the codification of a process-norm based on a new set of evolving post-Reformation social conventions. Within the new cooperative equilibrium, a dialectic process begins to refine sets of local conventions into an emerging point of international coordination—a new international legal system based on Justice-As-Sovereignty.

Considerable argument exists over what Westphalia really accomplished and whether or not it was the origin point for the state.[24] But from a Humean perspective, the creation of a two-tiered international system based on secular social conventions, and a process-norm of Justice-As-Sovereignty with both local and universal rules of recognition, is a significant event. It offered a modern scale of forms for international law that, since 1648, has rendered both contemporary international legal practice and the state system upon which it is based.

Overall, Hume's philosophical-policy illuminates a sovereignty-based definition of international law that is more complex than contemporary theory can offer. It creates a two-tiered world system procedurally adaptable to an ever-greater scope and complexity of culture and society than was envisioned by Suarez, but which rendered the same result: "peace in a universal law of nations."[25]

Opinio Juris *as a Function of Social Convention*

As international social convention evolves along its scale of forms, it moves through two levels of complexity as a concept of law. In the same way that the balance of SPPs will dictate the evolving conceptualization of Justice-As-Sovereignty, this idea of justice will regulate the three sources of international law.[26] Applying Hume's philosophical-policy to the progressive codification of these primary sources (i.e., principle, custom, and treaty) creates a hierarchy where *principle* is the most primitive level of law, contextual to process and a creature of preexisting *social convention*. Social convention will also be the source for *general customary law* as those practices and rules necessary to the stability of diplomacy and Justice-As-Sovereignty. *Treaty*, although a form of conscious contract, is still based on contract as convention and is the most codified level of the hierarchy. Within this framework, international markets thrive, especially with contract-by-convention when treaty becomes possible and the legal design space is complex enough to have the minimal background institutions for functioning markets. As sovereignty evolves, its translation of social convention into customary international law lies at the heart of the process that is the international legal system. This is because both are based in practice and contain the essential normative character of the law, as it evolves from human interaction with the aim of a stable social order.

Within sovereignty's scale of forms, social cooperation first evolves from unconscious behavior, which is supportive of social stability. The refinement of the idea of justice then establishes a more conscious pattern that is repeated on the municipal level to create states, then on the "interstate" level to create levels of transnational sanctions. These include diplomacy (i.e., approbation), then sovereignty as a process-norm (i.e., justice), and, finally, contract-by-convention with its multi- or supranational law and institutions (i.e., political society). These sanctions protect social order and coordination through Justice-As-Sovereignty.

The definition of customary law is invigorated through Hume's philosophical-policy and legal design, by redefining it as law derived from social convention. This makes general international law a creature of the SPPs as relative presuppositions within the metaphysics of Justice-As-Sovereignty. Justice becomes the standard of *effective* practice that establishes the delineation between valid and invalid customary law. The number of states that participate or acknowledge a rule of customary law, or a state's expressed obligation to its rules through opinio juris, are no longer the most crucial factors for law's validity. Rather, the implications of a proposed custom for maintaining the established coordination equilibrium mark it as a valid piece of general international law.

This requires a reconsideration of *opinio juris et necessatis*, or the consent and acknowledgment dimension of customary international law. We should expect that if opinio juris is a creature of the governance stage of progressive codification, produced through contract-by-convention, it will have no foundational or conventional priority. It will be independent from, and an afterthought of, and not necessary to the origin, but only the persistence of, international customary law. Within Humean legal design, opinio juris is not an equal and fundamental component, with practice, of customary international law.[27]

The history of general or customary international law, from the standpoint of Hume's philosophical-policy, begins with the solid dominance of evolving conventional practice. As that observable dimension of Justice-As-Sovereignty it sets expectations and can be depended on to protect the interests of constituent states in maintaining the Westphalian Equilibrium. Initially, international social conventions are sustained by diplomatic approbation. Eventually, they will require more definitive defense against the growing numbers of distinct conventional solutions to municipal collective action problems and the increasing challenge, in a growing world system, provided by the generation of alternative points of coordination. With the advent of the process-norm of Justice-As-Sovereignty to further stabilize international property, sovereign coordination may be protected by the tacit practice that any behavior not specifically prohibited by international constraints is permissible.[28] At this point, sovereignty becomes the core norm for any future governance institutions created through contract-by-convention at the third and last level of sanctions: political society.

Hume's logic of concepts suggests that social convention and, therefore, the original legitimacy of international custom should cause obligation to be generated from iterated practice, where the sanction of approbation is enough to secure initial cooperation. Humean *social* convention is established as a *legal* convention by interaction and the "mutual" acceptance of that behavior through the systematic coordination of actors at the Westphalian Equilibrium. Consent is not tacit or real, but simply inferred from the fact that states act in response to their reciprocal responsibilities within the coordination game. In this way, consensus is secured without opinio juris, through the operation of Justice-As-Sovereignty which is partially defined by a synthesis of the dialectic of local and universal rules of recognition.

But where does opinio juris originate? Practice is initially sufficient to support customary law as social convention. With the advent of stronger governance structures and intentionally codified law, Hume's logic of concepts, ever vigilant to protect Justice-As-Sovereignty, may require the positive accession of states to customary law. The additional level of political sanction reinforces Justice-As-Sovereignty by adding, to the *acceptance* of practice, the requirement that states need to consciously demonstrate a further obligation to custom and the universal rule of recognition through opinio juris.[29]

Given Hume's focus on social convention as practice, the requirement of *opinio jus et necessatis* is unnecessary because social convention, within the context of a coordination game, regulated by Justice-As-Sovereignty, is self-reinforcing. It would also have no utility because the moral obligation in the first two stages of Hume's progressive codification of sanctions is informal and focused on the creation of practice as this must preexist for rules to be possible. Only with the evolution of contract-by-convention as the third level of sanctions in the international system is the addition of a separate obligation to the practice of a rule of law possible and perhaps necessary to stabilize the complexity of an expanding society of states.

With the advent of contract-by-convention in the international legal system, critical principle becomes more fully engaged in the process⇆principle dialectic. Another reason for opinio jus et necessatis may be that it has utility in identifying those states that have consented to customary law. In a world of both contextual and critical principles, and with the universal validity of what is agreed to be customary law, Justice-As-Sovereignty may require a potentially disruptive principle to meet more than the standard test of conformity to practice. With the use of opinio juris et necessatis to establish more active assent to customary law, Justice-As-Sovereignty can better protect its coordination equilibrium from critical principle. If general international law is increasingly populated by critical principle, which then becomes universally applicable to states that heretofore have been obligated to custom as a direct product of social convention, then an extra gatekeeper is reasonable. This assures that no state need violate its sovereignty for the sake of a critical principle to which it did not consent. Hume's philosophical-policy sets opinio juris apart from custom as practice and assigns it to the third stage of sanctions, as a conscious reaffirmation of Justice-As-Sovereignty in customary law.

The International System and Hume's "State of Nature"

The two-tiered international system derived from Hume's philosophical-policy must deal with the traditional definition of the international state of nature assumed within international legal theory. Even without the enforcement abilities of a fully-developed municipal-type governance system, Hume's international state of nature must successfully coordinate states through approbation and justice connected to customary international law as a manifestation of social convention, even before the advent of contract-by-convention and formal codification of treaty. But how can Hume's concept of law navigate the "war of all against all"?

International legal theory has assumed that the international system existed within a state of nature where anarchy threatens individual nations with war and, in Hobbes' words, an "existence" that is "solitary, poore, nasty, brutish and short."[30] If any one state were to defect from this assumed international PD, the stability of the entire system would be fundamentally threatened. For Hobbes and the standard positivist' theory of international law, power is a currency necessary to maintain a very precarious system made up of noncooperative components constantly on the verge of meltdown.

The Humean "state of nature" is a less violent and more inconvenient or inefficient set of circumstances. Here, humanity is faced with questions of justice, which it has confronted before on a local level; that is, as an instability of property lessened by the evolution of social convention. It may be that states at the international level, when they have solved the municipal collective action problem, are more conscious of the distinct dimensions of the global coordination game facing them. Nevertheless, the solution lies in the utility of the Westphalian Equilibrium and the evolution of Justice-As-Sovereignty. With the process-norm of sovereignty, the recognition and operationalization of legal practice as an outgrowth of social convention makes an inconvenient and unstable world collectively better off. With convention, Justice-As-Sovereignty, and the evolution of rules first made evident in customary international law, the state of nature is tamed by the application of practical reason.

This is a dramatically different context for the international system from that described as Hobbesian anarchy. First, from a Humean standpoint, it lacks a desperate motivation to leave the state of nature. The incentive to create international social convention is a move prompted by the circumstances of justice that juxtaposes the metaphysical need for wider social relations against the limited generosity of individual sociopolitical actors. It is a move toward effectiveness and improved peaceful coexistence, convenience, and a more stable municipal⇆international world order. In a world of evolving social convention, the constant development of coordination equilibria offers an inherently prudent basis for improving human social relations.

This emphasizes Hume's insight that the international system has its own strategic reality. International collective action involves a solved PD at the municipal level and an international coordination game that has a distinct strategic framework and set of expectations for the actors. Specifically, the multiple coordination equilibria are competitive but, because this is a unique strategic context, the idea of coordination is in everyone's interest regardless of which equilibrium is chosen. This requires less incentive as the state of nature is populated by many solved PDs that make it more hospitable and less uncertain than its counterpart for municipal law. Expectations on the international tier are such that it is in everyone's interest to live by the accepted social conventions, especially when these involve a dialectic of municipal⇆international law that simultaneously supports Justice-As-Sovereignty.

The choice of equilibrium is indifferent between the players and will arise by social convention and then the codification of that convention through contract-by-convention. The resulting two-tiered system of rules from practice, both more efficient and effective, form what Schelling calls a prominent or "focal point" solution to the peace and reciprocity foundational to the international legal system.[31] This type of solution does not reflect or create a state of nature but a state of reciprocal social convention, which is a more stable manifestation of the universal rule of recognition. It is insured against the potential loss of cooperation because the process of coordination itself is the core value; that is, where the moral quality of the system itself is to be found. The option for those coordinating is not chaos or utopia, but different moments of the process-norm of Justice-As-Sovereignty that can rebalance its inherent dialectics to maintain a coordinated system of social convention.

Hume's logic of concepts defines a "state of nature" for the emerging international system that is uncoordinated and inefficient but not anarchic. It does not present the stark Hobbesian specter of the threat of death in disorder, but the social fact of unstable property relations that require social convention for international stability. This foundation provides the origin story for general or customary international law as a creature of practice. It also allows for the progressive codification of international legal practice that changes over time, as more states are created and seek Justice-As-Sovereignty for both local effective control and universal reciprocal participation. Hume's legal design imperatives give international law a core of utility and grant international society a distinct sense of public interest based on the coordination of the choices of states as social constructions.

A Stratified Dialectic for International Law

Hume's philosophical-policy suggests two distinct but dialectically related levels of social organization that compose the international rule of law: municipal and international. Each of these strata has evolved in dialectic relation to one another, where each tier is dependent for its stability on the amount of order in the other as mitigated by Justice-As-Sovereignty. The scale of forms for the evolution of sovereignty requires that the international social order be adaptable to its context and circumstances, which includes a distinct strategic situation and a unique definition of those sanctions necessary to maintain cooperation over time given the growth of social complexity.

At the municipal level, the solution to the PD requires that law be a more centralized set of sanctions that provide enforcement against defection and exploitation involving more critical risks. Given Hume's logic of concepts, the definition of governance at the international level is more effective while being much less centralized. Justice faces a coordination game and the need for choice between equally eligible equilibria, not a "war of all against all." Although these levels of social organization are dialectically related, each layer of social convention is distinct with different approaches to, and solutions for, the effective establishment of sovereignty. This places Hume in the dualist, or modified dualist, school of international legal theory.[32]

Specifically, dualists regard the stratification of municipal and international law as separation between two distinct eristic systems where law at the international level cannot be automatically incorporated into municipal law but must be transformed by the action of internal government institutions to affect the municipal level of social organization. Dualists also argue that these two parallel lines of institutions and processes do not necessarily have any connection with one another because they treat very distinct areas of law. For dualists, the transformation of international into municipal law is a process only to be considered in those rare instances when the two interact.

Dualism deciphered from Hume's philosophical-policy, however, is not traditional. It contains an inherent dialectical mechanism that treats these tiers of law as interrelated components of social convention represented by the process-norm of Justice-As-Sovereignty on its single scale of forms. Hume's legal design does not ignore the international level of the rule of law nor does he ignore the interaction of both levels given their specific solutions to distinct dilemmas. The focus of Justice-As-Sovereignty on the stability and persistence of cooperation at both tiers of social organization must simultaneously protect domestic security as it invigorates international cooperation.

To the degree that continued social stability can be disturbed at either level of organization, either internally or externally by the other level of evolving social convention, the policymakers obligated to the persistence of social convention at one level need to be aware of the requirements of all levels of law and how each tier can be channeled in mutual aid to the other. The process-norm of Justice-As-Sovereignty is the means of doing this. As a whole, justice in the international legal system has a single goal: the persistence and empowerment of social order. Both tiers have different strategic situations and a distinctly adapted legal process to solve their separate contextual requirements. But they find a common imperative in the absolute presupposition of the passion for society, which requires solving collective action problems from within a process⇆principle dialectic. Justice-As-Sovereignty both separates and simultaneously integrates many municipal legal systems into a single international legal order.

But this simultaneous action of sovereignty on both tiers of the system seems to put Hume into the monist camp of stratification theory. Again, however, this seeming contradiction is only superficial. Hume's logic of concepts expresses not the traditional dichotomy between monist and dualist models, but a more critical delineation of *eristic* from *dialectic* systems of stratification. Within Hume's legal design, the "transformation" or "incorporation" of international law must be understood within this framework.

Traditional monist or dualist theory is eristic in that it suggests strict classification of law where the normative role of sovereignty is reduced in complexity by only one or the other being considered true. A dialectic model of stratification synthesizes both models and identifies a single moral standard, the process-norm of Justice-As-Sovereignty, as the basis for judgments of incorporation or transformation. The dialectic approach to stratification suggests that hard and fast rules that always make treaty a subject of transformation and custom always a subject of incorporation are not necessarily effective nor supportive of justice. Each item of international law should be judged as to whether it empowers Justice-As-Sovereignty. If so, then incorporation is called for; if not, or if there is a question as to its relation to sovereignty, then transformation is required.

However, Hume's philosophical-policy also explains why custom is usually addressed by incorporation, while treaty is not. His argument assumes a moral base in the evolution of social convention, which is argued to be the core of international legal practice. To the degree that customary law is conventional, it can be expected to empower Justice-As-Sovereignty. It would therefore become part of practice to municipally incorporate customary law without undue concern for its disruptive nature. Treaty, on the other hand, is a product of contract-by-convention and potentially contains unconventional critical principle as well as process-norms. This makes it a riskier proposition to social order and requires that Justice-As-Sovereignty allow municipal legal systems a higher degree of scrutiny.[33]

Within Hume's logic of concepts, practical reason demands that the social stability of property, not power, dictate the validity of law. This redefines those interests in terms of Justice-As-Sovereignty: locally, in municipal governance, where each nation adapts the process of evolving international social convention to its particular circumstances; and internationally, in support of a system of sovereign reciprocity meant to stabilize property between states through peaceful coexistence. Justice-As-Sovereignty is therefore not only a process-norm for the coordination of international relations through transnational law, but a general dialectic standard for the protection of municipal social order.

The metaphysical evolution of Justice-As-Sovereignty provides a solution to both international and municipal social order. It recognizes the world system as a coordination game with nested PDs. The existence of a series of stable governments at a local level of organization creates the background conditions for the universal strategic framework of the coordination game. Justice-As-Sovereignty sets the terms of the legal relationship between tiers of social organization.

The municipal level of organization has no moral priority, as it would for the dualist, but finds purpose in the empowerment of social and legal universality and complexity at the international level. But it is also true that no single all-encompassing strategic situation exists, as assumed by the monist. The national agents of cooperation are simultaneously components of two levels of law that must be dialectically considered as they inherently affect one another. The transformation/incorporation of international into municipal law is a dialectic process where both levels are intimately engaged in a common pursuit of social order. Whatever is useful to either level to help the refinement of social convention on its scale of forms is part and parcel of that nation's reciprocal moral obligation to the evolutionary process of the whole as expressed in the dialectic of local and universal rules of recognition.

Specifically, it is legitimate to incorporate international law into municipal law if the validity of the law on both levels is necessary to the refinement of Justice-As-Sovereignty. Dialectic interaction and a synthesis of law at both tiers stabilizes both domestic and global patterns of interaction through social convention. A state may develop transformation rules that will protect fundamental domestic law, like constitutions, from international law,[34] but also directly incorporate international law that supports elective convention within the society. The approach to stratification suggested by Hume's concept of law may consider transformation by municipal legislative bodies when the stability of property on the municipal level would be further enhanced by this process, but not when the legislative process would disrupt international legal relations and the comity of states.[35]

Traditional stratification theories, whether monist or dualist, are replaced with *dialectic stratification*. To secure local and universal cooperation simultaneously, legal design must yield to the fundamental dialectic imperatives of Justice-As-Sovereignty. Effectiveness and peaceful coexistence, as rules of recognition, cannot exist separately. Unless effective control is dialectically balanced by the reciprocal responsibilities of states, the world system breaks down, as it did in the Thirty Years War.

Only through the adoption of an international coordination equilibrium, and the process-norm synthesized to inform and protect it, is the dialectic genesis of an international legal system possible. Any policy of transformation or incorporation should monitor these ongoing interactions to determine how the definition of Justice-As-Sovereignty is changing. The goal is to replace a debate between dualism and monism, or transformation and incorporation, with a definition of stratification based on the shifting metaphysical complexity of Justice-As-Sovereignty.

Only in understanding the structure of dialectic interactions between the SPPs with their variant definitions of sovereignty can we understand the background conditions of international law as a expression of practical reason. With this understanding, law becomes the synthesis renderings of social convention on its scale of forms, motivated by the need for social stability and regulated by Justice-As-Sovereignty. Only then can the survival and empowerment of both municipal and international governance be assured.

II. Legal Design Implications for Policy Investigation: Social Convention in a System of Nested Games

Hume's philosophical-policy suggests a dialectic international system in which cooperation between local municipal systems creates, and is created by, the need to establish international coordination with progressively codified legal institutions. With a foundation of social convention, both local and universal social orders act to secure the public utility of a stabilized meta-system through the process-norm of Justice-As-Sovereignty. The strategic complexity of the whole system, and its distinct yet interdependent definitions of sovereignty, combines to allow greater flexibility in the way the legal design space responds to changing circumstances with synthetic practice.

The Strategic Reality of the International Design Space

Scholars have utilized game theory as a heuristic device to clarify the logic of Hume's social theory as applied to the rise of law and sociopolitical order.[36] This analysis, however, has been essentially positivist and cannot accommodate the requirements of philosophical method. Consequently, the dialectic of international and municipal social orders, their tension, and both their separate and joint contributions to Hume's greater concept of law is overlooked. The strategic creation of social convention is examined one game matrix at a time, assuming that development is independent, eristic, and value-free. Generally, analysts have preferred using bare-bones strategic rationality where self-interested persons seek utility in collectively optimal outcomes that show some type of efficiency gain.

> Strategic rationality is based on the assumption that the results of action are not what any one person chooses but the concurrence of the choices of many "players" in the strategic context.[37]

And, while Humean exegesis is sometimes honored, acknowledging, for example, Hume's idea of "limited generosity," and, assuming agents are required to play the game because they are facing particular "circumstances of justice," these disembodied bits and pieces of Hume's argument ignore the systemic nature of his thought and its inherent metaphysics.

No effort is made to understand Hume holistically, as the author of a standalone argument about human society and its conventional roots with applications to contemporary society. This position is akin to Christian fundamentalists who see the Bible as an eristic, self-contained, literal truth, where every statement is fixed in time and place without the option of allowing its truths to evolve as a philosophical basis for modern application. Positivists, as textual fundamentalists, study a philosopher only in terms of what they literally argue and the applications they literally make, freezing them and their "truths" in the past. It is assumed that, since Hume wrote in the eighteenth century, the historical context totally encases the use of his argument rather than acting as a point of departure for further evolution and application. This neglects the possibility that Hume has created a whole, systemic, and timeless argument about human nature. Because positivist method encourages the discovery or search for "new" theory, it devalues the acknowledgment and refinement of systematic philosophical argument that already exists. This prevents the Positivist from viewing Hume's work as a logical system of concepts whose integrity transcends the vagaries of his circumstances to shine light on a variety of social, political, and legal topics that he may never have imagined.

The ramifications of this scholastic fundamentalism are evident in the many minutia-based arguments about whether, for example, Kant's idea of autonomy is absolute; whether Hegel's idea of ethical life is mirrored in the Prussian state; or, in the case of Hume, whether he is describing social convention as the product of a *pure coordination game* or a PD. Positivism and its social science methodology limits the possibilities for the use of game theory in the clarification of Hume's argument as it also limits the possibilities of a broader understanding of the actual legal design space that practice works within.

Michael Taylor, in *Anarchy and Cooperation*,[38] makes a definitive positivist argument that Humean social convention is a PD. First, he distinguishes between the iterated or multiple-play and single-play versions of the PD. Then, he uses the iterated game to explain Hume's social theory. Taylor finally denies that social convention is the real subject of Hume's analysis. He contends that social convention can only be produced by a Lewis coordination game, which denies the public goods nature of the PD and therefore the essential collective action problem that Hume means to solve: stable social order. This paradox is then "solved" by Russell Hardin[39] who, through manipulation of the PD through iteration, is able to generate "contract by convention" and with it the possibility of multiple equilibria within the PD, so that it can mimic the multiple indifferent equilibria of a Lewis coordination game.

These logical acrobatics, however, are only necessary if one accepts the premise that strategic realities, and the social practices meant to address them, should be definitively classified, dichotomized, and studied as isolated, eristic, and strictly empirical subjects. This entire discussion is unnecessary if one simply acknowledges that social life is a more complex philosophical proposition with dialectically engaged logics of concepts.

Taylor is correct to note that, in the creation of social convention on the municipal level of social organization, we face a situation that makes the strategic reality of those involved unlike a Lewis coordination game. Specifically, for a pure coordination convention, like formal dress at a social gathering, it can never be in anyone's interest to unilaterally ignore the social convention and wear jeans. One need only know which mode of dress the social convention requires and coordinate their behavior with the other agents.

Hume's original social conventions of property at the municipal level, however, are different because they originate to create (or recreate after flux) social order as a collective good and to counteract the human tendency to forsake the collective interest for one's own in situations of high risk. Once created, municipal-level governance institutions generate social rules that are counted on to redirect individual self-interest toward the social or public good. Justice and government, as Humean levels of social sanction, buttress social convention and act to supplement the limited generosity of the players in the provision of collective goods. In a pure coordination game, limited generosity is sufficient to establish and maintain coordination, but it is not enough within the PD.

Governance must evolve to overcome the pressure on the individual to forsake the public interest for his own, requiring the coercive sanctions of "political society." A social convention from a pure coordination game need only act as a road sign that informs players where coordination is to be established. But for Hume, municipal-level convention provides more, namely a coercive incentive package to each agent, delivering enforcement guarantees for society that correct for any motivation to defect from established patterns of cooperation, at least until these social conventions take full affect and property is stabilized.

Hume's municipal-level of social convention compensates for the fact that when each individual is pursuing what she believes to be in her immediate interests she will produce a collectively deficient outcome in terms of a lack of coordination. Each agent will come to regard this outcome as worse than an alternative that could have been achieved had all parties acted differently and cooperated for the long-term public good. This is the psychology of a PD, not a coordination game.

> [the] "prisoner's dilemma" escaped the domain of game theory and became shorthand for a commonly occurring situation between two individuals, the one in which two people hurt each other more than they help themselves in making self-serving choices and could both be better off if obliged to choose the opposite.[40]

Lewis' coordination game also does not require a strong central government with enforcement powers, since all any potential cooperator needs to know is where the established coordination is taking place in order to cooperate. Like Lewis' example of the development of language, a coordination game definition of social convention needs neither the strong disapprobation of one's peers, nor the further sanctions of centralized justice or government, to guarantee the basic origin and persistence of social stability. Since Hume's political thought primarily addresses the specific issues related to the evolution of these sanctions, the argument against a Lewis coordination game is that Hume must be describing a PD at the strategic foundation of municipal social convention. Although this is accurate, a full examination of Hume's philosophical-policy demonstrates that a more complex argument exists.

Rapoport in his 1966 book *Two-Person Games*, classifies only one game in which the individual rationality of the players produces a collectively deficient outcome. This game is the PD (see Matrix 4.1). In its one-play version, the PD can be described as a game of isolation, where each player chooses his strategy independently, without regard for the action of the other agent. The one-play game has an atmosphere of high risk where each player's primary motivation is to insure himself of the maximum/minimum

Matrix 4.1 Prisoner's dilemma game: 1>2>3>4

	C1 [Cooperate]	C2 [Defect]
R1 [Cooperate]	(2, 2)	(4, 1)
R2 [Defect]	(1, 4)	(3, 3)

(i.e., maximin) payoff. Unlike the pure coordination game, the one-play PD has a dominant strategy: each player has a choice, namely defection from cooperation, that is best for him no matter what the other does. Row will play R2 and column C2 for, even if one should ignore his dominant strategy and choose to cooperate, it remains in the other player's interest to stay with his dominant strategy and exploit that cooperation. The result of playing dominant strategies is an equilibrium on (R2,C2) which is the result of rational choice, but collectively deficient to (R1,C1). Herein lies the dilemma.

The classic philosophical example of the one-play PD is Hobbes' description of the origin of government.[41] Humanity desires the creation of civil society but remains in an anarchic "state of nature" (R2,C2) through playing their dominant strategy. Even though civil society (R1,C1) is a preferred condition, it is unstable because each agent is cognizant that to cooperate may result in personal disadvantage; that is, exploitation, harm, or even death. As long as noncooperation is a dominant strategy (R2,C2) will be the only point of equilibrium. Hobbes solves the game by instituting a strong centralized *Sovereign*. The sovereign guarantees that, in cooperating, one will not be exploited, in effect changing the structure of the payoffs by making the (1,4) and (4,1) exploitation cells legally off-limits.

In the one-play game, there is no sense of strategic interaction: one player functions in isolation from the other. The PD in this form is a game where it is always in the interest of each player to protect himself by not cooperating as long as the collectively nonoptimal equilibrium (R2,C2) has less risk and more stability than the cooperative outcome (R1,C1). The one-shot model, however, is generally acknowledged to be incompatible with Hume's logic.

First, Hume's fundamental assumption is that the agent is not entirely self-interested, but is defined by a "limited generosity" (i.e., the dialectic synthesis of self-interest and sympathy) and part of the universal circumstances of justice. Second, the entire basis for the evolution of social convention is the iterated interactions of people. Third, although the state of nature is for Hume a "wretched" state, he argues that Hobbes' description is as much a "fiction" as the positive mythology of the "golden age."[42] Lastly, Hume's idea of governance allows for more variation than an all-or-nothing Hobbesian Sovereign.

Like all dialectic philosophical concepts with a scale of forms, Hume's concept of governance requires only that level and type of sanction necessary to the persistence of a stable social order given the context of the circumstances of justice. Social convention creates just enough coercion to address the cooperation problem at hand. On the international level, these circumstances include multiple solved PDs on the municipal level that provide a more secure basis for cooperation than the agent had at the municipal level, where no experience with secure cooperation preexisted.

Basic to Hume's argument is the absolute presupposition that humans are social creatures, incomplete without stable interaction and dynamic exchange, the pattern of which creates social convention. Social convention is assumed to be a product of multiple trial and error interactions, what game theorists call iteration. This pattern of human interaction is a product of the strategic situation in which the evolution of society takes place both locally and universally; that is, in terms of domestic and international social order.

Michael Taylor argues that an iterated PD describes the philosophies of both Hobbes and Hume. The eristic argument in *Anarchy and Cooperation* is based on the assumption that cooperation (R1,C1) can be achieved within an iterated PD, with or without the external sanctions of government. Taylor contends that, with iteration, the players become more interested in coordinating their choices with the choices of others. One agent's strategic choice affects the other's, and the players now care what the others do.[43] In a single-play PD, one should play his dominant strategy no matter what the other does. But in an iterated game, one is encouraged by the ongoing interaction to cooperate if one has reason to believe that other player(s) also will. Taylor maintains that with the advent of contingent strategies, the choice of cooperation becomes rational for players without the sanctions of government. But this positivist conclusion encounters problems with two dimensions of collective action that, considered from the standpoint of philosophical method, are less troublesome: size and discounting.[44]

Within the parameters of philosophical method and Hume's philosophical-policy, these two factors are not isolated and argued eristically, but understood as dialectic components of Hume's description of human nature. From this perspective, one recognizes that size and discounting are interrelated components of the metaphysics of social convention on its scale of forms. The capability of one to compensate for the other through the reconstitutions of the process-norm of justice makes each less separately risky to collective action.

Taylor bases the success of cooperation in the iterated PD on the assumption that discount rates will remain below a threshold. However, as Hume argues, the larger and more complex the society, the more probable it is that the requisite critical mass of individuals, necessary to maintain collective action, will not materialize. As Hume describes in his example of draining the meadow,[45] with size comes increased discounting.

Taylor[46] stipulates that his PD is not only iterated, but also an n-person game with many players. He must do so if he intends to deal with the social requirements of cooperation on the society-wide scale of forms that interested both Hume and Hobbes. However, without the secure strategic context of a pure coordination game, one faces the self-interested psychology of the iterated PD and the inevitability of low discount rates in high-risk situations.

The cooperative strategy within the PD will only be maintained as long as each player has the expectation that, first, they will not be exploited by others who choose to free-ride on their cooperation, and second, they will be prevented from exploiting others. This guarantee is difficult for the sanction of approbation to accommodate as society grows more pluralistic and populous. Here, Hume's logic of concepts on a scale of forms allows us to acknowledge something that Taylor denies.

Taylor argues that government is unnecessary to the proper coordination of players in an iterated PD. But increasing size makes it very hard for any individual to monitor other player's performance and know what to expect collectively from their choices without government signals. As Hume states, only with "political society," or the evolution from justice-conventions to governance processes and institutions, can growing numbers of players, and a more complex understanding of convention on the scale of forms, be included in cooperation without causing instability. In effect, with justice and then government, Hume's systemic approach to the question of collective action evolving on its scale of forms allows justice to compensate for both size and discounting. It allows both the PD and the pure coordination game to characterize interactions as mutually-nested, dialectic elements of that scale of forms.

Taylor's theory does not do this. He accepts Lewis' argument that social convention is fundamentally a creature of a pure coordination game. Here, positivism creates a paradox for Taylor that requires him to deny the obvious. Because Hume creates government to maintain cooperation, but since coordination conventions do not require government to create self-sustaining cooperative equilibria, Taylor states that Hume could not be describing social convention.

> Conventions not only emerge but also persist spontaneously; for a convention is an equilibrium, from which no individual has an incentive unilaterally to deviate. It follows that everyone will conform to a convention without being coerced by a government or by any other agency. Yet Hume goes on to argue that men will not voluntarily observe the conventions they make about property, and government is necessary to constrain them to conform. [Therefore]...men find themselves not in a recurrent coordination game, but in a recurrent or iterated prisoner's dilemma game (with future payoffs discounted). If this is the case, then the laws of justice cannot be conventions.[47]

Hume's logic, however, does recommend government as the third level of sanction to assure collective action, given the circumstances of justice.[48] Hume also describes the individual's normally high discount rate when he discusses the tendency of individuals to prefer present personal interest to more distant collective interests.[49] Clearly Hume is also arguing for social convention. The trouble with discounting and the need for coercive governance structures comes from the specific strategic situation and the degree of governance it requires given the scale of forms and the metaphysical balance of dialectics involved.

While Taylor has to deny social convention to embrace the PD, Russell Hardin demonstrates how convention can be the solution to an iterated PD when it is described as producing multiple coordination equilibria with the background conditions of the governance stage of sanctions.[50] Hardin's "multiple coordination equilibria" arise from the variety of strategy combinations, or patterns of interactive choices to cooperate or defect, that are available to each player. These render multiple strategic patterns of choice that each produce cooperation, and indifferent equilibria, over iterations of the game.

As choice becomes regularized, setting general expectations, the players settle on one of the multiple and utility-indifferent patterns of interplay that produce the (R1, C1) outcome. The establishment of one of the PD's "coordination equilibria" becomes more advantageous than the standard equilibrium of total defection. Coordination equilibria allow the PD to produce social convention from a multiple-equilibrium ersatz coordination game. When joint habit settles the players on a specific outcome within the PD, everyone has an incentive to cooperate and to encourage others to cooperate, if this can be done at little or no cost to them. This sets mutual expectation of behavior that creates social convention as a low cost means to resolve the PD.

The specific stage of convention Hardin describes is the same as we have attributed to Hume's origin of governance: *contract-by-convention*.[51] But social convention for Hume is supported by both approbation and justice before political society. Specifically, Hume argues[52] that government is the third and most coercive level of sanctions, dependent on a preexisting and conventional process-norm of justice. Therefore Hardin's contention that social convention originates from multiple strategies at the contract-by-convention stage ignores Hume's presupposition that social convention is a prerequisite to any contract.

Hume's philosophical-policy creates a global scale of forms for social convention that begins at the smallest human group interaction and evolves to an international level of society. Humanity seeks greater and more complex expressions of the passion for society and requires the progressive codification of law to make this happen. While the international level is different, Hume's logic assumes that, at the municipal level, this requires property stabilization from within the strategic context of a PD; he stipulates that government is necessary to create social order.

What Taylor and Hardin fail to grasp is that each level of social organization has its own strategic context. Although at the municipal level a PD is being played out, with many stable municipal states, Hume's concept of law acknowledges a more universal definition of society that requires a transnational coordination game. On a scale of forms, with the background of established cooperation within states, the need to coordinate states at a new level of social interaction begins again at the approbation stage. Given the unique characteristics of the Humean agent, and this new context for the international circumstances of justice provided by the changing strategic reality of a coordination game, the task of social convention is different. The coordination game allows a lower level of sanction to support international relations. With the evolution of Justice-As-Sovereignty, approbation in a world of *Lotus* prohibitions is more than sufficient. Only with the advent of critical principle and the looming transition to a Stage-II international legal system in the twentieth century, do the further requirements of international political society become an issue.

Social convention for Hume's philosophical-policy is not the privileged product of a single type of game, but a dialectic multi-tiered process where one level of solved games creates a new strategic reality for the next level of social interaction on an extended scale of forms. Social convention is intended to establish social order by adapting to its strategic reality and creating a distinct system of practice given the unique circumstances of each level of social organization.

However, Hume argues that the origin of justice and governance on the municipal level tests the circumstances of justice in a more drastic way. While individuals need society, states need a law of nations less desperately.[53] The imperative to move up the scale of forms in terms of a larger and more global sense of society motivates the creation of international relations, which necessitates international law. But higher and more complex levels of organization depend on the level below for sufficient stability to initially coordinate social convention and, so, with municipal law and the stability of many component states having solved their PDs, international society becomes more stable and is less in need of higher-order sanctions or greater centralization. Hume's philosophical-policy describes a dialectic and holistic system of tiers of social convention that fight instability at one level of social organization with compensating stability at another.[54]

When international social convention seeks a point of coordination, a stable set of solved PDs at the local level are relied upon to supply enough security so that basic international social conventions can be realized in practice. What matters is how all of these sanctions dialectically interact to create an overall global equilibrium. Hume, like Kelsen, argues that social order is the specific idea of social convention for a particular context and may require distinct sanctions to coordinate in any particular constituent circumstance.

> [even] approval and disapproval by the fellow members of the community are as reward and punishment and may therefore be interpreted as sanctions...It is therefore doubtful whether a distinction between social orders with and without sanctions is possible. The only relevant difference is...that they [social orders] prescribe different types of sanctions.[55]

> The first characteristic, then, common to all social orders designated by the word "law" is that they are orders of human behavior. A second characteristic is that they are *coercive orders*.[56]

With layers of sanction within tiers of social convention, Hume departs from Hobbes one-size-fits-all idea of a centralized sovereign covenant as the solution to the PD. The reality of Hume's scale of forms, for both the size and complexity of the society and the sanctions involved, is a more practical and effective alternative reality for a world system with more complex recognition and stratification requirements (viz. local, national, and international social dimensions). Hume does, eventually, solve the collective action problem presented by the municipal PD with the creation of government that involves a conscious contract to create the institutions of "political society," so it can "maintain peace,...execute justice,...chuse magistrates, determine their power, and promise them obedience."[57] But the origin of government in contract or promise does not establish society, morals, promising, or justice, as they do in Hobbes; all exist prior to the origin of the Humean state. This distinguishes Hume's philosophical-policy from Taylor's analysis, which concludes that the collective action theories of both Hobbes and Hume are essentially the same because both solve a PD with government.[58] Philosophical method suggests that this comparison lacks adequate attention to metaphysical detail.

Governance for Hume is always *process* as an end-in-itself, and neutral to the specific values of the social order. Hume argues that humanity imposes layer-upon-layer of formal sanctions when and where they are needed, and because the other more fundamental layers exist, governance at the international level solves a different strategic dilemma with different sanctions than are needed for the PD. On an international level, the initial configuration of governance institutions need only be modest and decentralized. What is important is to seek the coordination equilibrium between indifferent institutional options, and then to allow all the constituents to find it. Those who defect on the municipal level have the enforcement of the law by central institutions and complex legal systems to dissuade them. While international defectors have no such "police" to concern them, the conventional conditions of membership in the international system, and the inherent advantages of that transnational point of equilibrium, are at stake in their coordination with a zero payoff for the defector. Hume's philosophical-policy recognizes that the solution to the international coordination game is a more secure outcome without the noncooperative characteristics of a PD. Even under these less strict conditions, Hume argues that only "the most extreme necessity"[59] would produce a nation's defection from the international coordination game.

Hume, after all, suggests that the "Knave" chooses his immediate advantage because he feels that his defection will not hurt the provision of collective goods for anyone else.[60] Hume describes the Knave as one who does not see himself as part of the critical mass necessary to establish collective action. But critical mass is a less significant concept within a pure coordination game because all the players are motivated to cooperate and have no reason to question whether they need to or if others will. In the same way that one has an inherent interest in learning one's "native" language, all states have an inherent interest in coordinating themselves within a self-enforcing framework of social convention based on Justice-As-Sovereignty at the Westphalian Equilibrium. This is where the stability of international society exists.

Hume's state agent, the idea of the Knave notwithstanding, has already been socialized, at the municipal level, through moral approbation, the process-norm of justice, and government when the further evolution of the international system presents itself. At the international level, it is the artifice of state leaders that is primary and, while it is possible that Knaves may be among these personages, their socialization, or what Hume calls their "artifice," is such that arguments for cooperation are less necessary here than for those whose personal and professional interests do not merge with the municipal public good.

This illustrates another way in which Hume's argument is both much simpler and more complex than either Taylor's or Hardin's: inherent metaphysical content. On both tiers of the world system, the advent of social convention creates a moral and then legal obligation to these conventions, as justice is added to approbation and governance institutions to justice. While both Taylor and Hardin acknowledge the iteration of human interactions that create social convention, in solving either a PD or a coordination game, they nevertheless fail to see that the critical element in these iterations is the norms created from them. Hardin, for example, contends that the number of players is less of a problem because of what he calls "the overlapping nature of activities" and that "large-scale contract by convention [is] a product of overlapping small-group interactions."[61] This allows the PD to be solved for large societies without government.[62]

> a convention covering the behavior of a very large class of people, none of whom interacts personally with more than a fraction of the class, can be built up out of smaller sub-group interactions in a large class situation.[63]

In the same way that multilateral treaties are more likely because of a state's experience with bilateral negotiation, Hardin depends on an unacknowledged scale of forms for the concept of collective action and accepts the idea that habit leads to custom which in turn leads to social convention, first locally, then, perhaps, even nationally, and internationally.

Hume's philosophical-policy, however, transcends Hardin's empirical dependence on validated experience, to focus more on the norms generated by the dialectic interaction of metaphysical presuppositions that transfigure human experience into a pattern of practice with universality, certainty, and duty. The normative dialectic creates the conditions under which one's experience, as well as their expectations, reinforce one another and establish moral obligation to the resulting social conventions as a prerequisite to justice. For international law, approbation, justice, and government are simply different expressions of the same process-norm: Justice-As-Sovereignty.

With a passion-based natural law, Hume's philosophical-policy can accommodate any size state with any level of political or social complexity, even international relations between states, with the same metaphysical argument.[64] Hardin must, in the end, admit the limitations of depending solely on positivist assumptions in a large society without government.

> contract by convention depends on knowledge conditions—the more people whose behavior one must know well enough to consider it predictable, the less one will be able to know about each of them on average. Hence, the prospects for successful contract by convention decline as group size increases.[65]

As Hardin admits, knowledge alone is insufficient for sustained cooperation. Knowledge must be backed by norms that speak to a deeper and more inherent set of metaphysical presuppositions; they infuse behavior with duty in order for it to influence choice persistently. Facts alone do not grant universality and certainty to legal rules; their inherent normative standards do.

Hume's simpler argument dismisses the Taylor–Hardin debate and simultaneously gives the analyst a more complex, flexible, and multilayered idea of social convention and governance. For Hume, the task for social groups forming states, and for states forming an international system, is not as simple as the appointment of an absolute sovereign. Social convention provides a conscious and unconscious process by which flexibility allows for "free" or "mix'd"[66] government, able to utilize process-norms for the benefit of mutually interactive tiers of social organization. Because of their common roots in evolving social convention, different systems of law can more easily interact and coordinate themselves around a process-norm like Justice-As-Sovereignty.

> For besides that nothing is more essential to public interest, than the preservation of public liberty; "tis evident, that if such a mix'd government be once suppos'd to be establish'd, every part or member of the constitution must have a right of self-defense, and of maintaining its ancient bounds against the encroachment of every other authority.[67]

Law in an Evolving International System

Convention arises on the municipal level to solve PDs. On the international level, it evolves from within the strategic context of a tiered coordination game to establish coordination through Justice-As-Sovereignty. The evolution of the international system, as sovereignty moves on its scale of forms from the regulation of a Stage-I legal system into Stage-II, requires explanation. During the international evolution of the rule of law, the full engagement of the process⇆principle dialectic in Stage-II provides a challenge to social convention established in Stage-I. Assuming that the dialectic reflects, and is reflected in, the strategic situation met by Justice-As-Sovereignty, then the possibilities for change in the strategic space become significant.

In the evolution of a Humean international legal system, social convention creates a new layer of interface between states to find a coordination equilibrium for the relations of a group of nested PDs. This takes place within a design space characterized by a definition of Justice-As-Sovereignty that regulates a more decentralized and prohibition-based legal space, granting local effective control the dominant role. In this first moment of its essence, sovereignty represents a dialectic between process⇆principle that is significantly weighted toward process. Principle, as a source of law, is limited to its contextual rather than its critical role in codification.

As the demands of the international strategic space become institutionalized, with the introduction of the sanction of governance through contract-by-convention, the transition to a Stage-II legal system is initiated. At this point, the process-norm of Justice-As-Sovereignty, and its legal design space, must accommodate the more complex metaphysical demands of the evolving legal system. This means that the process-norm will need to more fully incorporate, or compensate for, critical principle in its confrontation with established conventions. These metaphysical changes also have the potential to change the character of the strategic situation regulated by Justice-As-Sovereignty.

Hume's philosophical-policy illustrates that law is drawn predominantly from process-norms, but in the transition to Stage-II, social convention and its contextual principle no longer fully represent the requirements of law on either level (see Figure 2.1). The full introduction of aetiological-norms into the design space finds its origin in the human tendency, once a social milieu is stabilized, to seek a deeper level of moral satisfaction in terms of rights and rules from reasoned critical principles. These critical principles refine the essence of the law to account for humanity as an intrinsic value. In representing the more essential value of the person and their living environment, critical principles require that the law operate on more than a means-driven instrumental level focused on utility, order, and the social conventions that secure them. Critical principle is about substance rather than procedure, making humanity, rather than the means of cooperation, the end-in-itself.

If critical principle empowers revolutionary change through contract and legal design in the name of aetiological-norms, that change will disrupt, and may even drastically rearrange, the strategic background conditions of established social convention. The full engagement of the process⇆principle dialectic has the potential to create alternative points of coordination or potential equilibria that challenge the predominance of the Westphalian Equilibrium.[68] These alternative equilibria may advocate, for example, critical principles like the right to protect (R2P) or international human rights, resulting in the erosion of *Lotus* sovereignty.

Maintaining convention, or replacing one process-norm with another over an extended period of time, is a less disturbing alternative, and is always, initially, the risk-dominant[69] equilibrium. Critical principle as a source for a new equilibrium can be resisted if Justice-As-Sovereignty can be refined without losing its core. That is, if sovereignty can rebalance its inherent dialectics and find a new moment in its scale of forms, this will allow it, as a process-norm, to regenerate, which is a less risky alternative to the international social order. For example, perhaps a more absolute sense of *Lotus* sovereignty can be replaced by a manifestation of sovereignty that focuses on collective security regulating the influence of critical principle. In this scenario, the focus remains on process and social convention while sovereignty is amended in a way that maintains its regulatory force as a process-norm even at a new equilibrium.

In any case, moving to a new equilibrium takes a critical mass of cooperators defecting from status quo convention. This also requires, in Hume's terms, a redefinition of the public interest, a reorientation and empowerment of trust to lower the risk of change to overall social order, and refocusing the sanctions of social convention to a rebalanced set of relative metaphysical presuppositions.

The context of this dynamic rebalancing will require a readjustment of human expectations. Because the bulwark of established social convention is powerful, no one person or small group can dramatically or immediately reorient the system alone. Consequently, it will require the support, or total destruction, of political and legal institutions to fully implement change. This is a scenario for revolution rather than evolution. In the same way that long-term patterns of interaction, the Thirty Years War, and extended negotiations were necessary to locate the equilibrium codified by the Treaties of Westphalia, a new point of coordination will require enough incentives for change to cause a conscious reevaluation of the strategic situation by citizens and politicians alike.[70]

In effect, this reorientation of the point of coordination acquires the characteristics of an assurance type of coordination game. Here, the agent's choice is not dominated by the need to defect, as it would be in the PD, but neither is it self-evidently cooperative as in a pure coordination game. Each state's action will depend on its perception of what choices other states will make, as the changing conditions of the game progress. Under these conditions, choices and expectations will become self-reinforcing. If one is assured that they can switch equilibria without exploitation, they will; if no assurance is forthcoming, they will stay where they are.

Any assurance game is significantly affected by signals given to the players by the legal system. If a new equilibrium is validated in law, through custom, treaty, or principle, it gains a persuasive edge in creating that critical mass necessary to move to an alternative equilibrium. Whether based on another process-norm or a critical principle, in order to make headway against the established control of status quo social convention, the codification of, for example, a human right must take Justice-As-Sovereignty into account. As the conventional definition of justice attempts to readjust its dialectic balance to maintain its regulatory control of the international legal system, there will be a space when the first moment of its essence can be transcended (e.g., a transition will begin between a Stage-I and Stage-II legal system), but the established equilibrium will still command allegiance. In effect, the players will have two equilibria, but equilibria that are not yet of indifferent value to them. This means that another strategic situation will be in effect until the equilibria are again indifferent and the pure coordination game is reestablished.

This transitional strategic situation may be most readily compared to a *Stag Hunt* game.[71] In this case, the preestablished equilibrium, focused on social convention, process, and legal practice, is equivalent to hunting the *Hare*, while the newly competitive alternative can be described as hunting the *Stag* (see Matrix 4.2).

The Stag Hunt is a variant of a coordination game in which the players are accustomed to an equilibrium where each is able to provide their own social order through an idea of Justice-As-Sovereignty. Here, the bulwark of social convention supports *Lotus* prohibitions, effective control, and reciprocal coordination in terms of general rules of nonintervention. This established social convention, from the first essential moment of Justice-As-Sovereignty, is akin to "hare hunting." It breeds a situation where each state, within the context of an international Stage-I legal system, becomes very good at self-help or "independent hare hunting" and where the collective or public interest of the international system as a whole is invested in the practice of strict sovereignty as social order for the sake of a system of independent, hare-hunting states.

Historically, sovereignty as self-sufficiency was selected from a pair of indifferent equilibria, perhaps Westphalia (i.e., hunting hare), or a system of royal alliances (i.e., hunting beaver), where the former was somehow more reasonable given the context of the Reformation, the Thirty Years War, and the disintegration of the Papal System. The evolution of law on the international level created social convention from customary law, contextual principle, and treaty, where the codified rules of this basic international society were derived from the choice of equilibrium. But then, one of two things happens as the idea of international society grows in complexity,

Matrix 4.2 Stag hunt game

	Stag	Hare
Stag	(4, 4)	(1, 3)
Hare	(3, 1)	(2, 2)

No Hunt = 1, Hunting Hare Together = 2, Hunting Hare Alone = 3, Hunting Stag = 4

A. The hunters each have the choice of hunting hare or hunting deer.

B. The chances of getting a hare are independent of what any other player does. Although if one hunts hare alone one can get more food than competing for the limited population together. 3>2.

C. There is no chance of bagging a deer by oneself.

D. The chances of a successful deer hunt go up sharply with the number of hunters.

E. A deer is more collectively valuable than a hare.

progressively codifies, and makes a transition toward a more complex Stage-II legal system.

On the one hand, for some reason, perhaps circumstantial, or more probably because of the introduction of critical principle that causes vast disruption, hunting hare becomes impossible in one sudden and violent episode. States can no longer survive within a convention of self-sufficiency because hares are extinct (e.g., the universality of Papal revelation ceases to exist). This sudden rise and transition to substantive or critical principle as the core of a new coordination equilibrium can be called the *revolution scenario*.[72] While this option is both interesting and relevant, Hume's philosophical-policy gives us little by way of strategic description for it. This is because Hume's argument is mostly concerned with his primary route to the law: the evolution and maintenance of a stable pattern of social convention. As we have seen, critical principle is understood to be generally disruptive and therefore to be deflected, slowed down, or avoided altogether.

The other, more common, scenario is less violent and more gradual. A new imperative, for example, *reciprocity* in terms of *trade efficiency*, creates an alternative point of equilibrium (i.e., hunting stag). This makes a persuasive argument for the dialectic rebalancing of Justice-As-Sovereignty away from its *Lotus* moment in order to promote global markets as a more advantageous basis for international coordination and sovereign interaction. Although the prospect of an international system coordinating reciprocal trade may be of higher value, like a stag, it is also more dependent on collective action, more difficult to create, and more risky to international coordination than maintaining the existing process-norm of Justice-As-Sovereignty and its Westphalian Equilibrium.

Because the new imperative for change remains based on process rather than critical principle, this allows the process-norm of Justice-As-Sovereignty to maintain itself in the transition through a redefinition of the idea of reciprocity within its inherent dialectics. The transition to hunting stag can be more gradual as both moments for the concept of sovereignty seek process-based social conventions for coordination, but in different ways. The resulting equilibrium may be based on, for example, the World Trade Organization treaties rather than the treaties of Westphalia, but the process-norm will have maintained international coordination to the stability of international society. As long as the basis for change is biased toward process rather than critical principle, there is less risk that Justice-As-Sovereignty will be unable to compensate for change and maintain international social order.

In addition, with the advent of contract-by-convention, progressive codification may validate the alternative under a multilateral treaty, providing further assurance that hunting stag will not be in vain. As the social convention of hunting hare is overtaken by stag hunting, the former can be relied upon to provide the background conditions in which the latter can become established at minimal risk to the "food supply" (i.e., international legal order).

Replacing one convention with another requires a collective effort on the part of the players, and depends on the revitalized process-norm utilizing political society to create that critical mass of cooperators necessary to establish a new allegiance to a refined social convention. At first, this alternative will be the subject of antagonistic preferences, then indifference, but eventually it will attract players with its ability to maintain the overall coordination of the international system. But with one social convention replacing another, both honor the passion for society through the same process-norm, avoiding the dominance of critical principle.

The value of the new trading norm (i.e., its physical and metaphysical dimensions) to the long-term stability and empowerment of society makes it a viable challenger to the dominance of self-sufficiency, the hunting hare convention. The status quo convention gives way after increasing numbers of stag hunting groups stabilize and the new equilibrium becomes the point of coordination by providing a more certain and universal social order than its predecessor for the new strategic reality. Let's call the situation where one point of equilibrium replaces another, both regulated by process-norms, the *evolutionary scenario.*

> Over time there is some low level of experimentation with stag hunting. Eventually a small group of stag hunters comes to interact largely or exclusively with each other. This can come to pass through pure chance and the passage of time in a situation of interaction with neighbors [evolution]. Or it can happen more rapidly when stag hunters find each other by means of fast interaction dynamics [revolution]. The small group of stag hunters prospers and can spread by reproduction or imitation....As a local culture of stag hunting spreads, it can even maintain viability in an unfavorable environment of a large, random-mixing population by the device of signaling.[73]

Finding and maintaining an equilibrium within a coordination game is based on the ability of players to signal one another to the desired point of coordination. The stag hunt is a type of coordination game, except that the two competitive equilibria are not indifferent between the players. The stag hunt equilibrium is preferred by the players, but is also a higher risk than the conventional equilibrium of hare hunting. The solution to the game is to create assurance signals that lessen risk, so that the stag hunt can become a truly accessible choice. The existence of governance institutions helps with this signaling requirement.

When a critical mass of states have elected the new equilibrium, this suggests that the process norm has redefined itself from, for example, *Justice-As-Hare Hunting* to *Justice-As-Stag Hunting*. This lessens the risk to the stability of the system during transition, because a common process-norm, with the same dialectic web of presuppositions, defines the metaphysics of both manifestations of Justice-As-Sovereignty. The change in the risk implied by a switch of social convention from hare to stag hunting is more rapidly assimilated because it draws on the allegiance already established to its inherent metaphysics and the moral support thus guaranteed in its new form (i.e., Justice-As-Stag Hunting).

Progressive codification from one essential moment of sovereignty to the next creates a single pattern of practice where "once a small group... is formed... justice becomes contagious and rapidly takes over the entire population."[74] A common process-norm provides a common standard for trust and a common means to the ends of society. Its stability, like all social conventions, gradually creates a new worldview by rebalancing its metaphysical presuppositions. Rather than the simple utility of one's payoffs, moving from the hunting of hare to stag is a matter of new signaling norms, trust, belief, and assurance, based on a common metaphysical substructure adjusting to a changing strategic situation. The vital metaphysics of the change grants insight. But it is specifically this dimension of the change that positivism, alone, is helpless to analyze.

> assuming that everyone must cooperate for a successful outcome to the hunt—the problem of trust is multiplied. But if we ask how people can get from a hare hunt equilibrium to a stag hunt equilibrium, it does not have much to offer. From the standpoint of rational choice, for hare hunters to decide to be stag hunters, each must *change individual beliefs* about what the other will do. But rational choice-based game theory, as usually conceived, has nothing to say about how or why such a change of mind might take place.[75]

A Root Metaphysics of Trust and Promise

Hume's "true metaphysics" creates obligation to process-norms, duties in promising, and trust for participation in society, all from the reaction of agents to the dynamics of their strategic context. The risk of stag hunting to the hare hunter is that it takes collective rather than individual action and the payoffs must be shared rather than consumed directly by the hunter who did the work. The key to both understanding and controlling this risk is in the metaphysics of promise-keeping and trust, as normative ideas.

Hume's philosophical-policy anticipates the transitional games between layers of social convention and stages of the legal system. This is achieved by the evolution of social convention that dialectically compensates for change. These conventions, and their steadfast process-norm of Justice-As-Sovereignty, flesh out the payoff structure of these dynamic games. Specifically, they grant them stability with moral obligation to convention in *promising* and the duty to keep those promises in *trust*.

Within the context of the alternative equilibria of a transitional Stag Hunt, the metaphysical background conditions imbue a qualitative value on the payoffs of one's obligation and duty. Because of the common nature of this metaphysics to both alternatives, an effective environment of promise-keeping and trust can be maintained while the point of coordination changes. Justice-As-Sovereignty, whether made manifest in hunting hare or stag, remains the representative of the absolute presupposition of the passion for stability in society (or the food supply). Therefore, shifting one's obligation from one equilibrium to the other is a matter of transferring a conventional sense of trust based on the same underlying end: coordination in the provision of a collective good.

Comprehending the inherent stability of the strategic dynamics of the international system from within Hume's philosophical-policy requires us to understand the metaphysical presuppositions of his idea of natural law. An examination of how his exegesis supports both stability⇆change in the legal design space is helpful.

As with all applications of Hume's philosophical-policy, we begin with the individual's need for society. It "[t]is by society alone he is able to supply his defects."[76] Through the division of labor, small social groups create and empower themselves to continue the evolution of social convention up a scale of forms to its essence in universal society.

> When every individual person labors a-part, and only for himself, his force is too small to execute any considerable work; his labors being employ'd in supplying all his different necessities, he never attains a perfection in any particular art; and his force and success are not at times equal, the least failure in either of these particulars must be attended with inevitable ruin and misery. Society provides a remedy for these three inconveniences. By the conjunction of forces, our power is augmented: By the partition of employments, our ability encreases: And by mutual succour we are less expos'd to fortune and accidents. 'Tis by this additional *force, ability, and security,* that society becomes advantageous.[77]
>
> The passion for society is accompanied by the instability of property. This progression is inherently normative. Hume states that "all property depends on morality; and...all morality depends on the ordinary course of our passions."[78]

Property is an empirical obstacle to the full expression of the passion for social stability as it has the potential, given the circumstances of justice, to disrupt cooperation on the municipal level, or coordination on the international tier, by its inherent instability. Property is built on the absolute presupposition of one's need for society, but acts as a material condition to the dialectic balance of relative presuppositions in the production of that stability through social convention. The lasting affect of social convention comes from a combination of the utility of property to the individual, the relationship of pain and pleasure to that utility,[79] and the role of causality in understanding one's relationship to and definition of property itself.

> But nothing has a greater effect both to encrease and diminish our passions, to convert pleasure into pain, and pain into pleasure, than custom and repetition. Custom has two *original* effects upon the mind, in bestowing a *facility* in the performance of any action or the conception of any object; and afterwards a *tendency or inclination* toward it; and from these we may account for all its other effects, however extraordinary.[80]

The stability of property is necessary to the successful expression of the passions. Human understanding is based on customary reoccurrence signifying causality and its resultant universality and certainty to the observer. In addition, the social conventions for the stability of property, as well as the definition of the concept itself, become a type of normative causality within Hume's logic of concepts.

> property may be defin'd, [as] such a relation betwixt a person and an object as permits him, but forbids any other, the free use and possession of it, without violating the laws of justice and moral equity. If justice, therefore, be a virtue, which has a natural and original influence on the human mind, property may be look'd upon as a particular species of causation; whether we consider the liberty it gives the proprietor to operate as he pleases upon the object, or the advantages, which he reaps from it…[as] the mention of the property naturally carries our thought to the proprietor, and of the proprietor to the property; which being a proof of a perfect relation of ideas is all that is requisite.[81]

This metaphysical substructure is crowned by the evolution of justice as an artificial virtue created by humanity to overcome the circumstances preventing the requisite stability of society. The need for society gains legitimacy in those legal sanctions evolved as social conventions to reinforce the stability of property through coordination on a strategic equilibrium. With sanctions of approbation, justice, and then codified law, Hume argues that "[p]roperty must be stable, and must be fix'd by general rules."[82] Hume builds rules from practice and its metaphysical underpinnings, giving positive law a common goal in the passion for social stability, and a firm foundation in a morality of public utility, breeding trust, and obligation.

Hume's theory of consent is also compatible with the same metaphysical root as stability of property. Consent is not important to Hume in and of itself, but only as a means for the transference of property and its stability during transition. Consent is a contextual principle and the means to the end of secure coordination when an established equilibrium is challenged.

How property is initially owned, and how just ownership persists afterward is the point of departure for understanding any legal system based on social convention. For Hume, all property conventions can be seen in only one light, which is also our SPP for universal recognition within the international system: *reciprocal cooperation in a peaceful social order*.[83] In turn, this peace can only be preserved within an international legal process where changes in specific points of coordination share the same root metaphysics. Hume's idea of natural law generates rules universally, without regard for the idiosyncrasies of the individual state.

> The convention concerning the stability of possession is enter'd into, in order to cut off all occasions of discord and contention; and this end wou'd never be attain'd, were we allowed to apply this rule differently in every particular case, according to every particular utility, which might be discover'd in such an application…It follows, therefore, that the general rule, *that possessions*

> *must be stable*, is not apply'd by particular judgments, but by other general rules, which must extend to the whole society, and be inflexible either by spite or favour.[84]

However, since approbation and justice precede government and codified rules, Hume also provides for a prelaw conventional rule by which property can be stabilized: "constancy of possession."[85] This is the local rule of recognition or "effective control." It is the key to any "first" conventional allocation of property within the municipal PD, but also marks the obligation of a state to cooperate in a minimal set of international laws that broker peace and resolve disputes not resolvable by municipal systems, but necessary to their nested stability.

Because his argument for social conventions of justice is process-based, and therefore neutral between specific ends that might give moral definition to first allocation of ownership, Hume opts for the idea that one maintains possession of what one has in the first iteration of property conventions as the normative standard for legal design. Hume's philosophical-policy seeks, primarily, to explain the "general convention for the establishment of society"[86] that creates the original stability of property and the basis for peaceful cooperation in a Stage-I system. In considering the future transfer of property, consent becomes more important.

> But we may observe, that tho' the rules of the assignment of property to the present possessor be natural, and by that means useful, yet its utility extends not beyond the first formation of society...We must, therefore, seek for some other circumstance, that may give rise to property after society is once establish'd; and of this kind, I find four most considerable, *viz.* Occupation, Prescription, Accession, and Succession.[87]

The core of Hume's metaphysics, within the first essential moment of Justice-As-Sovereignty, is *reciprocity* in the transference of property. This is the only *peaceful* or valid means to stabilize international society as it progressively codifies and moves toward a full dialectic of process⇆principle in a Stage-II legal system. Conquest is contrary to Justice As Sovereignty and unjust. The other four means of legitimate transference may be just, but only through the sanction of Justice-As-Sovereignty. All shifting of property can create "very considerable inconveniences...which calls for a remedy."[88] The remedy combines trust and promise in mutual or reciprocal consent.

> To apply one [remedy] directly, and allow every man to seize by violence what he judges to be fit for him, wou'd destroy society; and therefore the rules of justice seek some medium betwixt a rigid stability, and this changeable and uncertain adjustment. But there is no medium better than the obvious one, that possession and property shou'd always be stable, except when the proprietor agrees to bestow them on some other person. This rule can have no ill consequence, in occasioning wars and dissentions; since the proprietor's consent, who alone is concern'd, is taken along in the alienation.[89]

The dialectic dynamic between the SPPs creates the common basis for social convention as it regulates the material condition of property with the process-norm of Justice-As-Sovereignty. Consent, in terms of promise, and trust in that promise, create a stable foundation for both convention and change. Hume's concept of natural law grounds the idea of change: "the translation of property by consent is founded on a law of nature."[90]

Stable property relations are the Humean motivation for social convention. Property therefore has a logical and metaphysical connection to human passion, the SPPs as rules of recognition, and the process-norm of Justice-As-Sovereignty. The peaceful maintenance of these conventional practices, at the most universal level of organization, becomes the end-in-itself for the political society. On all levels of social organization, rules are metaphysically legitimate to the degree they support the peace and stability of international coordination and the underlying passion for social order that this represents. When the allegiance to one point of coordination is traded for another, this same metaphysical footing provides the trust and obligation necessary to stabilize the dynamic evolution of the international rule of law.

Hume's philosophical-policy has a series of implications for how one understands the international system. First, international relations is not defined by superficial power struggles within a chaotic state of nature, but is about improving collective social life by providing social convention as a procedural and continuing means for the stability of international property.

Second, Hume's concept of the international system and its stratification does not fit neatly into either monism or dualism. His idea of stratification suggests that incorporation and transformation should be applied as legal standards given their adherence to Justice-As-Sovereignty. The choice between incorporation and transformation should be made on the basis of which causes the pertinent case to have the most positive effect on international stability.

Third, the international legal system is a complex metaphysics based on the absolute presupposition of the passion for society, containing the interaction of the SPPs of reciprocal cooperation, effective control, and progressive codification and regulated by the process-norm of Justice-As-Sovereignty. In the transition from a Stage-I into a Stage-II legal system, the full engagement of the process⇆principle dialectic creates both a new strategic situation and a new moment for Justice-As-Sovereignty as it grapples with change, depending on a common metaphysics of trust and obligation to maintain its authority.

Fourth, general or customary international law becomes the most critical and foundational manifestation of law as social convention within the international system. The value of custom, as a source of international law is not principally in consent or opinio jus et necessatis, which must await contract-by-convention and subsequent promising. Its value is in those *practices* that render the process-norm of Justice-As-Sovereignty and the SPPs as procedural rules of recognition (local and universal), adjudication, and change. Customary law as social convention is the point of departure for all other sources of international law. This is true both in terms of contextual *principle*, which predates its critical counterpart, and *treaty* that requires contract-by-convention and an institutional structure for legitimacy.

Hume's philosophical-policy, as an application of practical reason to international law, promotes a concern for the collective, or in this case, international stabilization of property, over a concern for private power as the core of international relations. Utility, specifically public utility, lies at the center of Hume's philosophical and political argument. Justice-As-Sovereignty finds its genesis, or its first essential moment, in terms of justice-as-utility, which is also the first moment on the scale of forms for practical reason applied to international law.

Hume focuses on the collective ramifications of utility as it transforms human passions into concrete social agency. He acknowledges that "interest" is a necessary basis for law, but this is a distinctly social definition of interest, reacting to specific strategic situations that create social convention for the protection of society. The specific legal and moral content of social convention in terms of justice and governance may differ on the municipal, as opposed to the international, level of social organization. But all social convention has a common metaphysics of public utility and a common absolute presupposition in the persistence of society. The power to create collective order grants all "social" convention its metaphysical point of origin in human passion, and its progressive goal in a system of law that seeks the essence of society in its most complex and all-inclusive manifestation at the global level.

The Humean perspective upsets the positivist's priority for preference or interest as the currency of international relations. Hume focuses on private interests only to the extent that they provide public utility in the stable coordination of international social order. Hume introduces a metaphysical argument for public utility as a prerequisite to the empirical facts of the international system. With its inherent and evolving scale of forms, Justice-As-Sovereignty seeks to encompass the widest possible complexity and diversity of human society in its evolving definition of public utility. This makes law at the international level more pertinent to, if not more important than, its municipal counterpart for the persistence and expansion of both a local and a universal sense of social stability.

The artificial nature of justice means that it is only of utility when considered in the general rather than the specific application. Hume denies that justice is a natural virtue specifically because, if it were, all private applications would be of interest, and therefore of utility, to both the individual and the society. Instead, he defines the artificial virtues dialectically in terms of their overall long-term capacity to consistently favor public over private good.

Unlike positivism, Hume's argument focuses, not on the individual agent but, upon "the happiness of human society"[91] and states that "public utility is the *sole* origin of justice."[92] He argues that "justice evidently tends to promote public utility and to support civil society,"[93] providing that for all governance institutions the moral imperative is in the "safety of the people [as] the supreme law."[94]

While Hume does not deny the existence of private interests and a private sphere,[95] and even acknowledges that sometimes it can be advantageous for individual agents to act on their own preferences and against the law,[96] private interests occupy a recessed role in his conceptual logic, beneath public utility. For Hume's philosophical-policy, if private concerns and private "national" interests were the motivating force behind international justice and law, they would exacerbate rather than tame the circumstances of justice, cause self-interest to transcend limited generosity, and add to the chaos of the international system, against humanity's primary passion for society and social order. With a focus on the public utility of social order and cooperation, Hume's philosophical-policy describes an equality of individual social power as a basic circumstance of justice and contends that power, over people or things, is of value only to the degree that it empowers cooperation and the production of public utility in society.

Hume's dialectic approach balances the social with the individual as mutually interdependent dimensions of Justice-As-Sovereignty. As the public utility of social convention is created from the interactions of individuals with limited generosity, so the private power over property as the medium of social convention is only legitimate in the service of public order and stability. Justice, through the private power or "artifice" of politicians, exists in Hume's philosophical-policy to facilitate public spirit and to assure the persistence of society; private preferences are assumed to be part and parcel of the public good, rather than focused on narrow personal advantage.

In the end, Hume's focus is on the justice necessary to maintain the persistence of international peace and cooperation between states as they move through various strategic contexts. Instead of the positivist assumptions of power and self-help, as the watchwords of the international system, Hume's philosophical-policy focuses on how Justice-As-Sovereignty balances local effectiveness with universal cooperation to produce social convention as a foundation for public utility. In this way, justice compensates for specifically those qualities of life that positivists, without a metaphysical sense of justice, assume are determinative.

nature has put man in an unfortunate position due to "the numberless wants and necessities, with which she has loaded him, and in the slender means, with which she affords to the relieving these necessities."[97] In other animals, "these two particulars generally compensate each other"[98] in that they have few and simple needs which are easily satisfied. Society provides a remedy for three specific kinds of problems, relating to *force, ability, and security*. First, self-sufficiency is extremely time-consuming, and we lack the power to adequately fulfill our own needs when we work in isolation or in competition with each other. Second, the sheer number of skills involved in having to provide all one's own food, protect oneself from the elements and each other, and so on, are a tax on even the most able of us. Third, even if one could temporarily achieve this self-sufficiency, one would then be at the mercy of those less capable, who could band together and take the results of one's efforts—Society remedies all three inconveniences.[99]

III. Evidence in Legal Practice

Applying Hume's idea of practical reason to the concept of international law, through Justice-As-Sovereignty, produces two manifestations of a rule of recognition: locally, in terms of the *effectiveness* of the state in stabilizing its internal social order; and universally, in terms of the external *peaceful coordination* of one state with all others in an international society of states.

The universal definition of recognition is concerned with two interdependent dimensions of international legal practice, both contained in the SPP of *peaceful reciprocal cooperation*. The first of these is the specific legal practice aimed at the establishment and maintenance of *peace*, or the "force, ability and security" necessary to the stability of property considered from the international frame of reference. The second dimension is more succinctly concerned with *reciprocal cooperation*, or that synthesis of international policy and law that sets the parameters of both responsibility between states and stratification between municipal and international law.

One insight of Hume's philosophical-policy, that process-rules of recognition are primary and provide the foundation for the rule of law, can be applied to the universal obligations on states that come with the rise of international social conventions and the Westphalian Equilibrium. Peace, based on reciprocal coordination, is a function of which international obligations are imposed upon municipal systems of law by Justice-As-Sovereignty in its regulation of dynamic nonviolence between states.

Unlike its local counterpart, the universal rule of recognition invokes the idea of legal stabilization from the perspective of the international system, not the state. This concept of law is based on the common project of regulating relations between states, so as to minimize violence and discord, maintain the Westphalian Equilibrium, and stabilize international society. According to Hume's logic of concepts, an examination of international legal practice should render a definition of peace that has evolved from the dominance of process and social convention in Stage-I, to a more refined and complex definition on the scale of forms as international society seeks a Stage-II legal system. Complexity in the logic of investigation that is legal practice is defined both in terms of the persistence of the two-tiered logic of property stabilization that is the Humean international system, and the degree, and terms of, the synthesis of international and municipal law by Justice-As-Sovereignty.

An important manifestation of the synthesis of international and municipal law is the distinction between the sovereignty of the state and the sovereignty of its government. These two dimensions of Justice-As-Sovereignty must be disentangled in order to set priorities between that component of a municipal state that is of interest to international social convention, and that which holds less salience in defining the responsibilities of any society toward peace and universal cooperation. The 1923 *Tinoco* Arbitration[100] is authoritative practice on this issue.

In 1917, the Costa Rican government of Alfredo Gonzales was overthrown by Frederico Tinoco, who created a new constitution with new currency and oil exploration laws favorable to Canadian and British Corporations within the country. After his retirement, a new government reverted to the old constitution and invalidated Tinoco's reforms.

Arbitration was taken on behalf of British Petroleum and the Royal Bank of Canada and their interest in making the new Costa Rican government recognize their investments in the economy under the old rules. The point of contention, and our interest in this case, stems from the argument over whether Justice-As-Sovereignty supports the legitimacy of the Tinoco government through its rules of recognition.

The arbitrator, William Howard Taft, Chief Justice of the United States, dismissed Costa Rica's arguments and found for the British. The importance of this case is that it validated a universal rule of recognition for the international system that segregated the state as the only legitimate subject that the coordination equilibrium and its rules must recognize. This arbitration defined the synthesis of local and universal rules of recognition as principally a matter of legal focus on the legitimacy of the state, with an assumption of the government's effective control.

Specifically, the decisive element in the *Tinoco* decision was the arbitrator's willingness to pronounce that, as long as the state remained a legal entity in international affairs, its government need only have effective control to render both levels legitimate agents in the international system.

> The non-recognition by other nations of a government claiming to be a national personality, is usually appropriate evidence that it has not attained the independence and control entitling it by international law to be classed as such. But when recognition of a government is by such nations determined by inquiry, not into its *de facto* sovereignty and complete governmental control, but into its illegitimacy or irregularity of origin, their non-recognition loses something of evidential weight…[it] cannot outweigh the evidence disclosed by this record before me as to the *de facto* character of Tinoco's government.[101]

The arbitrator's argument separates the state of Costa Rica from any particular municipal government. It was as if the ebbs and flows of the ongoing local PD were an internal concern as long as the state maintained its *effective* control and participated in *reciprocal coordination*, satisfying the two international rules of recognition. As *Lotus* and *Palmas* would reconfirm, the bulwark of social convention is contained within the international perception of effective control matched with the validity of the state and its obligation to continued peaceful cooperation within the international system.

Legal practice proceeds as if the process-norm of Justice-As-Sovereignty has biased the core dialectic (i.e., process⇆principle) toward process. In this decision, critical principle, in the form of political or moral concerns about the "origin" or moral character of the Tinoco government, is dismissed as an illegitimate subject for international legal deliberation.

> Foreign powers deal with the existing *de facto* government, when sufficiently established to give reasonable assurance of its permanence and of the acquiescence of those who constitute the state in its ability to maintain itself and discharge its...external obligations.[102]

This arbitration created a specific refinement of the synthesis of the local and universal rules of recognition empowering "*de jure* state, *de facto* government." In a synthesis of local and universal rules of recognition that combines universal *legal* legitimacy of the state in international reciprocity with the local *factual* or effective control of its government, *Tinoco* defines the baseline for Justice-As-Sovereignty in terms of legal recognition.

By establishing the basic parameters of a state's reciprocal obligations, within the international system, the maintenance of a coordinated peace would not require that international society make specific judgments regarding governments. These would be assumed to be factual, as long as the state's effective reciprocity remained intact. Peace was delimited in the decision to that between states regardless of the moral or legal idiosyncrasies of their municipal governments. These are assumed, by Hume's philosophical-policy, to be the results of distinct internal circumstances of justice and a PD. An exception would be made only if a change in government was so disruptive as to destroy the reciprocal or cooperative role of the state in international relations, as was the case for Yugoslavia (see chapter 2).

A universal rule of recognition, as regulated by Justice-As-Sovereignty, should do more than just separate government from state. It also has a role in the dialectic evolution of Justice-As-Sovereignty as nonstate actors are recognized in global institutional forums as a result of contract-by-convention at the international level of social organization. A universal rule of recognition should therefore empower Justice-As-Sovereignty to validate, not only states, but international institutions as subjects of the international rule of law. Here, the 1949 *Reparations* case widens international legal personality past, but nevertheless on behalf of, the prior conventional status of states.

After the Second World War, the status of Justice-As-Sovereignty had been worn thin by municipal government atrocities and the massive interventions and dislocations necessitated by armed conflict. In response, the victors in the war created the United Nations (UN) as an international institution meant to reinvigorate the Westphalian Equilibrium and to offer a point of international coordination still protected by social convention and its process-norm. However, for Justice-As-Sovereignty to maintain its status in this new world system, it needed to be refined. The UN, as a manifestation of a potential Stage-II international legal system, provided a forum for the reconsideration of international *process*, while it also acknowledged the need to recognize the growing relevance of critical *principle* and incorporate aetiological-norms to rebalance the dialectic between process⇆principle.

In the *Reparations* case,[103] a Swedish national who was a representative of the UN was killed supervising the peace in the new state of Israel. The question before the International Court of Justice (ICJ) was whether the UN had international legal personality, or legal standing, to approach the Court for reparations on behalf of him and his family.

Before this case, the international system of social convention, through its synthesis of local and universal rules of recognition, only granted "states" legal standing. The Court was limited to hearing only those cases brought by these singular legal entities who had already qualified under the local rule of recognition.[104] Thus, a Swedish national would have to depend on his state to seek reparations for his death. However, in its opinion, the Court recognized that dependence on one's state in a situation where one was not working on behalf of that state alone, but on behalf of the international community, would disrupt the peace by denying the required "independence" of those who work for the UN.

> To ensure the independence of the agent, and consequently, the independent action of the Organization itself, it is essential that in performing his duties he need not have to rely on any other protection than that of the Organization.... In particular, he should not have to rely on the protection of his own State. If he had to rely on that State, his independence might well be compromised, contrary to the principle applied by Article 100 of the Charter.[105]

If the purpose of international law is the stabilization of property and this property is by definition not regulated by states, then the peace of the two-tiered system of law requires refinement. An institutional setting must be created and recognized, so that, in addition to states, the refined coordination equilibrium that is the heart of the international system can be maintained. The Court recognized the international legal personality of the UN Organization. While the argument offered in doing so reveals the Judges' recognition that the dynamic nature of the equilibrium required a widened concept of Justice-As-Sovereignty, the Court also showed a predisposition to maintain the internal balance of process⇆principle to the advantage of the former.

First, the legal opinion in *Reparations* acknowledged the bulwark of social convention by a focus on *functional effectiveness* as the proper representation of Justice-As-Sovereignty in granting legal personality to states or other entities. The Court seemed interested in law founded on social convention and the need to maintain international coordination at the Westphalian Equilibrium. It did not express any concern for rights or critical principle, which were still assumed to be a lesser part of the inherent legal dialectic between process⇆principle.

> Competence to bring an international claim is, for those possessing it, the capacity to resort to customary methods recognized by international law for the establishment, the presentation, and the settlement of claims...This capacity certainly belongs to the State.[106]

Second, the opinion recognized that the legitimacy of an international agent is in their ability to participate in reciprocal coordination as part of the international community. In this way, the preexisting rules of recognition dealing with local effectiveness and the universal ability to engender reciprocal or peaceful cooperation remain the basis for the admission of the UN into the legal system. The Court did not change the definition of Justice-As-Sovereignty, but merely judicially recognized a postwar legal fact.

> Throughout its history, the development of international law has been influenced by the requirements of international life, and the progressive increase in the collective activities of States has already given rise to instances of action upon the international plane by certain entities which are not States. This development culminated in the establishment...of an international organization whose purpose and principles are specified in the Charter of the United Nations. But to achieve these ends the attribution of international personality is indispensable.[107]

In addition to the idea of a bulwark of international social convention supporting UN standing, the decision reflected the fact that the UN is a creation of sovereign states who can be said to have delegated authority to it. The Court also anticipated that an international institution like the UN might require legal personality to adapt to the dynamic nature of the dialectic between process⇆principle.

Hume's philosophical-policy anticipates a Stage-I⇆Stage-II transition and the need for legal design to accommodate the time when critical principles made salient in the postwar international system would more fully determine the synthesis legal product of the core dialectic. While the Court insisted it was not treating the UN like a state, let alone a "super-state,"[108] it does appear to acknowledge that international institutional structures are contributing members of international society. Only with legal personality could the UN bring this claim. In so doing, the UN contributed to the refinement of Justice-As-Sovereignty making progressive codification push the process-norm up its scale of forms.

> the Court has come to the conclusion that the Organization is an international person. That is not the same thing as saying that it is a State, which it certainly is not, or that its legal personality and rights and duties are the same as those of a State....What it does mean is that it is a subject of international law and capable of possessing international rights and duties.[109]

The fact that the states of the UN had, in effect, delegated their power to the international organization was decisive in the Court granting international legal standing to the UN. The universal rule of recognition gained salience within the dialectic in relation to the preexisting local rule of recognition. In *Reparations*, Justice-As-Sovereignty begins to be defined, not only in terms of effective control of territory but also by the state's duties to the international community. With the recognition of the UN as an institutional framework with international legal personality, the Court refined the concept of Justice-As-Sovereignty to include a wider definition of the universal component of its inherent dialectic. This allows both states and organizations of states to cooperate for the benefit of international society. But given this amended definition of Justice-As-Sovereignty, can the idea of a distinct international society be further enhanced?

The answer can be found in an examination of two more judicial decisions, both by the ICJ: *Nicaragua* and *Spain v. Canada*. In both cases, the parameters of the universal rule of recognition were further refined in its dialectic with local recognition and effective control. In effect, the Court refined the local idea of state sovereignty to acknowledge the legitimate universal obligations of states without overriding the dominant role of process in sovereignty's core dialectic.

Military and Paramilitary Activities In and Against Nicaragua[110] involves the actions of the United States in support of the "contras," a group of insurgents fighting the Sandinista government of Nicaragua. The Court first had to decide, in the jurisdictional phase of the case, if a reluctant United States could be obligated to come before the Court to justify its backing of the contras. Then, in the merits phase, the Court had to decide the legal basis on which intervention would be defined and justified. Through Hume's legal design, the pertinent question answered by the Court, in its logic of legal investigation, can be identified as whether critical principle is a sound legal basis for intervention within the accepted definition of Justice-As-Sovereignty.

In *Nicaragua*, the sources of international law were used to set limits within which a state could be required, by the international system, to act or cease action that interferes with their reciprocal obligations to peace. How that "peace" is recognized and what law governs it are the key matters of concern. With Hume's philosophical-policy, the case can be interpreted as if Justice-As-Sovereignty was the core process-norm. Its status is dependent not only on state-level effective control but also its capacity to universally regulate peacekeeping at the Westphalian Equilibrium.

The argument proceeds as if the core of international law is stable property relations between states. The judges write as if this stability is only assured by layered sources of international law that mutually reinforce one another and which should be judged by their mutual respect for the process-norm of Justice-As-Sovereignty. But, as we shall see, they also appear to recognize that the international system is a constantly evolving dialectic between process⇆principle.

In the first phase of this case, the United States considered itself protected from the jurisdiction of the Court by its Optional Clause declaration. This made America subject to the Court in a contested matter brought from points of law contained within a multilateral treaty, only if all the parties to the treaty were also made defendants. Therefore, since the UN Charter was the source of the concepts of self-defense and nonintervention relied upon by Nicaragua, the United States considered itself outside the Court's jurisdiction. However, the Court managed to bring the United States into its jurisdiction without involving all the parties to the Charter.

In effect, *Nicaragua* required that a synthesis be struck between the needs of a state to protect itself from outside interference, and the validity or recognition that international peace requires conscious and responsible choices on the part of a state in its role as a member of a larger international society. These responsibilities, related to the maintenance of the coordination equilibrium through the universal rule of recognition, are legally assessed in this decision.

The Court appears to have reconceptualized the established Westphalian coordination equilibrium to compensate for the reality that the stability of that equilibrium might be at risk. With the growing strength and scope of customary international law since the 1920s, the process of rule-making was changing to accommodate a refined dialectic between state sovereignty and state responsibility based on local and universal rules of recognition. Therefore, the role of the UN as an example of multilateralism, as well as its growing place in the delineation of what counts as legal intervention in state practice, required that the postwar scope of international law be reconsidered.

With the growing interaction between the sources of law, as these progressively codify, the Court was faced with a decision demanding an argument as to the legitimacy of custom in the face of treaty. Does treaty law, as a more obvious act of state consent, replace redundant custom, rendering its universal jurisdiction moot? Or, does the primary status of customary law, as the most direct manifestation of international social convention, remain powerful and valid in the face of redundancy, mutually reinforcing Justice-As-Sovereignty and giving it a more three-dimensional character? Like the mutation of standard coordination games into Stag Hunts, does the growing role of international organizations as recognized subjects of international law make those coordination equilibria that require interstate cooperation (e.g., hunting stag instead of hare) more available as qualitative refinements of the conventional Westphalian Equilibrium? *Nicaragua* answers these questions.

The majority opinion in *Nicaragua* begins in the jurisdictional phase with the assumption that customary international law, with what Hume's philosophical-policy would recognize as its *contextual* principles, continued to apply to the conduct of states in the international system, even if these same contextual principles found their way into multilateral treaty law.

> The fact that the above-mentioned principles, recognized as such, have been codified or embodied in multilateral conventions does not mean that they

> cease to exist and to apply as principles of customary international law, even as regards countries that are parties to such conventions. Principles such as those of the non-use of force, non-intervention, respect for the independence and territorial integrity of States, and the freedom of navigation, continue to be binding as part of customary international law, despite the operation of provisions of conventional law in which they have been incorporated.[111]

With the simultaneous existence of principle, custom, and treaty as valid international law, the scope of law at this level of the two-tiered system was greatly expanded. No longer could a state, like the United States, seek to avoid the accounting of international legal regulation by claiming that its consent to treaty trumps custom and was the only valid law it need recognize. In addition, this interpretation of legal infrastructure validated contextual principles, regardless of their source in the law, as support for the process-norm of Justice-As-Sovereignty without the further consent of states. Under these conditions, the synthesis product of the dialectic rules of recognition was more complex, requiring that states define reciprocal cooperation in terms of contextual principle, custom, and treaty, simultaneously rather than selectively.

> even if two norms belonging to two sources of international law appear identical in content, and even if the States in question are bound by these rules both on the level of treaty-law and on that of customary international law, these norms retain a separate existence.[112]

Ostensibly, the *Nicaragua* Court made the international dimension of the two-tired system more legally complex. In deciding that the sources of law were distinct, yet interdependent lines of legal argument, they also added dynamic potential to the core dialectic (process⇆principle). Not only were the process-based definitions of nonintervention and self-defense considered as contextual principles for Justice-As-Sovereignty (in defense of Nicaragua), but these ideas were also examined as critical principles in support of a "general right" to intervene on behalf of political or moral imperatives (in defense of the US position). But here the Court seemed cognizant of the bulwark of the former process definition of Justice-As-Sovereignty and was careful not to expand the legitimacy of critical principle too far or too quickly.

> The Court therefore finds that no such general right of intervention, in support of an opposition within another State, exists in contemporary international law.[113] The principle of non-intervention involves the right of every sovereign State to conduct its affairs without outside interference;...It is both an "essential foundation" and an "essential principle" of international law.[114]

Overall, the Court recognized an independent validity for each of the sources of international law, but stopped short of allowing the process⇆principle dialectic to render a synthesis solution dominated by critical principle. In the argument of this Court, we can see the first full differentiation between principles as contextual of social convention (i.e., the process-norm of sovereignty backed by nonuse of force) and critical principles as aetiological-norms representing moral necessity and rights defined in relation to ends-in-themselves (a general right of intervention based on defense of freedom). In their finding for Nicaragua, the Court supported the established balance of dialectics defining the process-norm of Justice-As-Sovereignty. Although they acknowledged critical principle as legitimate legal principle, and contemplated its role within Justice-As-Sovereignty, the fundamental nature of social stability at the Westphalian Equilibrium retained its preeminent status in their decision.

The universal rule of recognition, as a metaphysical element of Justice-As-Sovereignty, is further refined in our last decision: the *Spain v. Canada* fisheries case.[115] Although the Court refused jurisdiction in this case, the arguments by both majority and dissent demonstrated that, even in 1998, further expansion of the role of critical principle in the definition of Justice-As-Sovereignty was considered too disruptive of international peace and order to be tolerated.

Like the *Nicaragua* case, this dispute involved an effort, here by Canada, to avoid the jurisdiction of the Court through its Optional Clause statement. Meanwhile Spain, having suffered a grievance, wanted Canada's failure to respect international law adjudicated. Both litigants argued in terms of sovereignty and, in effect, the Court was asked to define the dialectic legal balance between the two rules of recognition within the metaphysics of Justice-As-Sovereignty: effective control with the obligations of peaceful reciprocity. Again, one side argued for empowerment of standing social convention while the other petitioned for its amendment by critical principle. Specifically, Canada's argument was based on the process side of Justice-As-Sovereignty, while Spain asked the Court to rebalance the core dialectic to the advantage of the universal rule of recognition and critical principle.

Spain-Canada advanced the effort to define the limits of the universal rule of recognition in international society. The case pitted a strong Spanish argument for the universal rule of recognition against a local, effective control argument about Canada's ability to limit its liability through the Optional Clause. Canada, for reasons related to the protection of their straddling fish stocks, had amended their Optional Clause declaration under Article 36 of the Court's Statute. This restricted the Court's jurisdiction in "disputes arising out of or concerning conservation and management measures taken by Canada with respect to vessels fishing in the . . . regulatory area."[116] At the same time, the Government of Canada submitted and passed Parliament Bill C-29 to amend the Coastal Fisheries Protection Act by extending its area of control to include this newly created "regulatory" area.

Subsequently, the Canadian Coast Guard captured and detained a Spanish vessel that was fishing the straddling stocks in the restricted regulatory area and argued that this action was "necessary to prevent further destruction of those stocks and to permit their rebuilding."[117] The Court recognized

Canada's new restriction on the Optional Clause and refused to hear the merits of the case,[118] but the majority recognized that "this dispute,...is not merely a matter of fisheries conservation and management."[119]

This opinion illustrates the point in the transition between a Stage-I and Stage-II legal system where the first essential moment of Justice-As-Sovereignty as the process-norm of social convention confronts pressure to rebalance its dialectics to provide a more prominent role for the universal recognition of a state's international responsibility. The *Spain-Canada* Court was charged with making a decision, akin to the one made in *Nicaragua*, as to what synthesis solution was necessary to stabilize effective control of property without ignoring the universal obligations of reciprocal or peaceful coordination.

Earlier in 1984, the Court refined the idea of customary international law, so that its universal application as social convention remained intact and the United States was forced to move to the "merits" phase of the *Nicaragua* case. In *Spain-Canada*, the Court, in weighing the merits of the two approaches to Justice-As-Sovereignty, sided with process and the local rule of recognition yet again and allowed Canada to protect itself by altering its Optional Clause statement. Why? Using Hume's logic of concepts, the decision can be explained precisely in the dialectic between process⇆principle.

Canada justified its actions leading up to the maritime incident in terms of its effective control over conservation of its environment and sustainability of its sovereign resources. Canada's amendment to the Optional Clause, its new domestic legislation, and its use of force, were all premised on the argument that Canadians had a right to defend the sustainability of their property against nonstate use.[120] The Canadian argument was not derived from critical principle where the environment would have to be considered intrinsically rather than instrumentally. It is an argument derived from the process-norm of Justice-As-Sovereignty, as determined primarily by the local rule of recognition, where effective control dominates its dialectic with the universal rule of recognition.

Canada defined the dialectic balance of rules of recognition, and therefore its concept of sustainability, as instrumentally supportive of the process-norm of Justice-As-Sovereignty. The use of the Article 36 Optional Clause as an established process, the amendment of municipal law by legislative action, and the use of force within one's own waters to protect sovereign resources, were all conventionally accepted means to maintain a rule of recognition as effective control. The idea of reciprocal or peaceful cooperation existed in the legal arguments but was dominated by the local rule of recognition that was allowed to maintain a stronger position in the dialectic by the Court's majority. A faith in the bulwark of international social convention and the fear of international responsibilities negating *Lotus* sovereignty can explain why the Court's majority accepted the sovereign right of Canada to amend its Optional Clause commitment, even at the last moment, and even if it was aimed at frustrating the Court itself.[121] Ultimately, this adjudication protects the established essence of Justice-As-Sovereignty. But to what extent has the role of critical principle and international responsibility gained ground since *Nicaragua*?

In a series of separate and dissenting opinions, the Judges laid out a more detailed argument about the relationship between the sovereign rights of a State and the power of international law to regulate that sovereignty in the interests of international society. These interests include such critical principles as nonaggression, freedom of the seas, and protection of the environment. Spain's argument can be characterized as being focused on critical principle and the universal responsibility of states to international society, where the universal rule of recognition dominates the dialectic structure of sovereignty and the practice of international law. Fourteen years after the US' argument for a general right of intervention for aetiological ends in the *Nicaragua* case, Spain's dependence on critical principle met the same fate. However, Spain's argument also engendered more dissent and wider concern for the state of critical principle and international responsibility in the conceptualization of Justice-As-Sovereignty.

Vice-President Weeramantry, in his dissent, admitted that Canada was "entitled" to amend its declaration to the Optional Clause, but considered Spain's argument in terms that advocate a synthesis judicial decision weighted to critical principle over process, universal over local recognition.

> to violate the basic principle of freedom of the high seas, to violate the peremptory norm of international law proscribing the use of force, to violate thereby a fundamental principle of the United Nations Charter, to violate the well-established principle of the complainant State's exclusive sovereignty on the high seas over vessels carrying its national flag, to endanger the lives of its seamen by a violation of universally accepted conventions relating to the safety of lives at seas—can all these alleged fundamental violations of international law, which would engage the jurisdiction of the Court under the general principle of submission, be swept away by the mere assertion that all these were done as a measure of conservation of fisheries resources? Reservations do not constitute a vanishing point of legality within the consensual system.[122]

The majority read Canada's claim as within the social conventions of process that define Justice-As-Sovereignty. "A declaration of acceptance of the compulsory jurisdiction of the Court, whether there are specified limits set to that acceptance or not, is a unilateral act of State sovereignty."[123] But Weeramantry and his dissenting colleagues contended that the list of alleged violations of critical norms, as well as the Canadian failure to act responsibly by the universal rule of recognition, should be the transcendent basis of the Court's decision, not Canada's "right" to amend Article 36.

Weeramantry maintained that Canada's actions "cannot be framed so as to undermine the declaration of which they form a part."[124] Overall, he called for the "dominance of international law within the system once it is entered."[125] But his understanding of "international law" is one of principle over process, universal over local recognition, which makes this a case that "goes far beyond the question of fisheries conservation."[126] Weeramantry's view was shared by Judges Vereshchetin[127] and Kooijmans,[128] and even the majority seemed to acknowledge a dialectic between process and principle-based definitions of state responsibility as posed in the "different perceptions by the Parties of the rights and obligations which a coastal State may or may not have in a certain area of the sea."[129]

If the dissenting judges had had their way, this would have been a case about critical principles and peremptory norms in both customary and treaty law as they affect the environment. Their arguments support a need to rebalance the dialectic of local-universal recognition so that Canada's obligations under the rule's universal manifestation would have trumped its rights defined by the outmoded local dimension. If the consensus of the Court had leaned toward the principled reading of Justice-As-Sovereignty, as defined by the dissent, then it would have supported a new balance between rules of recognition empowering the legitimacy of international society (or "the dominance of international law within the system once it is entered") and moved to undertake the merits phase of the case.

> [o]nce a State has entered the consensual system, submission to the basic rules of international law inevitably follows, and there can be no contracting out of the applicability of those rules. Once within the system, the rules of international law take effect, and apply to the entirety of the matter before the Court, irrespective of State approval.[130]

From the standpoint of Hume's philosophical-policy, the dissent called for a new definition of Justice-As-Sovereignty that elevated the universal rule of recognition over its local counterpart for the purposes of making the international obligations of states as important as their effective control of property. As an application of Justice-As-Sovereignty, the decision crafts a dialectic synthesis for practice with a more complex definition of sovereignty than the *Lotus* Court would allow.

However, by not advancing to consider the merits of the case, where the nature of sovereignty could be more fully specified, the majority was able to admit the complexity of the issue without having to fully debate definitive legal refinement of the idea of Justice-As-Sovereignty. The power of the conventional state-of-affairs in which the decision was made is dispositive in that no new idea of sovereignty, placing more weight on the responsibility of Canada to be judged by universal standards and critical principle, was made necessary. But then the ICJ in *Spain-Canada* is hardly the first appeals court to dismiss a case on a point of process rather than wrestle with a more substantial question of critical principle.

While it is true that, in the *Nicaragua* case, the Court refined the definition of international legal sources, the Judges stopped short of any refinement that would drastically rebalance the process⇆principle dialectic in favor of an American position pushing for international law to include the critical-normative consideration of a regime's character as a legal reason for intervention. Some 14 years later, in *Spain-Canada*, the same threshold for Justice-As-Sovereignty was again defended by the Court but in the face of more vehement dissent. If Hume's logic of concepts is correctly informing our analysis of practice, even if *Spain-Canada* had proceeded to the merits stage, the separate opinions demonstrate that the discussion would not have centered on the necessity of Canadian conservation measures or their legality. The debate would have rested on whether Justice-As-Sovereignty had evolved to a point where metaphysical rebalancing was required to compensate for changes in the demands of the modern international system.

These cases, interpreted through Hume's philosophical-policy, provide a pattern of evidence for an international legal system based on social convention. Here, the rules of local and universal recognition, and the consequent concepts of *effective control* and *responsible peace*, are creatures of the process⇆principle dialectic. The case chain also supports the contention that the bulwark of process and social convention continue to dominate the future refinement of Justice-As-Sovereignty in international law.

A full consideration of the SPP of *reciprocal peaceful cooperation* requires that we examine its influence on the degree of integration between municipal and international law, or legal stratification. Each sovereign state has its own approach to the acknowledgment and integration of international into municipal law. Primarily, I will utilize the experience of the United States as representative of a definitive argument about the usual way in which international law is synthesized by municipal legal systems. The three American cases are all Supreme Court Decisions: *Paquete Habana* (1900), *Missouri v. Holland* (1920), and *Reid v. Covert* (1957). Heard over a period of nearly 60 years, these cases represent the effort of the United States to find a synthesis of effective control and reciprocal responsibility in the integration of municipal and international law.

Normally, international legal theory treats stratification in terms of monist and dualist ideas of international legal practice. From within Hume's logic, a dualist approach definitively classifies international from municipal law and therefore violates philosophical method. Philosophical method considers the relationship of such social concepts as dialectic in nature, where refinement toward essence, not classification and discovery, are the point of intellectual exploration. Neither is Hume's logic conducive to monism, which totally integrates municipal and international law into a single entity. On the contrary, Hume recognizes that international and municipal law are distinct systems with distinct strategic and normative circumstances of justice, albeit with a common metaphysical foundation.

Hume's philosophical-policy replaces the hard division between municipal and international law with a range of possible synthesis solutions to the dialectic between municipal⇆international legal practice. Examining the selected cases is an attempt, within a representative municipal system, to chart the refinement of Justice-As-Sovereignty, over time, as a synthesis of the dialectic of process⇆principle represented in the balance between local and universal rules of recognition.

The first case[131] concerns "prize-taking" in the Spanish-American War. The Cuban fishing smack, *Paquete Habana*, was taken by United States naval forces as a prize of war. The international legal practice of the time was not to seize fishing boats due to their noncombatant nature. But the United States argued that taking the boat was not a violation of international law, but only of the less restrictive idea of *comity* between nations, which was suspended by the conditions of war. The lawyer for the *Paquete Habana*, J. Parker Kurlin, had to demonstrate to the Court that since the last case like this was adjudicated, international legal practice had evolved to make such an action on a fishing vessel a violation of not just comity but of customary international law, and therefore, of Justice-As-Sovereignty.

Precedent was traced to eighteenth-century British law where taking a boat named the *Young Jacob* was deemed, by Lord Stowell, to be a matter of rules "of comity only and not a legal decision."[132] However, this precedent was not honored by the Supreme Court which, in deciding for the owners of the fishing smack, elevated the ban on this type of prize-taking from comity to customary law, giving Kurlin the win. This decision acknowledged that justice in international law could evolve, as on a scale of forms. It also set the stage for the refinement of the universal rule of recognition in American legal practice.

First, the Court, in what has since been recognized as a seminal paragraph, acknowledged that customary international law is directly incorporated as justiciable by American courts when there is no treaty or domestic written law to say otherwise.

> International law is part of our law, and must be ascertained and administered by the courts of justice of appropriate jurisdiction, as often as questions of right depending upon it are duly presented for their determination.[133]

Next, the Court utilized Lord Stowell's judgment in *Young Jacob* not as a definitive precedent for this case, but as a point of departure for the refinement of international law. In doing so, it acknowledged that international law was not a static system of rules. With the hindsight of Hume's philosophical-policy, this acknowledgment can be further explained as an appreciation of international law as a process-based system of dialectic where the two rules of recognition interact with the adjudicatory standard of progressive codification to create an evolving international legal system. In effect, the Court recognized dialectics between all three of the SPPs heretofore examined.

> The word "comity" was apparently used by Lord Stowell as synonymous with courtesy or good will. But the period of a hundred years which has since elapsed is amply sufficient to have enabled what originally may have rested in custom or comity, courtesy or concession, to grow, by the general assent of civilized nations, into a settled rule of international law.[134]

In acknowledging that international customary law is directly applicable to municipal law in the United States, and that this system of legal practice is not static but evolutionary and dynamic, the Court suggests a multi-tiered international system as an overlapping system of sovereign rights and cooperative responsibilities characterized by the dialectic relations of the SPPs and the refinement of Justice-As-Sovereignty over time.

These predispositions on the part of the Court, to consider more than a traditional synthesis between the local and universal rules of recognition, was enhanced by their further acceptance of a definition of the rule under scrutiny in terms of critical principle. The majority accepts Kurlin's argument that, because of the specific evolution of humanitarian critical principles (i.e., a substantive aetiological-norm for protection of human dignity), the status of the rule against taking fishing vessels as naval prizes had been "accepted as a rule of conduct"[135] and therefore elevated from "comity only" to a matter of customary international law.

> This review of precedents and authorities on the subject appears to us abundantly to demonstrate that at the present day, by the general consent of civilized nations of the world, and independently of any express treaty or other public act, it is an established rule of international law, founded on consideration of humanity...that coast fishing vessels,...honestly pursuing their peaceful calling...are exempt from capture as prize of war.[136]

Within the legal parameters of international responsibility, the next refinement in the American synthesis between municipal⇆international law occurred in the *Missouri v. Holland* case.[137] It involved the Constitution of the United States, the State of Missouri, the United States Congress, and a Migratory Bird Treaty between the United States and Britain, representing Canada.

> On December 8, 1916, a treaty between the United States and Great Britain was proclaimed by the President. It...provided for specified close seasons and protection in other forms, and agreed that the two powers would take or propose to their lawmaking bodies the necessary measures for carrying the treaty out. (39 Stat. 1702). The above mentioned Act of July 3, 1918, entitled an act to give effect to the convention...the question raised is the general one whether the treaty and statute are void as an interference with the rights reserved to the States.[138]

The case involves the Constitution of the United States, first, in granting the federal government the power to make treaties, and second in the application of its 10th Amendment, which had previously been interpreted to reserve to the States all rights it had not specifically given to the federal branch of government. This latter category was assumed to include the regulation of waterfowl because of a previous wildlife statute of the US Congress that had been struck down by the Court under the 10th Amendment.

However, in this case, the statute under scrutiny was backed by a treaty and this allowed the Court to use international law to empower federal legislation and its supremacy. In the same way that the *Paquete Habana* Court integrated customary international law into American municipal law, by allowing a more dynamic and evolutionary definition of its inherent content, Oliver Wendell Holmes, writing for the majority, expanded the idea of federal supremacy under Article VI of the Constitution by connecting it to America's international treaty responsibility.

> by Article II, §2, the power to make treaties is delegated expressly, and by Article VI treaties made under the authority of the United States, along with the Constitution and laws of the United States made in pursuance thereof, are declared the supreme law of the land. If the treaty is valid, there can be no dispute about the validity of the statute under Article I, §8, as a necessary and proper means to execute the powers of the Government. The language of the Constitution as to the supremacy of treaties being general, the question before us is narrowed to an inquiry into the ground upon which the present supposed exception is placed.[139]

In this way, Holmes integrated international law into the Constitution, so that the responsibilities of reciprocal cooperation from a universal rule of recognition validated federal law. In addition, he accepted an evolutionary definition of Justice-As-Sovereignty, first acknowledged by his colleagues in 1900, as the basic point of departure for refinement of international law and America's municipal responsibility to it.

> The case before us must be considered in the light of our whole experience, and not merely in that of what was said a hundred years ago. The treaty in question does not contravene any prohibitory words to be found in the Constitution.[140]

The Court defines international law and the Constitution as evolving systems that have developed to the point where the supremacy of the federal government includes a responsibility to treaty law that trumps the 10th Amendment. Especially where title to the birds is the basis for the state's invocation of the 10th.[141] The irony in this case is that international law, in terms of treaty, was used to transform the federal wildlife statute, rather than the other way around.

> Here, a national interest of very nearly the first magnitude is involved. It can be protected only by national action in concert with that of another power. The subject matter is only transitorily within the State, and has no permanent habitat therein. But for the treaty and the statute, there soon might be no birds for any powers to deal with. We see nothing in the Constitution that compels the Government to sit by while a food supply is cut off and the protectors of our forests and our crops are destroyed. It is not sufficient to rely upon the States. The reliance is vain, and were it otherwise, the question is whether the

> United States is forbidden to act. We are of opinion that the treaty and statute must be upheld.[142]

In what can be defined as a Humean argument about the stabilization of "winged" property, the Court placed international treaty law, and its transformation by municipal statute, securely into federal law, where both local and universal recognition play a dialectic role in the definition of Justice-As-Sovereignty. Building on the incorporation of customary law from *Paquete Habana*, *Holland* integrates international treaty law as a component of federal supremacy, so that in dealing with the international legal system America will speak with one federal voice rather than 50 state voices.

The last case to be considered in this second chain is the 1957 Supreme Court decision in *Reid v. Covert*.[143] Here, the Court reestablished the Constitution as the ultimate principle-driven governor of the synthesis between local and universal recognition. *Reid v. Covert* revolved around a murder on an American military base in Britain. According to an executive agreement (i.e., treaty) between the two states, military personnel as well as their dependents who violated the law would be tried by American military courts rather than British Courts. Thus, the civilian wife of a murder victim was tried under this treaty by military court martial. She subsequently sued in US federal court on the basis that the Uniform Code of Military Justice (UCMJ) did not afford her the rights she was entitled to as a civilian citizen of the United States. The Court agreed and struck down the executive agreement between the United States and Great Britain as an international law that violated the Constitution of the United States.

> At the beginning we reject the idea that when the United States acts against citizens abroad it can do so free of the Bill of Rights. The United States is entirely a creature of the constitution...no agreement with a foreign nation can confer power on Congress, or on any other branch of Government, which is free from the restraints of the Constitution.[144]

Reid v. Covert established that the obligation to international society, refined and empowered in the first two cases, was nonetheless limited by any violation of the US Constitution. Domestically, all law is a "creature" of the Constitution that promotes its substantive critical principles over both municipal and international process. Unlike the dialectic between principle⇆process at the international legal level, within American municipal law, critical principle has equal dialectic status with process because of the Constitutional framework of what is a well–established, Stage-II critical legal system. In this way, *Holland* is reconfirmed, as setting the Constitutional baseline for Justice-As-Sovereignty, at least in terms of the universal rule of recognition.

> There is nothing in *Missouri v. Holland*...which is contrary to the position taken here. The Court carefully noted that the treaty involved was not

> inconsistent with any specific provision of the Constitution....To the extent that the United States can validly make treaties, the people and the States have delegated their power to the National Government and the Tenth Amendment is no barrier.[145]

The American cases demonstrate that the synthesis definition of the responsibility to international society, or the American solution to the dialectic between effective control⇆reciprocal cooperation as rules of recognition, is defined in terms of the incorporation of customary law, the transformation of treaty law, the evolutionary nature of the international legal system, and the ultimate power of the US Constitution as the basic set of principle-based ends that all law must honor.

A Canadian case reconfirms this pattern of dialectic and synthesis in municipal law. In *R. v. Hape*,[146] the Court took the opportunity of a fact situation about police procedure and foreign criminal law to make a lengthy statement about the status of the Canadian Charter of Rights and Freedoms in relation to the protection of international rights, Canadian sovereignty, and the jurisdictional reach of Canadian constitutional law.

> While Parliament has clear constitutional authority to pass legislation governing conduct by Canadians or non-Canadians outside Canada, its ability to pass extraterritorial legislation is informed by the binding customary principles of territorial sovereign equality and non-intervention, by the comity of nations, and by the limits of international law to the extent that they are not incompatible with domestic law...Since it is a well-established principle of statutory interpretation that legislation will be presumed to conform to international law, in interpreting the scope of application of the *Charter*, a court should seek to ensure compliance with Canada's binding obligations under international law where the express words are capable of supporting such a construction.[147]

This opinion could be considered an ultimate statement on the dialectic between the balance of effective control and the responsibility of states within Justice-As-Sovereignty. The Canadian Charter is acknowledged as both foundational municipal law and as the standard by which Canada's international responsibility to reciprocal cooperation should be measured. The Canadian Constitution's critical principles, however, were interpreted by the Court in terms of Justice-As-Sovereignty where "[s]overeign equality remains a cornerstone of the international legal system."[148]

> In order to preserve sovereignty and equality, the rights and powers of all states carry correlative duties, at the apex of which sits the principle of non-intervention. Each state's exercise of sovereignty within its territory is dependent on the right to be free from intrusion by other states in its affairs and the duty of every other state to refrain from interference.[149]

The Court recognized that constitutional law, while the ultimate standard for municipal law, should not be used to violate international law. In a step beyond *Reid v. Covert*, the *Hape* Court reestablished a conservatism with critical principle as it is applied to international law and the definition of a stable coordination equilibrium. The Court, in addition to using the *Charter* as a definitive document for substantial limitations on international law, also argued for it as an aid to the process-driven balance or synthesis sought by international rules of recognition.

> in an era characterized by transnational criminal activity, the principle of comity cannot be invoked to allow Canadian authorities to participate in investigative activities sanctioned by foreign law that would place Canada in violation of its international obligations in respect of human rights. Deference to the foreign law ends where clear violations of international law and fundamental human rights begin.[150]

Overall, international legal practice examined through the lens of the SPP of reciprocal or peaceful cooperation defines both the *effective control⇆reciprocal cooperation* dialectic and the *process⇆principle* dialectic in terms of the preeminence of international process and municipal constitutional principle in the definition of Justice-As-Sovereignty. The international legal system is a well–established, Stage-I procedural structure sustaining pressure to incorporate critical principle, but, to date, resisting a full transition to a Stage-II critical legal system. We continue to understand the universal rule of recognition, like its local counterpart, to have been codified from social convention as dialectic components of justice. This status as relative presuppositions of Justice-As-Sovereignty comes from their proven success in the stabilization of property and the maintenance of coordination at the Westphalian Equilibrium.

The scale of forms or evolutionary dimension of international law, which Hume's logic of concepts defines as the rule of adjudication represented by the SPP of progressive codification, has also been legally acknowledged as a dialectic element of stratification. Consequently, the two-tiered social organization that is the international system is constantly adjusting and readjusting its local and universal rules of recognition at the behest of a third relative presupposition in the metaphysics of sovereignty. This constant testing of the bulwark of established international social convention has been adjudicated by the Courts, revealing the tension and stress on the Stage-I legal system as it struggles with the pressure to more fully integrate the universal definition of recognition and critical principle into the practical conceptualization of Justice-As-Sovereignty.

5

"Non-Intervention": A Rule of Change Protecting "Process" from "Principle"

Abstract

Hume's philosophical-policy does not characterize the sovereign state *as a moral individual but as a* social construction *promoting the systematic policy precept of* nonintervention *as its international rule of change. This lens dramatically redefines both the state's sovereign status and its purpose within international law. The state becomes an elective institutional structure, created by social convention settling on one equilibrium within the global coordination game rather than another. Next, a case study involving the ascendance of* World Trade *Organization (WTO) dispute settlement is used to extrapolate the legal design implications of change. Lastly, the erosion of Justice-As-Sovereignty is tracked through a series of jurisdictional and immunity cases.*

I. Hume's Philosophical Insight: The State as a Social Construction

Another remnant of modern positivism is the conviction that the state ought to be treated as a moral person. This is traced back to Thomas Hobbes' *Leviathan*. Hobbes' assumption was that the institutional structure of the sovereign state is a necessary prerequisite to justice in collective action. Sovereign power was treated as a product of critical principle establishing the state as an end-in-itself with self-interest, power, and the natural law imperative to self-preservation, making the state the moral equivalent of a person.

However, an examination of the state from within Hume's philosophical-policy makes a much more complex, yet conceptually simple, argument for the state. It is based on the same absolute presupposition of the passion for society and the social conventions evolved to affirm social stability. From a Humean perspective, the state is an elective structure derivative of the metaphysics of social order, as made evident in the specific circumstances of justice for the coordination of humanity at the Westphalian Equilibrium. Further, sovereignty is that attribute of this social construction, derived from process rather than principle, that gives the state its public utility. If the state is essential at all, its indispensability is for the persistence of social convention, the particulars of Justice-As-Sovereignty, and the coordination equilibrium it maintains. For Hume's legal design, society, and not the state, is the absolute presupposition for moral, political, and legal evolution; the state is not an individual but a product of collective action given the international circumstances of justice. The state has instrumental value sufficient to stable coordination, given its conventional context, but not necessary to the persistence of generic social organization at the transnational level.

The idea of an international "society" is controversial[1] and often used in argument for the transcendence of the state. For example, Christian Wolff argues for a "society of the entire human race,"[2] but he makes this society conditional on the legal existence, not of states, but on the evolution of a "Supreme State."[3] His idea of a *civitas maxima* contains his universalist argument that global values leading to a transnational society require a corresponding centralization of policy to make international law equivalent to a global municipal government.

Because individuals are the sole carriers of rights,[4] and nation-states are individuals that carry particularized rights for a local society, a Supreme State is necessary to support a global set of rights adequate to maintain a social *jus gentium*.[5] Wolff's argument makes international society dependent on the global state. More specifically, he makes continued social cooperation dependent on the governance structure of centralized institutions as a precondition of peaceful international social cooperation or international society.[6] The state, in both local and universal forms, is, for Wolff, as it is for Hobbes, a prior, principled, and necessary "individual free person" living in an anarchic "state of nature," which is a prerequisite to the advent of a global civil society.[7]

Wolff considers the state "immutable"[8] in the same way that the law of nature is. Consequently, the state carries a "necessary and immutable"[9] obligation that has two levels of expression. First, the individual is obliged to create the nation-state in order to extricate himself from local chaos. Second, the state is obliged to struggle for centralized law in the anarchy of an international state of nature. Here, the "supreme state" becomes a whole and "free" person,[10] or a fixed and principled end for the international system.[11]

Hume's philosophical-policy envisions the world system in diametrically reverse order. For Hume, the existence of a stable society, at all stages of organization, is the focus of human coordination and convention and, therefore, the absolute presupposition of his metaphysical framework. Meanwhile, the state, as one among many potential governance structures, within the choice of indifferent equilibria of an international coordination game, exists and is dependent upon a world of evolving social convention. The state, and its sovereignty, are elective social constructions given the Westphalian circumstances of justice. Because the core dialectic of Hume's philosophical-policy is weighted in favor of process and, further, because progressive codification supports the evolution of society and not the state in particular, the development and persistence of society is paramount. For Hume, international social stability is a prerequisite to the state's institutional structure, which remains elective.

Within a Humean legal design argument, society is not only independent of the state, but the state and its process-norm of Justice-As-Sovereignty are products of social coordination and the human passion for society, created by collective action for its own sake, prior to any institutional setting. After all, international society develops in terms of approbation and justice before the advent of the state in contract-by-convention.

In the evolution of international law, the nation-state has an instrumental value only to the persistence of society itself; it loses its utility when it no longer provides for the persistence of stable international social cooperation. Therefore, within Hume's philosophical-policy, the state is not an inevitable or even primary form of governance structure. Thus it can hardly be "immutable" and a necessary or morally imperative "individual"[12] with constituent validity invoking a substantive obligation. The state is a means to an end, not an end-in-itself. It is an elective social construction, pure and simple, that international society has survived without, and could again.[13]

Although current practice indicates that the international system is, and will continue to be, made up of sovereign states, the process-norm of Justice-As-Sovereignty is neither substantive nor a priori, but procedural and conditioned on the specific circumstances of justice that have created the particular historical line of practice of our experience. Hume's idea of law and legal systems, as well as the imperative for progressive codification, is based on the central role of society in the creation of Justice-As-Sovereignty and its inherent metaphysics of procedural rules. This stabilizes the coordination of states even as legal practice is challenged by the rise of critical aetiological-norms in the evolution from a Stage-I to a Stage-II international legal system.

For Hume's philosophical-policy, the state-in-practice has no independent validity, but carries normative weight only so long as it promotes the process-norm of Justice-As-Sovereignty and, more specifically, empowers the coordination and stability of the international system to maintain the

Westphalian Equilibrium. With the state so defined, as a social construction and not an inevitable moral fixture of the legal landscape, the dialectic process inherent in the evolution of Justice-As-Sovereignty creates a more dynamic definition of jus gentium than is possible within positivism.

The dynamics of the international legal system are focused first on a global society of people who eventually organize themselves through states. The social stability of this society predates the institutions of the state, and is able to transcend or change the state structure. Change is a product of the demands of international society that forces movement on the scale of forms for Justice-As-Sovereignty that then, by rebalancing its inherent dialectics, seeks that political structure best able to secure social convention at its new point of coordination.

Explicitly, in this context, international law is not required to create Wolff's Supreme State in order to provide a stable international social order. There are many other ways to support or redefine Justice-As-Sovereignty as a process-norm focused on the coordination of the social-system itself. Hume's philosophical-policy does not require a Supreme State or any other state structure to maintain an international society, for as social convention predates and creates the state in its image, the state is a construction of inter-societal coordination, not a prerequisite to it.

Many institutional structures could replace the state as long as society and social order persist. Just as municipal societies create states as one means of fostering cooperation (i.e., presumably to achieve the most justice-as-utility), international society, fostered by the foundation of municipal law, can create many different vehicles for the further cohesion of a global society as this evolves with different requirements or circumstances of justice (e.g., world government; centralized federation of states; system of international organizations).

Hume's idea of the state as a social construction requires us to examine the ramifications of an emphasis on the collective nature of the state, as well as the dynamic international society in which states interact. Departing from the idea of the state as a moral person places new emphasis on the distinction between ethical and political or juridical motivation, will, and legal personality, as well as the state's role as an elective "means" to the cooperative ends of international society, rather than as an essential or substantive ideal end-in-itself.

Describing the state as an elective form of governance requires a closer look at the ramifications of doing so. Of particular interest is the difference between two connotations of nonintervention: one derived from the traditional idea of the state as a moral individual, the other from a process-based idea of the state.

The SPP of Nonintervention

If the state is a social construct, and its sovereignty is therefore conditioned on the stability and progress of international society, then the idea of change within the international legal system should be marked by the synthesis between process⇆principle as made manifest in the subsidiary dialectic of sovereignty⇆intervention. Although the state is instrumental to Justice-As-Sovereignty, it has come to be a very important instrumental value. Consequently, the idea of state intervention as the prime dialectic counterweight to sovereignty makes nonintervention a particularly important element in the metaphysics of sovereign justice.

Specifically, within Hume's philosophical-policy, a procedural *rule of change* is defined by the SPP of *nonintervention* and how this acts to balance sovereignty⇆intervention as a means to the persistence of a changing international society. This precept is similar to Krasner's definition of *Westphalian sovereignty*, which "refers to political organization based on the exclusion of external actors from authority structures within a given territory."[14]

A critical presupposition of Hume's logic of concepts, both in terms of the foundation of his idea of natural law and the dispositive product of legal practice, is that agency or legal personality within the international system is not rendered by the "interests" or "power" of states, but the social cohesion and stability of each municipal system and the international society of which it becomes a component part. The absolute metaphysical presupposition of the Humean agent, whether individual or collective, is to seek and coordinate an ever-wider social complexity.

Within Hume's concept of law, the basic motivational assumption is not one based upon the narrow self-interest or individual power, liberty, or right of the agent involved, as Hobbes and his positivist descendents argue. Nor is it about a critical principle of "self-preservation" that is sought by the choices and actions of states-as-moral-persons. Rather, the process of social cooperation is the end-in-itself for Justice-As-Sovereignty. International society, as a growing community-of-states, is a dialectic product of a more balanced or limited generosity that is social in nature and that seeks *coordination conventions*, for the sole purpose of *property stabilization*, deriving *moral and societal obligation* from the contextual process of finding and preserving a *Westphalian* coordination equilibrium.

The institutional structure of the state is, by this logic, the result of these presuppositions and a process of contract-by-convention that creates law for the primary purpose of shoring-up social convention and cooperation in the face of the inevitable and constant change that comes with growing complexity. This *Societal-State System* is assumed to react to the circumstances of justice by overcoming scarcity and limited sympathy to reinforce the stability of society as a collective good. This is accomplished through the creation of legal rules of de jure possession as defined by Justice-As-Sovereignty, an expression of international public utility.

The state, therefore, is not and, cannot be, treated philosophically as an individual person,[15] but must be assumed to be a collective entity. Nor is the state a strictly empirical phenomenon; the state is a social idea, the perfection of which lies in its evolution across boundaries of population, geography, and institutional complexity. Under this definition, Justice-As-Sovereignty arises not from the will of a person or government, nor to hold men "in awe."[16] Rather, justice is a joint expression of natural, initially unconscious, pro-social behavior and the expectations of all persons regarding the settlement of their joint-agency on one of a number of possible coordination equilibria, all valued for their provision of a stable international social order.

This conventionally-created coordination equilibrium is protected by the refinement of sympathy as a philosophical concept and the conventions made necessary to assure the fundamental expression of the human passion for society within an ever-more complex and larger framework. Justice-As-Sovereignty increases the levels of sanctions as it moves up its scale of forms from its first level of complexity as a Stage-I system toward its second level or moment of essence in a Stage-II legal system with a fully engaged process⇆principle dialectic.

At the heart of the concept of Justice-As-Sovereignty lies the absolute presupposition of an inherent sociability or sympathy with the good of the whole, actualized through the stabilization of property. The imperative of each state cooperator becomes *prudential mutual-aid* not "self-help"[17] in isolation, as the realists would have it. Mutual aid is defined as the creation of the conditions in which an international social system can be rendered with appropriate institutions that compensate for each societal-state's limited collective generosity.

An axiom of Hume's philosophical-policy is the human struggle between self-interest and sympathy. This dialectic occurs within a metaphysical context where one's interest in the stability and security of their own life is dependent on the consciousness that social and personal security are interdependent variables. Within this dialectic, the social level of organization dominates. Hume argues that the "collective" is more than an aggregate of individuals; it is a distinct systemic level of analysis generating justice and moral obligation.[18] It is also a product of social interaction, built from the individual to the global level through various strategic situations where policy design adapts legal solutions to fit the empirical context.

As the dominant level of individual concern, the society, as an entity, must be protected. This makes change dependent on the empowerment of the passion for society and the state structure that represents it. While the state, over time, may be replaced, it must also be protected from change that is too sudden or too vast to allow for the persistence of stability and social order. Consequently, the SPP of nonintervention is the rule of change for Hume's metaphysics of sovereignty. In the definition of Justice-As-Sovereignty, any progressive codification of international law, any rebalancing of the rules of recognition toward universal responsibilities rather than local control (i.e., any change in the essential *Lotus* definition of sovereignty as social convention) must clear the hurdle set by the SPP of nonintervention.

Social convention at the wider international level is assumed to seek a coordination equilibrium that allows distinct domestic societal regimes to find consensus and cooperate in stabilizing the more encompassing level of social organization while protecting the boundaries of their municipal strategic situation. The dialectic between international and municipal stability generates the circumstances for the rise of Justice-As-Sovereignty as a conventional process-norm representing practical reason applied to the evolution of international law. As a process-norm, Justice-As-Sovereignty focuses on procedure and is neutral as to specific "cultural" values. The international framework of the state system therefore protects all municipal solutions to the prisoner's dilemma (PD) without discrimination by simultaneously providing its own single coordination equilibrium at the international level that, in a dialectic tradition, is generally agreeable to, and in the interest of, all participants. It is this reality that the SPP of nonintervention is meant to protect.

But does Hume's philosophical-policy provide a more dynamic model of the state with more inherent utility than the dominant Hobbesian model? Applying philosophical method to Hobbes' logic of concepts will provide us with his philosophical-policy and create a systematic paradigm to foster comparative consideration. Especially in the contrast between the Hobbesian and Humean definitions of nonintervention, the full advantages of the Humean argument over the traditional axioms of realism/positivism should become clear.

Hobbes' Philosophical-Policy: State and Sovereignty

In *Leviathan*,[19] Thomas Hobbes logically integrates a moral and political chronicle of the origin and structural progression of men forming states from within a *prior* "natural" or unregulated state of war. The Hobbesian evolution from the State of Nature to Civil Society, is not a creature of process, as it is for Hume, but is based on three critical principles that should be considered universal and essential to Hobbes' metaphysics: *Power*, *Liberty*, and *Right*. These prior principles lie at the root of Hobbes' argument for prudential morality and political covenant, as well as his idea[20] of natural law. The interaction and dialectic dilemmas of power, liberty, and right, in the state of nature, are the variables that explain the human conditions in Hobbes' "pre-political" or prelegal world. Simply, the "willful" control of these three factors by a sovereign(ty) forms the law, which moves man into a Civil-Political State where justice is the sovereign's will.

Hobbes defines *Power* in *Leviathan*, at the beginning of Chapter 10. "The Power of a Man (to take it Universally), is his present means, to obtain some future apparent Good." Power is subsequently broken down into "Naturall Power"[21] or genetic eminence, and "Instrumentall Power,"[22] which is a means to acquire more of a thing. The latter can be based on the former, but is not dependent upon it. Instrumental power is one of the most important presuppositions in Hobbes' argument.

For Hobbes, an agent's value (individual or state-as-individual) is based on the importance of their power to others; value as a general concept involves the acquisition and maintenance of instrumental power, for the security of the agent, as well as his/its prestige. The culmination of individual power is in the creation of the civil aggregation of the powerful and autonomous state, or commonwealth understood as a "person" with sovereignty.[23]

> The Greatest of human Powers, is that which is compounded of the Powers of most men, united by consent, in one person, Naturall, or Civill...such as in the Power of a Commonwealth.[24]

The range within which an individual's power functions can be defined as their *Liberty*. Liberty, is the "absence of externall Impediments," which "may oft take away part of a mans power to do what he would; but cannot hinder him from using the power left him, according as his judgement, and reason shall dictate to him."[25] Liberty is also the antecedent stage of deliberation:

> And it is called Deliberation; because it is a putting an end to the Liberty we had of doing, or omitting, according to our own Appetite, or Aversion.[26]

Deliberation results in the placement of an impediment to the Liberty of the agent, in the form of something willed. The range of Liberty, in which agents use their power, is limited by their will.

In terms of the international system, and the state as a person within it, Hobbes philosophical-policy suggests that the liberty of a state is what we would now call its negative freedom,[27] or freedom from constraint by other states or laws. The power and liberty of the state are therefore measured in terms of one's empirical circumstances and the quantity of both attributes that allow one's political will to exercise one's individual or national interest, free of interference. This renders a very strict and inflexible definition of nonintervention.

To ensure Liberty, the individual seeks the construction of the State, for Hobbes contends that: "there is no other way by which a man can secure his life and liberty."[28] In fact, a second definition of Liberty, in Chapter 21 of *Leviathan*, reaffirms the definition of Liberty as a *negative range* of applied agency. Here Hobbes draws an even deeper distinction between Power and Liberty as he defines Liberty in the State.[29]

> Liberty, or Freedom, signifieth (properly) the absence of Opposition; (by Opposition, I mean externall Impediments of motion);...But when the impediment of motion, is in the constitution of the thing it selfe, we use not to say, it wants the Liberty; but the Power to move;[30]

In this case, the state, as a moral person, is created as the end or focus of the Power of aggregate wills, within a range of its Liberty, which, in turn, defines one's Right of Nature.[31] This right of the state, based on negative freedom, is the "summe of the Right of Nature; which is, By all means we can, to defend our selves."[32]

A specific and near-absolute right to self-defense or self-preservation defines the dialectic synthesis of the multiple dialectics of power⇆liberty⇆right for Hobbes. The absolute presupposition of his argument is a Right of nature, or to one's nature, that implies self-defense and is a substantive end that is assumed to be universal and unlimited. "It followeth, that in such a condition, every man has a Right to everything: even to one anothers body."[33] This is the civil society's dilemma in the international state of nature. In the state of nature the individual state has a right to everything but power over nothing; this puts its self-preservation at risk, unless it seeks a centralized covenant, exiting the state of nature for its own protection.

But the fundamental presupposition of self-preservation remains. In order to answer its imperative, the agent is motivated to leave the state of nature for inherently normative reasons; that is, because of his obligation to his right of self-preservation. The most specific definition of Natural Right in *Leviathan* involves the relationship between our three variables as relative presuppositions for the single end of self-preservation.

> The Right of Nature,...is the Liberty each man hath, to use his own Power as he will himselfe, for the preservation of his own Nature.[34]

The agents are here given an unlimited range of Liberty, by Right, within which they may utilize whatever Power (including violence) they possess as a means to the basic substantive end of their fundamental right.

Whether in terms of the creation of municipal or international law, Hobbes focuses on the centralized conscious and contractual solution to the PD that protects the fundamental right of all agents to their own self-preservation by providing the negative freedom of nonintervention necessary to it. In terms of international "covenant," the only difference is that one must contract the creation of the municipal state, escaping the *general* state of nature, before one can contract with other states, internationally, to escape the *global* state of nature.[35] In effect, Hobbes' logic of concepts creates a philosophical argument where power, motivated by self-interest and expressed as self-preservation, is the metaphysical core of both his definition of the state, its sovereignty, and the imperative of nonintervention.

The problem for both Hobbesian municipal and international law arises when one considers that Hobbes has also presupposed that all agents are, overall, equal to one another. In Chapter 13 of *Leviathan*, Hobbes states that agents are by their "Naturall Condition"[36] equal when they are "reckoned together."[37] This equality of power, when integrated with Hobbes' definition of the unlimited Right of Nature, leads to intense and self-interested eristic contact between agents with unlimited right, and a will predisposed to claim that right in interactive competition.

These circumstances, on any level of operation, breed the fundamentally noncooperative strategic environment of a PD. Here, the only stabilization of municipal affairs is in the conscious contractual creation of a substantive sovereignty or state personhood that compels cooperation by eliminating exploitative payoffs coercively from the top down.[38] Without the willingness of agents to trade unlimited right for conditional power in the creation of the sovereign state as a "moral person" in substantive command, the equality of Right and Liberty, along with a utilization of power toward identical but competitive ends, results in chaos.

> From this equality of ability, ariseth equality of hope in the attaining of our Ends...And from this (resulting) diffidence of one another, there is no way for any man to secure himself, so reasonable, as Anticipation; that is, by force, or wiles, to master that persons of all men he can, so long, till he see no other power great enough to endanger him.[39]

This conflict of power is further fueled by the general inclination of all agents toward "a perpetuall and restlesse desire of Power, that ceaseth onely in Death," [40] and, consequently, this results in, within the nonregulated "State of Nature"...a "warre; as is of every man, against every man."[41]

If one assumes that war, in the Hobbesian state of nature, is caused by the competition for power, in an environment of unregulated Liberty as granted by the Right of Nature, then law in the form of a centralized municipal-style sovereignty is a logical answer for both the local and universal states of nature. In any condition of unimpeded power, each agent's standard of reason by which they reach judgments, will be a strictly insular one. Because of this, the will of a sovereign is critical to creating one will that acts in the name of the collective. Only then can the chaos of joint decision-making end in the sovereignty and strict nonintervention necessary to create that ordered international relations of states that is the sole path to the regulation of the war of all against all. Under these extreme circumstances, the state of nature allows each agent to establish his own "Right Reason" in the transfer of right for the continuation of one's own sovereign preservation into the sovereignty of the state.[42]

The war created by the principles of power, right, and liberty, as representative of the presupposition of self-preservation, further causes the self-interested exercise of the Right of Nature to turn on itself. Agents with unlimited Right, and an unencumbered range of Liberty, compete for Power over one another. In this unrestricted competition, the less powerful loose their security to the more powerful, who themselves hold onto this power without civil stability.[43] Though equality of means is an overall reality, inequality of means is the individual situation that causes loss of Right, in death, to some, and fear of the loss of security to all the rest.

The answer to the problem of war in any State of Nature is *Peace in the Sovereignty of the State*. This is a "peace" that insures the security of all, or each agent's right to their self-preservation in the limitation of everyone's right to intervene in others' affairs. It is a partial transfer to a new moral "person": the artificial *person* of the state's sovereign or sovereignty. The fundamental moral desire to preserve one's inherent nature leads one's reason to a set of "theorems"[44] for the regulation of behavior. Hobbes calls these the Laws of Nature.

> The Passions that encline men to Peace, are Feare of Death; Desire of such things as are necessary to commodious living; and a Hope by their Industry to obtain them. And Reason suggesteth convenient Articles of Peace, upon which men may be drawn to agreement. These Articles, are they which otherwise are called the Laws of Nature.[45]

In accordance with the Laws of Nature, agents maintain their Right of Nature by a mutual and balanced limit of this Right as agreed to by conscious covenant that only then brings justice in ordered collective action. Agents will agree among themselves to transfer their unlimited Rights and unobstructed Liberty to a third party in legal contract, an artificial construct called the Sovereign. This social contract[46] is an expression of will at the posterior stage of deliberation, where unlimited Liberty ends and is replaced by the negative freedom of order and one's moral duty to it. Wherever deliberation ends in willing (i.e., choice and action), Liberty is limited by its dialectic with duty. As Hobbes puts it: "[f]or where liberty ceaseth, there beginneth obligation."[47]

For Hobbes, moral obligation comes only after contract, with government and the creation of a system of state sovereignty based on the negative freedom of each state. Moral obligation comes from substantive principle that limits liberty for Hobbes' individual (i.e., person or state). But with obligation, and the construction of the role of the sovereign, self-preservation is assured. To preserve their inherent value, the agent limits his/its individual Right, constricts his/its Liberty, and restricts the use of his/its Power, all to insure peace.

The variables of individual Power, Liberty, and Right that establish intolerable conditions in the State of Nature, lead to the creation of a new artificial construct in the form of the state, and the subsequent extrication of each agent from that state of war, which is the state of nature. The structured state is the result of reasoning individuals willing its constituent elements. The Hobbesian state, by solving the noncooperative strategic situation of the person, and by granting them a more secure context, is a necessary institutional expression of the absolute metaphysical presupposition of self-interested self-preservation.

Two Definitions of Nonintervention

Both Hobbes' and Hume's ideas about the normative status of sovereignty begin in a dialectic between sovereignty↔intervention. Hobbes frames nonintervention in terms of the negative freedom of the state as agent within a principle-driven PD that is the international state of nature. Here, law manifests itself through that limited level of intervention in local sovereignty necessary to the self-preservation of the agent.

For Hume, nonintervention is measured by the process-based standard of how the state contributes to the stability of international society. International law finds its genesis in the nonintervention of states as a metaphysical element of Justice-As-Sovereignty. Here, justice sanctions intervention only when the state no longer supports the cooperative equilibrium of the coordination game and loses its capacity to balance local and universal rules of recognition. But, this is where the common ground shared by Hobbes and Hume ends.

Hobbes' substantive principles of power, liberty, and right protect the self-preservation of the state, on the international level, as a substantive end in itself.[48] The state and its sovereignty are fundamentally the same thing. Although the state exists on different levels of social organization, both state and sovereignty exist within a single strategic reality, where they are the solution to unregulated human interactions creating PDs. Consequently, if there is no equivalent to the state on the international level, then the transnational PD will remain unsolved, and sovereignty will only be an "organized hypocrisy." Hobbes' logic ends in the same place where Wolff's begins: the Supreme State.

The Hobbesian argument relies on the solved municipal PD as the backbone for the future development of an international state and its sovereignty. The legally-mature state breeds stringent municipal enforcement institutions in the name of the sovereign, who is made necessary by the strategic reality of the PD on the local level. For Hobbes, the same dilemma exists on the international stage. The global PD cannot be solved by the agreement of states not to intervene in one another's affairs. Nonintervention can only be established within the PD by central institutions that regulate peace from the top down as an expression of the principle of self-preservation in the face of war. Consequently, our decentralized world system and its legal practice are merely pre-legal by Hobbesian standards.

When the international legal system is a state of nature constantly on the brink of a war of annihilation, and self-interest is expressed through an absolute presupposition of state self-defense or "self-preservation," then the metaphysical foundation of the argument for the state is essentially based on its' moral individuality and is disruptive to cooperation. This narrow concept of an international system does not allow much room for law except when it is based on absolute sovereignty (i.e., liberty, power, and right).

For Hobbes' philosophical-policy, law is an individual metaphysics of aetiological-norms and principles, specifically, an overlapping interaction of power, liberty, and right, where self-preservation is the absolute presupposition. For Hume, law is a social metaphysics, culminating in a cooperative process that is an end-in-itself and that focuses justice on the overall collective pattern of unconscious cooperation with its resulting social conventions that stabilize property. Instead of Power, Hume focuses on property stability; instead of Liberty, he focuses on coordination conventions; and instead of Right, he focuses on obligation to the collective order, which predates government in the social conventions of approbation and justice.

The focus on *process* gives Hume a more flexible definition of change or nonintervention within a two-tiered international strategic environment. Society is the focus of moral and legal personality, rather than the individual or the state, and a dialectic is created between the "ethical" and the "juridical."[49] This is not present in Hobbes' philosophical-policy, where morality is antecedent, encompassed by, and rendered from, the contractual emergence of the state and its sovereignty.

While Hobbes argues for one route to covenant that assumes a violent state of nature and a self-interested agent, Hume's approach provides for two distinct levels of social convention: one solving a PD at the municipal level and the other solving a coordination game for the sake of international society. By forsaking principle for process, Hume's logic can also accommodate many more distinct value systems or substantive ends than Hobbes' approach, which assumes that the Laws of Nature are a universal set of common and independent critical principles. Further, Hume's idea of nonintervention is not as an absolute and essential principle, but a protective and flexible rule of legal change within the metaphysics of Justice-As-Sovereignty.

Hume offers a nested strategic environment that allows different levels of complexity and governance requirements to be incorporated into each tier of evolving social convention. Within two distinct, but interrelated, levels of strategic interaction, Hume's focus on society and its persistence is concerned with collective action and how the use of institutional or administrative structures compensate for contextual complexity. Instead of a one-time covenant from which the sovereign state becomes an end-in-itself, Hume presents an argument for a scale of forms in which social convention evolves to protect the process of coordination, which is derived from the human passion for society. Nonintervention allows for the steady pace of this change, protecting the process-norm of Justice-As-Sovereignty while allowing for the increasing influence of critical principle in the process⇆principle dialectic. Hume's philosophical-policy is able to recognize law in a variety of governance structures including, but not limited to, the state, and does not require centralized enforcement as a perquisite to the existence of a legal system.

Hobbes presupposes that individual self-preservation overrides society, state, and all collective forms of expression, and that this substantive norm has a common, agreed-upon definition. For Hume, the idea of social convention makes the specific content of a society's shared values irrelevant to the more critical and universal cooperative process-requirements of all circumstances of justice. On all levels of social organization, the social conventions for order and stability determine the character of general legal practice as it overcomes any noncooperation to create states within an international system that equally preserves any and all human values not antithetical to the stability of society.

As Hume's philosophical-policy illustrates, the international level of coordination may not be as critical as the municipal, but this grants governance flexibility and a distinct character that is not accessible through Hobbes' logic of concepts. Hobbes' argument is unable to recognize anything but a strong centralized sovereignty as law, and therefore must decline to recognize that law exists on the international level, as do many positivists.[50]

Considering these paradigms as philosophical wholes, for Hobbes, the state has intrinsic moral status; for Hume, it has only instrumental moral status. With the individual agent as the source of intrinsic moral value in Hobbes, and with the state considered as an agent, it too is granted a moral status by its existence as a separate and sovereign person with the absolute presupposition of an existence to protect.[51] While Hobbes allows some flexibility in the specific organization of his sovereignty, once created, its structure becomes necessary to the maintenance of peace and is always the origin of moral value and justice for the civil society.

In defending itself, Hobbes' state, like the individual before it, fights off others in the state of nature to protect its absolute rights, and seeks the persistence of prudential morality under the laws of peace, where a strict negative freedom of nonintervention is the point of departure for international prelegal relations. But it is the private interest of the individual state and its power, liberty, and right that are the currency of the international system created by Hobbes' philosophical-policy. Here is where justice lies. But it is not justice-as-utility, but justice from right-in-existence.

Reading Hobbes and Hume as whole philosophical systems points out the difference between treating the state as an individual or as a collective entity. Hobbes' philosophical-policy is an argument for private interest, whether represented in a person or the state. He contends that the state, like a moral person, is an integrated unitary and static interest, looking inward to its own longevity and uninterrupted independence.

Hume's philosophical-policy is inherently collective because public utility trumps individual considerations. With a focus of limited generosity, Hume's logic of concepts promotes the public interest, which he argues is the primary source of the "moral approbation" that supports the idea of "justice."[52] Hume's society is not just looking inward; it acknowledges the dialectic interdependence of the international and domestic strategic spaces, as well as the interdependence of the ethical and juridical dimensions of that social utility that solves the municipal PD and preserves coordination on the global level.

Hobbes' idea of the state makes no distinction between ethical and juridical dimensions. For Hobbes, the juridical sovereignty of the state is a direct result of, and persists because of, the ethical power of the right in self-preservation. The ethical personality of the agent is directly translated into the juridical personality of the state. The power, liberty, and right originating in the individual is the foundation of the state and the source of its control and sanctioning power. The juridical is a direct outgrowth of the ethical.

Order in society is the core of Hume's analysis; order maintains its ethical status throughout the refinement of Justice-As-Sovereignty on its scale of forms and allows more flexibility to social evolution than is available from Hobbes. The juridical is an entirely distinct and primarily contingent element of Hume's logic of concepts. The governance structure and the definition of justice on which it is built are not of moral concern except to the extent that they diminish or empower the process of social cooperation. In this sense, Justice-As-Sovereignty is a juridical, and therefore artificial, construction, created in aid of the natural passions toward the coordination of society and bent to its persistence. The elective juridical personality of society informs, and gives reason to, the juridical personality of the state. The juridical is a separate concern that must be judged in terms of its facilitation of the morality or ethics of social order in context, making Hume's approach less dependent on the state per se as the necessary juridical currency of international society.

Hobbes' and Hume's philosophical-policy paradigms also have distinct approaches to how policy and law relate to certainty and universality. For Hume, a person finds certainty internally as an individual and faces uncertainty externally within the social collective; that is, individuals seek their universality and certainty internally in their humanity, which is under their control, and face uncertainty and local isolation in their external dealings with collective social interactions that require a solution to collective action problems beyond the control of any one agent. Meanwhile, social order seeks universality and certainty externally, in coordination with other social units, and experiences uncertainty internally in the atomistic complexity of a system of pluralistic values and overlapping consensus.[53]

If the state is assumed to be an individual, then Hobbes is logical to think that its universality would be internal to the creation of centralized sovereignty for the purposes of leaving the state of nature. Further, it could be posited that the sense of uncertainty would be in its international relations where a strong central governance structure has no jurisdiction. Such a state has moral status and would only cooperate in the international system to the extent that cooperation was perceived as self-interest. No dialectic would exist between layers of covenant, but only an eristic relationship between sovereign municipal states and the uncertain world outside. Universality becomes local in this context; the state is a necessary institutional structure, and uncertainty causes a lack of expansion of the covenant internationally.

However, if the state is considered a *social* construction, this provides a model that is more complete and more familiar to our experience of international legal practice. As the state is an instrumental creation of societal convention that exists to preserve the sociocultural pluralism or uniqueness of society, then one would expect that when the international layer of social convention evolves, uncertainty within the state has already been addressed in the solution to its PD. With this uncertainty satisfied, the collective state system is better able to address universality by externally seeking coordination through Justice-As-Sovereignty; it solves the internal clash of values through empowering a process-consensus similar to the one at the municipal level. Because Hume's philosophical-policy acknowledges the distinct yet dialectic tension between uncertainty and universality at both the individual and social levels of organization, universality is more achievable in international relations.

Justice-As-Sovereignty addresses the uncertainty of local society, which, through the process of evolving social convention, can then jointly create those instrumental institutions necessary to secure universality in the international system. Here, the dialectic between layers of social convention and the refinement of the concept of Justice-As-Sovereignty differentiates the concept of sovereignty from the institutional structure of the state and allows it to adapt both metaphysically and empirically on a scale of forms that may or may not include the state. This is not an option in Hobbes' paradigm.

The distinct definitions of sovereignty in Hobbes and Hume provide, in dialectic terms, the starkest contrast between these two philosophical systems. Calling Hobbes' philosophical-policy "Justice-As-Self-Preservation," it may, like Justice-As-Sovereignty, recommend nonintervention as a measure of change within the international system. However, Hobbes describes nonintervention in terms of the strict negative freedom necessary for state self-preservation, regulated by an absolute sovereignty defined by a top-down universal application of principle to the needs of individual states as ends-in-themselves. Hume's logic uses nonintervention as a flexible procedural rule that gauges the changing utility of Justice-As-Sovereignty. Sovereignty is consequently more than absolute nonintervention. It is both a top-down and bottom-up manifestation of the public interest in social stability.

Within international legal practice, as based on a positivist version of Hobbes philosophical-policy, sovereignty locates its imperative in the top-down process that insures control over territory and the equal status of any state to control its internal affairs under its own aegis. However, there are also a number of arguments about human rights and democratic institutions that suggest these must be considered as bottom-up sources of sovereignty.[54] Instead of the Hobbesian focus on the critical right of the state to preserve itself with control of its dominion, substantive or critical principles, like self-determination, universal rights, and personal autonomy are identified as defining sovereignty from the grass roots.[55] This seeming contradiction between what might be called the "two-faces of sovereignty" is, from the vantage point of Hume's philosophical-policy, not a contradiction at all, but simply different moments in the dialectic metaphysics of Justice-As-Sovereignty.

Effective control and critical rights are both top-down and bottom-up sources of sovereignty. Hume integrates his concept of sovereignty, dialectically, in a set of procedural rules including a rule of change defined by nonintervention. Hobbes creates a definition of nonintervention with a less complex and flexible metaphysics, allowing for a less dynamic international system. He defines nonintervention in terms of the fundamental right of self-preservation for the state. This requires the negative freedom necessary for the expression of a state's sovereignty; this negative freedom is contained within the nonintervention rule. For Hobbes' philosophical-policy, the dimensions of sovereignty as a concept, the ideas of self-determination, autonomy, rights, and democratic freedom, all find their origins with the advent of the state. The state is necessary to law and justice, which are in turn necessary to the rise of any of these moral ideals. In terms of causation, the creation of the state is a bottom-up exchange of private right that creates the essential platform from which all the subsequent components of justice are ostensibly dictated through the top-down establishment of effective control.

For Hobbes, the only moral or legal obligation is to the contractual establishment and preservation of the state. Any change in the state's main task of self-preservation must come from within in a top-down fashion. In this way, the bottom-up creation of sovereignty from a state of nature is replaced and consumed by the establishment of the state in a covenant that is, thereafter, the sole depository of top-down sovereignty. Nonintervention in the sovereignty of each municipal state then becomes the sole focus of the right to self-preservation at all levels of analysis.

This critical or substantive end for each state discourages cooperation between states and imposes the strategic atmosphere of a one-shot PD on the international system. This all-or-nothing empirical reality exists in the form of a global state of nature that imposes the uncertainty of a "war of all against all" as a punishment for any significant intervention. This environment is subsequently protected by a strict definition of nonintervention sanctified by the critical principles of liberty, right, and power. The liberty of the state is then designated as a repository of all considerations of right that are subject to the top-down power of the state subsequent to its basic imperative for survival in an international state of nature.

Hobbes' replacement of bottom-up with top-down sovereignty conflicts with those advocating human rights and the self-determination of peoples as fundamental (i.e., bottom-up) components of state sovereignty. For example, John Hoffman, in his book *Sovereignty*, argues for the abandonment of the idea of the state as a modern governance structure.[56] He seeks to find a point of integration between the "two sovereignties." He separates sovereignty from the state and makes it an independent, standalone principle with substantive content but without legal form, which, from the vantage point of legal practice, presents a more fundamental problem than Hobbes' top-down approach.

The state as a governance structure is and remains the primary possessor of legal personality within the world system.[57] The state has a central role to play in the definition and evolution of the idea of the rule of law. Thus, just as we may not want to abandon the bottom-up grass-roots component of sovereignty as Hobbes requires, we also may not want to abandon the idea of the state as Hoffman recommends. This returns us to Hume's philosophical-policy and legal design and its dialectic answer to this dilemma.

Hume consistently describes international society as a coordination process and Justice-As-Sovereignty as an instrumental process-norm involved in the persistence of social convention as it creates stability on all levels of social organization. Hume's philosophical-policy connects the public utility of justice and society with the process of coordination thereby defining state sovereignty. Specifically, from the perspective of Hume's logic of concepts, nonintervention is a rule of change that, with the other procedural SPPs, tractably protects, measures, and mediates Justice-As-Sovereignty as it responds to the contingencies of the international system.

For Hume, a society or "people" have the right to self-determination, not the individual agent as either a state or a person. That same social order, able to measurably defend itself through nonintervention, has the character of collective policy and social obligation, not private will. This local sense of recognition is complemented by the responsibilities of reciprocal or peaceful coordination at the universal level. Meanwhile, the international system is adjudicated through a process of progressive codification that depends on an institutional or administrative structure able to change and respond to the inevitable shifts in the need for nonintervention, as defined by the stability of international society.

Throughout the dialectic interactions of these procedural rules, there is no institutional form, substantive moral end, or inherent, principled value necessary to the stability of the Humean argument for international law. The instrumental value contained in the state is only coextensive with the moral obligation to create those sanctions necessary to assure the persistence and cohesion of human society through the refinement of Justice-As-Sovereignty on its scale of forms.

Although Hume's philosophical-policy does not require the establishment of the state per se, the value of the state and Justice-As-Sovereignty come from their utility to the chosen coordination equilibrium. The stability of any coordination equilibrium and its resulting process-norm is dependent on the institutional structure that evolves to support social convention; the modern state fulfills this role. For Hume's philosophical-policy, sovereignty is not a free-standing principle or aetiological-norm as it is for Hobbes. The normative background of the argument from Hume's conceptual logic is an ongoing dialectic between aetiological- and process-norms, where the latter, containing Justice-As-Sovereignty has the advantage.

Specifically, Hume's philosophical-policy solves the conundrum of sovereignty through philosophical method. First, like Hobbes, sovereignty is essentially a normative rather than an empirical concept for Hume. It is not just the observable practice of states that matters, but also the underlying metaphysics or presuppositions built on humanity's passion for society. The resulting logical system of normative social conventions and regulative moral principles that form the foundation of legal norms and invoke human obligation to them[58] evolve to protect and foster social interaction at increasing levels of complexity. This is the imperative of Hume's entire sociolegal system.

Second, sovereignty, and its SPPs, are not dichotomous, independent variables for Hume, but are connected dialectically. Justice-As-Sovereignty is, and continues to be, the synthesis of both a bottom-up process of creating and forming obligation to social convention, and a top-down process of solidification and institutionalization of property that provides for the persistence of social cooperation over time, through the governance structure of the state as a social construction.

Third, Hume confirms the dialectical nature of sovereignty through his contention that legal norms have both a *primary* (process-based) and a *secondary* (principle-based) source of moral authority that must be ultimately reconciled in order to establish a stable international legal system (see Figure 2.1). Although his definition of natural law makes the former more fundamental than the latter, together, in the reconciliation of the dialectic between them, they provide a more complete and dilemma-free argument for the concept of Justice-As-Sovereignty.

Hume's *primary* path for moral or normative authority for law is the process-norm created by social convention, which is not based upon a priori moral principle but is rendered by the bottom-up, iterated, and unconscious desire for social cohesion, breeding sets of expectations and social order out of the extrapolation of habitual behavior. These procedural rules of *recognition*, *adjudication*, and *change* are the metaphysical building blocks of a legal system and must respond to the progressive codification of the law over layers of social sanctions.

As we know, Hume's idea of social convention has three layers of sanction: moral approbation, justice, and contract-by-convention. Each of these layers of sanction reinforces the previous one, buttressing the terms of mutual property ownership, transfer, and stability, as well as refining the responsibilities of reciprocal cooperation as social systems become larger and more heterogeneous. The progressive development of governance institutions, defined by the scale of forms for Justice-As-Sovereignty, create the state as a social construction in answer to the imperatives of coordination at the Westphalian Equilibrium.

The *secondary* path for moral or normative authority in a Humean international legal system are those aetiological-norms that are ideal-regarding,[59] self-referential,[60] and based upon inherent ends or critical principles. They are not conventional, but created through debate and conscious policy design or contract, supporting the ability of human reason to morally sanction a nonproducible end as an imperative of human agency through legal design. Unlike Hoffman who argues that the critical principles behind rights reflect the bottom-up dimension of sovereignty, Hume argues that these critical principles are secondary to the establishment of social convention, but nevertheless a top-down phenomenon, requiring contract-by-convention and governance institutions to be legal.

For Hume's philosophical-policy argument, reasoned principle is not *prior* to, but *posterior* of, the existence of both social convention and the governance institutions created through contract-by-convention at the third level of sanctions. With the aid of these legal institutions, regulative moral principles become legal principles, and then legal norms through their persuasive success within the top-down legal governance structure.

Critical principle, for Hume, presupposes *prior* ends for political decision and a political/legal contract structure. It also presumes that social convention and contract-by-convention have preceded it, and that the fundamental governance structure of the legal system has been created to process critical moral principles and sort them for their potential status as legal principles, norms, and then dispositive rights and rules in law.

The secondary route to law is, by definition, dialectically supplemental for Hume, while the metaphysical foundation of social convention in reciprocal cooperation is more fundamental and essential. In the latter, Hume refines the dialectic in the process of the evolution of social convention and its layers of sanction. But the dialectic process also allows principle to remain in the mix, once introduced. Principle exists as a critical and disruptive element of the dialectic between process⇆principle in contention for the determination of synthesis solutions in the legal design process. This is especially true as international society moves from a Stage-I into a Stage-II legal system.

The primary evolution of social convention as a bottom-up process of social construction first frames the definition of Justice-As-Sovereignty for Hume. Individuals preserve their social predispositions and solve collective action problems through binary and group interaction, progressively compensating for discounting and free-riding as the social milieu becomes more complex.

Only with the evolution of institutional layers of sanction can Justice-As-Sovereignty create contract-by-convention and become the foundation of governance and a top-down solution to the persistence of social convention. At this phase of social integration, critical principle plays a larger role without the necessity of a concentrated Hobbesian state or its narrow focus on self-preservation as an end-in-itself.

No matter how decentralized or voluntary international law may initially be, the coordination of states at the Westphalian Equilibrium requires territory to be stabilized and general cooperation to be maintained; this becomes a top-down exercise of complying with Justice-As-Sovereignty. In terms of critical principle, the existence of governance institutions makes the integration of aetiological-norms another dimension of top-down property stabilization. But, unlike in Hobbes' concept of law, Humean governance also allows for another bottom-up venue for principle in the grass-roots generation of rights and substantive ends for the legal system.

Hobbes argument for the state prohibits any further bottom-up processes. Hume, however, provides for social convention that creates an institutional or democratic process from fundamental cooperation that can also advocate critical principle in the law. By forming obligations to established social conventions, political society also allows for both top-down and bottom-up processing of aetiological-norms, thus providing an integrated synthesis solution to the core dialectic where both dimensions of Justice-As-Sovereignty exist simultaneously. The core dialectic between process⇆principle expressed through sovereignty is simultaneously a top-down and a bottom-up norm for the consolidation of international law.

The measure of Justice-As-Sovereignty is how the bottom-up value of cooperation integrates with the top-down sanctions of the law. Here non-intervention plays the role of gatekeeper. This dialectic synthesis is revealed through a changing definition of nonintervention in international law. If a default sense of absolute nonintervention is the point of departure for the genesis of international law, then as critical principle becomes more fully engaged and more effective in shifting the legal synthesis away from process, the SPP of nonintervention will be redefined and change Justice-As-Sovereignty in measurable ways.

Within Hume's concept of Justice-As-Sovereignty, nonintervention, as a rule of change, is in dialectic with both the two rules of recognition and the rule of progressive codification. Specifically, in a Stage-I system, a stricter sense of nonintervention will limit the progressive codification of international law as well as the universal sense of state responsibility to the transnational community in order to support a *Lotus* definition of sovereignty as effective control. Here all the SPPs support Justice-As-Sovereignty, where the dialectic balance is weighted to the local rule of recognition. Within a Stage-II legal system, the dialectic of process⇆principle becomes more fully engaged. Now nonintervention must continue to protect effective control as the local rule of recognition, but also deal with pressure from both the universal rule of recognition and the rule of adjudication. Fundamentally, Justice-As-Sovereignty is moving on its scale of forms and the previously dominant process side of international sovereignty (i.e., effective control as a local rule of recognition) must change, requiring a more flexible definition of nonintervention that redefines sovereignty in terms of specific instances when intervention will aid in the persistence of justice. Here, as substantive principle affects the international procedural responsibilities of reciprocal cooperation and progressive codification, nonintervention will relax its hold and allow gradual changes to the Hobbesian or *Lotus* idea of sovereignty as international law.

Although Justice-As-Sovereignty is predominantly a top-down concept, it inherently provides for bottom-up moral principles in two ways. *Ex ante*, it initiates the dialectic between agency and obligation within the evolution of social convention, before top-down institutions are created. *Ex post*, Justice-As-Sovereignty provides a secondary route for ideal moral principle to become law through contract-by-convention. Sovereignty has both its roots (process-norm) and its secondary moral authority (aetiological-norm) in bottom-up moral precepts. In this way, Hume's Philosophical-Policy not only finds a specific solution to the dialectic for any circumstance, but creates a multidimensional argument for Justice-As-Sovereignty applicable to a changing international system. In its transition to a Stage-II legal system, Justice-As-Sovereignty may be required to regulate sets of nonconventional moral concepts "which denote empowerment and development—a concept which embraces democracy, autonomy and self-government."[61]

Overall, in Hobbes' philosophical-policy, self-preservation is the absolute presupposition represented by the relative presuppositions of power, liberty, and right against a background of the chaotic state of nature where the need for a Sovereign is the contractual solution to both the local and international PD. The state functions as a moral person where the critical moral standard for the law is its capacity to affect the preservation of the state as an end-in-itself. Nonintervention as an international measure of change is defined entirely by a virtually static idea of top-down sovereignty, which is a creature of critical principle and the requirements of the state. The absolute presupposition of Hobbes' argument provides a critical standard for his international legal philosophy, as well as an overlapping systemic framework for how power, liberty, and right synthesize to create an international system to maintain the negative freedom of the state.

Without a Wolffian "Supreme State," the Hobbesian approach results in the static dominance of an anarchic state of nature and the critical principles, like self-preservation and peace, that it threatens. This limits the possibilities of international law in the future as well as its dynamic qualities in the present. Hobbes' philosophical-policy, although the point of departure for positivist interpretations of international law, offers no concept of progressive codification, but only a single definition of universal morality, a single collective action problem, and a static creation of covenant that establishes a one-size-fits-all international rule of pre-law through centralized sovereign power.

Hume, by contrast, argues for "society" as the absolute presupposition that has come to be represented in the instrumental value of the state and its process-norm of Justice-As-Sovereignty. Nonintervention measures both the process and principle side of Justice-As-Sovereignty and allows for both more flexibility and a greater variety of possibilities for the influence of principle in the legal design process. As a measure of change, nonintervention is a function of local recognition in effective control, universal recognition in reciprocal cooperation, and adjudication in progressive codification. These SPPs allow Hume's philosophical-policy to process critical principle while circumventing both Hobbes' reliance on one manifestation of principle-in-covenant as a definitive determination of the law or Wolff's dependence on the *civitas maxima*.

Justice-As-Sovereignty is a process-norm that can respond to change in terms of the level of *nonintervention* prescribed by the demands of social order. To the degree that process cannot integrate human autonomy, self-determination, or democratic responsiveness, these values will be sacrificed to the evolution of social order and nonintervention will severely limit change. But if the persistence of society, within the context of a Stage-II legal system, requires the law to reflect a higher level of critical principle (inherently disruptive of process), then nonintervention will slowly relax its grip allowing for specific rights, duties, and substantive ends to become components of Justice-As-Sovereignty. The specific nature of the process⇆principle dialectic, as the latter competes for status in the legal design space that is a Stage-II International Legal System, will be considered next.

II. Policy Extrapolation for Legal Design: Process⇆Principle, the WTO, and the Logic of Change

Hume's Philosophical-Policy identifies the SPP of nonintervention as the procedural rule of change within Justice-As-Sovereignty. The degree to which the process-norm cedes ground to intervention in sovereign affairs will be a direct result of how the SPP interacts with the internal and external rules of recognition and the rule of adjudication also contained within the metaphysical elements of justice. Here, the ascendance of the World Trade Organization (WTO) will be examined to see how the process⇆principle dialectic affects the role of the rule of change in Justice-As-Sovereignty as the legal system sorts out the policy design implications of one alternative equilibrium based on critical principle and another based on process and reciprocity.

Of specific concern is the challenge to conventional sovereignty presented by the rise of the WTO and its dispute settlement structure. One claim is that WTO law is robust enough to be the constitutional center for a new and expanded idea of international practice that would transcend traditional Justice-As-Sovereignty and encompass all areas of legal concern.[62] Another perspective[63] is that essential principles connected to human rights and environmental quality may be discounted within such a constitutional structure. To understand this controversy requires a deeper understanding of the struggle between process⇆principle exemplified in the confrontation between environment, trade, and sovereignty within WTO dispute settlement.

Within the metaphysics of Justice-As-Sovereignty, the rule of change (i.e., nonintervention) has dialectic relationships with both the universal rule of recognition (i.e., peaceful cooperation) and the rule of adjudication (i.e., progressive codification). These pairs then have dialectic connections to the local rule of recognition (i.e., effective control) as the central agent in the established conceptualization of Justice-As-Sovereignty. The details of this dialectic map will be considered in the next chapter, but, for now, the dialectic forces balancing nonintervention can be characterized as the essential elements of a *Lotus* type of sovereign equality. This definition of sovereign justice will have to yield for change to occur. *Lotus*, however, is confirmed by the human passion for society, social convention, and the persistence of an established coordination equilibrium. *Lotus* provides a synthesis snapshot of public utility in legal practice that continues to focus on the international stabilization of property. The utility of *Lotus* sovereign equality, for both the municipal and international levels of social organization, lies in *reciprocity* as the means to social stability; specifically, first in unconscious reciprocity, and then in reciprocity sanctioned by approbation, then justice and, finally, by law.

For Hume's logic of concepts applied to the international legal system, reciprocity is sanctioned as public utility by the norm of Justice-As-Sovereignty. As a procedural idea reciprocity protects the absolute presupposition of the passion for society and its progressive evolution. It is reflected within the policy design space by a social construction of the state and contains a systematic and integrated metaphysical system of SPPs supporting the persistence of coordination. The state is, from this perspective, both a creature of, and a contributor to, its own social construction.

The instrumental value contained in the state is coextensive with the moral obligation to create those sanctions necessary to the refinement of conventions of process-reciprocity on a scale of forms, and the persistence of Justice-As-Sovereignty, necessary to the cohesion of human society and its inherent order. Justice-As-Sovereignty is a manifestation of the passion for society and has utility in one metaphysical moment only to the degree that it maintains that coordination equilibrium necessary to systemic stability. It does this on the international level by rendering legal rules created from that practice rendered by the interaction of the SPPs, which represent process⇆principle and affect the inherent dialectic balance defining the concept of justice.

As the Stage-I international system yields to a Stage-II configuration, an established synthesis snapshot weighted toward a law of *Lotus* sovereignty is increasingly challenged by many other policy considerations, which enliven and more fully engage the core dialectic of process⇆principle. Some of these challenges come from other process-norms suggesting alternative points of equilibrium through the persistence of reciprocal cooperation. But other norms are aetiological, representing critical principles, which seek to become an equal participant in the process⇆principle dialectic through contract-by-convention and conscious policy design. This particular challenge also suggests new equilibria, but with more inherent disruption to social convention, that is trumped in the synthesis snapshot by a necessary end rather than another instrumental means. These challenges to Justice-As-Sovereignty put more demands on the elasticity of its metaphysical elements and tax its dialectic nature.

Considering the rise of the WTO within the framework of Hume's philosophical-policy, and the inherent tension between process⇆principle, we can gauge the power of the state, its process-norm of Justice-As-Sovereignty, and the SPP of *Lotus* nonintervention, as these navigate the alternative arguments for coordination equilibria introduced by both alternative process-norms and critical principles. We shall consider the reaction of the WTO's panel and appellate bodies to three cases where critical principle, defined by the integrity of nature, challenges the process-norm of trade reciprocity as a variant of Justice-As-Sovereignty. These cases involve an effort on the part of the United States to determine its public policy priorities between trade and environmental protection in the face of international obligations that may run counter to them.

It is not surprising that the core documents of the WTO promote efficient and reciprocal trade as the dominant norms of its system of international law. The Panel decision in the *Shrimp/Turtle* case (examined in more detail below) stated categorically that "trade concerns outweigh environmental concerns…[o]ur reading of the object and purpose of the WTO Agreement led us to conclude that the central focus of that agreement is the promotion of economic development through trade."[64]

However, contrary to expectations, seeming critical principles, in terms of "protecting and preserving"[65] a sustainable environment, also play a role in the preamble to the WTO agreement.[66] The commitment to the preservation of a sustainable environment is a marked change from the singular focus on the "full use of the world's resources" agreed to by the state parties in the original language of the 1947 General Agreement on Tariffs and Trade (GATT) treaty, later used as a template for the WTO Agreement.[67] This change can be characterized as the beginnings of a transition from a Stage-I definition of sovereignty. Formerly, a state's right both to use its own resources to the full and coordinate with others to do the same globally is fully protected, but in a Stage-II system critical principle (e.g., human dignity, preservation of the environment) are factors legally petitioning to intervene in *Lotus* sovereignty and disrupt reciprocal trade.

In Stage-I, GATT worked in support of Justice-As-Sovereignty, placing the norm in a powerful position by promoting a balance of its rules of local and universal recognition, heavily weighted toward the former. In this way, the legal design based on social convention dominates and blocks the disruptive force of critical environmental principle, which, to trump "maximum use," would change the metaphysical balance of Justice-As-Sovereignty and its established synthesis definition of nonintervention.

But the coming of Stage-II, and an international concern for environmental values, will not be blocked forever, and evidence emerges for the acknowledgment by the WTO dispute settlement system that the introduction of alternative norms, some from critical principle, is a necessary element of the evolving legal system to which Justice-As-Sovereignty must respond. For example, the Panel in *Shrimp/Turtle* explains the shift from full use to be "a recognition by WTO negotiators that optimal use of the world's resources should be made in accordance with the objective of sustainable development."[68]

The WTO has also established a permanent Committee on Trade and Environment (CTE)[69] that, in the preamble of its constitution, acknowledges critical principle in the form of a tacit commitment to the ex ante "protection" and "promotion" of the environment.[70] In the agreement-proper, the CTE calls upon the parties to "identify the relationship between trade measures and environmental measures in order to promote sustainable development"[71] and encourages the signatories of the WTO to work for law that reflects critical principle toward the end of a "sustainable" natural world. More specifically, the CTE creates "rules to enhance positive interaction between trade and environmental measures for the promotion of sustainable development, [and] to ensure responsiveness of the multilateral trading system to environmental objectives set forth in Agenda 21 and the Rio Declaration."[72]

A note on the "principle" of sustainability is necessary. As I have argued elsewhere,[73] controversy exists as to whether sustainability should be classified as primarily a critical principle, because of its imperatives for precaution, prevention, and the right to environmental quality for future generations, or as what I have called a "contextual" principle, because of its reflection of international social convention in the right to resources and sovereign development. It is sufficient that the meta-principle of sustainability contains elements that invoke specific, universal, and necessary ends (e.g., precaution in the face of environmental risk; the health of future generations). Consequently, this argument will consider sustainability a critical principle because it contains imperatives that seek to trump established social conventions and force the balance of dialectics within Justice-As-Sovereignty to shift, for the sake of nature, toward a more liberal conception of nonintervention.

This classification of sustainability as a critical principle is supported by the fact that, in addition to the prominent position the umbrella principle of sustainable development has in the international law of the WTO, its tribunals have also brought some of its "critical" subprinciples into their decisions. For example, the precautionary principle features in the *United States v. European Community–Beef Hormones* case of 1997.[74]

But the question remains as to the status of sustainability as a "perceived" critical principle in the *ratio* or *dicta* of the WTO Tribunals; that is, as either a full component of a vital Stage-II dialectic requiring change in the process-norm of Justice-As-Sovereignty, or simply as a side issue of the tribunal's decision-making in a less evolved international legal system. Three cases will help us answer this question: *Tuna/Dolphin I*, *Tuna/Dolphin II*, and *Shrimp/Turtle*.[75]

All three of these cases involve the use of Article XX(b/g) of the WTO treaty by the United States, to justify violations of the reciprocal or "fair" trading provisions of Articles III, IX, and XI in the name of environmental protection. Overall, the United States attempted to use the "General Exceptions" to the rules of fair trade to integrate protections for endangered species into trade policy. Specifically, Art.XX(b) and (g) were invoked, which allow member states to implement those measures "(b) necessary to protect human, animal or plant life or health or (g) relating to the conservation of exhaustible natural resources, if such measures are made effective in conjunction with restrictions on domestic production or consumption."[76]

In *Tuna/Dolphin* I and II the United States tried to ban the importation of tuna caught by technology that also allowed the incidental taking of dolphins. In both cases, even after the United States rewrote the monitoring and exception provisions to the Marine Mammal Protection Act and renegotiated with the parties involved in the dispute, the Panel did not allow the use of Article XX, refusing to promote critical environmental principle to trump the social conventions of reciprocal trade. Even though the Panel appeared to agree that the dolphins were at risk as a resource and that environmental protection may be a critical value, they were more strongly persuaded that the restriction on reciprocal trade was unnecessary. In their written opinion, the Panel made a series of decisions that, in effect, overruled American municipal law, while it promoted the social conventions of *reciprocal trade* as an alternative coordination equilibrium to Justice-As-Sovereignty. In the process, the Panel suppressed American sovereignty for the requirements of WTO reciprocal trade norms.

The Panel in *Tuna-I* set the burden of proof "on the party invoking Article XX to justify its invocation,"[77] arming the norm of reciprocal trade, as an established social convention, with the power of the legal default position. It also set a high threshold in terms of the "necessity" of interfering with trade reciprocity, by contending that "Article XX was [only] intended to allow contracting parties to impose trade restrictive measures inconsistent with the General Agreement to pursue overriding public policy goals to the extent that such inconsistencies were *unavoidable*."[78] This bulwark against the necessity of overruling process with critical principle again placed the WTO as a defender of trade-process, but also defined a competitive, and perhaps indifferent, equilibrium within the coordination game that produced Justice-As-Sovereignty.

The WTO was, in effect, redefining the metaphysical balance of Justice-As-Sovereignty to establish reciprocal trade as a better representative of the passion for society than a purer *Lotus* sovereignty. This is a first step in the reconfiguration of nonintervention from a more absolute definition to a more conditional definition that allows trade, but not environmental integrity, to trump sovereign self-determination. This alternative can be called "*Justice-As-Trade Reciprocity*."

In *Tuna-II*, the Panel went further, focusing specifically on the illegality of the United States insistence that other states "adopt a regulatory program"[79] aimed at equivalent conservation of fish (i.e., mammal) stocks. The Panel also articulated a three-step legal test[80] that can be interpreted, through Hume's philosophical-policy, as an effort to make the status of Justice-As-Trade Reciprocity more explicit in its confrontation for dominance of the legal process with both the first *Lotus* moment of Justice-As-Sovereignty and the critical principles of environmental protection.

First, the Panel required that the sovereign municipal policy had "to conserve" or "protect" health or life. Second, it had to be "necessary" to that protection and "in conjunction" with domestic measures. Third, it had to be free of "arbitrary or unjustifiable discrimination" under the chapeau of Article XX.[81] The Panel found that while the United States passed the first test, it failed both the second and third.

In their conclusion, the WTO Panel sorted environment principle, sovereign self-determination, and reciprocal trade, to the express advantage of the latter. The protection of the international environment, as well as a state's *Lotus* sovereignty, now have a limit in terms of the point at which reciprocal international trade and its norms and rules are to be threatened. [82]

The most recent case exploring the process⇆principle dialectic again concerns the United States and its efforts to use its municipal sovereignty to elevate critical principle over reciprocal trade. American environmental policy regarding turtle conservation resulted in a municipal ban on the importation of shrimp caught without the use of TEDs (i.e., Turtle Exclusion Devices). A case was brought against the United States by a group of Asian states and it proceeded through both a WTO Panel and the Appellate Body procedure, resulting in a definitive interpretation of Article XX within the WTO dispute settlement system.

With the previous experience of the Tuna cases, the United States ensured that the amendment to the Endangered Species Act (ESA)[83] requiring the use of TEDs for all shrimp harvesting, including both domestic and foreign imports, incorporated species of turtles already classified as endangered both domestically under the ESA and internationally under Appendix I of the Convention on International Trade in Endangered Species of Wild Fauna and Flora (CITES).[84] In addition to certainty that the species was under threat and that the law applied to domestic shrimp as well as foreign, the American argument for trade exception was supported by a series of bilateral negotiations aimed at averting the dispute through treaty law. Nevertheless, the WTO Panel found the practice a violation of reciprocal trade, "inconsistent with GATT Article XI" and "unjustifiable under Article XX."[85] The United States took their case to the Appellate Body for a more definitive judgment.

Although the Appellate Body did not reverse the Panel in terms of the ultimate decision, it made four points of interest to our argument that reflect an understanding of the dialectic between process⇆principle and the changing nature of Justice-As-Sovereignty. First, the Appellate Body "rationalized" the interpretation of Article XX, reversing the Panel's approach. Second, it established that environmental protection, and international law more generally, were factors within the province of WTO jurisprudence. Third, it used norms from conventional international law to argue that while critical environmental principle was not compatible with Justice-As-Sovereignty, an equilibrium based upon Justice-As-Trade Reciprocity was its natural extension or replacement. Fourth, the Appellate Body discounted environmental protection at the municipal tier of the international system, promoting global Justice-As-Trade Reciprocity instead.

Previously, the Panel's decision suggested that in order for a measure to be classified as a legal exception under Article XX, it had first to meet the requirements of the chapeau (viz. that it is not "a means of arbitrary or unjustifiable discrimination" or a "disguised restriction" on reciprocal international trade). Only then would the petition be judged as to whether it fell under one of the acceptable categories of Article XX exceptions (a to g). Since, from its perspective, the United States failed the chapeau test, the Panel never fully considered whether the American law was necessary for the protection of a living resource under XX (b or g).

The Appellate Body called the Panel's approach "chapeau-down,"[86] and reversed it, citing both previous GATT cases and international law.[87] It argued that a measure should first meet the criteria of one of the Article XX exceptions, and only then take the chapeau test. In applying this "exceptions-up" approach to Article XX, the Appellate Body used both the WTO agreement and the international law of treaty to decide that the American import restrictions for non-TED shrimp were acceptable as falling under XX(g), passing the first Article XX test. From within Hume's logic of concepts, this decision acknowledges that international law was in transition to Stage-II and that consequently, critical principle was a pertinent subject within the process⇆principle dialectic that merited legal consideration.

In addition, the Appellate Body, in turning the Panel's approach upside-down, made itself the international arbiter of the legality of both critical environmental principle and the sovereign state's right to protect it, not just for trade law but for general international law as well. In examining the case from the "exceptions up" standpoint, the Appellate Body postponed the full application of the norm of Justice-As-Trade Reciprocity until the issue of environmental exceptions was dealt with, expanding the reach of the WTO dispute settlement system into more general international law. By fiat, the Appellate Body demonstrated that its dispute settlement system was able to accommodate concerns for environmental protection and Justice-As-Sovereignty within the context of trade reciprocity.

> we hold that, in line with the principle of effectiveness in treaty interpretation, measures to conserve exhaustible natural resources, whether *living* or *non-living*, may fall within Article XX(g).[88]

The use of the word "may" is significant. While the core of the paragraph seems to encourage a state's consent to treaty limitations on its sovereignty that would support a conventional reliance on Justice-As-Sovereignty, "may" suggests that the Appellate Body reserves the ultimate decision on these matters.

Although the American argument was found to qualify for an Article XX exemption under section (g), it was ultimately unsuccessful as it "constitutes arbitrary and unjustifiable discrimination between Members of the WTO, contrary to the requirements of the chapeau of Article XX."[89] Examined from the standpoint of Hume's philosophical-policy and legal design, one could argue that the Appellate Body ultimately created a hierarchy among critical environmental principle, Justice-As-Sovereignty, and its alternative, Justice-As-Trade Reciprocity, the latter having priority. By discounting what it admits are "necessary conservation measures" pertaining to nonsustainable resources in favor of reciprocal or efficient trade, the WTO Appellate Body intervenes in American sovereignty to regulate the extraterritorial reach of its municipal law in the name, not of Justice-As-Sovereignty, which supported the American position, but the alternative process-norm of Justice-As-Trade Reciprocity.

In a seeming effort to make Justice-As-Trade Reciprocity a more appealing alternative to Justice-as-Sovereignty, without the disruptive presence of the critical principle of environmental protection, the Appellate Body chastised the United States for trying to force other nations to change their environmental law to preserve a living species. Then it argued, that to preserve the equality of states, the United States should cease expressing its sovereignty in terms of critical environmental principle that is "plainly discriminatory,"[90] and therefore inherently disruptive to international order.[91]

Utilizing Hume's philosophical-policy, one can see that the Americans may have lost this case, not because they violated the established practice of Justice-As-Sovereignty, but because they utilized it to make the sovereign decision to promote critical principle in international law. Instead of moving to the full international institutionalization of critical principle, which is potentially a greater disruption to the Westphalian Equilibrium, the Appellate Body made the easier move from one process-norm to another that, while distinct, is also based on reciprocity.

The Appellate Body also makes a case for its jurisdiction as the proper venue for environmental decision making. By segregating trade from environmental law, the Appellate Body reduces the status of the latter, raises the affect of the former, and promotes itself as the best judge of the correct "trade" synthesis between *Lotus* sovereignty⇆nonintervention. Justice-As-Sovereignty's rule of change is made more flexible by the dispute settlement structure of the WTO, so that international reciprocity can be simultaneously protected from American sovereignty and critical principle in the name of Justice-As-Reciprocal Trade. Meanwhile, critical environmental principle is reduced to *dicta*, within a WTO rendition of international environmental law.[92] The implied conclusion is that the ultimate judge of when and how much of these actions are acceptable should be left to international law as interpreted through the WTO Dispute Settlement System and its alternative process-norm of Justice-As-Trade Reciprocity.

What the WTO did demonstrates that their alternative equilibrium for international law stabilizes sovereignty and the international system with little or no disruption of the established bulwark of social convention. This highlights at least an unconscious appreciation that Justice-As-Trade Reciprocity is a much-less threatening alternative to the status quo than any adoption of critical environmental principle in international law. The fact that trade continued to focus on the stabilization of international property and reciprocal peaceful relations makes the move to Justice-As-Trade Reciprocity akin to the move from hunting rabbit to hunting stag. Specifically, such a move can be accommodated within the existing Westphalian coordination game. Justice-As-Trade Reciprocity is, therefore, only a rebalance of the inherent metaphysical dialectics of Justice-As-Sovereignty, rather than its wholesale replacement. By maintaining critical principle in its proper, that is, subservient place, the shift to Justice-As-Trade Reciprocity holds out the prospect of a less disruptive shift in international legal practice that retains a considerable amount of the process-norm of Justice-As-Sovereignty while still suppressing critical principle. This argument becomes even more transparent with the Appellate Body's decision in what might be called *Shrimp/Turtle II*.[93]

In 2001, the dispute settlement system examined the actions taken by the United States in the wake of the first *Shrimp/Turtle* case. In this decision, the

WTO adjudicators dismissed a complaint by Malaysia and ratified the new American approach to Shrimp protection policy. However, the reasons why the United States won the approval of the WTO are telling. Specifically, they shed light on the evolution of the international legal system in terms of the utility of Hume's philosophical-policy and legal design.

First, the United States had "comparable"[94] negotiations with all the relevant parties, and second, presented the parties with "flexible"[95] conservation options to gain proper certification. In other words, the WTO allows sovereign action by a state if it first, pays "serious, good faith"[96] efforts to gain the sovereign consent of the other states involved, and when it makes the "single, rigid and unbending requirements"[97] of critical principle much less necessary and less universal. Although aetiological-norms represent ends that are substantive, necessary, and, sometimes a degree unbending, the Appellate Body requires those ends to be compromised for "comparable effectiveness" in relation to their standards of Justice-As-Trade Reciprocity.[98] Comparable effectiveness is a term more applied to means than ends, but it has the effect of ensuring that critical principle does not trump process under the WTO alternative definition of justice.

Second, a case is made for the WTO alternative by its capacity to achieve vindication in an important dimension of reciprocity: consent. All of this occurs within a context where the new approach of the Americans supported process-norms over critical principle as the core of justice. International trade was no longer faced with the threat of disruption from aetiological-norms, while stable property relations became accessible by either of two equilibria: *Lotus* sovereignty (hunting hare) or Justice-As-Trade Reciprocity (hunting stag).

As the process refines itself, and a Stage-I legal system moves into Stage-II, the conventional or status quo norm will, ceteris paribus, fight off any newly competitive aetiological-norms or critical principles that will, by design, cause disruption in reciprocal expectations and interfere with the conventional social equilibrium. While social convention downplays the legitimacy of critical principle within international legal practice, one might also expect that new contingencies of context will cause adjustment in the idea of nonintervention that portend change, and that established norms will be refined through legal design in adaptation to these shifting circumstances of justice.

In making the necessary changes, the social conventions undergirding the law will have a less drastic reaction when Justice-As-Sovereignty is challenged by another process-norm to which it can more easily readjust its inherent dialectic configuration. Justice-As-Sovereignty is after all, like Justice-As-Trade Reciprocity, a creature of reciprocal human interaction and the social conventions that spring from them.

The need for an alternative process-norm should only arise if the established process-norm (viz. Justice-As-Sovereignty) no longer adequately protects reciprocal interaction at social equilibrium, and, in this way, ill-serves social convention and the stability of property that represent the passion for society. However, a new process-norm, rather than a new aetiological-norm, has the advantage of maintaining the reciprocal effectiveness of the process of social convention as evolution, without the "revolutionary" disruption of moving from a moral focus on *means* to a moral focus on substantive *ends*.

Applying Hume's philosophical-policy to a system faced with the need to hunt stag instead of hare, one should expect that the established evolutionary pattern within the legal design space will trend toward collective action that seizes on a seemingly "indifferent" point of coordination based on another process-norm akin to Justice-As-Sovereignty. Here the rule of change simultaneously empowers a point of transnational coordination through an alternative, but still neutral, means-based, norm that avoids having critical principle threaten the long-established order of international society. Under these conditions, Justice-As-Sovereignty is able to absorb change and redefine itself. It accommodates trade reciprocity through a less drastic rebalance of metaphysical elements, which may shift coordination equilibria but within the same Westphalian coordination game.

The predisposition to refine social convention by replacing one process-norm with another may account for the tendency of current international legal practice to demote moral discourse, and the critical principles it renders, to "soft"[99] rather than "hard" legal status. The alternative process-moment will place an additional obstacle in the way of critical principle as it seeks a more definitive status within the dialectic of process⇆principle, and therefore, in codified international law. The potential shifting of equilibria between process-norms within the coordination game further disadvantages critical principle for now change can be experienced without drastic disruption of social stability. Meanwhile, all aetiological-norms seeking legal status will continue to be vetted through a legitimation process defined by the process side of the core dialectic, further protecting social convention. Only the most tenacious critical principles will prevail.

The WTO, as is generally acknowledged, is currently making a case for its dispute settlement system to become the core constitutional-governance system for general international law. From the point of view of Hume's philosophical-policy, this effort offers the advantage of attempting to refine one process-norm with another. If the WTO is seeking to refine Justice-As-Sovereignty with Justice-As-Trade Reciprocity, while it simultaneously assures states that its ascension to constitutional status will protect social convention while keeping critical principle at bay, its argument has an inherent advantage within contemporary international legal practice, over any arguments based on critical principle. This is especially true because the majority of states, in their acknowledgment and compliance with WTO decisions, already accept the priority of trade reciprocity and its fundamental market assumptions, even to the detriment of their sovereign effective control.

On the other hand, those interested in critical principle (e.g., environmental protection or human rights) should expect that the WTO dispute settlement system will continue to recognize these ends as disruptive to the established coordination equilibrium. Critical principle will largely continue in its role as "soft" law, and it will be disadvantaged, as it was in the cases examined in this chapter, under the requirements of trade reciprocity. Nonintervention may relax to allow for global markets and trade equality, but this does not mean that the *responsibility to protect* or the *precautionary principle* will receive the same consideration. In fact, with the new and stronger equilibrium of trade reciprocity, and social convention rescued from more major disruption without the need of critical principle, "justice" may become more entrenched against critical principle.

Whatever the specific outcome, within a two-tiered system of reciprocal municipal and international social orders, all critical regulative principles that compete for the status of international law and threaten one or another definition of nonintervention, will only gain legitimacy if states are willing to compromise the bulwark of international social convention for the sake of these moral or legal ends. This is a high threshold to cross.

III. Evidence in Legal Practice

In the transition from a Stage-I to a Stage-II legal system, the balance of SPPs that constitute the metaphysical elements of Justice-As-Sovereignty will be refined. Within this dialectic balance, the rule of choice plays a specific role by providing counterbalance to both the universal rule of recognition and the rule of adjudication as they try to open up and then regulate a state's exposure to international law. Within this structure, nonintervention is the gatekeeper for change because its metaphysical weight will determine how much and what kind of affect international law will have on the municipal legal system and vice versa. In this way, the dialectic balances between the rule of change, universal recognition, and adjudication will determine the overall weight of the local rule of recognition, or the effective control of the state over its sovereign affairs within Justice-As-Sovereignty.

Stress on the rule of change arises when a primary definition for nonintervention as *Lotus* sovereignty is faced with a more fully-engaged dialectic between process⇆principle. The full engagement of nonintervention with critical international principle may result in a situation where the Westphalian Equilibrium is of less utility to the stability of international society. This would result in the redefinition of the rule of change within the dialectic, to both deal with critical principle and maintain the viability of Justice-As-Sovereignty.

The following series of jurisdiction and immunity cases provide insight as to whether or not the evolution of the international system, since the *Lotus* decision codified its first level of complexity, has rebalanced the social conventions of Justice-As-Sovereignty. Within this examination, the role of nonintervention as the gatekeeper of change will be specifically noted. These cases measure the changing definition of local recognition given the rebalancing of universal recognition and adjudication as measured in the rule of change with its SPP of nonintervention. All were heard in United States Appellate Courts.

In 1812, within a very young republic, the new Supreme Court recognized the social conventions of international law, the absolute status of Justice-as-Sovereignty, and a strong default definition of nonintervention in their opinion regarding *The Schooner Exchange v. McFaddon & Others* 11 U.S. 116 (1812).[100] Here, the balance of dialectics rendered a strong definition of effective control as a local rule of recognition.

> The jurisdiction of the nation within its own territory is necessarily exclusive and absolute. It is susceptible of no limitation not imposed by itself. Any restriction upon it, deriving validity from an external source, would imply a diminution of its sovereignty to the extent of the restriction, and an investment of that sovereignty to the same extent in that power which could impose such restriction.[101]

Chief Justice John Marshall laid out the definitive argument for an international system with a strong sense of Justice-As-Sovereignty determined by effective control. Within the framework of Hume's legal design, this decision is evidence in the creation of an international legal system that would, 100 years later, codify a law of prohibitions with a *Lotus* definition of justice-as-utility. His argument was reinforced by the Supreme Court some 85 years later in *Underhill v. Hernandez* 168 U.S. 250 (1897).

> Every sovereign state is bound to respect the independence of every other sovereign state, and the courts of one country will not sit in judgment on the acts of the government of another, done within its own territory.[102]

More recently, the International Court of Justice (ICJ) reinforced the default definition of nonintervention, particularly against the prospect of critical principle, in its *Nicaragua* decision.

> The principle of non-intervention involves the right of every sovereign State to conduct its affairs without outside interference;...the Court considers that it is part and parcel of customary international law....It is both an "essential foundation" and an "essential principle of international law."[103]

From the standpoint of Hume's philosophical-policy, one would expect this lineage. Within a Stage-I international legal system based on Justice-As-Sovereignty, the rule of nonintervention is calibrated as a bellwether of change for the maintenance of *Lotus* sovereignty and its Westphalian Equilibrium, with a predisposition toward local effective control. The purpose of the process-norm, under these circumstances of justice, is to empower social convention as it defers change through a strong definition of nonintervention. This gives the process-norm, at best, a latent rule of change and, at worst, a rule of nonchange.

But, with the further evolution of contract-by-convention, and a stronger sense of international legal institutions and policy, social convention will be faced with substantive rules and rights from critical principle. During this potential shift to a Stage-II system, critical principle, the natural agent of disruption within a Humean view of law as established practice, gains influence and requires that the strong definitions of effective control and nonintervention be rebalanced in favor of reciprocal cooperation and progressive codification.

As social convention stabilizes international society, it also ignores substantive ends to the requirements of processes that, over time, produce a resurgence of critical principle in defense of such ends, whatever they may be (e.g., human rights; protection of nature; equality; freedom; self-determination). This balances the dialectic between process⇆principle more evenly and makes the possibility of critical principle becoming law more probable. This consequent refinement of the idea of nonintervention is reflected in the evolution of American case law on jurisdiction.

By 1945, an appellate court in the United States began to consider exceptions to the strong definition of nonintervention, indicating that change to the established system of international social conventions, and correspondingly, a new definition of nonintervention within Justice-As-Sovereignty, was worth considering to maintain the utility of the Westphalian Equilibrium. In the case of *U.S. Aluminum Co. of America*, 148 F.2d 416 (2nd Cir. 1945)[104] the Second Circuit Court of Appeal refined the SPP of nonintervention as a rule of change. This refinement was not in response to political or moral concerns of critical principle, but to support the utility of Justice-As-Sovereignty in its dialectic with reciprocity in international commerce. It allowed jurisdiction for the United States when international action created an "effect" on its municipal anti-trust law.[105]

> it is settled law,...that any state may impose liabilities, even upon persons not within its allegiance, for conduct outside its borders that has consequences within its borders which the state reprehends; and these liabilities other states will ordinarily recognize....we shall assume that the [Sherman] Act does not cover agreements,...unless its performance is shown actually to have had some effect upon them.[106]

The so-called *effects doctrine* separated the economic ramifications of foreign behavior in terms of commercial effect and then created, by default, the dialectic partner of the effects doctrine in the *act of state doctrine*. Specifically, the court separated the political or moral acts of a state from their commercial actions and designated the latter as no longer strictly protected by the default definition of immunity or nonintervention that held sway for "acts of state."[107]

The full judicial codification of this matter occurred in 1964 with the Supreme Court case of *Banco National de Cuba v. Sabbatino* 376 U.S. 398 (1964).[108] In this judgment, the Court recognized the Act of State Doctrine by, again, delineating between political and economic fields of international action. But it also made a strong case not to move as far as the *Alcoa* Court had gone in transforming nonintervention from its default definition. As if the Court were concerned that too powerful an "effects" exception would threaten Justice-As-Sovereignty, they made an effort to connect the degree of change in the SPP of nonintervention to sovereignty without allowing the process-norm to overwhelm the immunity of an act of state.

> If a transaction takes place in one jurisdiction and the forum is in another, the forum does not by dismissing an action or by applying its own law purport to divest the first jurisdiction of its territorial sovereignty;...While historic notions of sovereign authority do bear upon the wisdom of employing the act of state doctrine, they do not dictate its existence.[109]

Nonintervention as evidence of change was protected by the Court in two ways. First, when political acts of state are separated from economic action, the former retain full default nonintervention and are free from the "constitutional" jurisdiction of the Court. Second, while commercial activity may become subject to extraterritorial jurisdiction, this is only when it is not considered antithetical to Justice-As-Sovereignty.

> The doctrine as formulated in past decisions expresses the strong sense of the Judicial Branch that its engagement in the task of passing on the validity of foreign acts of state may hinder rather than further this country's pursuit of goals both for itself and for the community of nations as a whole in the international sphere.[110]

Political acts of state become equivalent to comity rather than international law, where comity is no longer the purview of the Court. In their finding that the Act of State Doctrine should be narrowly interpreted by the Court, the Justices also indicated that the "political" nature of the issue involved might also have moral/legal implications best left to the "political branches."

> However offensive to the public policy of this country and its constituent States an expropriation of this kind may be, we conclude that both the national interest and progress toward the goal of establishing the rule of law among nations are best served by maintaining intact the act of state doctrine in this realm of its application.[111]

In effect, the court maintained as absolute a definition of nonintervention as they could, given their simultaneous epiphany that commercial transactions were now to be transcendent of sovereignty and subject to extranational regulation. Trade was acknowledged as an alternative process-norm (e.g., Justice-As-Trade Reciprocity), which must be integrated, by amending the established rule of change, in order to maintain the utility of

Justice-As-Sovereignty. However, in dissent, Justice White argued for a more all-encompassing role for modern international law.

> I am dismayed that the Court has, with one broad stroke, declared the ascertainment and application of international law beyond the competence of the courts of the United States in a large and important category of cases....This backward-looking doctrine, never before declared in this Court, is carried a disconcerting step further: not only are the courts powerless to question acts of state proscribed by international law but they are likewise powerless to refuse to adjudicate the claim founded upon a foreign law; they must render judgment and thereby validate the lawless act....No other civilized country has found such a rigid rule necessary for the survival of the executive branch of its government; the executive of no other government seems to require such insulation from international law adjudications in its courts; and no other judiciary is apparently so incompetent to ascertain and apply international law.[112]

From the perspective of Hume's philosophical-policy, White's dissent is an argument for a further amendment of the rule of change to allow for a wider definition of universal recognition and progressive codification than in *U.S. Aluminum Co. of America*. It acknowledges the first twitches of a transition toward a fully engaged Stage-II international legal system. This dissent is a call for a refined rule of change adequate to the new requirements of the dialectic between process⇆principle for both political and commercial activity.

White argued that the majority, by classifying a large area of customary international law as comity, severely restricts its own proper adjudication of international law. He contended that the Court's focus on the Act Of State Doctrine, as a device to protect a status quo sense of nonintervention, was "backward-looking." He maintained that the Court was actually violating international law by validating what amounts to "lawless" acts. White also identifies the nature of these lawless acts in the aetiological-norms of racial, religious, and national nondiscrimination.

From the perspective of Hume's philosophical-policy, one might expect that while law from critical principle would be more evident in political action, commercial action is characterized by a focus on the processes involved with exchange and reciprocity, which make it more amenable to Justice-As-Sovereignty. Logically then, a Court trying to protect a default rule of change in defense of Justice-As-Sovereignty would find a way to remove itself from decisions that will frequently involve critical principle, limiting its decisions only to those instances where less disruptive "commercial" process-norms are involved.

This position is evident, by default, in White's dissent. His suggestion that critical principle can no longer be ignored by the niceties of comity, and delegated to the political branches of government, speaks of a Court resisting change while facing the realities of an impending Stage-II international legal system. By avoiding the issues presented by progressive codification of international law, White argued that the Court was granting validity to what the world now defines as not only immoral, but illegal acts, in the name of a static and strong definition of nonintervention.[113]

> The reasons for non-review, based as they are on traditional concepts of territorial sovereignty, lose much of their force when the foreign act of state is shown to be a violation of international law....Although a state may reasonably expect that the validity of its laws operating on property within its jurisdiction will not be defined by local notions of public policy of numerous other states...it cannot with impunity ignore the rules governing the conduct of all nations and expect that other nations and tribunals will view its acts as within the permissible scope of territorial sovereignty....Finally, the impartial application of international law would not only be an affirmation of the existence and binding effect of international rules of order, but also a refutation of the notion that this body of law consists of no more than the divergent and parochial views of the capital importing and exporting nations, the socialist and free-enterprise nations.[114]

White's dissenting position, however, did not gain momentum against the bulwark of established social convention. In the 1976 *Timberlane* case,[115] it appears to have had little influence.

In *Timberlane*, the Court reinforced the distinctions made in *Banco* with a set of specific tests they defined as the "Substantial Effects Doctrine." First, the Court accepted that commercial extraterritorial jurisdiction was a fact of contemporary legal practice. Consequently, they acknowledged that an absolute, or *Lotus*, rule of change was no longer necessary for the protection of a stable international economic order. The Court stated that "[t]here is no doubt that American antitrust laws extend over some conduct in other nations." However, the Court balanced this codification of extraterritorial commercial jurisdiction with the creation of a two-part test that insured that critical principle in the form of political acts of state would be "balanced by the foreign harmony incentive" and, in effect, remain immune from judicial scrutiny.

The test outlined in *Timberlane* allows a court to define when a "substantial effect" on commerce exists in the United States. Specifically, it has three parts:

1. there had to exist in the legal evidence some specific effect, actual or intended, on American foreign commerce;
2. this economic effect needed to be sufficiently large to create a "cognizable injury" and a "civil violation" of antitrust law; and
3. the magnitude of the effect on "American foreign commerce" needed to be great enough to convince the Court that the issue was not one of comity and that they "should" assert jurisdiction.[116]

In order to decide the third part of the test, a second set of written standards defining comity, as opposed to law, was also created by the Court.

This requirement codified the delineation between political acts of states, subject to a strong default definition of nonintervention by the Courts, and commercial nonacts of state susceptible to judicial intervention. Since courts do not want to disrupt the foreign relations of the United States, which is constitutionally a venue of the executive branch, comity, as opposed to international law, was to be judged by the "degree of conflict" generated "if American authority is asserted" by the Courts. This was to be measured by:

1. the degree of conflict with foreign law;
2. the nationality of parties;
3. the location of business;
4. the enforcement potential of United States law;
5. significance of the economic effect on the United States as compared to elsewhere;
6. if there is evidence of an explicit purpose to harm;
7. the foreseeability of this effect;
8. the relative importance of violations.[117]

These "tests" reveal that, within the jurisprudence of municipal courts in the United States, the parameters of a transition to a Stage-II international legal system were beginning to have affect, but only in terms of the reciprocity of commerce, not in terms of political acts involving critical principle. The judges' allegiance to a strict conventional rule of nonintervention, as we might expect, was slow to change.

In balancing the metaphysical elements of Justice-As-Sovereignty, given its rule of change, there are certain legacies from these cases. First, that the American Federal Courts tinkered with the effects doctrine and created elaborate tests for its application betrays discomfort with the idea of refining the default definition of nonintervention supported by Justice-As-Sovereignty and the Westphalian Equilibrium. This case chain also divulges a fear of disrupting established international social convention and its definition of international society. But the role of the act of state doctrine as a palliative for the refinement of nonintervention in the international system is the best evidence for the Court's acknowledgment that the conventional rule of change and its parent process-norm are being stressed by the transition to a Stage-II international legal system and the concurrent rise of alternative process-norms and critical principles in international law.

The Act of State Doctrine separates political from economic acts, assuming that the former are still completely protected by Justice-As-Sovereignty's rule of change (i.e., nonintervention), and therefore not a concern for the courts. This is a common way for judiciaries to defend social convention and devalue a specific system of law. For example, the designation of actions as political has been recognized as a major impediment in the progressive codification of international law.[118] But Hume's philosophical-policy informs us that this division may also be justified by the predisposition of those in a convention-based system to recognize that commerce deals in reciprocity, as does Justice-As-Sovereignty, and is not as threatening to the status quo as political dealings that are more likely to involve a conflict with critical principle.

If nonintervention, as a rule of change, was to submit to any refinement, then a commercial exception should not be an unexpected first step. Understanding the Act of State Doctrine through Hume's philosophical-policy alerts us to the fact that the inherent distinction between political and commercial considerations has its roots in the acknowledgment of the process of reciprocity as social convention in the foundation of the international legal system. More specifically, in a conventional system of rules, the protection of Justice-As-Sovereignty as a representative of the core dialectic will be marked by the extent to which gatekeepers have the opportunity to refine nonintervention through process-based, rather than principle-based, norms which favor commercial interests. If the legal system can inhibit change for the sake of critical "political" principle, then disruption to the Westphalian Equilibrium can be minimized.

Economic transactions are about market process; that is, a system of reciprocal exchange that establishes the validity of trade in terms of its Kaldor efficiency within the process. The market ideal, at its essence, is that any transaction accepted within established exchange procedures, or occasioned by the process itself, is inherently valid. These reciprocal trading procedures can be described as creatures of social convention.[119] Meanwhile, "political acts" are left to the executive branch, not as matters of law but as acts of international comity.

The advantage of using Hume's logic of concepts is that one can simultaneously understand that, first, aetiological-norms and critical principle are inherent in the core dialectic, while also expecting, second, that they are not foundational, but characteristics of a secondary path to legal validity during the evolution to a Stage-II legal system. Consequently, by disrupting an established point of coordination with a proven definition of justice, one should expect that critical principle will have difficulty infiltrating the established system of reciprocal social convention to become dispositive in law. This is, in general, because change toward critical principle is always both slower and easier to reverse than maintenance of social convention.

In dichotomizing the political from the commercial, Justice White was correct that "the Court has, with one broad stroke, declared the ascertainment and application of international law beyond the competence of the courts of the United States." White's dissent in *Sabbatino* made no distinction between political and economic acts, but only those behaviors that were lawful or not. White's seeming ability to see the full synthesis of process⇆principle, within a transforming Stage-II international legal system, was unique and farsighted, when viewed through Hume's logic of concepts. However, Hume's argument about the power of social convention also substantiates that this viewpoint had a low probability of being shared.[120] Instead, the result is the incremental evolution of the rule of change that allows only specific extraterritorial or interventionist jurisdiction for other process-norms connected to commerce.[121]

If aetiological-norms and critical principles, even those encased in *jus cogens* or *erga omnes* designations, do not find full and easy application in international law, this may be why. Even the most universally accepted critical principles struggle with "soft law" designations and questions of true legal status in the face of the stability requirements of Justice-As-Sovereignty.

Overall, we should understand the evolution of nonintervention as an international rule of change, from the standpoint of a judiciary whose expectation is to defend a bulwark of social convention based on reciprocal coordination. Because change frequently comes from critical principle as disruptive of established social convention, any general realization that nonintervention needs refinement is met by trepidation.

To confirm that pressure nevertheless exists to weaken the conventional power of effective control and nonintervention, in the move toward a Stage-II international legal system, two non-American cases will be examined: the 1999 House of Lords Decision in the *Pinochet* extradition case, and the 2002 opinion of the ICJ in the *Arrest Warrant* case. Both show the first glimmers of legal recognition for critical principle, while also reflecting abiding timidity to legalize nonprocess norms in the face of established social convention.

Spain's attempt to extradite Senator Augusto Pinochet for acts of torture,[122] as heard and decided in the British House of Lords, demonstrates the universality of the "effects" and "act of state" doctrines as incremental palliatives for the full engagement of the dialectic of process⇆principle in international law. As in the American cases, the range of synthesis solutions expressed in the opinions of the Lords illustrates the struggle of the judges to adapt Justice-As-Sovereignty to a shifting process⇆principle dialectic without losing the Westphalian Equilibrium. In an analysis of this case, Christine Chinkin argues that the ultimate "[d]enial of the immunity *ratione materiae* claimed by a former head of state for official acts of torture represented a choice between two visions of international law: a horizontal system based upon the sovereign equality of states and a vertical system that upholds norms of *jus cogens* such as those guaranteeing fundamental human rights."[123]

On one end of the spectrum, Lord Browne-Wilkinson suggests a synthesis decision supportive of critical principle as law.[124] He first acknowledges the general acceptance of freedom from torture as a matter of jus cogens, and then connects this with universal jurisdiction, or the ability of a state with no territorial or nationality connections to an act to, nevertheless, bring that act before a court as a matter of law.

> the Republic of Chile accepted before your Lordships that the international law prohibiting torture has the character of jus cogens or a peremptory norm, i.e. one of those rules of international law which have a particular status....The jus cogens nature of the international crime of torture justifies states in taking

> universal jurisdiction over torture wherever committed. International law provides that offenses jus cogens may be punished by any state because the offenders are "common enemies of all mankind and all nations have an equal interest in their apprehension and prosecution."[125]

Browne-Wilkinson supports universal jurisdiction as further codified in international treaty law, specifically in the Convention Against Torture, and concludes that immunity for acts of state cannot therefore be extended to acts of torture. In this way, he extends what was formerly an established commercial exception to encompass critical political and legal principle.

> Can it be said that the commission of a crime which is an international crime against humanity and jus cogens is an act done in an official capacity on behalf of the state? I believe there to be strong ground for saying that the implementation of torture as defined by the Torture Convention cannot be a state function.[126]

His conclusion, however, is basically justified by the perception that the adjudicatory rule of progressive codification in international law requires, in this case, a refinement of the rule of change, making substantive and principled exceptions to nonintervention. Such a refinement of the rule of change allows aetiological-norms a more active role in the core or essential dialectic between process⇆principle.

> I have doubts whether, before the coming into force of the Torture Convention, the existence of the international crime of torture as jus cogens was enough to justify the conclusion that the organization of state torture could not rank for immunity purposes as performance of an official function....But in my judgment the Torture Convention did provide what was missing: a worldwide universal jurisdiction. Further, it required all member states to ban and outlaw torture...How can it be for international law purposes an official function to do something which international law itself prohibits and criminalises?[127]

On the opposite end of the spectrum of synthesis arguments in the Pinochet case is Lord Goff. He defended the bulwark of social convention, and the security of the socially-constructed state, in his advocacy of a solution based squarely on a more traditional idea of Justice-As-Sovereignty defined by its local rule of recognition: effective control, supporting the strong sense of nonintervention as a rule of change. He denied that the Torture Convention granted universal jurisdiction. He based his argument on the instability of the international system that would result from allowing critical principle in the form of jus cogens to trump conventional sovereign process.

> Obviously the mere fact that the conduct is criminal does not of itself exclude the immunity, otherwise there would be little point in the immunity from

> criminal process;...It follows, in my opinion, that the mere fact that the crime in question is torture does not exclude state immunity.[128]

Lord Goff delineated between torture as a "specific crime" and torture as a crime that "offends against the public order of the international community,"[129] and argued that the latter comity-based definition,[130] should be exempt from immunity. He found no "settled practice" on the public dimension "in respect of torture outside the context of armed conflict."[131] With the stability of the international system at the Westphalian Equilibrium a preeminent concern, his argument then turned to the problems inherent in refining nonintervention from its default definition.

Lord Goff's concern, like the US Supreme Court before him, was to protect states as sovereign social constructions with effective control of their affairs through the ability of their political leaders to carry on international affairs. An allegiance to Justice-As-Sovereignty also provides Lord Goff with a contrasting interpretation of the Torture Convention.

> if immunity ratione materiae was excluded, former heads of state and senior public officials would have to think twice about traveling abroad. For fear of being the subject of unfounded allegations emanating from states of a different political persuasion....Reasons such as these may well have persuaded possible state parties to the Torture Convention that it would be unwise to give up the valuable protection afforded by state immunity. Indeed, it would be strange if state parties had given up the immunity ratione materiae of a head of state which...would only imperil the very substantial advantages which could be achieved by the Convention even if no waiver of state immunity was included in it.[132]

A concern for the social convention at the roots of international law, and the protection of Justice-As-Sovereignty, dominates his argument. States as social constructions require mutual nonintervention in order to maintain the stability of the international system that protects the moral imperative of social order for all states. Lord Goff's opinion that Pinochet remained entitled to state immunity[133] is best defended through an allegiance to social convention in the face of rising critical principle, which he recognized as a disruptive force, except during wartime.

Overall, the "double criminality rule" was used by the Lords to limit the specific crimes of torture and, consequently, the allowable extraterritorial jurisdiction for matters of critical principle. The decision in this case was described by Hazel Fox, an expert in the law of immunity, as "surprising."[134] But that certain international crimes were disentangled from absolute sovereign protection by the Lords is only surprising to the degree that the evolution of law toward a greater role for critical principle, and a rebalancing of the metaphysical components of Justice-As-Sovereignty, goes unacknowledged.

From the perspective of Hume's philosophical-policy, there would be an expectation that, in the transition to a Stage-II international legal system, critical principle will present a greater challenge to established process but, eventually, cause a refinement of nonintervention in its favor.[135] Both Lord Hutton and Lord Phillips acknowledge this changing reality.

> Had the events with which this appeal is concerned occurred in the 19th century, there could have been no question of Senator Pinchot being subjected to criminal proceedings in this country in respect of acts, however heinous, committed in Chile....This accorded with the fundamental principle of international law that one state must not intervene in the internal affairs of another.[136]
>
> since the end of the second world war there has been a clear recognition by the international community that certain crimes are so grave and so inhuman that they constitute crimes against international law and that the international community is under a duty to bring to justice a person who commits such crimes. Torture has been recognized as such a crime.[137]

Overall, Chinkin is correct that there were two distinct visions of the international system at work in these separate opinions. She calls them "horizontal" and "vertical." But, what is more important, than the distinction between a system based on the equality of states versus one that acknowledges a wider role for international legal standards, is the suggestion that there may be two dialectic ideas of practice existing simultaneously with common roots.

Hume's philosophical-policy and legal design proffers illumination. It suggests that the superficial dichotomy represents a more fundamental legal dialectic between process⇆principle that refines the metaphysical essence of Justice-As-Sovereignty as it anticipates transition from a Stage-I to a Stage-II international legal system. Here, a dialectic of legal design solutions is evolving incrementally from Stage-I, when the bulwark of social convention remains unchallenged, to Stage-II where critical principle is codified and takes on a larger role in determining international law. As such, a new understanding of the underlying metaphysics of Justice-As-Sovereignty is possible; one that manifests a systematic and logical application of practical reason in the law. From the standpoint of practical reason, Chinkin's models are not separate and isolated realities, but both manifestations of a single process⇆principle dialectic, representing the absolute presupposition of the passion for international society. If these alternative descriptions of legal practice have a systematic interdependence, it provides a richer, more complete, and logical understanding of from whence they came, where they are going, and why. As two separate models, all these questions remain unasked.

An examination of the *Arrest Warrant* case,[138] as decided by the ICJ, demonstrates the same transition at the international level. The struggle is, again, over whether, and to what extent, critical principle should be allowed to change the conventional definition of nonintervention and affect the status of a state's effective control of its territory.

In *Arrest Warrant*, the State of Belgium issued an arrest warrant for an official of the Congo on the basis of universal jurisdiction. In the same dynamic that was identified in the Pinochet case, the international Court divided itself primarily in terms of whether or not the Judges understood the international system to be what Hume's philosophical-policy would define as a Stage-I or Stage-II legal model. The majority settled on defending a Stage-I model with a default sense of nonintervention and rejected the power of critical principle to significantly redefine the parameters of change through the SPP of nonintervention.

> The Court accordingly concludes that the functions of a Minister for Foreign Affairs are such that, throughout the duration of his or her office, he or she when abroad enjoys full immunity from criminal jurisdiction and inviolability. That immunity and that inviolability protect the individual concerned against any act of authority of another State which would hinder him or her in the performance of his or her duties.[139]

In another separation of comity from law, the majority opinion delineated between immunity and impunity, in terms of the former being process and the latter being principle. This distinction recognized the fundamental difference between social conventions of practice that are a subject of law, and deeper questions of morality and responsibility that are removed from their immediate jurisdiction.

> The Court emphasizes, however, that the *immunity* from jurisdiction enjoyed by incumbent Ministers of Foreign Affairs does not mean that they enjoy *impunity* in respect of any crimes they might have committed, irrespective of their gravity....Jurisdictional immunity may well bar prosecution for a certain period or for certain offences; it cannot exonerate the person to whom it applies from all criminal responsibility.[140]

The Judges exhibited the expected predisposition to be wary of the full engagement of the process⇆principle dialectic and attempted to limit the effects of critical principle on the established conceptualization of Justice-As-Sovereignty. In the Stage-I system, process is the end-in-itself, while principle is contextual and consumed by the same social conventions that elevate process over any critical moral precept or aetiological-norm. In trusting the familiarity of a Stage-I system, the Court discourages any challenge from a new and more fully engaged dialectic. It is therefore not surprising that the majority squashed the warrant.

> Accordingly, the Court concludes that the circulation of the warrant, whether or not it significantly interfered with...diplomatic activity, constituted a violation of an obligation of Belgium toward the Congo, in that it failed to respect the immunity of the incumbent Minister for Foreign Affairs of the Congo and, more particularly, infringed the immunity from criminal jurisdiction and the inviolability then enjoyed by him under international law.[141]

The opposite approach, exhibiting an inherent understanding of the core dialectic and the inevitable evolution of critical principle within a Stage-II legal system, is represented in the joint/separate opinions of Judges Higgins, Kooijmans, and Buergenthal.

First, they chided the Court for not acknowledging the idea of universal jurisdiction which the dissent holds as a pertinent matter in law. They then used the idea of, if not the word, dialectic, to argue that jurisdiction is an integrated component of the concept of immunity.

> In our opinion it was not only desirable, but indeed necessary, that the Court should have stated its position on the issue of jurisdiction....The Court, in passing over the question of jurisdiction, has given the impression that "immunity" is a free-standing topic of international law. It is not. "Immunity" and "jurisdiction" are inextricably linked. Whether there is "immunity" in any given instance will depend not only upon the status of Mr. Yerodia but also upon what type of jurisdiction, and on what basis, the Belgian authorities were seeking to assert it.[142]

Jurisdiction was argued to contain what Hume's philosophical-policy recognizes as two dialectically-related positions. The first, rooted in social convention and characteristic of the submissions of the Congo, is that critical principle is a matter of effective control and not subject to international law but only to comity.[143] The other position, while not codified in international law, acknowledged the need to rebalance the dynamics of progressive codification and the other SPPs within the metaphysics of Justice-As-Sovereignty in response to critical principle (i.e., universal jurisdiction). This suggests that critical principle is worthy of consideration and promotion as law by a Stage-II Court.

> That there is no established practice in which States exercise universal jurisdiction, properly so called, is undeniable. As we have seen, virtually all national legislation envisages links of some sort to the forum State; and no case law exists in which pure universal jurisdiction has formed the basis of jurisdiction. This does not necessarily indicate, however, that such an exercise would be unlawful.[144]
>
> There are, moreover, certain indications that a universal criminal jurisdiction for certain international crimes is clearly not regarded as unlawful. The duty to prosecute under those treaties which contain the *aut dedere aut prosequi* provisions opens the door to a jurisdiction based on the heinous nature of the crime rather than on links of territoriality or nationality.[145]

Like all the dissenting arguments we have analyzed, that promote critical principle over process, the opinion here is evolutionary in nature. *Arrest Warrant* supports the idea that, while Justice-As-Sovereignty in its first moment representing practical reason in the law has heretofore been the cornerstone of the international system, aetiological-norms should have an ever-greater part in its changing dialectic balance. Specifically, process, in the form of conventional jurisdiction, requires a refined sense of nonintervention to adjust to the contingencies of a Stage-II international legal system.

> The contemporary trends, reflecting international relations as they stand at the beginning of the new century, are striking. The movement is toward bases for jurisdiction other than territoriality. "Effects" or "impact" jurisdiction is embraced both by the United States and, with certain qualifications, by the European Union. Passive personality jurisdiction, for so long regarded as controversial, is now reflected not only in the legislation of various countries,...and today meets with relatively little opposition.[146]

In turn, the requirements for relaxing the rule of change are substantive and translate a concern for aetiological-norms of human rights and their globalization.[147]

> [i]t is equally necessary that universal criminal jurisdiction be exercised only over those crimes regarded as the most heinous by the international community.[148]...The substantive content of the concept of crimes against humanity and its status as crimes warranting the exercise of universal jurisdiction, is undergoing change....Crimes against humanity are now regarded as a distinct category.[149]

The dissenting Judges in *Arrest Warrant* make an argument for the refinement of the idea of nonintervention from its strong default position to allow a greater role for critical principle in shaping the law. What this suggests is not radical, but incremental, change. It focuses on the most basic critical principles relating to the dignity or human rights of the individual and the most egregious actions against such substantive ends.

> Reflecting these concerns, what is regarded as permissible jurisdiction and what is regarded as the law on immunity are in constant evolution. The weights on the two scales are not set for all perpetuity. Moreover, a trend is discernible that in a world which increasingly rejects impunity for the most repugnant offences, the attribution of responsibility and accountability is becoming firmer, the possibility for the assertion of jurisdiction wider, and the availability of immunity as a shield more limited. The law of privileges and immunities, however, retains its importance since immunities are granted to high State officials to guarantee the proper functioning of the network of mutual inter-State relations. Which is of paramount importance for a well-ordered and harmonious international system.[150]

In effect, the *Arrest Warrant* joint dissent makes the case that, under specific circumstances, universal jurisdiction should be recognized as customary international law.[151] By not recognizing the dialectic between process⇆critical principle and the characteristics of universal jurisdiction that place it in the latter category the dissent invokes *Lotus*, against itself. They argue, ironically, that without a specific prohibition, universal jurisdiction should be considered an act of the state that should be protected, as if it is supportive of the Westphalian Equilibrium rather than inherently disruptive of a process-based definition of justice.[152] However, this use of *Lotus* speaks to a lack of understanding that what it established was a system of process-prohibitions in defense of sovereignty, while the argument for universal jurisdiction is based on a concern for critical principles (e.g., human dignity-autonomy) that require disruption of process and the transcendence of Justice-As-Sovereignty.

Overall, the examined cases, as seen through the lens of Hume's philosophical-policy and legal design, form distinct municipal and international reactions to the rise of an international Stage-II legal system. They illustrate two points of view on jurisdiction and immunity law, but also, given Hume's logic of concepts, offer evidence of a much deeper and more substantive debate that deals with the future form and content of Justice-As-Sovereignty, in general as well as in the specific issues each considers.

First, the subjects of argument highlighted in these cases are not ideas that can be definitively classified and treated in isolation; they are overlapping legal concepts that are components of a dialectically driven metaphysics of justice as utility. Justice-As-Sovereignty is evolving toward its essence and, in doing so, must continue to represent the point of coordination that is the international system by rebalancing its metaphysical components as demanded by the prime dialectic: process⇆principle. Second, the real issue in debate is the rule of change and how its adjustments to the contingencies of an evolving legal practice moderate the originally strong sense of nonintervention identified with Justice-As-Sovereignty. Can the process-norm adjust its SPPs in a way that maintains order and property stability as primary concerns, while also recognizing that nonintervention must be moderated to allow for critical principle to have a role in matters of jurisdiction and immunity?

Overall, the evolution of critical principle in law is a natural characteristic of the pattern of social convention in the transition from a Stage-I into a Stage-II legal system. All refinement of the rule of nonintervention is determined within an evolving dialectic where the pride of place for process-dominance is challenged by the rise of critical aetiological-norms in the form of concern for the most basic human rights and jus cogens principles.

6

Conclusion: The Metaphysical Elements of Sovereignty

Abstract

The metaphysical essence of Justice-As-Sovereignty is revealed in a dialectic model that integrates the four systematic policy precepts representing the rules of adjudication, change, and local/universal recognition. No longer relegated to the status of "organized hypocrisy," sovereignty becomes the "genuine" product of the evolution of international law from its genesis in social convention. The state becomes simply one of a number of possible social constructions available for the continued stability of international society as it evolves within a unique strategic environment that is not a state of nature but a transition from the "rule of convention" to the "rule of law." As a result of the application of Hume's philosophical-policy as legal design, the essence of Justice-As-Sovereignty is revealed as the logical source of the definition of practical reason as utility.

From the vast interdisciplinary literature on the concept of sovereignty, at least three points of agreement emerge. First, sovereignty is the keystone of the international legal system.

> Of all the rights that can belong to a nation, sovereignty is, doubtless, the most precious....[1]
>
> "Sovereignty" is undoubtedly a key concept of international law. It has been appropriately described as "the supreme political characteristic" and "the central legal formula" of the international system.[2]
>
> ...sovereignty constitutes the unthought foundation of political knowledge...[3]
>
> The territorial integrity of States, this great principle of peace, indispensable to international stability...has today acquired the character of a universal and pre-emptory norm.[4]
>
> So long as many in the society of states view sovereignty as contributing to world stability, security, and peace, the concept will remain a sturdy foundation for the superstructure of international politics.[5]

Second, general agreement exists that sovereignty is a complex idea with multiple definitions that seem to work at odds with one another, lessening the utility of the concept, and according to Eli Lauterpacht, the rational and decisional use of the term.

> to invoke the concept of national sovereignty as in itself a decisional factor is to fall back on a word which has an emotive quality lacking meaningful specific content. It is to substitute pride for reason.[6]
>
> Sovereignty as supreme authority, which is independent of any other earthly authority, may be said to have different aspects.[7]
>
> The term sovereignty has been used in...different ways....[8] [which] are not logically coupled, nor have they covaried in practice.[9]
>
> Sovereignty,...is not a single norm, but an institution comprising several sometimes conflicting norms, and is associated with a bundle of properties....[10]
>
> But sovereignty sorely needs definition. Its tortuous evolution since its first recorded usage in the thirteenth century renders quixotic the attempt to find a single, specific, historically valid formulation.[11]

Third, sovereignty is treated as a creature of context and in continuous evolution in response to the empirical conditions of the international legal and political environment.

> Throughout the course of history, the meaning of sovereignty has undergone important changes and transformations...[12]
>
> ...no particular characteristics inhere in the concept of sovereignty, but...its nature depends very much on the customs and practices of nation-states and [the] international system.[13]
>
> Sovereignty thus reveals itself as an idea that, on the one hand is constant over time, but on the other hand is subject to significant variation in its historical manifestations.[14]
>
> Conceiving of sovereignty as caught up in an endless process of becoming[15]...sovereignty is...a continuous rather than...a dichotomous variable. And its movement along the continuum between the convenience-of-the-states extreme and the states-are-obliged-to-go-along extreme is...shaped by situational, domestic, international and legal determinants.[16]...Supplemented by situational and domestic determinants, in short, the international milieu also appears to be contributing to movement toward the states-are-obliged-to-go-along extreme of the sovereignty continuum.[17]
>
> Sovereignty has many different aspects and none of these aspects is stable. The content of the notion "sovereignty" is continuously changing, especially in recent years.[18]

Hume's philosophical-policy can integrate these three points of agreement within a single metaphysical model, so that the multiple definitions deciphered by positivists can be tied together as dimensions of a single timeless and universal conceptualization of Justice-As-Sovereignty that is nonetheless plural and evolutionary due to its dialectic structure. As demonstrated by the case analysis of the previous chapters, these dialectic relationships create an evolutionary conceptualization of sovereignty that can accommodate the changing context of international law and politics. Hume's philosophical-policy also reveals a distinction between empirical surface and philosophical essence, so that we can understand that the changing context of sovereignty is anchored by a single metaphysical substructure that establishes a baseline for continuity and change inaccessible through positivist analysis alone. For example, the dialectic between surface⇆essence established by Hume's logic of concepts makes Krasner's seemingly distinct definitions of sovereignty (i.e., domestic sovereignty, interdependent sovereignty, international legal sovereignty, and Westphalian sovereignty) not contradictory and "hypocritical," but, through the application of Hume's philosophical-policy as practical reason, "sincere" and dialectically self-reinforcing elements of a single dynamic conceptualization of sovereignty on a scale of forms (see Table 6.1).

Under Hume's philosophical-policy we can approach the nature of the international legal system as a set of overlapping components dialectically engaged on a scale of forms. This scale of forms establishes the process-norm of Justice-As-Sovereignty as its first moment of essence in a Stage-I legal system. The scale of forms then initiates movement toward Stage-II status as the dialectic of process⇆principle becomes more fully engaged with the advent of contract-by-convention and the consequent rise of critical principle in policy and law. This evolving system of global social convention provides a procedural superstructure for the core process⇆principle dialectic that arises from the passion for society and that coordinates states in the Westphalian Equilibrium through the process-norm of Justice-As-Sovereignty.

The Stage-I phase of international legal evolution is characterized by a nonanarchic set of nested games with distinct strategic situations and corresponding institutional governance requirements. Here, the logic of concepts that is Hume's philosophical-policy and legal design creates, through its systematic policy precepts (SPPs), a set of relative presuppositions for the international system. These relative presuppositions arise from, and for the protection of, the absolute metaphysical presupposition of the human passion for stable social interaction at growing levels of complexity.

Table 6.1 Justice-As-Sovereignty: Transcending hypocrisy

Procedural Rule	Local Rule of Recognition	Rule of Adjudication	Universal Rule of Recognition	Rule of Choice
SPP	Effective Control	Progressive Codification	Reciprocal Cooperation	Non-Intervention
Krasner's Taxonomy	Domestic Sovereignty	Interdependence Sovereignty	International Legal Sovereignty	Westphalian Sovereignty

With Hume's philosophical-policy, the evolution of Justice-As-Sovereignty is a "process of becoming," a dialectic of practice⇆metaphysics that makes sovereignty the process-norm of the international legal system. Our case analysis suggests that with the codification of a Stage-I international legal system in the *Lotus* decision, the balance of dialectics defining Justice-As-Sovereignty has been weighted toward the local rule of recognition and the rule of change.

In the dialectics of Justice-As-Sovereignty, these two SPPs have protected the bulwark of social convention at the Westphalian equilibrium against both other process norms (e.g., Justice-As-Trade Reciprocity) and the rise of critical principle (e.g., human rights, *jus cogens*). Since the Second World War, the universal rule of recognition and the rule of adjudication have simultaneously been gradually pulling their counterparts (the local rule of recognition and the rule of change) toward a more fully institutionalized Stage-II international legal system with a more prominent role for critical principle.

The rule of change, in the case evidence, counteracted the nonsovereign aspects of both the rule of adjudication and the universal rule of recognition, being dialectically paired, separately, with each (Figure 6.1). In these dialectics, the counterweight of nonintervention as the rule of change has allowed for some reciprocal cooperation and the gradual progressive codification of transnational law. But it has acted primarily to protect the local rule of recognition (i.e., effective control) as the most immediate systematic policy precept involved with the conventional status of the state as representative of stability and order within a Stage-I international legal system.

Meanwhile, the weight of the local rule of recognition in the determination of Justice-As-Sovereignty places "effective control" at the center of the model (see Figure 6.1). This centrality is a direct product of the relative power of nonintervention, as a dominant rule of change, to determine synthesis results of its dialectic relations with both reciprocal cooperation as the universal rule of recognition and progressive codification as the rule of adjudication. Because of this balance, the core dialectic of process⇆principle continues to be weighted in favor of social convention and its process-norm of Justice-As-Sovereignty.

Because of the dynamic quality of these SPPs as dialectic relative presuppositions in the metaphysics of sovereignty, the persistence of this balance is not written in stone. For example, as the international system changes, as it has since the Second World War, with rise of critical principal in the call for acknowledgment of international human rights as transcendent of Justice-As-Sovereignty, the metaphysical elements of sovereignty have been readjusting. This happens as reciprocal cooperation on these issues forces progressive codification to make international law that further weakens sovereign nonintervention and allows easier international coordination in the violation of sovereignty on humanitarian grounds (e.g., compare North Atlantic Treaty Organization (NATO) in Kosovo with NATO action in Libya). Perhaps, eventually, the power of the universal rule of recognition

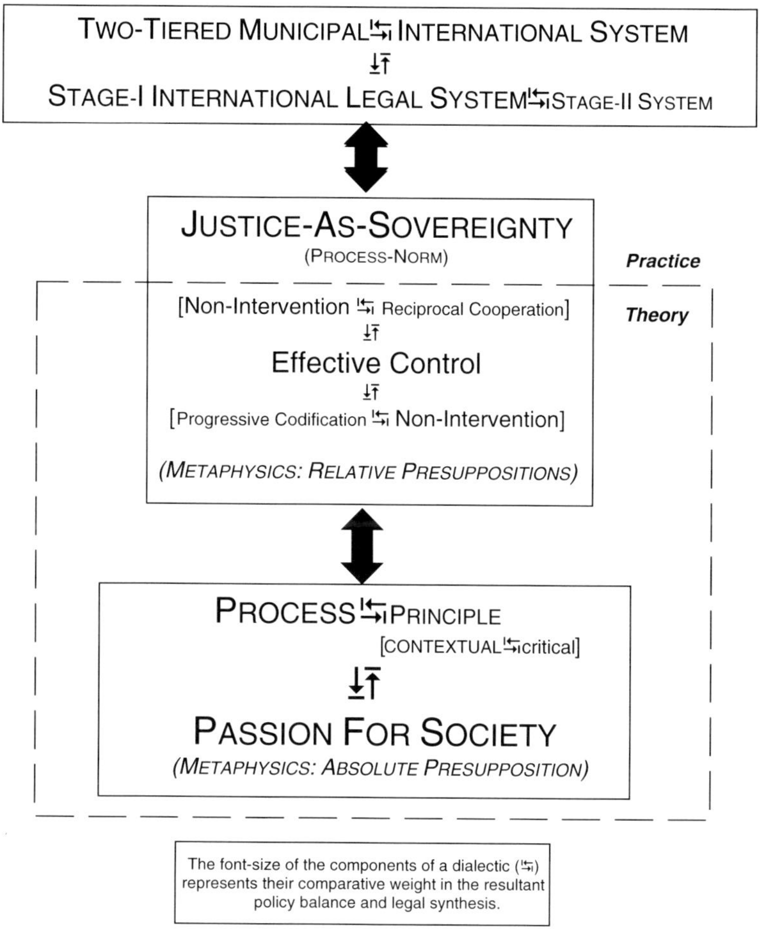

Figure 6.1 The metaphysics of sovereignty.

will replace effective control as the centerpiece of the model, re-sorting the four SPPs accordingly.

Within the context of a Stage-I international legal system, the current status of Justice-As-Sovereignty emphasizes nonintervention for the purposes of effective control, while also allowing the international legal system to achieve a basic level of stability in terms of reciprocal cooperation and a slowly growing level of progressive codification. Our case analysis has demonstrated that there is growing pressure on the sovereign state to give a larger role to critical principle and, consequently, a larger role, within the metaphysics of sovereignty, to the universal rule of recognition and progressive codification. This allows the principle side of the core dialectic to be more fully engaged as a Stage-II system comes to fruition.

Hume's philosophical-policy allows us to see the parameters of modern international law in a definition of Justice-As-Sovereignty that has two component SPPs pulling in the direction of a greater role for international law, and two others trying to balance this trend by protecting international social convention. Evidence for the ongoing tension between these trends is best given by attention to the various dissents we have considered (e.g., Weeramantry in *Spain-Canada*). These arguments decry the apparent and lasting power of the conventional or *Lotus* definition of Justice-As-Sovereignty and argue for its transcendence by critical principle in the form of human rights, or transcendent consideration of the obligations a state has to the law of the international system before its own.

Hume's logic of concepts not only allows us to describe the metaphysical elements of sovereignty for a Stage-I system but also sets up a dialectic map with which the evolution of sovereignty on its scale of forms can be traced, not just in terms of practical context, but also in terms of philosophical balance. Specifically, the metaphysics of Justice-As-Sovereignty (i.e., its SPPs) can integrate all of Krasner's definitions of sovereignty, but they also account for both the evolution of the idea of sovereignty over time, as Bartelson and Rosenau do, as well as the intuition that sovereignty is a result of both continuity and change. In addition, because the conceptual evolution of sovereignty is described within a philosophical scale of forms with dynamic dialectic balances, Justice-As-Sovereignty not only accommodates the changing empirical context of the idea of sovereignty but also its absolute and relative presuppositions, or essential metaphysics, as this determines and is determined by the dynamics of international law as practice.

The substructure or metaphysical essence of the model, revealed through the dialectic interaction of the SPPs, now allows one to understand what is behind the apparent practice of international law.[19] They explain the core of international law as a dialectic of process⇆principle, derived from the imperative for social stability and the evolution and primacy of social convention. These international conventions provide a support structure for the fundamental sources of the rule of law: first contextual then critical principle, custom, and treaty. As our case analysis demonstrates, allegiance to international social convention through Justice-As-Sovereignty remains the primary criterion for the condition of statehood as well as the terms of legal stratification and the jurisdiction and immunity of states. Social convention provides a foundation for positive law and legal practice. It also demonstrates how collective action problems at both levels of organization are solved and how the solutions to the range of municipal prisoner's dilemmas[20] influence the formation and persistence of the international coordination game and the society of states that are its agents.

With international social convention and its stratified stability, the concept of law and the evolutionary pattern of legal practice find validity in a process-based common law.[21] This result is a response to the circumstances of Justice-As-Sovereignty. However, the complexity of this Stage-I system and its imperative favoring progressive codification provides a means for more than a single route to the law, resulting in the need for process to grow to accommodate a more fully realized and critical definition of principle as this dialectic becomes more fully formed. The resulting policy design space is complex and requires that law protecting convention respond to progressive codification to "balance" process and principle in synthesis legal solutions that define the international legal system as it evolves to Stage-II.

The greater role for critical principle is continually suppressed by the bulwark of social convention that has defined the predispositions and expectations of decision-makers to date. But Hume's philosophical-policy provides an argument for the concept of state sovereignty that describes it as the evolutionary result of particular sets of circumstances in dialectic with a set of metaphysical presuppositions that change over time requiring social convention to respond. This response, as it comes from codified law and more complex governance institutions, allows critical principle to challenge the established process-norm and its procedural rules of recognition (i.e., local and universal), adjudication, and change, constantly amending Justice-As-Sovereignty. Therefore, this dialectical legal model gives international law more flexibility than positivist international legal theory has heretofore allowed.

The state as a social construction of the human passion for society makes it an instrument for justice-as-order and a variable in the course of legal progress among many possible competitors. Therefore, Justice-As-Sovereignty, as a metaphysical and material presupposition, must be constantly reinforced through the use of conscious legal design within contract-by-convention if it is to maintain the Westphalian coordination equilibrium.

When the status of this basic metaphysical system of sovereignty-based social convention is challenged, as it constantly is, Hume's logic of concepts suggests that one should expect a confrontation by alternative process-norms to find more salience than options based on critical principle. The examination of the World Trade Organization (WTO) and its process-norm of Justice-As-Reciprocal Trade in chapter 5 demonstrated the logic of this contention. However, when aetiological-norms are added to process-norms, critical principle can influence policy argument and legal design. This brings into play the full power of the dialectic between process⇆principle and tests Justice-As-Sovereignty and the established power of the Stage-I international legal system.

Hume's philosophical-policy provides a metaphysics that demonstrates the true complexity and flexibility of the international rule of law. The subsequent scale of forms can be understood in terms of a two-stage definition of the legal system in which, at Stage-I, the sources of international law, namely custom, treaty, and contextual principle, find a coordination equilibrium that stratifies the overall system of nested games, all defined by the process-norm of Justice-As-Sovereignty as an absolute presupposition for a specific set of circumstances.

Hume's philosophical-policy and its inherent sense of natural law as social convention create a comprehensive metaphysical source for the concept of sovereignty as it relates to both the municipal and international dimensions of statehood. At the local level the focus is on what Krasner distinguishes as "domestic sovereignty" and "Westphalian sovereignty." At the international level of social stability, Krasner's other two definitions of sovereignty, "international legal sovereignty" and "interdependence sovereignty," are acknowledged. However, in contrast to Krasner's understanding of these definitions as independent and contradictory, Hume's philosophical-policy and legal design, through its metaphysics of process⇆principle, simultaneously integrates all four within a single definition of international law (Table 6.1). This conceptualization is able to map the rules of recognition, change, and adjudication onto the SPPs, which then transform Krasner's definitions into multiple dimensions of one integrated and dialectic idea: Justice-As-Sovereignty.

Moving toward Stage-II, contract-by-convention allows the legal design space to become more complex as critical principle competes more effectively in the process⇆principle dialectic. Justice-As-Sovereignty is then threatened by the progressive codification of critical principle and nonintervention, which, as its rule of change, weakens its dialectics with reciprocal cooperation and progressive codification, allowing the latter more scope. This changes the power of effective control to determine the law defending Justice-As-Sovereignty. The incremental acceptance of critical principle may be resisted but cannot be ignored or deferred. With the absolute presupposition of Justice-As-Sovereignty, together with its component procedural SPPs, Hume's philosophical-policy adds a depth, complexity, and dynamism to the role of justice by highlighting an evolutionary pattern and teleological definition of sovereignty for international law.

Hume's philosophical-policy allows us to understand the *process* by which social convention is refined into law. It provides a more three-dimensional philosophical basis for international law as a well-integrated legal system where procedural rules predate substantive rules and where convention predates, but ultimately must be reconciled with, reason and critical principle. This allows for a more specific understanding of the normative genesis of international law and offers a more robust ability to understand how legal systems exist, what threatens them, and how to anticipate changes to them and, if possible, effectively regulate these changes. Hume offers a key, not only to an understanding of the genesis of international law, but to how these foundations for legal practice have evolved; what dilemmas modern international legal practice should expect to face; and the dynamics of specific elements of a changing rule of international law. That key is his understanding of the fundamental role of social convention in the creation of law.

Fundamental Discontinuity Stabilized by a "Forbidding Jungle of Philosophical Argument"?

Ruggie opines that "no shared vocabulary exists in the literature to depict change and continuity,…[so] we are not very good…at studying the possibility of fundamental discontinuity in the international system."[22] Perhaps the model offered here, developed from Hume's logic of concepts, helps to address this problem. Applying Hume's philosophical-policy to the legal design of international law through its foundational concept of Justice-As-Sovereignty allows us to see that the pattern of development in the law between states reflects the characteristics of Hume's argument for the evolution of social convention. Through philosophical method, the dialectic of process⇆principle is identified and a series of SPPs are derived from this dialectic that rationalize the concept of sovereignty as both a single and plural idea of overlapping concepts, dynamic on a scale of forms. This provides a single vocabulary of change and continuity for international law.

Applying Hume's paradigm demonstrates that the synthesis of his logic of concepts with the current legal logic of practice is accessible and more enlightening than the former unrealistic separation of surface and essence. Hume's philosophical-policy establishes that social convention, and its Justice-As-Sovereignty process-norm, are at the core of international legal development. But it also supports the further refinement of this definition of justice through legal design as the circumstances of international justice change. Contemplating the current dilemmas of globalization and its ensuing social, political, and moral implications, Hume's philosophical-policy offers a fuller understanding of the superficial rules of international law.

Hume's argument demonstrates that law has both an empirical superstructure and a philosophical substructure. The perceived superstructure of the positive law, its fact situations, and its context of legal practice is built upon a substructure of ideas, ideals, normative principle, moral precepts, and competing definitions of justice, all organized and categorized for us by philosophical method, philosophical-policy, and legal design. This substructure may not be as susceptible to identification and processing by empirical means, but it is, nevertheless, a vital component of the law. Consequently, a more useful understanding of the international legal environment requires that we investigate both the *empirical* superstructure and the *philosophical* substructure of the law. In this way, the legal design created by Justice-As-Sovereignty for international law is a genesis description, a first "moment" for the further evolution of both layers of legal-philosophical phenomena as distinct but dialectically interdependent entities.

Even though H. L. A. Hart[23] has called metaphysical substructure in law "the forbidding jungle of philosophical argument" philosophical method can provide the continuity for empirical change that Ruggie seeks. Hart is suggesting that such inquiry will blur and confuse the study of practical law and policy, not clarify it. But Hume's philosophical-policy demonstrates that Hart's trepidation may not just be overstated but actually misguided in terms of the ability of a philosophical-policy argument to tie law dialectically to its inherent metaphysics or philosophical foundation, providing illumination to positive practice and making the jungle more hospitable terrain.

Philosophical-policy provides the tools to decipher both the logic of concepts and the policy paradigms that inform that logic of investigation seeking continuity in the rise of justice as order, or sovereignty, in the international system. But while Hume's argument about the genesis of social convention grants insight into the rise and role of the system of ordered states within an international social system, defined by its process-norm of Justice-As-Sovereignty, contemporary dispute settlement demands more.

The critical questions in globalizing legal practice now deal with international human rights, the freedom of the person, and the protection of the global environment. How these public order precepts, based not on process but critical principle, can be promoted within a predominantly conventional legal system based upon state sovereignty must be addressed by philosophical method. Today, a lawyer or policymaker within an infant Stage-II international system can be helped if they understand the ramifications of a more evenly balanced process⇆principle dialectic, where critical principle is more important in legal decision-making.

Hume cannot enlighten us here. Hume's argument for social convention is focused on the public good and not the good, let alone the rights, of individual persons or the natural environment. Human freedom, which is the basis of universal rights claims, has no status as a locus for policy, independent of the process-norm of Justice-As-Sovereignty and its social conventions that define it as disruptive to stable collective action. This makes Hume's philosophical-policy of less utility to the pertinent dilemmas of current international law.

Luckily, philosophical method, with its contention that concepts overlap and are refined over time toward their essence, allows legal design to incorporate additional paradigms to continue the refinement process. Hume's philosophical-policy argument has described the genesis phase of the refinement of modern international law toward its essence. However, when transitioning from the genesis of the international legal system, in Stage I, to the dynamics of contemporary international law, in Stage II, the next chosen philosophical-policy must integrate human freedom with social convention and better accommodate both the changing dialectic of process⇆principle and the arising role of critical reason in the definition of justice as legal right.

This book sought the essence of sovereignty as the baseline "source" of practical reason. Next we shall seek the "locus" of international law in contemporary dispute settlement through G. W. F. Hegel's philosophical-policy and its arguments for individual freedom, mutual recognition, and legal right as a definition of practical reason.

Notes

Preface

1. Alf Ross, *A Textbook of International Law* (London: Longmans, 1947), 34.
2. Paul W. Ward, *Sovereignty: A Study of a Contemporary Political Notion* (London: Routledge, 1928), 178.
3. Hen Kalmo and Quentin Skinner, *Sovereignty in Fragments: The Past, Present and Future of a Contested Concept* (Cambridge: Cambridge University Press, 2010), 1.
4. Philip Allott, *The Health of Nations: Society and Law Beyond the State* (Cambridge: Cambridge University Press, 2002), 154.
5. Allott, *Health*, 154.
6. Allott, *Health*, 154.
7. Allott, *Health*, 157
8. R. G. Collingwood, *An Essay on Philosophical Method* (Oxford: Clarendon Press, 1933), 97–98.
9. Here bias is avoided by the application of a variety of philosophical paradigms to the same case to gauge their comparative persuasiveness.
10. Allott, *Health*, 156.
11. Allott, *Health*, 155.
12. Stephen D. Krasner, *Sovereignty: Organized Hypocrisy* (Princeton: Princeton University Press, 1999), 40.
13. Jutta Brunneé and Stephen J. Troope, *Legitimacy and Legality in International Law: An Interactional Account*, Cambridge Studies in International and Comparative Law (Cambridge: Cambridge University Press, 2010).
14. Jens Bartelson, *A Genealogy of Sovereignty*, ed. Steve Smith, vol. 39, Cambridge Studies in International Relations (Cambridge: Cambridge University Press, 1995)—see Prologue.

Prologue

1. Stephen D. Krasner, *Sovereignty: Organized Hypocrisy* (Princeton: Princeton University Press, 1999), 3–4.
2. Jens Bartelson, *A Genealogy of Sovereignty*, ed. Steve Smith. Vol. 39, Cambridge Studies in International Relations (Cambridge: Cambridge University Press, 1995).
3. Bartelson, *Genealogy*, 14.
4. Bartelson, *Genealogy*, 21.
5. Bartelson, *Genealogy*, 49.
6. Bartelson, *Genealogy*, 51.
7. Bartelson, *Genealogy*, 15

8. Bartelson, *Genealogy*, 49–52.
9. Immanuel Kant, *Critique of Pure Reason*, Vol. 4 Gesammelte Schriften (Berlin: Prussian Academy of Sciences, 1781), Bx; R. G. Collingwood, *The New Leviathan or Man, Society, Civilization & Barbarism* (Revised ed. Oxford: Oxford University Press, 2005. Reprint, 1992), §14.3.
10. Collingwood, *Leviathan* §§14.65–14.68; *Essays in Political Philosophy*, ed. David Boucher (Oxford: Clarendon Press, 1995), 7, 33,41.
11. Bartelson, *Genealogy*, Ch. 2.
12. See third sections of chapters 2–5.

1 Philosophical Method, Hume's Philosophical-Policy, and Legal Design

1. Neil MacCormick, *Practical Reason in Law and Morality*, Law, State, and Practical Reason (Oxford: Oxford University Press, 2011), 2.
2. John W. Danford, *David Hume and the Problem of Reason: Recovering the Human Sciences* (New Haven: Yale University Press, 1990).
3. Both his *Treatise* and *Enquires* are so divided, treating theoretical and then practical reason.
4. Duncan Forbes, *Hume's Philosophical Politics* (Cambridge: Cambridge University Press, 1975), Ch. 1.
5. R. G. Collingwood, *An Essay on Philosophical Method* (Oxford Clarendon Press, 1933), *passim.*
6. Collingwood, *Method*; *An Essay on Metaphysics*, revised ed. (Oxford: Oxford University Press, 2002. Reprint, 1998); *The New Leviathan or Man, Society, Civilization & Barbarism*, Revised ed. (Oxford: Oxford University Press, 2005. Reprint, 1992).
7. I choose Hume after applying philosophical-policy and legal design to a range of alternative philosophical systems.
8. John Martin Gillroy, *Justice & Nature: Kantian Philosophy, Environmental Policy & the Law* (Washington, DC: Georgetown University Press, 2000), Ch. 1; John Martin Gillroy, Breena Holland, and Celia Campbell-Mohn, *A Primer for Law & Policy Design: Understanding the Use of Principle and Argument in Environment and Natural Resource Law*, American Casebook Series (St. Paul, MN: West Group, 2008), Ch. 1.
9. Jonathan Francis Bennett, *Locke, Berkeley, Hume: Central Themes* (Oxford: Clarendon Press, 1971); Elie Halevy, *The Growth of Philosophical Radicalism* (London: Faber And Faber, 1928).
10. Max Horkheimer and Theodor W. Adorno, *Dialectic of Enlightenment: Philosophical Fragments* (Stanford: Stanford University Press, 2002), 5.
11. John Martin Gillroy, "Review of William Ophuls, Requiem for Modern Politics: The Tragedy of the Enlightenment and the Challenge of the New Millennium," *Americal Political Science Review* 91, no. 4 (1997): 948–949.
12. My interpretation is supported in Wayne Waxman, *Kant and the Empiricists: Understanding-Understanding* (Oxford: Oxford University Press, 2005) and Henry E. Allison, *Custom and Reason in Hume: A Kantian Reading of the First Book of the Treatise* (Oxford: Clarendon Press, 2008).
13. Louis E. Loeb, *Stability and Justification in Hume's Treatise* (Oxford: Oxford University Press, 2002).
14. As detailed by G. W. F. Hegel, *Phenomenology of Spirit*, trans. A. V. Miller (Oxford: Oxford University Press, 1977), 523, 541.

15. John Rawls, *A Theory of Justice* (Cambridge, MA: The Belknap Press of Harvard University Press, 1971). A catholic argument limited by its author to modern western liberal democracies.
16. Robert Jackson, *The Global Covenant: Human Conduct in a World of States* (Oxford: Oxford University Press, 2000), 130, 178.
17. Collingwood, *Leviathan*, 181–182.
18. J. W. Harris, *Law and Legal Science: An Inquiry into the Concepts "Legal Rule" and "Legal System"* (Oxford: Clarendon Press, 1979), Ch. 1.
19. Collingwood, *Method*, 41–42.
20. Gillroy, *Justice*, Ch. 5.
21. Collingwood, *Method*, 61.
22. Collingwood, *Method*, 161.
23. I understand that the word "metaphysical" invokes primarily negative reactions among modern scholars and that it is a word of many meanings. However, here it represents the search for what Aristotle called "first principles" (Aristotle, "The Basic Works," ed. Richard McKeon (New York: Random House, 1941), 987). More specifically, it is the search for the logical pattern of absolute and relative presuppositions that lay behind the objects of experience. "Thus philosophy as a whole is like a tree whose roots are metaphysics" (Rene Descartes, "Principles of Philosophy," in *The Philosophical Works Vol. 1*, ed. Elizabeth S. Haldane and G. R. T. Ross (Cambridge: Cambridge University Press, 1975), 211.
24. Collingwood, *Metaphysics*, 31.
25. Collingwood, *Metaphysics*, 41.
26. Collingwood, *Metaphysics*, 154, 176.
27. Collingwood *Metaphysics*, 173.
28. Collingwood *Metaphysics*, 31.
29. Cynthia Weber is an exception (*Simulating Sovereignty: Intervention, the State and Symbolic Exchange*, ed. Steve Smith. Vol. 37, Cambridge Studies in International Relations (Cambridge: Cambridge University Press, 1995)). She would rather state the relationship between sovereignty and intervention in terms of the language of post-modernism as "a logic of simulation" rather than dialectic, but they amount to the same thing.
30. Gillroy et al., *Primer*, Ch. 1.
31. Weber, *Sovereignty*, 126–127.
32. Hans-Georg Gadamer, *Hegel's Dialectic: Five Hermeneutical Studies*, trans. P. Christopher Smith (New Haven: Yale University Press, 1982), 3.
33. Thomas Hobbes, *Leviathan*, ed. C. B. Macpherson, Pelican Classics (Harmondsworth, Middlesex, England: Penguin Books, 1979), 189.
34. Hobbes, *Leviathan*, 190.
35. Charles R. Beitz, *Political Theory and International Relations* (Princeton: Princeton University Press, 1979), 28–30; Alexander Wendt, *Social Theory of International Politics*, ed. Steve Smith. Vol. 67, Cambridge Studies in International Relations (Cambridge: Cambridge University Press, 1999), 264–266; Wight, *Thinkers* 141ff., Martin Wright, *Four Seminal Thinkers in International Theory: Machiavelli, Grotius, Kant & Mazzini*, ed. Gabriele Wright and Brian Porter (Oxford: Oxford University Press, 2005); and Hedley Bull, *The Anarchical Society: A Study of Order in World Politics*, 3rd. ed. (London: Palgrave, 2002), 4.
36. David Hume, *A Treatise of Human Nature*, ed. L. A. Selby-Bigge and P. H. Nidditch, 5th ed. (Oxford: Oxford University Press, 1978), 363.
37. Hume, *Treatise*, 103.
38. Hume, *Treatise*, 488.
39. Inherent in the person—Hume, *Treatise*, 443.

40. Hume, *Treatise*, 488
41. Hume, *Treatise*, 487.
42. Hume, *Treatise*, 487.
43. Hume, *Treatise*, 484.
44. Hume, *Treatise*, 487–488.
45. Hume, *Treatise*, 492.
46. Hume, *Treatise*, 483.
47. Hume, *Treatise*, 534.
48. Although the conventional idea of dialectic concerns pairs of concepts, there is also the idea that a concept can be in more than one dialectic at a time. For example, Hume defines the concept of the "circumstances of justice" in the interdialectic dynamics of three concepts: (Equality⇆Scarcity)⇆(Equality⇆Generosity)⇆(Scarcity⇆Generosity).
49. This is essentially the historic pattern of diplomatic practice. Robert H. Ferrell, *American Diplomacy: A History*, 3rd ed. (New York: Norton, 1975).
50. David Hume, *Enquiries Concerning Hume Understanding (E1) and Concerning the Principles of Morals (E2)*, ed. L. A. Selby-Bigge and P. H. Nidditch, 3rd ed. (Oxford: Oxford University Press, 1975), 80–86.
51. Hume, *Treatise*, 501–502.
52. *International Court of Justice Statute* art. 38 (1)(c); Hume, *Treatise*, 489.
53. This is a nonlinear dynamic with forward progression, backward movement, and plateaus.
54. R. Duncan Luce and Howard Raiffa, *Games and Decisions: Introduction and Critical Survey* (New York: Wiley, 1957); Jon Elster, *Ulysses and the Sirens: Studies in Rationality and Irrationality* (Cambridge: Cambridge University Press, 1979).
55. See chapter 4 for more detail.
56. Russell Hardin, *Collective Action* (Baltimore, MD: Johns Hopkins University Press, 1983), 90–100; David K. Lewis, *Convention: A Philosophical Study* (Cambridge, MA: Harvard University Press, 1969); Michael Taylor, *Anarchy & Cooperation* (London: John Wiley & Sons, 1976).
57. Hardin, *Collective*, Chs 9, 10.
58. These are strict Nash-equilibria meaning not only that no other equilibrium makes anyone better off, but that any other equilibrium makes them worse off.
59. Lewis, *Convention*, 8–14.
60. A dominant strategy is a choice option (to cooperate or defect) that is better for one player no matter what choice the other player makes.
61. Lewis, *Convention*, 78.
62. Lewis, *Convention*, 42.
63. Lewis, *Convention*, 3, 6, 48.
64. Although argument exists that iteration alone can solve the prisoner's dilemma (Hardin, *Collective*, 90–100), overall, the Hobbesian legal solution is necessary in any complex social context (David P. Gauthier, *The Logic of Leviathan: The Moral and Political Theory of Thomas Hobbes* (Oxford: Clarendon Press, 1969), 88–89).
65. Edward Keene, *Beyond the Anarchical Society: Grotius, Colonialism and Order in World Politics* (Cambridge: Cambridge University Press, 2002), Ch. 3.
66. Hume, *Treatise*, 497.
67. It is important to note that Lewis equilibria are indifferent for the players only until one is chosen. At that point the parties have a stake in this equilibrium and will no longer be indifferent to change but strongly favor the status-quo. This asymmetry is defined as *hysteresis*. Hardin, *Collective*, 82–83.
68. These are core criteria for a definition of legitimate constitutional authority (Daniel Philpott, *Revolutions in Sovereignty: How Ideas Shaped Modern International Relations* (Princeton: Princeton University Press, 2001), 15–16) as begun with the

treaties of Westphalia (Stephane Beaulac, "The Westphalian Legal Orthodoxy: Myth or Reality?" *Journal of the History of Philosophy* 2 (2000), 148).

69. Kenneth Neal Waltz, *Theory of International Politics*, 1st ed. (Long Grove, Illinois Waveland Press, 2010), 107—*passim*.
70. This is Hume's generic definition of justice. "The origin of justice explains that of property" (*Enquiries*, 491). "In fact, Hume takes the very concepts (or 'ideas') of 'property'…to emerge only in the establishment of the rules of justice" (James Baillie, *Hume on Morality* (London: Routledge, 2000), 171).
71. Hume, *Treatise*, 486.
72. Hume, *Treatise*, 486.
73. Hume, *Treatise*, 489.
74. Ferrell, *Diplomacy*, 3–7.
75. *International Court of Justice Statute* Art. 38(1c).
76. Hume, *Treatise*, 492.
77. Hume, *Treatise*, 490.
78. One could argue here that Humean convention, on the international level, would focus on the law of war first, as this was the most prominent point that lacked coordination.
79. Hume, *Enquiries*, 310.
80. Hume is not concerned with how particular objects are assigned to particular people, but with the public utility of stable coordination. Hume, *Enquiries*, 310.
81. Hardin, *Collective* and Gillroy, *Justice*, 200–229 to compare the collective action problems of Hobbes, Hume, and Kant.
82. The treaties of Westphalia established this axiom.
83. *Charter of the United Nations*, Art. 2(7).
84. This stricture does not hold for "uncivilized" nations, as the circumstances of justice and "society" itself, are not shared. *Enquiries*, 190–191.
85. James Crawford, *International Law as an Open System: Selected Essays* (London: Cameron May, 2002), 17–38.
86. Hume, *Treatise*, 497.
87. "*particular breaches* of the laws of nations do much more harm than particular breaches of the rules of private justice," Harrison, *Justice*, 231.
88. See Stag Hunt, chapter 4.
89. Harrison, *Justice*, 541.
90. Harrison, *Justice*, 499–500.
91. Concepts of "producible" and "non-producible" as defined in Alan Donagan, *The Theory of Morality* (Chicago: University of Chicago Press, 1977), 224–232.
92. Hobbes, *Leviathan*, 228.
93. Hume, *Treatise*, 490; Hardin, *Collective*, 155–172.
94. Hobbes, *Leviathan*, 227–229.
95. See chapter 2.
96. Hume, *Treatise*, 568.
97. Hume, *Treatise*, 569.
98. Hume, *Treatise*, 535.
99. Jack Donnelly, *Realism and International Relations* (Cambridge: Cambridge University Press, 2000), 6–42; Anthony Clark Arend, *Legal Rules and International Society* (New York: Oxford University Press, 1999), 111–164.
100. Hume, *Treatise*, 538.
101. See WTO case study chapter 5.
102. Wilhelm G. Grewe, *The Epochs of International Law* (Berlin: Walter de Gruyter, 2000), 337.
103. As when the United States ignored the League of Nations for a series of bilateral treaties (Ferrell, *Diplomacy*, 514–518).

104. Hume, *Treatise*, 205.
105. Hume, *Treatise*, 541.
106. Hume, *Treatise*, 538.
107. Hume, *Treatise*, 546.
108. Hume, *Treatise*, 501.
109. Hume, *Treatise*, 483.
110. Hume, *Enquiries*, 282–283.
111. Hume, *Enquiries*, 283.
112. Hume, *Treatise*, 500.
113. Hume, *Treatise*, 538–539.
114. Hume, *Treatise*, 546.
115. Hume, *Treatise*, 543.
116. H. L. A. Hart (*The Concept of Law*, Clarendon Law Series (Oxford: Clarendon Press, 1961), 80–81), makes a distinction between "having" and "being under" an obligation. For Hume, both are matters of social convention where the evolving levels of sanction first create the former, and then the latter with the advent of political institutions and positive law.
117. Or snapshots of a concept in its process of evolution on a scale of forms (Hegel, *Phenomenology*, 2).
118. This is only one way of characterizing international law. But as it has no constitutional or legislative institutions I will consider its jurisprudence as the most fruitful inventory of law for the purposes of gauging the practical implications of Hume's argument for unearthing the essence of Justice-As-Sovereignty in the law.
119. The distinction is one between "why should I do X" and "why should I use the coercive power of government to make everyone do X" (John Martin Gillroy and Maurice Wade, eds, *The Moral Dimensions of Public Policy Choice: Beyond the Market Paradigm* (Pittsburgh: University of Pittsburgh Press, 1992), xi.)
120. Gillroy, *Justice*, Ch. 9.

2 "Effectiveness": A "Local" Rule of Recognition and the Foundation for Justice-As-Sovereignty

1. Francisco de Vitoria, *Political Writings*, ed. Anthony Pagden and Jeremy Lawrance, Cambridge Texts in the History of Political Thought (Cambridge: Cambridge University Press, 1991); Anthony Anghie, *Imperialism, Sovereignty and the Making of International Law*, Cambridge Studies in International and Comparative Law (Cambridge: Cambridge University Press, 2005), 17–23.
2. St. Thomas Aquinas, *Treatise on Law (Summa Theologica, Questions 90–97)*, ed. Ralph McInerny (Washington DC: Gateway Editions, Regnery Publishing, 1956), Q91.
3. Vitoria, *Writings*; Anghie, *Imperialism*, 15–16.
4. Vitoria, *Writings*, 123; Anghie, *Imperialism*, 18.
5. Vitoria, *Writings*, 127.
6. Vitoria, *Writing*, 262–266, 292. He lists a number of presuppositions distinguishing legitimate from illegitimate rule among the "barbarians."
7. I use the English rendering of "aetiological" rather than the American (etiology) because it is closer to the Greek root of the word "aitia" meaning causal and "logia" meaning logic. I use this term to signify the causal logic of the underlying principle that gives this norm its ideal-regarding and regulative moral value as a critical standard.

8. David Hume, *The History of England* (Indianapolis, IN: Liberty Fund, 1983), vols. 3, 4.
9. David Hume, *A Dissertation on the Passions and the Natural History of Religion*, ed. Tom Beauchamp, The Clarendon Edition of the Works of David Hume (Oxford: Clarendon Press, 2007).
10. Jonathan Francis Bennett, *Locke, Berkeley, Hume: Central Themes* (Oxford: Clarendon Press, 1971).
11. James Baillie, *Hume on Morality* (London: Routledge, 2000), 10–11; Stephen Buckle, *Natural Law and the Theory of Property: Grotius to Hume* (Oxford: Clarendon Press, 1991), 244; Knud Haakonssen, *The Science of a Legislator: The Natural Jurisprudence of David Hume and Adam Smith* (Cambridge: Cambridge University Press, 1981), 4, 7–8.
12. Notwithstanding Hume's "Law" which is argued to be an invention of nineteenth-century positivism. See Buckle, *Property*, 282 n.275; John Martin Gillroy, *Justice & Nature: Kantian Philosophy, Environmental Policy & the Law* (Washington, DC: Georgetown University Press, 2000), 131.
13. Robert Sugden, *The Economics of Rights, Co-Operation & Welfare* (Oxford: Basil Blackwell, 1986), 162.
14. Sugden, *Rights*, 80.
15. Sugden, *Rights*, 81.
16. Sugden, *Rights*, 143.
17. Sugden, *Rights*, 155.
18. David Hume, *Enquiries Concerning Hume Understanding (E1) and Concerning the Principles of Morals (E2)*, ed. L. A. Selby-Bigge and P. H. Nidditch, 3rd ed. (Oxford: Oxford University Press, 1975), 90.
19. R. G. Collingwood, *R. G. Collingwood: An Autobiography*, ed. Stephen Toulmin (Oxford: Clarendon Press, 1978), 110.
20. Hume, *Enquiries*, 12.
21. Hume, *Enquiries*, 10.
22. Buckle, *Property*, 298.
23. Milton Friedman, *Essays in Positive Economics* (Chicago: The University of Chicago Press, 1953). He defines theory in terms of behavior "as if" it were true.
24. Hume, *Enquiries*, 10.
25. Hume, *Enquiries*, 19.
26. Hume, *Enquiries*, 75.
27. Hume, *Enquiries*, 12.
28. The core of Hume's distinction between the artificial and natural; foundational to his contention that justice serves the public utility.
29. Hume, *Religion*.
30. Aquinas, *Law*.
31. Hume, *Enquiries*, 6.
32. Hume, *Enquiries*, 7.
33. Hume, *Enquiries*, 192.
34. Peter Abelard. *Ethical Writings*, trans. Paul Vincent Spade, ed. Marilyn McCord Adams (Indianapolis, IN: Hackett, 1995).
35. Hume, *Enquiries*, 205.
36. Hume, *Enquiries*, 205.
37. Hume, *Enquiries*, 206.
38. Hume, *Enquiries*, 199.
39. Hume, *Enquiries*, 188.
40. R. G. Collingwood, *An Essay on Philosophical Method* (Oxford: Clarendon Press, 1933).

41. Mackie, *Universe*.
42. Science is also used to this end. Gillroy, *Justice*, Ch.4.
43. Hume, *History*, Bk. I; R. G. Collingwood, *The Idea of History*, ed. Jan Van Der Dussen, revised ed. (Oxford: Oxford University Press, 1993).
44. Philip Allott, *The Health of Nations: Society and Law Beyond the State* (Cambridge: Cambridge University Press, 2002).
45. Jared Diamond, *Guns, Germs, and Steel: The Fates of Human Societies* (New York: W. W. Norton & Company, 2005).
46. Rodney Stark, *The Victory of Reason: How Christianity Led to Freedom, Capitalism, and Western Success* (New York: Random House, 2005), 99.
47. Stark, *Victory*, 31–32.
48. Harold J. Berman, *Law and Revolution : The Formation of the Western Legal Tradition* (Cambridge, MA: Harvard University Press, 1983), 95.
49. Berman, *Revolution*, 95.
50. Berman, *Revolution*, 516–517.
51. Berman, *Revolution*, 254, 95; Alexander Passerin d'Entreves, *Natural Law: An Introduction to Legal Philosophy* (Piscataway, NJ: Transaction Books, 1994).
52. Berman, *Revolution*, 254.
53. Stark, *Victory*, 99.
54. Berman, *Revolution*, 528–529.
55. Berman, *Revolution*, 527.
56. H. Patrick Glenn, *Legal Traditions of the World*, 2nd ed. (Oxford: Oxford University Press, 2004), Ch. 7.
57. Berman, *Revolution*, 95—dates from eleventh century.
58. Stark, *Victory*, 32, 105 and Galileo Galilei, *The Essential Galileo*, ed. Maurice A. Finocchiaro (Indianapolis, IN: Hackett 2008), 60–62.
59. Aquinas, *Laws*, Q91.
60. Berman, *Revolution*, 253.
61. Hugo Grotius, *The Rights of War and Peace*, ed. Knud Haakonssen; Richard Tuck ed. 3 vols, Natural Law and Enlightenment Classics (Indianoplis, IN: Liberty Fund, 2005)—separating god from *jus gentium*.
62. Emer de Vattel, *The Law of Nations*, ed. Knud Haakonssen, Bela Kapossy, and Richard Whatmore, Natural Law and Enlightenment Classics (Indianoplis, IN: Liberty Fund, 2008).
63. Berman, *Revolution*.
64. Berman, *Revolution*; Stark, *Victory*.
65. Berman, *Revolution*, 519.
66. Berman, *Revolution*, 29–30.
67. Berman, *Revolution*, 131.
68. Maurice de Wolf, *An Introduction to Scholastic Scholastic Philosophy, Medieval and Modern: Scholasticism Old and New* (Eugene, OR: Wipf and Stock Publishers, 2003); Wilfried Hartmann and Kenneth Pennington, eds, *The History of Medieval Canon Law in the Classical Period, 1140–1234 (from Gratian to the Decretals of Pope Gregory Ix)* (Washington DC: The Cathloic University of American Presss, 2008), 1,140–1,234.
69. *Westphalia. Art. LXIV–LXVII, XXVIII.*
70. Hendrik Spruyt, *The Sovereign State and Its Competitors* (Princeton: Princeton University Press, 1994), Part III.
71. Isaac Newton *Papers & Letters on Natural Philosophy and Related Documents* (Cambridge, MA: Harvard University Press, 1958), Introduction.
72. Collingwood, *Method*, 123, 177.
73. Newton *Papers*, 1, 9.

74. Hume, *Enquiries*, 11.
75. Hume, *Enquiries*, 11.
76. David Hume, *Selected Essays*, ed. Stephen Copley and Andrew Edgar (Oxford: Oxford University Press, 2008), 38ff; *Religion*, §11.
77. Hume, *Religion*, §14.
78. Hume, *Enquiries*, 11.
79. Hume, *Enquiries*, 12.
80. Hume, *Enquiries*, 415.
81. Hume, *Religion*, §§1–3.
82. Hume, *Religion*, §11.
83. Hume, *Enquiries*, 44.
84. Stephen D. Krasner, *Sovereignty: Organized Hypocrisy* (Princeton: Princeton University Press, 1999), 4.
85. H. L. A. Hart, *The Concept of Law*, Clarendon Law Series (Oxford: Clarendon Press, 1961), Ch. 1.
86. Baillie, *Morality*, 172.
87. Thomas Hobbes, *Leviathan*, ed. C. B. Macpherson, Pelican Classics (Harmondsworth, Middlesex, England: Penguin Books, 1979), Ch. 17.
88. David Hume, *A Treatise of Human Nature*, ed. L. A. Selby-Bigge and P. H. Nidditch, 5th ed. (Oxford: Oxford University Press, 1978), 345.
89. Hart, *Concept*, 10.
90. Hart, *Concept*, 9–11.
91. Hart, *Concept*, 10–12 for Hart's rejection of metaphysical content in law.
92. Hart, *Concept*, 55.
93. Hart, *Concept*, 78.
94. Hart, *Concept*, 209.
95. Hart, *Concept*, 26.
96. Hart, *Concept*, 92 for confirmation of universality-certainty in law.
97. Hart, *Concept*, 93.
98. Hart, *Concept*, 94.
99. Hart, *Concept*, 92.
100. Hart, *Concept*, 93.
101. Hart, *Concept*, 94.
102. Hart, *Concept*, 78–79.
103. John Austin and Wilfrid E. Rumble, *The Province of Jurisprudence Determined*, Cambridge Texts in the History of Political Thought (Cambridge: Cambridge University Press, 1995), Lecture 1.
104. Hart, *Concept*, 79.
105. Hart, *Concept*, 91.
106. Hart, *Concept*, 209.
107. Hart, *Concept*, 6.
108. Hart, *Concept*, 163.
109. Hart, *Concept*, 206.
110. Louis E. Loeb, *Stability and Justification in Hume's Treatise* (Oxford: Oxford University Press, 2002), Ch. 1.
111. Hume, *Treatise*, Bk 3:6
112. Kenneth Pennington, *The Prince and the Law 1200–1600: Sovereignty and Rights in the Western Legal Tradition* (Berkeley: University of California Press, 1993), 121, 134–135, 147–149, 160, for historical evidence in support of my reversal of primary and secondary rules.
113. Which is now but a boundary condition of process.
114. Hume, *Treatise*, 132.

115. Berman, *Revolution*, 8 (meta-law); Giandomenico Majone, *Evidence, Argument & Persuasion in the Policy Process* (New Haven: Yale University Press, 1989), 146–149 (meta-policy).
116. *International Court of Justice Statute* Art. 38(c).
117. This may be the origin of the categorization "soft law."
118. Hans Kelsen, *Introduction to the Problems of Legal Theory: A Translation of the First Edition of the Reine Rechtslehre or Pure Theory of Law*, ed. Bonnie Litschewaki Paulson and Stanley L. Paulson (Oxford: Clarendon Press, 2001).
119. Henry Sidgwick, *The Methods of Ethics*, 7th ed. (Indianapolis: Hackett Publishing, 1981), 440.
120. Antonio Casssese, *International Law*. 2nd. ed. (Oxford: Oxford University Press, 2005), 12–13 and Ch. 3.
121. Lotus PCIJ Ser. A, No. 10, p. 4 (1927).
122. *Lotus*, 19.
123. Gillroy, *Justice*, Ch.4.
124. *Lotus*, 18.
125. *Lotus*, 21.
126. *Lotus*, 1.
127. Isle of Palmas case (Scott, Hague Court Reports 2d 83 (1932).
128. *Palmas*, 2.
129. *Palmas*, 3.
130. *Palmas*, 1.
131. Badinter Opinion #1: 31 I.L.M. (1992).
132. *Badinter* #1, 164.
133. *Badinter* #1, 166.
134. *Badinter* #1, 163.
135. South West Africa Cases (Ethiopia vs. South Africa; Liberia vs. South Africa), Second Phase, Judgment, I.C.J. Reports 1966, p. 6.
136. *Africa*, para.3.
137. *Africa*, para.33-see also 24, 26.
138. *Africa*—Jessup 433.
139. Richard A. Falk, "The South West Africa Cases: An Appraisal," *International Organization* 21, no. 1 (1967): 1–23; Alexander J. Pollock, "The South West Africa Cases and the Jurisprudence of International Law," *International Organization* 23, no. 4 (1969): 767–87; Rosalyn Higgins, "The International Court and South West Africa: The Implications of the Judgment," *International Affairs* 42, no. 4 (1966): 573–599; and James Crawford, *The International Law Commission's Articles on State Responsibility: Introduction, Text, and Commentaries*, ed. United Nations International Law Commission (Cambridge: Cambridge University Press, 2002).
140. *Africa*, para. 50—see also 44, 49, 51.
141. 163 U.S. 537 (1896).
142. *Africa*, para. 52, 53.
143. Thomas M. Franck, "The Emerging Right to Democratic Governance," *American Journal of International Law* 86 (1992): 46 and *The Power of Legitimacy among Nations* (New York: Oxford University Press, 1990), 16.
144. John H. Jackson, "Sovereignty-Modern: A New Approach to an Outdated Concept," *American Journal of International Law* 97 (2003): 801.
145. *Africa*, para. 91.
146. *Africa*—Tanaka, 289.
147. In the United States it took violence and the civil rights movement, 100 years after *Plessy*, to replace the social conventions affirmed in the laws of separate-but-equal with law based on the critical principle of equality.
148. Legality of Nuclear Weapons 35 I.L.M. 809 (1997).

149. *Weapons*, para. 21.
150. Orakhelashvili, *Peremptory Norms in International Law* (Oxford: Oxford University Press, 2006), Ch. 2.
151. *Weapons*, para. 29.
152. *Weapons*, para. 33.
153. *Weapons*, para. 42.
154. Laurence Boisson de Chazournes and Philippe Sands, eds, *International Law, the International Court of Justice and Nuclear Weapons* (Cambridge: Cambridge University Press, 1999).
155. *Weapons*, para. 96. "the Court cannot lose sight of the fundamental right of every State to survival, and thus its right to resort to self-defense, in accordance with Article 51 of the Charter, when its survival is at stake."
156. Chazournes and Sands, *Weapons.*
157. *Weapons*—Weeramantry, S. 9.

3 "Progressive Codification": A Rule of Adjudication and the Evolution of Justice-As-Sovereignty

1. Emer de Vattel, *The Law of Nations*, ed. Knud Haakonssen, Bela Kapossy, and Richard Whatmore, Natural Law and Enlightenment Classics (Indianoplis, IN: Liberty Fund, 2008), 78.
2. Hugo Grotius, *The Rights of War and Peace*, ed. Knud Haakonssen. Richard Tuck ed. 3 vols., Natural Law and Enlightenment Classics (Indianoplis, IN: Liberty Fund, 2005), 22.
3. John Martin Gillroy and Maurice Wade, eds, *The Moral Dimensions of Public Policy Choice: Beyond the Market Paradigm* (Pittsburgh: University of Pittsburgh Press, 1992), 6–8.
4. Philip Allott, *The Health of Nations: Society and Law Beyond the State* (Cambridge: Cambridge University Press, 2002), 411–412.
5. Stephen Buckle, *Natural Law and the Theory of Property: Grotius to Hume* (Oxford: Clarendon Press, 1991), 45.
6. Grotius, *Peace*, para. 16.
7. David Hume, *A Treatise of Human Nature*, ed. L. A. Selby-Bigge and P. H. Nidditch. 3th ed. (Oxford: Oxford University Press, 1978), 490, 547.
8. Hume, *Treatise*, 538.
9. Thomas Hobbes, *Leviathan*, ed. C. B. Macpherson, Pelican Classics (Harmondsworth, Middlesex, England: Penguin Books, 1979), Ch. 13.
10. Jack L. Goldsmith and Eric A. Posner, *The Limits of International Law* (Cambridge: Cambridge University Press, 2005).
11. John F. Murphy, *The United States and the Rule of Law in International Affairs* (Cambridge: Cambridge University Press, 2004), 4–6.
12. H. L. A. Hart, *The Concept of Law*, Clarendon Law Series (Oxford: Clarendon Press, 1961), 94.
13. Hume, *Treatise*, 505.
14. Bin Cheng, *General Principles of Law as Applied by International Courts and Tribunals* (Cambridge: Cambridge University Press, 2006).
15. Hart, *Concept*, Ch. 4.
16. Progressive in evolutionary terms, capable of moving forward, backward and holding in place.
17. Buckle, *Property*, Ch. 6.
18. Hume, *Treatise*, 520.

19. Hume, *Treatise*, 522.
20. Hume, *Treatise*, 522–523.
21. Hume, *Treatise*, 518.
22. Hume, *Treatise*, 518.
23. Hume, *Treatise*, 516.
24. Hume, *Treatise*, 523.
25. Hume, *Treatise*, 518.
26. Hume, *Treatise*, 518.
27. Stephen D. Krasner *Sovereignty: Organized Hypocrisy* (Princeton: Princeton University Press, 1999), 4.
28. Hume, *Treatise*, 523.
29. Hume, *Treatise*, 522.
30. John Martin Gillroy, "Adjudication Norms, Dispute Settlement Regimes and International Tribunals: The Status of 'Environmental Sustainability' in International Jurisprudence," *Stanford Journal of International Law* 42, no. 1 (2006): 1–52.
31. Christian Reus-Smit, *The Moral Purpose of the State: Culture, Social Identity, and Institutional Rationality in International Relations* (Princeton: Princeton University Press, 2009), Ch. 1–3; Robert H. Ferrell, *American Diplomacy: A History*, 3rd ed. (New York: Norton, 1975), Ch. 1 and 2; Arthur. Nussbaum, *A Concise History of the Law of Nations* (New York: Macmillan, 1947), Ch. 1 and 2.
32. *Vienna Convention On The Law Of Treaties* 63 *Am. J. Int'l L.* 875 1969.
33. Russell Hardin, *Collective Action* (Baltimore, MD: Johns Hopkins University Press, 1983), 196.
34. Martti Koskenniemi, *From Apology to Utopia: The Structure of International Legal Argument* (Cambridge: Cambridge University Press, 2005), §5.1.1.
35. *Vienna Convention On The Law Of Treaties* Art. 26.
36. Hume, *Treatise*, 516.
37. James Baillie, *Hume on Morality* (London: Routledge, 2000), 180–185.
38. Antonio Casssese, *International Law*. 2nd. ed. (Oxford: Oxford University Press, 2005), 176.
39. As when the Latin American approach to multilateral treaties (that was willing to accept reservations to gain parties to a treaty) became conventional in practice instead of the European approach (that chose unreserved participation over number of parties).
40. Hart, *Concept*, Ch. 2.
41. John Rawls, *The Law of Peoples* (Cambridge, MA: Harvard University Press, 1999), 172–174.
42. As exemplified by the "Safeguard Clause," *Declaration on Principles of International Law Concerning Friendly Relations and Co-operation Among States In Accordance With The Charter of The United Nations. GAR 2625 (XXV) (1970).*
43. Steven Kelman, *Making Public Policy: A Hopeful View of American Government*, Basic Series in American Government (New York: Basic Books, 1987), 6–8.
44. E. J. Mishan, *Cost-Benefit Analysis*, 3rd ed. (Boston: George Allen & Unwin, 1982), 100–109; Robin W. Boadway and David E. Wildasin, *Public Sector Economics*, 2nd ed. (Boston: Little Brown and Company, 1984), 176–180.
45. Gillroy and Wade, *Dimensions*, 5–11; John Martin Gillroy, *Justice & Nature: Kantian Philosophy, Environmental Policy & the Law* (Washington, DC: Georgetown University Press, 2000), Ch. 3.
46. Gillroy *Justice*, Ch. 3; Mishan, *Analysis*, Ch. 24.
47. Giandomenico Majone, *Evidence, Argument & Persuasion in the Policy Process* (New Haven: Yale University Press, 1989), 12–20.
48. Majone, *Evidence*, 12–13.

49. Hume, *Enquiries*, 201, 206, 305.
50. Hume *Enquiries*, 201.
51. David Miller, *Philosophy and Ideology in Hume's Political Thought* (Oxford: Clarendon Press, 1981), Ch. 4.
52. Miller, *Ideology*, Ch. 6.
53. R. G. Collingwood, *An Essay on Philosophical Method* (Oxford Clarendon Press, 1933), Pt II.
54. Miller, *Ideology*, Ch. 6.
55. In contrast, Miller, *Ideology*, 128.
56. E. E. Schattschneider, *The Semi-Sovereign People: A Realist's View of Democracy in America* (Hinsdale, IL: Dryden Press, 1960).
57. Cheng, *Principles*.
58. *Charter of the United Nations* Article 2.7.
59. My method allows for a more detailed taxonomy of normative standards in international law, transcending the practice of using the word "norm" to describe everything from a critical moral principle to a rule.
60. Gillroy, *Justice*, Ch. 5.
61. Michael H. Hoeflich and Jasonne M. Grabher, "The Establishment of Normative Legal Texts: The Beginnings of the *Ius Commune*," in *The History of Cannon Law in the Classical Period, 1140–1234: From Gratian to the Decretals of Pope Gregory Ix*, ed. Wilfried Hartmann and Kenneth Pennington (Washington, DC: The Catholic University of America Press, 2008).
62. Peter Stein, *Roman Law in European History* (Cambridge: Cambridge University Press, 1999), 87–88.
63. North Sea Continental Shelf, Judgment, I.C.J. Reports 1969, p. 3.
64. *Continental*—Sorensen 246—see also 256–257.
65. *Continental*—Tanaka 196—see also 186, 189.
66. *Continental*—Sorensen 244.
67. *Continental*, para. 81.
68. *Continental*, para. 19—see also para. 18.
69. *Continental*, para. 46—see also paras. 21, 39, 46, 55.
70. *Continental*, para. 55.
71. *Continental*, para. 85—see also para. 101.
72. *Continental*, para. 82.
73. *Continental*—Tanaka 180.
74. *Continental*—Tanaka 182.
75. Gabcikovo—Nagymaros I.C.J. Rep No. 92 (1997).
76. *Gabcikovo*, para. 40.
77. *Gabcikovo*, paras. 51, 53.
78. *Gabcikovo*, paras. 112
79. *Gabcikovo*, para. 114.
80. *Gabcikovo*, para. 57—see also paras. 54, 101, 48 (quoting *International Articles of State Responsibility*[old article 33]).
81. *Gabcikovo*, para. 112.
82. *Gabcikovo*, para. 140.
83. *Gabcikovo*—Weeramantry 2.
84. *Gabcikovo*—Weeramantry 18.
85. *Gabcikovo*—Weeramantry 18.
86. *Gabcikovo*—Weeramantry 21.
87. Re Separation of Quebec 1998 2 S.C.R. 217.
88. *Quebec*, para. 76.
89. *Quebec*, para. 77—see also para. 78.

90. *Quebec*, para. 135 (quoting para. 15–16 of an amicus curiae).
91. *Quebec*, para. 127.
92. *Quebec*, para. 111.
93. *Quebec*, para. 126.
94. *Quebec*, para. 130.

4 "Peaceful Cooperation": A Universal Rule of Recognition and the Strategic Context of Justice-As-Sovereignty

1. Stephen D. Krasner, *Sovereignty: Organized Hypocrisy* (Princeton: Princeton University Press, 1999), 4.
2. Francisco S. J. Suarez, *Selections from Three Works*, trans. Gwladys L. Williams, Ammi Brown, John Waldron, and S. J. Henry Davis, ed. James Brown Scott (Oxford: Clarendon Press, 1944. Reprint, Classics of International Law), 342.
3. Suarez, *Selections*, 352.
4. Suarez, *Selections*, 343.
5. Suarez, *Selections*, 341.
6. Suarez, *Selections*, 342.
7. Suarez, *Selections*, 342.
8. Suarez, *Selections*, 352.
9. Suarez, *Selections*, 346, 352.
10. Suarez, *Selections*, 343.
11. Suarez, *Selections*, 352.
12. Suarez, *Selections*, 345.
13. Suarez, *Selections*, 345.
14. Suarez, *Selections*, 346.
15. Suarez, *Selections*, 341.
16. Suarez, *Selections*, 352.
17. Suarez, *Selections*, 357.
18. Suarez, *Selections*, 352.
19. Harold J. Berman, *Law and Revolution: The Formation of the Western Legal Tradition* (Cambridge, Massachusetts: Harvard University Press, 1983), 267.
20. Ronald G. Asch, "The *Ius Foederis* Re-Examined: The Peace of Westphalia and the Constitution of the Holy Roman Empire," in *Peace Treaties and International Law in European History*, edited by Randall Lesaffer (Cambridge: Cambridge University Press, 2004), 321–322; Johnathan Scott, *Commonwealth Principles: Republican Writing of the English Revolution* (Cambridge: Cambridge University Press, 2004), 214; Joseph Strayer, *On the Medieval Origins of the Modern State* (Princeton: Princeton University Press, 1970).
21. Berman, *Revolution*, 519.
22. Randall Lesaffer, ed., *Peace Treaties and International Law in European History: From the Late Middle Ages to World War One* (Cambridge: Cambridge University Press, 2004), Pt. 1.
23. Lesaffer, "Lodi to Westphalia" in *Treaties*, 13–14.
24. Beaulac, *The Power of Language in the Making of International Law: The Word Sovereignty in Bodin and Vattel and the Myth of Westphalia*. Vol. 46, Developments in International Law (Leiden, The Netherlands: Martinus Nijhoff Publishers, 2004).
25. Suarez, *Selections*, 342.
26. *International Court of Justice Statute*, Art. 38.

27. Ian Brownlie, *Principles of Public International Law*, 6th ed. (Oxford: Oxford University Press, 2003), 8–10; Malcolm N. Shaw, *International Law*, 6th ed. (Cambridge: Cambridge University Press, 2008), 84–89; Michael Byers, *Custom, Power and the Power of Rules: International Relations and Customary International Law* (Cambridge: Cambridge University Press, 1999), 18–19.
28. Codified in *Lotus* 18.
29. *Continental Shelf* 3; *Nicaragua* 14; *Asylum* 3.
30. Thomas Hobbes, *Leviathan*, ed. C. B. Macpherson, Pelican Classics (Harmondsworth, Middlesex, England: Penguin Books, 1979). 186.
31. T. C. Schelling, *The Strategy of Conflict* (Cambridge, MA: Harvard University Press, 1963), 57–58.
32. Shaw, *Law*, 131–132.
33. This may explain why the United States Senate assumes that all Human Rights treaties are non-self-executing.
34. *Reid v. Covert* 354 U.S. 1 (1957).
35. *Paquete Habana* 175 U.S. 677 (1900).
36. Russell Hardin, *Collective Action* (Baltimore, MD: Johns Hopkins University Press, 1983); Michael Taylor, *Anarchy & Cooperation* (London: John Wiley & Sons, 1976); David K. Lewis, *Convention: A Philosophical Study* (Cambridge, MA: Harvard University Press, 1969).
37. Jon Elster, *Ulysses and the Sirens: Studies in Rationality and Irrationality* (Cambridge: Cambridge University Press, 1979), 18.
38. Taylor has written a more up-to-date version of this analysis, but in it he states that "the chapter dealing with the political theories of Hobbes and Hume is the only one to survive intact," Michael Taylor, *The Possibility of Cooperation*, Studies in Rationality and Social Change (Cambridge: Cambridge University Press, 1987), ix.
39. Hardin, *Collective*, Ch. 10.
40. Schelling *Strategy*, 110.
41. Hobbes, *Leviathan*, Ch. 14.
42. David Hume, *A Treatise of Human Nature*, ed. L. A. Selby-Bigge and P. H. Nidditch, 5th ed. (Oxford: Oxford University Press, 1978), 492–493.
43. Axelrod's analysis of game simulations supports this contention; Robert Axelrod, *The Evolution of Cooperation* (New York: Basic Books, 1984), 60–65.
44. Taylor, *Anarchy*, 8–9; *Possibility*, 81, 154, 161.
45. Hume, *Treatise*, 538.
46. The complications of size are not just numbers but the increasing tendency to be unable to maintain the tight interrelationship and sophisticated play necessary to monitor contingent strategy choice.
47. Taylor, *Anarchy*, 124.
48. Hume, *Treatise*, 534ff.
49. Hume, *Treatise*, 535.
50. Hardin, *Collective*, Ch. 10.
51. Hardin, *Collective*, 176.
52. Hume, *Treatise*, 535.
53. Hume, *Enquiries* 206.
54. "Political society" originates as a promise between men based on the preexisting conventions of social justice and the requirements of its scale of forms in maintaining social stability in the face of increasing complexity (*Treatise*, 541, 535, 541, 546; *Enquiries*, 205). Hume's iterated game coordinates larger n-person games by supplementing the conventions of justice with the "separate sanction of government" (*Treatise*, 546).
55. Hans Kelsen, *Introduction to the Problems of Legal Theory: A Translation of the First Edition of the Reine Rechtslehre or Pure Theory of Law*, ed. Bonnie Litschewaki Paulson and Stanley L. Paulson (Oxford: Clarendon Press, 2001), 27–28.

56. Kelsen, *Pure*, 33.
57. Hume, *Treatise*, 541.
58. Taylor, *Anarchy*, 127; *Possibility*, 162.
59. Hume, *Enquiries*, 206.
60. Hume, *Enquiries*, 282–284.
61. Hardin, *Collective*, 184.
62. Hardin *Collective*, 174; Chs. 11–12.
63. Hardin *Collective*, 186, 196.
64. Hume, *Treaties*, 567–569.
65. Hardin, *Collective*, 184.
66. Duncan Forbes, *Hume's Philosophical Politics* (Cambridge: Cambridge University Press, 1975), 153ff.
67. Hume, *Treatise*, 564.
68. Gene M. Lyons and Michaet Mastanduno, eds, *Beyond Westphalia: State Sovereignty and International Intervention* (Baltimore: Johns Hopkins University Press, 1995), Ch. 1.
69. Brian Skyrms, *The Stag Hunt and the Evolution of Social Structure* (Cambridge: Cambridge University Press, 2004), 3.
70. Axelrod, *Evolution*, Part II.
71. Skyrms, *Stag*, 1.
72. Daniel Philpott, *Revolutions in Sovereignty: How Ideas Shaped Modern International Relations* (Princeton: Princeton University Press, 2001), Ch. 1.
73. Skyrms, *Stag*, 123.
74. Skyrms, *Stag*, 29.
75. Skyrms, *Stag*, 10 (original italics).
76. Hume, *Treatise*, 485.
77. Hume, *Treatise*, 485.
78. Hume, *Treatise*, 532.
79. Hume, *Treatise*, 414.
80. Hume, *Treatise*, 422.
81. Hume, *Treatise*, 310.
82. Hume, *Treatise*, 497.
83. Russell Hardin, *David Hume: Moral & Political Theorist* (Oxford: Oxford University Press, 2007), Ch. 3.
84. Hume, *Treatise*, 502.
85. Hume, *Treatise*, 503.
86. Hume, *Treatise*, 503.
87. Hume, *Treatise*, 505.
88. Hume, *Treatise*, 514.
89. Hume, *Treatise*, 514.
90. Hume, *Treatise*, 514.
91. Hume, *Enquiries*, 198.
92. Hume, *Enquiries*, 183.
93. Hume, *Enquiries*, 201.
94. Hume, *Enquiries*, 196.
95. This is a major distinction between Hume and Adam Smith, with whom he is frequently compared. David Miller, *Philosophy and Ideology in Hume's Political Thought* (Oxford: Clarendon Press, 1981), 196–200.
96. Hume, *Enquiries*, 206.
97. Hume, *Treatise*, 484.
98. Hume, *Treatise*, 485.
99. James Baillie, *Hume on Morality* (London: Routledge, 2000), 160–161.

100. Tinoco Claims Arbitration (Great Britain v. Costa Rica) (1923) 1 R.I.A.A. 369.
101. *Tinoco.*
102. *Tinoco.*
103. Reparation for injuries suffered in the service of the United Nations, Advisory Opinion: I.C. J. Reports 1949, p. 174.
104. *International Court of Justice Statute* Art.35.
105. *Reparations*, 183.
106. *Reparations*, 177–178.
107. *Reparations*, 178.
108. *Reparations*, 179.
109. *Reparations*, 179.
110. Jurisdiction, Judgment, I.C.J. Reports 1984, p. 392; Merits, Judgment. I.C.J. Reports 1986, p. 14.
111. *Nicaragua*, para. 73.
112. *Nicaragua*, para. 177—see also para. 178.
113. *Nicaragua*, para. 209.
114. *Nicaragua*, para. 202.
115. Fisheries Jurisdiction (Spain v. Canada), Jurisdiction of the Court, Judgment, I. C.J. Reports 1998, p. 432.
116. *Spain/Canada*, para. 14.
117. *Spain/Canada*, para. 15.
118. *Spain/Canada*, para. 87.
119. *Spain/Canada*, para. 25.
120. *Spain/Canada*, para. 14, 15, 17–18, 20–21, 25–26, 45–46, 60–61, 65, 70, 72–73, and 87.
121. *Spain/Canada*—Kooijmans para. 8.
122. *Spain/Canada*—Weeramantry para. 25—see also para. 12.
123. *Spain/Canada*—Weeramantry para. 46.
124. *Spain/Canada*—Weeramantry para. 13.
125. *Spain/Canada*—Weeramantry para. 17. Also in para. 54 he argues that without a superior position for what I call 'critical principle' over sovereignty, the "integrity of the entire system" is at risk.
126. *Spain/Canada*—Weeramantry para. 40. Also fn. 14 from Spain's Memorial.
127. *Spain/Canada*—Vereshchetin para. 10–18.
128. *Spain/Canada*—Kooijmans para. 1, 5, and 11–13.
129. *Spain/Canada*, para. 8.
130. *Spain/Canada*—Vereshchetin para. 17.
131. Paquete Habana 175 U.S. 677 (1900).
132. *Paquete*, 694.
133. *Paquete*, 700.
134. *Paquete*, 694.
135. *Paquete*, 711.
136. *Paquete*, 708.
137. Missouri v. Holland 252 U.S. 416 (1920).
138. *Holland*, 431–432.
139. *Holland*, 423.
140. *Holland*, 433–434.
141. *Holland*, 434.
142. *Holland*, 435.
143. Reid v. Covert 354 U.S. 1 (1957).
144. *Reid*, I.
145. *Reid*, II.

146. R. v. Hape, [2007] 2 S.C.R. 292, 2007 SCC 26.
147. *Hape*, [53] [56] [68].
148. *Hape*, para. 46—see also para. 43.
149. *Hape*, para. 45—see also para. 59.
150. *Hape*, 52, 96, 99–100.

5 "Non-Intervention": A Rule of Change Protecting "Process" from "Principle"

1. Philip Allott, *The Health of Health: Society and Law Beyond the State* (Cambridge: Cambridge University Press, 2002), 33–34.
2. Christian Wolff, *The Law of Nations Treated According to a Scientific Method*, trans. Joseph H. Drake (Oxford: Clarendon Press, 1934. Reprint, The Classics of International Law), §7.
3. Wolff, *Law*, §10.
4. Wolff, *Law*, §2
5. Wolff, *Law*, §13.
6. Wolff, *Law*, §13.
7. Wolff, *Law*, §2.
8. Wolff, *Law*, §5.
9. Wolff, *Law*, §6.
10. Wolff, *Law*, §2.
11. In the same way that a single sense of necessary revelation was the glue for the international Papal System, Wolff assumes that all nations recognize necessity in the state structure itself.
12. Wolff, *Law*, §2.
13. Andreas Osiander, *Before the State: Systemic Political Change in the West Form the Greeks to the French Revolution* (Oxford: Oxford University Press, 2007).
14. Stephen D. Krasner, *Sovereignty: Organized Hypocrisy* (Princeton: Princeton University Press, 1999), 4–5.
15. Thomas Hobbes, *Leviathan*, ed. C. B. Macpherson, Pelican Classics (Harmondsworth, Middlesex, England: Penguin Books, 1979), Ch. XVII.
16. Hobbes, *Leviathan*, 185.
17. Kenneth Neal Waltz, *Theory of International Politics*, 1st ed. (Long Grove, IL: Waveland Press, 2010), 74, 91.
18. David Hume, *A Treatise of Human Nature*, ed. L. A. Selby-Bigge and P. H. Nidditch, 5th ed. (Oxford: Oxford University Press, 1978), 545; *Enquiries Concerning Hume Understanding (E1) and Concerning the Principles of Morals (E2)*, ed. L.A. Selby-Bigge and P. H. Nidditch, 3rd. ed. (Oxford: Oxford University Press, 1975), 192.
19. Hobbes, *Leviathan*, Parts I and II.
20. Hobbes, *Leviathan*, Ch. 15.
21. Hobbes, *Leviathan*, Ch. 10.
22. Hobbes, *Leviathan*, Ch. 10.
23. *Leviathan* is usually drawn as a giant made up of individuals.
24. Hobbes, *Leviathan*, Ch. 10.
25. Hobbes, *Leviathan*, 189.
26. Hobbes, *Leviathan*, 127.
27. Isaiah Berlin, *Four Essays on Liberty* (Oxford: Oxford University Press, 1969), 122; John Martin Gillroy, *Justice & Nature: Kantian Philosophy, Environmental Policy & the Law* (Washington, DC: Georgetown University Press, 2000), Ch. 5.
28. Hobbes, *Leviathan*, 163.

29. Hobbes, *Leviathan*, 163–164. The first definition of Liberty is in Chapter 14 and is applicable to man in the State of nature. The second definition, in Chapter 21, regards the "Liberty of Subjects" in a civil society, viz. Liberty as civil freedom.
30. Hobbes, *Leviathan*, 261.
31. Hobbes, *Leviathan*, Ch. 14.
32. Hobbes, *Leviathan*, 190.
33. Hobbes, *Leviathan*, 189–191.
34. Hobbes, *Leviathan*, 189.
35. Charles R. Beitz, *Political Theory and International Relations* (Princeton: Princeton University Press, 1979), 46–48.
36. Hobbes, *Leviathan*, Ch.13.
37. Hobbes, *Leviathan*, 183.
38. Hobbes, *Leviathan*, 184—Assuming scarcity, Hobbes argues that two men after the same end cannot be equally satisfied.
39. Hobbes, *Leviathan*, 184.
40. Hobbes, *Leviathan*, 161.
41. Hobbes, *Leviathan*, 185.
42. Hobbes, *Leviathan*, 185.
43. Hobbes, *Leviathan*, Ch. 13; S. I. Benn "Hobbes on Power," in *Hobbes and Rousseau: A Collection of Critical Essays*, ed. Maurice Cranston and Richard S. Peters, 21 (New York: Anchor Books, 1972), 21.
44. Hobbes, *Leviathan*, 217.
45. Hobbes, *Leviathan*, 188.
46. Hobbes, *Leviathan*, 190, 201—the second and third Laws of Nature.
47. Hobbes, *Leviathan*, 201.
48. In the same way that the individual creates the municipal state for the sake of his local preservation as such an end.
49. Immanuel Kant, *Metaphysics of Morals:* Vol. 6, Gesammelte Schriften (Berlin: Prussian Academy of Sciences, 1797), Ak214.
50. Jack L. Goldsmith and Eric A. Posner, *The Limits of International Law* (Cambridge: Cambridge University Press, 2005).
51. The concept of human and state *autonomy* might be used to replace Hobbes' use of *sovereignty*. Both, by his logic of concepts, are rendered from reason-based critical principles related to essential independence-preservation.
52. Hume, *Treatise*, 499–500.
53. John Rawls, *The Law of Peoples* (Cambridge, MA: Harvard University Press, 1999), 172–174.
54. Susan Marks, *The Riddle of All Constitutions: International Law, Democracy, and the Critique of Ideology* (Oxford: Oxford University Press, 2000), 38.
55. John Hoffman, *Sovereignty* (Minneapolis: University of Minnesota Press, 1998), 18–20.
56. Hoffman, *Sovereignty*, 19, Ch.10.
57. Janne Elisabeth Nijman, *The Concept of International Legal Personality: An Inquiry into the History and Theory of International Law* (The Hague: T.M.C Asser Press, 2004), Ch. 1.
58. John Martin Gillroy, "Adjudication Norms, Dispute Settlement Regimes and International Tribunals: The Status of 'Environmental Sustainability' in International Jurisprudence," *Stanford Journal of International Law* 42, no. 1 (2006): 55.
59. Brian Barry, *Political Argument* (Berkeley: University of California Press, 1992. Reprint, Reissue), 39–40.
60. Giandomenico Majone, *Evidence, Argument & Persuasion in the Policy Process* (New Haven: Yale University Press, 1989), 146–147.
61. Hoffman, *Sovereignty*, 20.

62. E. U. Petersmann, "The WTO Constitution and Human Rights," *Journal of International Economic Law* 3 (2000); "How to Constitutionalize International Law and the Gatt/Wto Dispute Settlement System," *Michigan Journal of International Law* 20 (1998); "Constitutionalization and International Adjudication: How to Constitutionalize the UN Dispute Settlement System," *New York Journal of International Law* 31 (1999).
63. Deborah Z. Cass, *The Constitutionalization of the World Trade Organization: Legitimacy, Democracy, and Community in the International Trading System* (Oxford: Oxford University Press, 2005).
64. *Shrimp/Turtle* 270/para. 6.7
65. Words we normally associate with intrinsic rather than instrumental values.
66. *Shrimp/Turtle*, 319/para. 129.
67. *Shrimp/Turtle*, 327/para. 152.
68. *Shrimp/Turtle*, 328/para. 153. Gillroy, *Justice*, Ch. 2, for a distinction between *full-* and *optimal*-use applied to Kaldor efficiency.
69. In negotiations at Marrakesh. *Shrimp/Turtle*, 328/para. 153.
70. *Shrimp/Turtle*, 328/para. 154.
71. *Shrimp/Turtle*, 329/para. 154.
72. *Shrimp/Turtle*, 329/para. 154.
73. Gillroy, "Adjudication".
74. *Shrimp/Turtle*, 355/para. 123.
75. United States—Restrictions on Imports of Tuna. September 3, 1991; United States—Restrictions on Imports of Tuna, June 16, 1994; United States—Import Prohibition of Certain Shrimp and Shrimp Products *WTO case Nos. 58 (and 61).*
76. *Shrimp/Turtle*, 313/para. 113.
77. *Tuna/Dolphin*, 71/para. 5.22.
78. *Tuna/Dolphin*, 72/para. 5.27 (emphasis added).
79. *Tuna/Dolphin*, 98/para. 5.3.
80. *Tuna/Dolphin, II* 102/para. 5.12 for XX(g); 108/para. 5.29 for XX(b).
81. The chapeau states that exceptions are limited "[s]ubject to the requirements that such measures are not applied in a manner that would constitute a means of arbitrary or unjustifiable discrimination between countries where the same conditions prevail, or a disguised restriction on international trade".
82. *Tuna/Dolphin, II* 112/para. 5.42.
83. Statute amendment §609 incorporated in 16 USCA §1537.
84. 2 IELR, 236.
85. *Shrimp/Turtle*, 241.
86. *Shrimp/Turtle*, 318/para. 127.
87. *Shrimp/Turtle*, 313/para. 114.
88. *Shrimp/Turtle*, 320–321/para. 131.
89. *Shrimp/Turtle*, 343/para. 186.
90. *Shrimp/Turtle*, 339/para. 172.
91. *Shrimp/Turtle*, 334/para. 164.
92. 2 *IELR*, 343/para. 185.
93. *Shrimp/Turtle II*, (WT/DS58/RW).
94. *Shrimp/Turtle II*, para. 122.
95. *Shrimp/Turtle II*, para. 136.
96. *Shrimp/Turtle II*, para. 131.
97. *Shrimp/Turtle II*, para. 140.
98. *Shrimp/Turtle II*, para. 143.
99. Dinah Shelton, ed., *Commitment and Compliance: The Role of Non-Binding Norms in the International Legal System* (Oxford: Oxford University Press, 2000), 22ff.

100. *Schooner* 116.
101. *Schooner*, 156–157.
102. *Underhill/Hernandez* 250.
103. *Nicaragua* para.126.
104. *Aluminum* 416.
105. Sherman Anti-Trust Act of 1890, 15 U.S.C. § 1–7.
106. *Aluminum*, 443
107. Justice-As-Sovereignty was amenable to markets/trade as definitions of reciprocity before the WTO, making *trade-reciprocity* less disruptive to established social convention than critical principle.
108. *Sabbatino*, 398.
109. *Sabbatino*, 421.
110. *Sabbatino*, 423.
111. *Sabbatino*, 436–437.
112. *Sabbatino*—White 439–440.
113. *Sabbatino*—White 186.
114. *Sabbatino*—White 457–458.
115. Timberlane v. Bank of America 549 F.2d 597 (9th Cir. 1976).
116. *Timberlane*, 597.
117. *Timberlane*, 597.
118. H. Lauterpacht, *The Function of Law in the International Community* (Oxford: Clarendon Press, 1933), 144–145.
119. David Miller, *Philosophy and Ideology in Hume's Political Thought* (Oxford: Clarendon Press, 1981), Ch. 6.
120. This acceptance of intervention on behalf of a process-norm, as distinguished from a critical principle, is evident in the Constitutional status of Congressional/Executive agreements under the Commerce Clause of Article 1. *USA Foundation v. US, 242 F. 3d 1300 (11th Circuit 2001).*
121. In *Argentina v. Weltover 504 U.S. 607 (1992)* and *Saudi Arabia v. Nelson* 507 U.S. 349 (1993) the Supreme Court established a process-based "commercial activities exception" ignoring the critical principle of protection from torture, even when the subject was a private citizen running a commercial enterprise.
122. *Regina v. Bow Street (No. 3) [2000] 1 A.C. 147.*
123. Christine Chinkin, "United Kingdom House of Lords: Regina V. Bow Street Stipendiary Magistrate, Ex Parte Pinochet Ugarte," *American Journal of International Law* 93, no. 3 (1999): 703–711.
124. *Pinochet*, this is also the position of Lords Millett-69, and Hope-41.
125. *Pinochet*, 9: quoting *Demjanjuk v. Petrovsky* 571.
126. *Pinochet*, 13.
127. *Pinochet*, 14.
128. *Pinochet*, 18.
129. *Pinochet*, 19.
130. Agreeing with the Supreme Court in *Sabbatino*.
131. *Pinochet*, 19.
132. *Pinochet*, 25.
133. *Pinochet*, 865.
134. *Immunity* 153.
135. At the threshold between Stage-I and Stage-II international legal systems municipal law is stabilizing as the municipal tier is made up of stable Stage-II states that have integrated, to a greater-or-lesser extent, critical principle in their constitutional structures
136. *Pinochet*, 72–3.

137. *Pinochet*, 55.
138. Arrest Warrant of April 11, 2000 (Democratic Republic of the Congo v. Belgium), Judgment, I.C.J. Reports 2002, p. 3
139. *Warrant*, para. 54.
140. *Warrant*, para. 60.
141. *Warrant*, para. 71.
142. *Warrant*—Dissent para. 3.
143. *Warrant*—Dissent para. 7
144. *Warrant*—Dissent para. 45.
145. *Warrant*—Dissent para. 46.
146. *Warrant*—Dissent para. 47.
147. Chinkin, "Pinochet," 711.
148. *Warrant*—Dissent para. 60.
149. *Warrant*—Dissent para. 62—see also para. 73.
150. *Warrant*—Dissent para. 75.
151. Kevin R. Gray, "Case Concerning the Arrest Warrant of 11 April 2000 (Democratic Republic of the Congo V. Belgium)," *European Journal of International Law* 13, no. 3 (2002), 11.
152. *Arrest Warrant*—Dissent para. 49.

6 Conclusion: The Metaphysical Elements of Sovereignty

1. Emer de Vattel, *The Law of Nations*, ed. Knud Haakonssen, Bela Kapossy, and Richard Whatmore, Natural Law and Enlightenment Classics (Indianoplis, IN: Liberty Fund, 2008), 289.
2. Joseph Frankel, *International Politics: Conflict and Harmony*, A Pelican Book (Harmondsworth, Middlesex, England: Penguin Books, 1973), 38—see also Daniel Philpott, *Revolutions in Sovereignty: How Ideas Shaped Modern International Relations* (Princeton: Princeton University Press, 2001), 16.
3. Jens Bartelson, *A Genealogy of Sovereignty*, ed. Steve Smith. Vol. 39, Cambridge Studies in International Relations (Cambridge: Cambridge University Press, 1995), 239—see also John H. Jackson, "Sovereignty-Modern: A New Approach to an Outdated Concept," *American Journal of International Law* 97 (2003): x.
4. A. Pellet, "The Opinions of the Badinter Abitration Committee," *European Journal of International Law* 3 (1982): 185.
5. Michael Fowler and Julie Marie Bunck, *Law, Power and the Sovereign State: The Evolution and Application of the Concept of Sovereignty* (University Park: Pennsylvania State University Press, 1995), 164.
6. Eli Lauterpacht, "Sovereignty—Myth or Reality?" *International Affairs* 73, no. 1 (1997): 141.
7. L. Oppenheim, *International Law: A Treatise*, ed. Ronald F. Roxburgh, 3rd ed. (London: Longmans, Green and Co., 1920. Reprint, Lawbook Exchange 2005), §123, 206–207—see also Jackson, "Sovereignty-Modern," 782.
8. Stephen D. Krasner, *Sovereignty: Organized Hypocrisy* (Princeton: Princeton University Press, 1999), 3–4.
9. Krasner, *Sovereignty*, 9—see also Jackson, "Sovereignty-Modern," xi.
10. Dominik Zaum, *The Sovereignty Paradox: The Norms and Politics of International Statebuilding* (Oxford: Oxford University Press, 2007), 3.
11. Daniel Philpott, *Revolutions in Sovereignty: How Ideas Shaped Modern International Relations* (Princeton: Princeton University Press, 2001), 16—see also Cynthia

Weber, *Simulating Sovereignty: Intervention, the State and Symbolic Exchange*, ed. Steve Smith. vol. 37, Cambridge Studies in International Relations (Cambridge: Cambridge University Press, 1995), 1.

12. Thomas J. Biersteker and Cynthia Weber, eds, *State Sovereignty as Social Construct*, Cambridge Studies in International Relations (Cambridge: Cambridge University Press, 1996), 14.
13. Jackson, "Sovereignty-Modern," 786.
14. Jackson, *Sovereignty*, 23.
15. James N. Rosenau, *Along the Domestic-Foreign Frontier: Exploring Governance in a Turbulent World*. Vol. 53, Cambridge Studies in International Relations (Cambridge: Cambridge University Press, 1997), 218.
16. Rosenau, *Domestic-Foreign*, 222.
17. Rosenau, *Domestic-Foreign*, 231.
18. Henry Schermers, "Different Aspects of Sovereignty," in *State, Sovereignty, and International Governance*, ed. Gerard Kreijen, Marcel Brus, Jorri Duursma, Elisabeth De Vos, and John Dugard (Oxford: Oxford University Press, 2002), 185.
19. Jutta Brunneé and Stephen J. Troope, *Legitimacy and Legality in International Law: An Interactional Account*, Cambridge Studies in International and Comparative Law (Cambridge: Cambridge University Press, 2010).
20. What Kant would define as a matter of "Gerechtigheit" rather than "Recht."
21. See Chester Brown, *A Common Law of International Adjudication* (Oxford: Oxford University Press, 2007) for evidence supporting the dominance of process in the international system.
22. John Gerard Ruggie, "Territoriality and Beyond: Problematizing Moderity in International Relations," *International Organization* 47 (Winter 1993): 140, 143–144.
23. H. L. A. Hart, "Definition and Theory in Jurisprudence," in *Essays in Jurisprudence and Philosophy*, ed. H. L. A. Hart (Oxford: Oxford University Press, 1983), 21.

Bibliography

Abelard, Peter. *Ethical Writings*. Translated by Paul Vincent Spade. Edited by Marilyn McCord Adams. Indianapolis, IN: Hackett, 1995.

Allison, Henry E. *Custom and Reason in Hume: A Kantian Reading of the First Book of the Treatise*. Oxford: Clarendon Press, 2008.

Allott, Philip. *The Health of Nations: Society and Law Beyond the State*. Cambridge: Cambridge University Press, 2002.

Anghie, Anthony. *Imperialism, Sovereignty and the Making of International Law*, Cambridge Studies in International and Comparative Law. Cambridge: Cambridge University Press, 2005.

Aquinas, St. Thomas. *Treatise on Law (Summa Theologica, Questions 90–97)*. Edited by Ralph McInerny. Washington DC: Gateway Editions, Regnery Publishing, 1956.

Arend, Anthony Clark. *Legal Rules and International Society*. New York: Oxford University Press, 1999.

Aristotle. "The Basic Works." Edited by Richard McKeon. New York: Random House, 1941.

Asch, Ronald G. "The *Ius Foederis* Re-Examined: The Peace of Westphalia and the Constitution of the Holy Roman Empire." In *Peace Treaties and International Law in European History*, edited by Randall Lesaffer, 319–337. Cambridge: Cambridge University Press, 2004.

Austin, John, and Wilfrid E. Rumble. *The Province of Jurisprudence Determined*, Cambridge Texts in the History of Political Thought. Cambridge: Cambridge University Press, 1995.

Axelrod, Robert. *The Evolution of Cooperation*. New York: Basic Books, 1984.

Baillie, James. *Hume on Morality*. London: Routledge, 2000.

Barry, Brian. *Political Argument*. Berkeley: University of California Press, 1992. Reprint, Reissue.

Bartelson, Jens. *A Genealogy of Sovereignty*. Edited by Steve Smith. Vol. 39, Cambridge Studies in International Relations. Cambridge: Cambridge University Press, 1995.

Beaulac, Stephane. "The Westphalian Legal Orthodoxy: Myth or Reality?" *Journal of the History of Philosophy* 2 (2000): 148–177.

———. *The Power of Language in the Making of International Law: The Word Sovereignty in Bodin and Vattel and the Myth of Westphalia*. Vol. 46, Developments in International Law. Leiden, The Netherlands: Martinus Nijhoff Publishers, 2004.

Beitz, Charles R. *Political Theory and International Relations*. Princeton: Princeton University Press, 1979.

Benn, S. I. "Hobbes on Power." In *Hobbes and Rousseau: A Collection of Critical Essays*, edited by Maurice Cranston and Richard S. Peters, 21. New York: Anchor Books, 1972.

Bennett, Jonathan Francis. *Locke, Berkeley, Hume: Central Themes*. Oxford: Clarendon Press, 1971.

Berlin, Isaiah. *Four Essays on Liberty*. Oxford: Oxford University Press, 1969.

Berman, Harold J. *Law and Revolution: The Formation of the Western Legal Tradition*. Cambridge, MA: Harvard University Press, 1983.

Biersteker, Thomas J., and Cynthia Weber, eds. *State Sovereignty as Social Construct*, Cambridge Studies in International Relations. Cambridge: Cambridge University Press, 1996.

Boadway, Robin W. and David E. Wildasin. *Public Sector Economics*. 2nd ed. Boston: Little Brown and Company, 1984.

Brown, Chester. *A Common Law of International Adjudication*. Oxford: Oxford University Press, 2007.

Brownlie, Ian. *Principles of Public International Law*. 6th. ed. Oxford: Oxford University Press, 2003.

Brunneé, Jutta and Stephen J. Troope. *Legitimacy and Legality in International Law: An Interactional Account*, Cambridge Studies in International and Comparative Law. Cambridge: Cambridge University Press, 2010.

Buckle, Stephen. *Natural Law and the Theory of Property: Grotius to Hume*. Oxford: Clarendon Press, 1991.

Bull, Hedley. *The Anarchical Society: A Study of Order in World Politics*. 3rd. ed. London: Palgrave, 2002.

Byers, Michael. *Custom, Power and the Power of Rules: International Relations and Customary International Law*. Cambridge: Cambridge University Press, 1999.

Cass, Deborah Z. *The Constitutionalization of the World Trade Organization: Legitimacy, Democracy, and Community in the International Trading System*. Oxford: Oxford University Press, 2005.

Casssese, Antonio. *International Law*. 2nd. ed. Oxford: Oxford University Press, 2005.

Chazournes, Laurence Boisson de and Philippe Sands, eds. *International Law, the International Court of Justice and Nuclear Weapons*. Cambridge: Cambridge University Press, 1999.

Cheng, Bin. *General Principles of Law as Applied by International Courts and Tribunals*. Cambridge: Cambridge University Press, 2006.

Chinkin, Christine. "United Kingdom House of Lords: Regina V. Bow Street Stipendiary Magistrate, Ex Parte Pinochet Ugarte." *American Journal of International Law* 93, no. 3 (1999).

Collingwood, R. G. *An Essay on Philosophical Method*. Oxford Clarendon Press, 1933.

———. *R. G. Collingwood: An Autobiography*. Edited by Stephen Toulmin. Oxford: Clarendon Press, 1978.

———. *The Idea of History*. Edited by Jan Van Der Dussen. Revised ed. Oxford: Oxford University Press, 1993.

———. *Essays in Political Philosophy*. Edited by David Boucher. Oxford: Clarendon Press, 1995.

———. *An Essay on Metaphysics*. Revised ed. Oxford: Oxford University Press, 2002. Reprint, 1998.

———. *The New Leviathan or Man, Society, Civilization & Barbarism*. Revised ed. Oxford: Oxford University Press, 2005. Reprint, 1992.

Crawford, James. *The International Law Commission's Articles on State Responsibility: Introduction, Text, and Commentaries*. Edited by United Nations. International Law Commission. Cambridge: Cambridge University Press, 2002.

———. *International Law as an Open System: Selected Essays*. London: Cameron, May 2002.

D'Entreves, Alexander Passerin. *Natural Law: An Introduction to Legal Philosophy*. Piscataway, NJ: Transaction Books, 1994.

Damrosch, Lori F. *International Law : Cases and Materials*. 4th. ed, American Casebook Series. St. Paul, MN: West Group, 2001.

Danford, John W. *David Hume and the Problem of Reason: Recovering the Human Sciences*. New Haven: Yale University Press, 1990.

De Wolf, Maurice. *An Introduction to Scholastic Philosophy, Medieval and Modern: Scholasticism Old and New*. Eugene, OR: Wipf and Stock Publishers, 2003.

Descartes, Rene. "Principles of Philosophy." In *The Philosophical Works Vol. 1*, edited by Elizabeth S. Haldane and G. R. T. Ross, 201–302. Cambridge: Cambridge University Press, 1975.

Diamond, Jared. *Guns, Germs, and Steel: The Fates of Human Societies*. New York: W. W. Norton & Company, 2005.

Donagan, Alan. *The Theory of Morality*. Chicago: University of Chicago Press, 1977.

Donnelly, Jack. *Realism and International Relations*. Cambridge: Cambridge University Press, 2000.

Elster, Jon. *Ulysses and the Sirens: Studies in Rationality and Irrationality*. Cambridge: Cambridge University Press, 1979.

Falk, Richard A. "The South West Africa Cases: An Appraisal." *International Organization* 21, no. 1 (1967): 1–23.

Ferrell, Robert H. *American Diplomacy: A History*. 3rd ed. New York: Norton, 1975.

Forbes, Duncan. *Hume's Philosophical Politics*. Cambridge: Cambridge University Press, 1975.

Fowler, Michael Ross and Julie Marie Bunck. *Law, Power and the Sovereign State: The Evolution and Application Od the Concept of Sovereignty*. University Park: The Pennsylvania State University Press, 1995.

Fox, Hazel. *The Law of State Immunity*. Oxford: Oxford University Press, 2008.

Franck, Thomas M. *The Power of Legitimacy among Nations*. New York: Oxford University Press, 1990.

———. "The Emerging Right to Democratic Governance." *American Journal of International Law* 86 (1992): 46–91.

Frankel, Joseph. *International Politics: Conflict and Harmony*, A Pelican Book. Harmondsworth, Middlesex England: Penguin Books, 1973.

Friedman, Milton. *Essays in Positive Economics*. Chicago: The University of Chicago Press 1953.

Gadamer, Hans-Georg. *Hegel's Dialectic: Five Hermeneutical Studies*. Translated by P. Christopher Smith. New Haven: Yale University Press, 1982.

Galilei, Galileo. *The Essential Galileo*. Edited by Maurice A. Finocchiaro. Indianapolis, IN: Hackett 2008.

Gauthier, David P. *The Logic of Leviathan: The Moral and Political Theory of Thomas Hobbes*. Oxford: Clarendon Press, 1969.

Gillroy, John Martin. "Review of William Ophuls, Requiem for Modern Politics: The Tragedy of the Enlightenment and the Challenge of the New Millennium." *Americal Political Science Review* 91, no. 4 (1997): 948–949.

———. *Justice & Nature: Kantian Philosophy, Environmental Policy & the Law*. Washington, DC: Georgetown University Press, 2000.

———. "Adjudication Norms, Dispute Settlement Regimes and International Tribunals: The Status Of "Environmental Sustainability" In International Jurisprudence." *Stanford Journal of International Law* 42, no. 1 (2006): 1–52.

———. "Justice-as-Sovereignty: David Hume and the Origins of International Law." *The British Year Book of International Law* 78 (2007): 429–79.

———. "A Proposal for 'Philosophical Method' in Comparative and International Law." *Pace International Law Review* Online. 1, no. 3 (2009): 1–14. http://digitalcommons.pace.edu/pilronline/3/

Gillroy, John Martin, Breena Holland, and Celia Campbell-Mohn. *A Primer for Law & Policy Design: Understanding the Use of Principle and Argument in Environment and Natural Resource Law*, American Casebook Series. St. Paul, MN: West Group, 2008.

Gillroy, John Martin, and Maurice Wade, eds. *The Moral Dimensions of Public Policy Choice: Beyond the Market Paradigm*. Pittsburgh: University of Pittsburgh Press, 1992.

Glenn, H. Patrick. *Legal Traditions of the World*. 2nd ed. Oxford: Oxford University Press, 2004.

Goldsmith, Jack L. and Eric A. Posner. *The Limits of International Law*. Cambridge: Cambridge University Press, 2005.

Gong, Gerrit W. *The Standard Of "Civilization" In International Society*. Oxford: Clarendon Press, 1984.

Gray, Kevin R. "Case Concerning the Arrest Warrant of 11 April 2000 (Democratic Republic of the Congo V. Belgium)" *European Journal of International Law* 13, no. 3 (2002): 677–684.

Grewe, Wilhelm G. *The Epochs of International Law*. Berlin: Walter de Gruyter, 2000.

Grotius, Hugo. *The Rights of War and Peace*. Edited by Knud Haakonssen. Richard Tuck ed. 3 vols, Natural Law and Enlightenment Classics. Indianoplis, IN: Liberty Fund, 2005.

Haakonssen, Knud. *The Science of a Legislator: The Natural Jurisprudence of David Hume and Adam Smith*. Cambridge: Cambridge University Press, 1981.

Halevy, Elie. *The Growth of Philosophical Radicalism*. London: Faber And Faber, 1928.

Hardin, Russell. *Collective Action*. Baltimore, MD: Johns Hopkins University Press, 1983.

———. *David Hume: Moral & Political Theorist*. Oxford: Oxford University Press, 2007.

Harris, J. W. *Law and Legal Science: An Inquiry into the Concepts "Legal Rule" and "Legal System."* Oxford: Clarendon Press, 1979.

Harrison, Jonathan. *Hume's Theory of Justice*. Oxford: Clarendon Press, 1981.

Hart, H. L. A. *The Concept of Law*, Clarendon Law Series. Oxford: Clarendon Press, 1961.

———. "Definition and Theory in Jurisprudence." In *Essays in Jurisprudence and Philosophy*, edited by H. L. A. Hart, 21–48. Oxford: Oxford University Press, 1983.

Hartmann, Wilfried and Kenneth Pennington, eds. *The History of Medieval Canon Law in the Classical Period, 1140–1234 (from Gratian to the Decretals of Pope Gregory Ix)*. Washington DC: Cathloic University of American Press, 2008.

Hegel, G. W. F. *Phenomenology of Spirit*. Translated by A. V. Miller. Oxford: Oxford University Press, 1977.

Higgins, Rosalyn. "The International Court and South West Africa: The Implications of the Judgment." *International Affairs* 42, no. 4 (1966): 573–99.

Hobbes, Thomas. *Leviathan*. Edited by C. B. Macpherson, Pelican Classics. Harmondsworth, Middlesex, England: Penguin Books, 1979.

Hoeflich, Michael H. and Jasonne M. Grabher. "The Establishment of Normative Legal Texts: The Beginnings of the *Ius Commune*." In *The History of Cannon Law in the Classical Period, 1140–1234: From Gratian to the Decretals of Pope Gregory Ix*, edited by Wilfried Hartmann and Kenneth Pennington. Washington, DC: Catholic University of America Press, 2008.

Hoffman, John. *Sovereignty*. Minneapolis: University of Minnesota Press, 1998.

Horkheimer, Max and Theodor W. Adorno. *Dialectic of Enlightenment: Philosophical Fragments*. Stanford: Stanford University Press, 2002.

Hume, David. *Enquiries Concerning Hume Understanding (E1) and Concerning the Principles of Morals (E2)*. Edited by L. A. Selby-Bigge and P. H. Nidditch. 3rd ed. Oxford: Oxford University Press, 1975.

———. *A Treatise of Human Nature*. Edited by L. A. Selby-Bigge and P. H. Nidditch. 5th ed. Oxford: Oxford University Press, 1978.

———. *The History of England*. Vol. 1. Indianapolis, IN: Liberty Fund, 1983.

———. *The History of England*. Vol. 3. Indianapolis, IN: Liberty Fund, 1983.

———. *The History of England*. Vol. 4. Indianapolis, IN: Liberty Fund, 1983.

———. *A Dissertation on the Passions and the Natural History of Religion*. Edited by Tom Beauchamp, The Clarendon Edition of the Works of David Hume. Oxford: Clarendon Presss, 2007.

———. *Selected Essays*. Edited by Stephen Copley and Andrew Edgar. Oxford: Oxford University Press, 2008.

Jackson, John H. "Sovereignty-Modern: A New Approach to an Outdated Concept." *American Journal of International Law* 97 (2003): 782–802.

Jackson, Robert. *The Global Covenant: Human Conduct in a World of States*. Oxford: Oxford University Press, 2000.

Kalmo, Hen and Quentin Skinner, eds. *Sovereignty in Fragments: The Past, Present and Future of a Contested Concept*. Cambridge: Cambridge University Press, 2010.

Kant, Immanuel. *Critique of Pure Reason*. Vol. 4 Gesammelte Schriften. Berlin: Prussian Academy of Sciences, 1781.

———. *Critique of Practical Reason*. Vol. 5, Gesammelte Schriften. Berlin: Prussian Academy of Sciences, 1788.

———. *Metaphysics of Morals:* Vol. 6, Gesammelte Schriften. Berlin: Prussian Academy of Sciences, 1797.

———. *Toward Perpetual Peace*. Vol. 8, Gesammelte Schriften. Berlin: Prussian Academy of Sciences, 1795.

———. *The Cambridge Edition of the Works of Immanuel Kant in Translation*. Edited by Reinhard Brandt Henry Allison, Paul Guyer, Ralf Meerbote, Charles D. Parsons, Hoke Robinson, J. B. Schneewind, and Allen W. Wood. Cambridge: Cambridge University Press, 1995–2007.

Keene, Edward. *Beyond the Anarchical Society: Grotius, Colonialism and Order in World Politics*. Cambridge: Cambridge University Press, 2002.

Kelman, Steven. *Making Public Policy : A Hopeful View of American Government*, Basic Series in American Government. New York: Basic Books, 1987.

Kelsen, Hans. *Introduction to the Problems of Legal Theory: A Translation of the First Edition of the Reine Rechtslehre or Pure Theory of Law*. Edited by Bonnie Litschewaki Paulson and Stanley L. Paulson. Oxford: Clarendon Press, 2001.

Koskenniemi, Martti. *From Apology to Utopia: The Structure of International Legal Argument*. Cambridge: Cambridge University Press, 2005.

Krasner, Stephen D. *Sovereignty: Organized Hypocrisy*. Princeton: Princeton University Press, 1999.

Lauterpacht, Eli. "Sovereignty—Myth or Reality?" *International Affairs* 73, no. 1 (1997): 137–50.

Lauterpacht, H. *The Function of Law in the International Community* Oxford: Clarendon Press, 1933.

Lesaffer, Randall, ed. *Peace Treaties and International Law in European History: From the Late Middle Ages to World War One*. Cambridge: Cambridge University Press, 2004.

Lewis, David K. *Convention: A Philosophical Study*. Cambridge, MA: Harvard University Press, 1969.

Loeb, Louis E. *Stability and Justification in Hume's Treatise*. Oxford: Oxford University Press, 2002.

Luce, R. Duncan, and Howard Raiffa. *Games and Decisions: Introduction and Critical Survey*. New York: Wiley, 1957.

Lyons, Gene M., and Michaet Mastanduno, eds. *Beyond Westphalia: State Sovereignty and International Intervention*. Baltimore: Johns Hopkins University Press, 1995.

MacCormick, Neil. *Practical Reason in Law and Morality*, Law, State, and Practical Reason. Oxford: Oxford University Press, 2011.

Mackie, J. L. *The Cement of the Universe*. Edited by L. Jonathan Cohen, Clarendon Library of Logic and Philosophy. Oxford: Clarendon Press, 1980.

Majone, Giandomenico. *Evidence, Argument & Persuasion in the Policy Process*. New Haven: Yale University Press, 1989.

Marks, Susan. *The Riddle of All Constitutions: International Law, Democracy, and the Critique of Ideology*. Oxford: Oxford University Press, 2000.

Miller, David. *Philosophy and Ideology in Hume's Political Thought*. Oxford: Clarendon Press, 1981.

Mishan, E. J. *Cost-Benefit Analysis*. 3rd ed. Boston: George Allen & Unwin, 1982.

Murphy, John F. *The United States and the Rule of Law in International Affairs*. Cambridge: Cambridge University Press, 2004.

Newton, Isaac. *Papers & Letters on Natural Philosophy and Related Documents*. Cambridge, MA: Harvard University Press, 1958.

Nijman, Janne Elisabeth. *The Concept of International Legal Personality: An Inquiry into the History and Theory of International Law*. The Hague: TMC Asser Press, 2004.

Nussbaum, Arthur. *A Concise History of the Law of Nations*. New York: Macmillan, 1947.

Oppenheim, L. *International Law: A Treatise*. Edited by Ronald F. Roxburgh. 3rd ed. London: Longmans, Green and Co., 1920. Reprint, Lawbook Exchange 2005.

Orakhelashvili. *Peremptory Norms in International Law*. Oxford: Oxford University Press, 2006.

Osiander, Andreas. *Before the State: Systemic Political Change in the West Form the Greeks to the French Revolution*. Oxford: Oxford University Press, 2007.

Pellet, A. "The Opinions of the Badinter Abitration Committee." *European Journal of International Law* 3 (1982): 178–85.

Pennington, Kenneth. *The Prince and the Law 1200–1600: Sovereignty and Rights in the Western Legal Tradition*. Berkeley: University of California Press, 1993.

Petersmann, E. U. "How to Constitutionalize International Law and and Foreign Policy for the Benefit of Civil Society." *Michigan Journal of International Law* 20 (1998): 1–30.

———. "Constitutionalization and International Adjudication: How to Constitutionalize the Un Dispute Settlement System." *New York Journal of International Law* 31 (1999): 753–790.

———. "The WTO Constitution and Human Rights." *Journal of International Economic Law* 3 (2000): 19–26.

Philpott, Daniel. *Revolutions in Sovereignty: How Ideas Shaped Modern International Relations*. Princeton: Princeton University Press, 2001.

Pollock, Alexander J. "The South West Africa Cases and the Jurisprudence of International Law." *International Organization* 23, no. 4 (1969): 767–87.

Rapoport, Anatol. *Two-Person Games: The Essential Ideas*. Ann Arbor: University of Michigan Press, 1966.

Rawls, John. *A Theory of Justice*. Cambridge, MA: Belknap Press of Harvard University Press, 1971.

———. *The Law of Peoples*. Cambridge, MA: Harvard University Press, 1999.

Reus-Smit, Christian. *The Moral Purpose of the State: Culture, Social Identity, and Institutional Rationality in International Relations*. Princeton: Princeton University Press, 2009.

Rosenau, James N. *Along the Domestic-Foreign Frontier: Exploring Governance in a Turbulent World*. Vol. 53, Cambridge Studies in International Relations. Cambridge: Cambridge University Press, 1997.

Ross, Alf. *A Textbook of International Law*. London: Longmans, 1947.
Ruggie, John Gerard. "Territoriality and Beyond: Problematizing Moderity in International Relations." *International Organization* 47 (Winter 1993): 143–144.
Schattschneider, E. E. *The Semi-Sovereign People: A Realist's View of Democracy in America*. Hinsdale, IL: The Dryden Press, 1960.
Schelling, T. C. *The Strategy of Conflict*. Cambridge, MA: Harvard University Press, 1963.
Schermers, Henry. "Different Aspects of Sovereignty." In *State, Sovereignty, and International Governance*, edited by Gerard Kreijen, Marcel Brus, Jorri Duursma, Elisabeth De Vos, and John Dugard, 185–192. Oxford: Oxford University Press, 2002.
Scott, Johnathan. *Commonwealth Principles: Republican Writing of the English Revolution*. Cambridge: Cambridge University Press, 2004.
Shaw, Malcolm N. *International Law*. 6th ed. Cambridge: Cambridge University Press, 2008.
Shelton, Dinah, ed. *Commitment and Compliance: The Role of Non-Binding Norms in the International Legal System*. Oxford: Oxford University Press, 2000.
Sidgwick, Henry. *The Methods of Ethics*. 7th ed. Indianapolis, IN: Hackett Publishing, 1981.
Skyrms, Brian. *The Stag Hunt and the Evolution of Social Structure*. Cambridge: Cambridge University Press, 2004.
Spruyt, Hendrik. *The Sovereign State and Its Competitors*. Princeton: Princeton University Press, 1994.
Stark, Rodney. *The Victory of Reason: How Christianity Led to Freedom, Capitalism, and Western Success*. New York: Random House, 2005.
Stein, Peter. *Roman Law in European History*. Cambridge: Cambridge University Press, 1999.
Strayer, Joseph. *On the Medieval Origins of the Modern State*. Princeton: Princeton University Press, 1970.
Suarez, Francisco S. J. *Selections from Three Works*. Translated by Gwladys L. Williams, Ammi Brown, John Waldron, and S. J. Henry Davis. Edited by James Brown Scott. Oxford: Clarendon Press, 1944. Reprint, Classics of International Law.
Sugden, Robert. *The Economics of Rights, Co-Operation & Welfare*. Oxford: Basil Blackwell, 1986.
Taylor, Michael. *Anarchy & Cooperation*. London: John Wiley & Sons, 1976.
———. *The Possibility of Cooperation*, Studies in Rationality and Social Change. Cambridge: Cambridge University Press, 1987.
Vattel, Emer de. *The Law of Nations*. Edited by Knud Haakonssen, Bela Kapossy, and Richard Whatmore, Natural Law and Enlightenment Classics. Indianapolis, IN: Liberty Fund, 2008.
Vitoria, Francisco de. *Political Writings*. Edited by Anthony Pagden and Jeremy Lawrance, Cambridge Texts in the History of Political Thought. Cambridge: Cambridge University Press, 1991.
Waltz, Kenneth Neal. *Theory of International Politics*. 1st ed. Long Grove, IL: Waveland Press, 2010.
Ward, Paul W. *Sovereignty: A Study of a Contemporary Political Notion*. London: Routledge, 1928.
Waxman, Wayne. *Kant and the Empiricists: Understanding-Understanding*. Oxford: Oxford University Press, 2005.
Weber, Cynthia. *Simulating Sovereignty: Intervention, the State and Symbolic Exchange*. Edited by Steve Smith. Vol. 37, Cambridge Studies in International Relations. Cambridge: Cambridge University Press, 1995.
Wendt, Alexander. *Social Theory of International Politics*. Edited by Steve Smith. Vol. 67, Cambridge Studies in International Relations. Cambridge: Cambridge University Press, 1999.

Wolff, Christian. *The Law of Nations Treated According to a Scientific Method*. Translated by Joseph H. Drake. Oxford: Clarendon Press, 1934. Reprint, The Classics of International Law.

Wright, Martin. *Four Seminal Thinkers in International Theory: Machiavelli, Grotius, Kant & Mazzini*. Edited by Gabriele Wright and Brian Porter. Oxford: Oxford University Press, 2005.

Zaum, Dominik. *The Sovereignty Paradox: The Norms and Politics of International Statebuilding*. Oxford: Oxford University Press, 2007.

Index

Italicized page numbers refer to tables and illustrations

Printed in the United States of America